Macroeconomics and Finance

Franco Modigliani celebrating the 1985 Nobel Prize in economics

Macroeconomics and Finance
Essays in Honor of Franco Modigliani

edited by
Rudiger Dornbusch,
Stanley Fischer, and
John Bossons

The MIT Press
Cambridge, Massachusetts
London, England

This book was set in Palatino by Asco Trade Typesetting Ltd., Hong Kong, and printed and bound by Halliday Lithograph in the United States of America.

Library of Congress Cataloging-in-Publication Data

Macroeconomics and finance.
  Includes bibliographies and index.
  1. Macroeconomics.   2. Finance, Public.   3. Economic policy.   4. Modigliani, Franco.
I. Modigliani, Franco.   II. Dornbusch, Rudiger.   III. Fischer, Stanley.
HB172.5.M3354   1987   339   86-16296
ISBN 0-262-04087-5

Contents

List of Participants

Andrew B. Abel
Harvard University

Albert Ando
University of Pennsylvania

Giorgio Basevi
University of Bologna

Olivier Blanchard
Massachusetts Institute of Technology

John Bossons
University of Toronto

Rudiger Dornbusch
Massachusetts Institute of Technology

Mario Draghi
World Bank

Jared J. Enzler
Federal Reserve System

Stanley Fischer
Massachusetts Institute of Technology

Benjamin Friedman
Harvard University

Francesco Giavazzi
University of Venice

Alberto Giovannini
Columbia University

Alfonso Jozzo
Istituto Bancario San Paolo di Torino

Pentti J. K. Kouri
New York University

Paolo Sylos Labini
University of Rome

Giorgio La Malfa
Chamber of Deputies, Italian Parliament

Robert C. Merton
Massachusetts Institute of Technology

Merton H. Miller
University of Chicago

David Modest
Columbia University

Franco Modigliani
Massachusetts Institute of Technology

Stewart C. Myers
Massachusetts Institute of Technology

Fiorella Padoa-Schioppa
University of Trieste

Tommaso Padoa-Schioppa
Banca d'Italia

Luigi Pasinetti
Catholic University, Milan

Paul A. Samuelson
Massachusetts Institute of Technology

Robert J. Shiller
Yale University

Robert M. Solow
Massachusetts Institute of Technology

Luigi Spaventa
University of Rome

Arlie Sterling
Marsoft

Giorgio Szego
University of Rome

James Tobin
Yale University

Preface

Most of the chapters in this *Festschrift* were delivered as papers at a conference held on Martha's Vineyard in September 1985. Note the date: though the participants did not know it, this was a pre-Nobel Prize event. Indeed, some of us had concluded that the Nobel Prize Committee, which had missed so many excellent opportunities to award the prize to Franco Modigliani, inexcusably might never do it.

The pre-Prize party was sweeter for its timing. Franco's friends and coauthors (the groups continue to overlap) were there to pay tribute to an outstanding economist and a person of rare warmth. In attendance were former students, many of whom came from Italy for the occasion, present and former colleagues, his wife Serena, his economist-in-training grand-daughter Leah Modigliani, and basking in the attention, affection, and the magnificent fall days, Franco himself.

The conference was an intellectual as well as sentimental event. The program contained papers on those parts of finance and macroeconomics in which Franco has made his major contributions. The quality of the papers was high, and we believe this volume includes substantive contributions to the literature as well as evaluations of Franco's work. There were two commentators for each paper: the formal commentator, whose comments are included in the volume, and Franco. It was appropriate that at his own conference Franco be given the right to speak freely—and lest the right wither from disuse, he exercised it.

The problem in setting the conference schedule was deciding how to keep it manageable. Franco has written with more than the average number of coauthors, knows everyone in Italy, and has countless admirers around the world. We can only apologize to those who should have been there but were not.

Two chapters in this volume were written after the conference: Franco's Nobel address and Paul Samuelson's evaluation of Franco for the journal

Science (volume 231, 21 March 1986). We are grateful to the Nobel Prize Committee and the editors of *Science* for allowing us to reprint them, and thereby give closure to the volume.

John Bossons of the University of Toronto and Jacques Drèze of C.O.R.E. at Louvain were responsible for the idea of the book. When the administrative burdens of coordinating an event over two continents became too great, Rudi Dornbusch and Stanley Fischer entered the picture, turning the difficult work over to Carol McIntire at MIT. She made the trains (and buses) run on time and even persuaded most of the authors to get their papers in on time while earning the gratitude of the participants. Takeo Hoshi of the MIT Economics Department helped speed the book through production.

We are grateful indeed to the conference's chief sponsor, the Istituto Bancario di Sao Paulo di Torino, and to Alfonso Jozzo in particular, for making this successful and happy event possible. The Department of Economics and the Sloan School of Management at MIT, Franco's homes, provided further financial and moral support.

Rudiger Dornbusch
Stanley Fischer
John Bossons

Macroeconomics and Finance

1

Life Cycle, Individual Thrift, and the Wealth of Nations

(Nobel Lecture Delivered in Stockholm, Sweden, 9 December 1985)

Franco Modigliani

Introduction

This paper provides a review of the theory of the determinants of individual and national thrift that has come to be known as the Life Cycle Hypothesis (LCH) of saving. Applications to some current policy issues are also discussed.

Section 1 deals with the state of the art on the eve of the formulation of the LCH some 30 years ago. Section 2 sets forth the theoretical foundations of the model in its original formulation and later amendment, calling attention to various implications distinctive to it and, sometimes, counterintuitive. It also includes a review of a number of crucial empirical tests, both at the individual and the aggregate levels. Section 3 reviews some applications of LCH to current policy issues, though only in sketchy fashion, as space constraints prevent fuller discussion.

1 Antecedents

1.1 The Role of Thrift and the Keynesian Revolution

The study of individual thrift and aggregate saving and wealth has long been central to economics because national saving is the source of the supply of capital, a major factor of production controlling the productivity of labor and its growth over time. It is because of this relation between saving and productive capital that thrift has traditionally been regarded as a virtuous, socially beneficial act.

Yet, there was a brief but influential interval in the course of which, under the impact of the Great Depression, and of the interpretation of this episode that Keynes suggested in the *General Theory* (1936), saving came to be seen with suspicion, as potentially disruptive to the economy and harmful to social welfare. The period in question goes from the mid-'30s to the late '40s or early '50s. Thrift posed a potential threat, as it reduced one component of demand, consumption, without systematically and automatically giving rise to an offsetting expansion in investment. It might thus cause "inadequate" demand—and, hence, output and employment lower than the capacity of the economy. This failure was attributable to a variety of reasons, including wage ridigity, liquidity preference, fixed capital coefficients in production, and investment controlled by animal spirits rather than by the cost of capital.

Not only was oversaving seen as having played a major role in the Great Depression, but, in addition, there was widespread fear that the problem might come back to haunt the postwar era. These fears were fostered by a widely held conviction that, in the future, there would not be too much need for additional accumulation of capital while saving would rise even faster than income. This combination could be expected to result, sooner or later, in saving outstripping the "need" for capital. These concerns were at the base of the "stagnationist" school, which was prominent in the '40s and early '50s.

1.2   Early Keynesian Theories of the Determinants of Saving

It is interesting and somewhat paradoxical that the present-day interest and extensive research activity about saving behavior owes its beginnings to the central role assigned by Keynesian economics to the consumption function as a determinant of aggregate demand and to the concern with oversaving as a source of both cyclical fluctuations and long-run stagnation. It is for this reason that the early endeavor to model individual and aggregate saving behavior was dominated by the views expressed on this subject by Keynes in the *General Theory*, and in particular by his well-known "fundamental psychological [rather than 'economic'] law" (1936, p. 96) to the effect that an increase in income can be counted on to lead to a positive but smaller change in consumption. Even when the analysis followed the more traditional line of demand theory, it relied on a purely static framework in which saving was seen as one of the many "goods" on which the consumer could spend his income. Thus, income was seen as the main systematic determinant of both individual and national saving, and, in line with Keynes's "law," it was regarded as a superior commodity (i.e., one on which "expenditure" rises with income) and most likely a luxury, for which expenditure rises faster than income. Also, in contrast to other goods, the "expenditure" on saving could be negative—and, accordingly, dissaving was seen as typical of people or countries below some "break-even" level of income. All these features could be formalized by expressing consumption as a linear function of income with a substantial positive intercept. This formulation appeared to be supported by the findings of numerous budget studies, and even by the newly developed National Income Accounts, spanning the period of the Great Depression, at the bottom of which saving turned small or even negative.

As is apparent, in this early phase the dominant approach could best be characterized as crudely empirical; little attention was given to why rational consumers would choose to "allocate" their income to saving. The prevailing source of substantial saving was presumably the desire of the rich to bequeath an estate (Keynes's "pride" motive, 1936, p. 108). Accordingly, the main source of the existing capital *stock* could be traced to inheritance. Similarly, there was little evidence of concern with how, and how long, "poor" people, or countries, could dissave without having saved first or without exceeding their means.

1.3 Three Landmark Empirical Studies

In the second half of the '40s three important empirical contributions dealt a fatal blow to this extraordinarily simple view of the saving process. First, the work of Kuznets (1946) and others provided clear evidence that the saving ratio had not changed much since the middle of the nineteenth century, despite the large rise in per capita income. Second, a path-breaking contribution of Brady and Friedman (1947) provided a reconciliation of Kuznets's results with budget study evidence of a strong association between the saving rate and family income. They demonstrated that the consumption function implied by family data shifted up in time as mean income increased, in such a way that the saving rate was explained not by the *absolute* income of the family but rather by its income *relative* to overall mean income.

Ways of reconciling these findings with the standard linear consumption function were soon provided by Duesenberry (1949) and Modigliani (1949), though within the empirical tradition of the earlier period. Duesenberry's "relative income hypothesis" accounted for the Brady-Friedman results in terms of imitation of the upper classes. This is an appealing explanation, though it fails to come to grips with the budget constraint in the case of would-be dissavers below mean income. Similarly, the "Duesenberry-Modigliani" consumption function tried to reconcile the cyclical variations of the saving ratio with its long-run stability by postulating that current consumption was determined not just by current income but also by its highest previous peak, resulting in a ratchetlike upward creep in the short-run consumption function. In my own formulation, primary stress was placed on reasons why the savings rate should more procyclically and on the consideration that in an economy with stable long-run growth, the ratio of the current to highest previous income could be taken as a good measure of cyclical conditions. Duesenberry, on the other hand, put more stress on consumers explicitly anchoring their consumption on the previous peak. This formulation was brought to its logical conclusion by Brown (1952) when he proposed that the highest previous income should be replaced by the highest previous consumption.

The third fundamental contribution was the highly imaginative analysis of Margaret Reid (not published), which pointed to a totally different explanation for the association between the saving ratio and relative income, namely, that consumption was controlled by normal or "permanent," rather than current, income.

This contribution was an important source of inspiration, both for the Life Cycle Hypothesis and for the roughly contemporaneous Permanent Income Hypothesis (PIH) of Milton Friedman (1957).

2   The Life Cycle Hypothesis

Between 1952 and 1954, Richard Brumberg and I wrote two essays, "Utility Analysis and the Consumption Function: An Interpretation of Cross Section Data" (Modigliani and Brumberg, 1954), and "Utility Analysis and the Aggregate Consumption Function: An Attempt at Integration" (Modigliani and Brumberg, 1979), which provide the basis for the Life Cycle Hypothesis of Saving (LCH). They will be referred to hereafter as MB-C and MB-A, respectively. Our purpose was to show that all the well-established empirical regularities could be accounted for in terms of rational, utility-maximizing, consumers, allocating optimally their resources to consumption over their life, in the spirit of Irving Fisher (1930). (For an earlier and extensive, but strictly theoretical, application of utility maximization to the theory of saving by households, see Ricci, 1926.)

2.1   Utility Maximization and the Role of Life Resources (Permanent Income)

The hypothesis of utility maximization (and perfect markets) has, all by itself, one very powerful implication—the resources that a representative consumer allocates to consumption at any age, t, will depend only on his life resources (the present value of labor income plus bequests received, if any) and not at all on income accruing currently. When combined with the self-evident proposition that the representative consumer will choose to consume at a reasonably stable rate, close to his anticipated average life consumption, we can reach one conclusion fundamental for an understanding of individual saving behavior, namely, that the size of saving over short periods of time, like a year, will be swayed by the extent to which current income departs from average life resources.

This conclusion is common to LCH and to Friedman's PIH, which differs from LCH primarily in that it models rational consumption and saving decisions under the "simplifying" assumption that life is indefinitely long. Accordingly, the notion of life resources is replaced by that of "permanent income," while the discrepancy between current and permanent income is labeled "transitory" income.

The notion that saving largely reflects transitory income has a number of implications, which have been made familiar by the contributions of Friedman and by our own 1954 paper, and which have received ample empirical support, even with some occasional controversy. Among these implications, the best known and well established is that relating to the upward bias arising in estimating the slope of a saving-income relation from budget data, when, as is usual, the individual observations are classified by current income classes. Because of the correlation between transitory and current income (relative to mean income), the regression line tends to be steeper than the underlying true relation between the (permanent) saving rate and permanent income. Thus, the estimated saving function departs from the true one by being rotated counter-clockwise around the mean, to an extent that is greater the greater the variability of transitory income, e.g., more for a sample of farmers than for one of government employees. It is this phenomenon that accounts for the finding of Brady-Friedman cited above, to the effect that the saving ratio, estimated from budget studies at different points of time, appears to depend on the income not in absolute terms but rather relative to overall mean income.

This same consideration provides an explanation for a famous counter-intuitive empirical finding first observed in a large survey conducted in the United States in 1936, namely, that black families appeared to save more (or dissave less) than white families at any level of income. The reason, of course, is that black families tend to have a much lower average level of permanent income, and, therefore, at any given level of *current* income the transitory component, and hence saving, tended to be larger—see, e.g., Fisher and Brown (1958).

The extent of bias in the cross-sectional saving function should tend to decline if the households are classified by some criterion less positively correlated with transitory income, and this prediction too has been extensively verified—see, e.g., Modigliani and Ando (1960).

However, we do not intend to pursue here any further the implications of the relation between saving and transitory income since, as already noted, these implications are basically the same for LCH as for PIH. We concentrate, instead, on those aspects that are specific to LCH.

2.2   LCH—The "Stripped Down" Version

By explicitly recognizing the finite life of households, the LCH could deal with variations in serving other than those resulting from the transitory deviations of income from life resources of PIH. In particular, it could focus on those systematic variations in income and in "needs" that occur over the life cycle, as a result of maturing and retiring, and of changes in family size—hence the name of Life Cycle Hypothesis. In addition, the LCH was in a position to take into account bequests and the bequest motive, which were not amenable to analysis within the approximation of infinite life.

In MB-C and in the first two parts of the MB-A, we made a number of simplifying, stylized, assumptions concerning the life cycle path of household opportunities and tastes, in order to draw out succinctly the essential implications of the LCH approach. These were (1) opportunities: income constant until retirement, zero thereafter; zero interest rate; and (2) preferences: constant consumption over life, no bequests.

For this "basic" or "stripped down" model, the life cycle path of saving and wealth is described in the, by now familiar, graph in figure 1.1. Because the retirement span follows the earning span, consumption smoothing leads to a humped-shaped age path of wealth holding, a shape that had been suggested earlier by Harrod (1948) under the label of hump saving (though "hump wealth" would seem like a more descriptive label).

In MB-A, it was shown that this basic model led to a number of implications that were at that time quite novel and surprising—almost counterintuitive. They included the following:

1. The saving rate of a country is entirely independent of its per capita income.

2. The national saving rate is not simply the result of differential thrift of its citizens, in the sense that different national saving rates are consistent with an identical individual (life cycle) behavior.

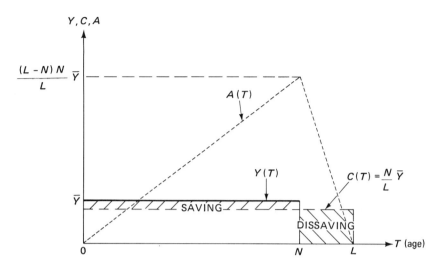

Figure 1.1
Income, consumption, saving, and wealth as a function of age.

3. Between countries with identical individual behavior the aggregate saving rate will be higher the higher the long-run growth rate of the economy. It will be zero for zero growth.

4. The wealth-income ratio is a decreasing function of the growth rate, thus being largest at zero growth.

5. An economy can accumulate a very substantial stock of wealth relative to income even if no wealth is passed on by bequests.

6. The main parameter that controls the wealth-income ratio and the saving rate for given growth is the prevailing length of retirement.

To establish these propositions, we begin by considering the case of a stationary economy, and then that of steady growth.

The Case of a Stationary Economy
Suppose that there is neither productivity nor population growth, and assume, conveniently, that the mortality rate is 1 at some age L and 0 before. Then, clearly, figure 1.1 will represent the age distribution of wealth, saving, consumption, and income, up to a factor representing the (constant) number of people in each age bracket. Hence, the aggregate wealth-income ratio, W/Y, is given by the ratio of the sum of wealth held at each age—the area under the wealth path—to the area under the income path. This has a number of significant implications.

a. It is apparent from the graph that W/Y depends on a single parameter, the length of retirement, M—which establishes proposition 6. The relation between M and W/Y turns out to be extremely simple, to wit:

$$W/Y = M/2 \tag{1}$$

(see MB-A, footnote 38).

b. In MB-A, for illustrative purposes, we conservatively took the average length of retirement as 10 years, implying a wealth-income ratio of 5. This result was an exciting one in that this value was close to the wealth-income ratio suggested by preliminary estimates of Goldsmith's (1956) monumental study of US savings. It implied that one could come close to accounting for the entire wealth holding of the United States without any appeal to the bequest process—proposition 5—a quite radical departure from conventional wisdom.

c. With income and population stationary, aggregate wealth must remain constant in time, and, therefore, the change in wealth or rate of saving must be zero, despite the large stock of wealth—proposition 3. The explanation is that, in the stationary state, the dissaving of the retired, from wealth accumulated earlier, just offsets the accumulation of the active population in view of retirement. Saving could occur only transiently if a shock pushed W away from $(M/2)\bar{Y}$, where $\bar{Y}$ is the stationary level of income; then, as long as Y remained at $\bar{Y}$, wealth would gradually return to the equilibrium level $(M/2)\bar{Y}$.

The Case of a Steadily Growing Economy
In this case, the behavior of the saving rates can be inferred from that of aggregate private wealth, W, through the relation $S = \Delta W$, implying[1]

$$s \equiv \frac{S}{Y} = \frac{\Delta W}{W}\frac{W}{Y} = \rho w, \qquad \frac{ds}{d\rho} = w + \rho\frac{dw}{d\rho}, \tag{2}$$

where w is the wealth-income ratio and ρ is the rate of growth of the economy, which in steady state equals the rate of growth of wealth, $\Delta W/W$. Since w is positive and is based on a level life cycle consumption and earnings, which ensures that it is independent of the *level* of income, we have established propositions 1 and 2. If, in addition, the age profile of the wealth-income ratio could be taken as independent of *growth*, then the saving rate would be proportional to growth with a proportionality factor equal to $M/2$, substantiating proposition 3. Actually, the model implies that w is, generally, a declining function of ρ—proposition 4—though with a small slope, so that the slope of the relation between s and ρ tends to flatten out as ρ grows.

When the source of growth is population, the mechanism behind positive saving may be labeled the Neisser effect (1944): younger households in their accumulation phase account for a larger share of population, and retired dissavers for a smaller share, than in the stationary society. However, w also falls with ρ because the younger people also are characterized by relatively lower levels of wealth holding. Thanks to the simplifying assumptions of the basic model, it was possible to calculate explicitly values for w and s: for $\rho = 2\%$, $w = 4$, $s = 8\%$; for $\rho = 4\%$, $w = 3\frac{1}{4}$, $s = 13\%$.

When the growth is due to productivity, the mechanism at work may be called the Bentzel (1959) effect (who independently called attention to it). Productivity growth implies that younger cohorts have larger lifetime resources than older ones, and, therefore, their savings are larger than the dissaving of the poorer, retired cohorts. It was shown in MB-A that, if agents plan their consumption as though they did not anticipate the *future* growth of income, then $w(\rho)$ and $s(\rho)$ for productivity growth are just about the same as for population growth, for values of ρ in the relevant range.

It should be noted that this conclusion is diametrically opposite to that reached by Friedman (1957, p. 234), namely, that productivity growth should tend to *depress* the saving ratio on the ground that a rise in income "expected to continue tends to raise permanent income relative to measured income and so to raise consumption relative to measured income." This difference in the implications of the two models—one of the very few of any significance—can be traced to the fact that, if life is infinite, there cannot be a Bentzel effect. To be sure, to the extent that agents anticipate fully future income, they will tend to shift consumption from the future to the present, and this will tend to reduce the path of wealth and perhaps even generate negative net worth in early life (see, e.g., Tobin, 1967). But this effect must be overshadowed by the Bentzel effect, at least for small values of ρ, which, realistically, is what matters. [This follows from the continuity of $ds/d\rho$ in equation (2).]

The model also implies that the short-run behavior of aggregate consumption could be described by a very simple aggregate consumption function, linear in aggregate (labor) income (YL), and wealth (W):

$$C = \alpha YL + \delta W. \tag{3}$$

An equation of this type had been proposed somewhat earlier by Ackley (1951), though both the functional form and the presumed stability of the coefficients rested on purely heuristic considerations. By contrast, it was shown in MB-A that, if income followed closely the steady growth path, then the parameters α and δ could be taken as constant in time and determined by the length of life (L), of retirement (M), and the rate of growth (MB-A, p. 135). For the standard assumption $L = 50$, $M = 10$, and $\rho = .03$, δ comes to .07 (see MB-A, p. 180). Furthermore, the parameters could be well approximated by the same constant even if income moved around the trend line, as long as the departures were not very long lasting and deep, except that YL should be interpreted as long run expected rather than current income. The short-run equation (3) is, of course, consistent with the long-run properties 1–6, as one can readily verify.

Empirical Verifications
None of these long- and short-run implications of the basic model could be explicitly tested at the time they were established. There were no data on Private Net Worth to test equation (3), except for some indirect estimates pieced together by Hamburger (1951) and some preliminary Goldsmith figures for a few selected years. Similarly, information on Private National Saving was available only for a couple of countries. We could only take encouragement from the fact that the model seemed to fit the single observation available, namely the United States. Both the wealth income ratio, 4 to 5, and the saving rate, S, "between 1/7 and 1/8" (Goldsmith, 1956), were broadly consistent with the prediction of the model, for a 3% growth rate, namely, $4\frac{1}{3}$ for w and 13% for s.

But the availability of data improved dramatically in the next decade. For the United States, an annual time series of Private Wealth was put together in the early '60s (Ando et al., 1963), and equation (3) was tested (Modigliani and Ando, 1963). It was found to fit the data quite well, and with parameter estimates close to those predicted by the model. By now the consumption function (3) has become pretty much standard, having been estimated for many countries and periods. The coefficient of wealth is frequently lower than the .07 quoted earlier, but this can be accounted for, at least in part, by the fact that Y is typically defined as total rather than just labor income.

Similarly, by the early '60s, the United Nations had put together National Account statistics for a substantial number of countries, characterized by wide differences in the growth rate, and it became possible to test the relation between the national saving ratio and the growth rate. The early tests were again quite successful (Houthakker, 1961, 1965; Leff, 1969; Modigliani, 1970). The newly available data also revealed the puzzling and

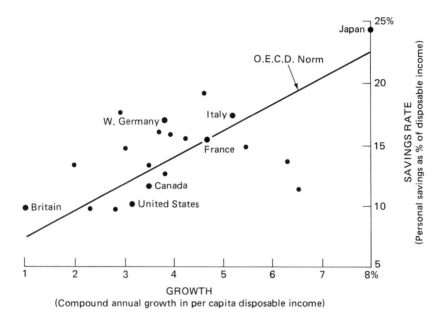

Figure 1.2
The relation between savings and growth: savings rate versus growth for 21 OECD countries, averages for 1960–1970. Source: Modigliani and Sterling (1983).

shocking fact that the saving ratio for the United States, by far the richest country in the world, was rather low compared with other industrial countries (see, e.g., figure 1.2). The LCH could account for the puzzle through a relatively modest growth rate. By now it is generally accepted that growth is a major source of cross-country differences in the saving rate.

2.3 The Effect of Dropping the Simplifying Assumptions

As was demonstrated in MB-A, most of the simplifying assumptions can be replaced by more "realistic" ones without changing the basic nature of the results, and, in particular, the validity of propositions 1–5.

Nonzero Interest
Allowing for a nonzero interest rate, r, has two effects. One effect is on income, as we must distinguish between labor income, say YL, property income, YP, whose "permanent component" may be approximated by rW and total income, $Y = YL + YP = YL + rW$. If we continue to assume a constant labor income till retirement, then the graph of income in figure 1.1

is unchanged. However, the graph of consumption changes through an income and substitution effect: the addition of rW increases income, but at the same time r also affects the opportunity cost of current, in terms of future consumption. It is possible that the consumer would still choose a constant rate of consumption over life (if the elasticity of substitution were zero). In this case, in figure 1.1, consumption will still be a horizontal straight line, but at a higher level because of the favorable "income effect" from rW. As for saving, it will be the difference between C and Y. The latter differs from the (piecewise) horizontal YL in the figure by rW, which is proportional to W. As a result, the path of W will depart somewhat from the "triangle" in figure 1.1, and, in particular, the overall area under the path can be shown to decline with r. This means that W and, a fortiori, $w = W/Y$, will fall with r.

This result has interesting implications for the much debated issue of the effect of interest rates on saving. Turning back to equation (2), we see that (i) in the absence of growth, a change in r has *no* effect on saving (which remains zero), and (ii) for any positive rate of growth, a higher interest rate means a lower saving rate. However, this conclusion depends on the special assumption of zero substitution. With positive substitution, consumption will start lower and will rise exponentially: this "postponement" of consumption, in turn, lifts saving and peak assets. If the substitution effect is strong enough, w will rise, and so will s, as long as ρ is positive.

This same conclusion can be derived from (3) and the definition of Y. These can be shown to imply

$$\frac{W}{Y} = \frac{1 - \alpha}{\rho + \delta - \alpha r}. \tag{4}$$

Numerical calculations in MB-A suggest that α is not much affected by r, but δ is. In (1975) I hypothesized that the effect of r on δ might be expressed as $\delta = \delta^* + \mu r$ when μ is unity for 0 substitution, and declines with substitution (possibly to a negative value). Substituting for δ in (4), one can see that, when the interest rate rises, saving may fall or rise depending on whether μ is larger or smaller than α.

Which of these inequalities actually holds is an empirical matter. Unfortunately, despite a hot debate, no convincing general evidence either way has been produced, *which leads me to the provisional view that s is largely independent of the interest rate.* It should be noted in this connection that, insofar as saving is done through pension schemes aimed at providing a retirement income, the effect of r on s is likely to be zero (or even positive) in the short run but negative in the long run.

Allowing for the Life Cycle of Earning and Family Size
Far from being constant, average labor income typically exhibits a marked hump pattern, which peaks somewhat past age 50, falls thereafter, partly because of the incidence of retirement, and does not go to zero at any age, though it falls sharply after 65. However, consumption also varies with age, largely reflecting variations in family size, as one might expect if the consumer smooths consumption *per equivalent adult* (Modigliani and Ando, 1957). Now the life cycle of family size, at least in the United States, has a very humped shape rather similar to that of income, though with a some-what earlier peak. As a result, one might expect, and generally finds a fairly constant rate of saving in the central age group, but lower saving or even dissaving in the very young or old. Thus, as in our figure 1.1, the wealth of a given cohort tends to rise to a peak around age 60 to 65 (see, e.g., Projector, 1968; King and Dicks-Mireaux, 1982; Avery et al., 1984; Ando and Kennickell, 1985; Diamond and Hausman, 1985).

It is also worth noting that available evidence supports the LCH predic-tion that the amount of net worth accumulated up to any given age in relation to life resources is a decreasing function of the number of children and that saving tends to fall with the number of children present in the household and to rise with the number of children no longer present (cf. Blinder, Gordon, and Wise, 1983; Ando and Kennickell, 1985; Hurd, 1986).

Length of Working and Retired Life
One can readily drop the assumption that the length of retired life is a given constant. As is apparent from figure 1.1, a longer retirement shifts forward, and raises, the peak of wealth, increasing w and the saving rate. This does not affect the validity of propositions 2–6, but could invalidate 1. It is possible, in fact, that, in an economy endowed with greater produc-tivity (and, hence, greater per capita income), households might take ad-vantage of this by choosing to work for fewer years. This, in turn, would result in a higher national saving rate. Note, however, that this scenario need not follow. The increase in productivity raises the opportunity cost of an extra year of retirement in terms of consumables, providing an incentive to *shorter retirement*. Thus the saving rate could, in principle, be affected by per capita income, but through an unconventional, life cycle mechanism, and, furthermore, in a direction unpredictable a priori. Empirical evidence suggests that the income effect tends to predominate but is not strong enough to produce a measurable effect on the saving rate (Modigliani and Sterling, 1983).

Aside from income, any other variable that affects the length of retirement could, through this channel, affect saving. One such variable that has received attention lately is Social Security. Several studies have found that the availability of social security, and terms thereof, can encourage earlier retirement (Feldstein, 1974, 1977; Munnell, 1974; Boskin and Hurd, 1978; Modigliani and Sterling, 1983; Diamond and Hausman, 1985). To this extent, Social Security tends to encourage saving, though this effect may be offset, and even more than fully, by the fact that it also reduces the need for private accumulation to finance a given retirement.

Liquidity Constraint

Imperfections in the credit markets as well as the uncertainty of future income prospects may, to some extent, prevent households from borrowing as much as would be required to carry out the unconstrained optimal consumption plan. Such a constraint will have the general effect of postponing consumption and increase w as well as s. But, clearly, these are not essential modifications, at least with respect to the aggregate implications—on the contrary, they contribute to ensure that productivity growth will increase the saving rate. However, significant liquidity constraints could affect quantitatively certain specific conclusions, e.g., with respect to temporary tax changes (see section 3.1).

Myopia

LCH presupposes a substantial degree of rationality and self-control to make preparations for retired consumption needs. It has been suggested— most recently by Shefrin and Thaler (1985)—that households, even if concerned in principle with consumption smoothing, may be too myopic to make adequate reserves. To the extent that this criticism is valid, it should affect the wealth income ratio in the direction opposite to the liquidity constraint, though the effect of transitory changes in income from any source would go in the same direction. However, such myopia is not supported empirically. The assets held at the peak of the life cycle are found to represent a substantial multiple of average income (on the order of 5, at least for the United States) and an even larger multiple of permanent income, which, in a growing economy, is less than current income. Such a multiple appears broadly consistent with the maintenance of consumption after retirement. This inference is confirmed by recent studies that have found very little evidence of myopic saving behavior. In particular, both Kotlikoff, Spivak, and Summers (1982) and Blinder and Gordon (1984, especially figure 4.1), working with data on households close to retirement, find that for most families the resources available to provide for retired consumption appear to be quite adequate to support retired consumption at a rate consistent with life resources.

2.4 The Role of Bequests and the Bequest Motive

Evidence on the Bequest Process
The basic version of the LCH that ignores the existence of bequests has proved quite helpful in understanding and predicting many aspects of individual and aggregate behavior. However, significant bequests do exist in market (and nonmarket) economies, as can be inferred from two sets of observations. One observation relates to the behavior of saving and assets of elderly households, especially after retirement. The basic LCH implies that, with retirement, saving should become negative, and thus assets decline at a fairly constant rate, reaching zero at death. The empirical evidence seems to reveal a very different picture: dissaving in old age appears to be at best modest (e.g., see Fisher, 1950; Lydall, 1955; Mirer, 1979; Ando and Kennickell, 1985). According to Mirer, the wealth-income ratio actually continues to rise in retirement. (Note, however, that his estimate is biased as a result of including education in his regression. Given the steady historical rise in educational levels, there will be a strong association between age, educational attainment, and socioeconomic status *relative* to one's cohort, if one holds constant the absolute level of education. Thus, his results could merely reflect the association between bequests, wealth, and relative income discussed below.)

Most other recent analysts have found that the wealth of a given cohort tends to decline after reaching its peak in the 60–65 age range (Shorrocks, 1975; King and Dicks-Mireaux, 1982; Diamond and Hausman, 1985; Avery et al., 1984; Ando, 1985), though there are exceptions—e.g., Menchik and David (1983), discussed below. To be sure, the results depend on the concept of saving and wealth used. If one makes proper allowance for participation in pension funds, then the dissaving (or the decline in wealth) of the old tends to be more apparent, and it becomes quite pronounced if one includes an estimate of social security benefits. But, when the saving and wealth measures include only cash saving and marketable wealth, the dissaving and the decline appear weaker or even absent.

However, the lastest US study by Hurd (1986), using a very large sample and relying on panel data, finds that, at least for retired people, marketable wealth systematically declines, especially so if one leaves out the very illiquid asset represented by owner occupied houses.

The finding that decumulation, though present, is slow, may partly reflect the fact that survey data give an upward biased picture of the true behavior of wealth during old age, and for two reasons. First, as Shorrocks has argued (1975), one serious bias arises from the well-known positive association between longevity and (relative) income. This means that the average wealth of successively older age classes is the wealth of households with higher and higher life resources. Accordingly, the age profile of wealth is upward biased. Second, in a similar vein, Ando and Kennickell (1985) have found evidence that aged households that are poor tend to double up with younger households and disappear from the sampled population so that the wealth of those remaining independent is again an upward biased estimate of average wealth.

But even allowing for these biases, the decline in wealth—especially of the bequeathable type—is unquestionably less fast than one would expect under a pure life cycle with certain time of death.

This conclusion is confirmed by a very different set of observations coming from probate data. These data, discussed further below, confirm that there is a nonnegligible annual flow of bequests.

How Important Is Inherited Wealth?
The next question is a factual one: Just how important is the bequests process in accounting for the existing stock of wealth?

I recently (1985) reviewed a substantial body of information on inherited wealth based on direct surveys of households and on various sources of estimates on the flow of bequests. This review yields a fairly consistent picture suggesting that the proportion of existing wealth that has been inherited is around 20%, with a margin of something like 5 percentage points.

This conclusion has recently found support in an interesting calculation carried out by Ando and Kennickell (1985) (hereafter A&K). Starting from estimates of national saving and allocating them by age, using the saving-age relation derived from a well-known budget study (the Bureau of Labor Statistics' Consumer Expenditure Survey, 1972–73), they are able to estimate the aggregate amount of wealth accumulated through life cycle saving by all the cohorts living in a given year. They then compare this with aggregate wealth to obtain an estimate of the shares of wealth that are, respectively, self-accumulated and inherited.

Even though the age pattern of saving they use involves relatively little dissaving in old age, their estimate of the share of inherited wealth turns out to be rather small. For the years after 1974, it is around 25%, which agrees well with, and thus supports, the findings of my 1985 paper. For the years 1960 to 1973, the share they compute is somewhat larger, fluctuating between 30 and 40%. But this higher figure may, at least partly, reflect an upward bias in the A&K estimate of inherited wealth. The bias arises from the fact that the change in total wealth includes capital gains, while the change in the self-accumulated portion largely excludes them. In the period before 1974, capital gains were unquestionably significantly positive, and hence self-accumulation is underestimated and the share of bequests over-estimated. In the years from 1973 to 1980, depressed conditions in the stock market reduce the significance of this effect, though this is partially offset by the boom in real estate values.

These estimates are conspicuously at odds with that presented in a pro-vocative paper of Kotlikoff and Summers (1981) (hereafter K&S). They endeavor to estimate the share of bequests by two alternative methods: (1) from an estimated flow of bequests, as above, and (2) by an approach methodologically quite similar to that of Ando and Kennickell expect that instead of allocating aggregate saving to households by age, they allocate labor income and consumption to individuals 18 and over by age. Through this procedure, they estimate the life cycle wealth, accumulated by every cohort present in a year. Using the first method, K&S reach an estimate of inherited wealth of over one half, while using the second—which they regard as more reliable—their estimate rises even higher, to above four-fifths.

In the 1985 paper, I have shown that the difference between all other estimates, including Ando and Kennickell, and their much higher ones can be traced (i) to some explicit errors of theirs, for example, their treatment of the purchase of durable goods, and (ii) to unconventional definitions, both of inherited wealth and of life cycle saving. I have shown that when one corrects the error and uses the accepted definitions, one of the K&S mea-sures—that based on bequest flows—coincides very closely with all other estimates. Their alternative measure remains somewhat higher, but it is shown to be subject to an appreciable upward bias, which could easily account for the difference.

K&S have suggested an alternative operational criterion of "importance" that should be independent of definitional differences: By what percentage would aggregate wealth decline if the flow of bequests declined by 1%? The suggestion is sound but is very hard to implement from available observations. However, a rough measure can be provided by considering the response of the representative household confronted with a larger bequest, but subject to the steady state conditions that he must, in turn, increase his bequest by even more (by a factor equal to the rate of growth of the economy times the average gap between inheriting and bequeath-ing). He may be better or worse off as a result. If we suppose that he is neither, then one shows that the "importance" of bequests is measured by total bequests received by those currently living—capitalized from date of receipt to the present—divided by total wealth. This happens to be the measure of the "share of bequests" advocated by K&S. But in reality, for realistic values of the return on wealth and of the growth of the economy one finds that the representative consumer can be expected to be notably better off. Under these conditions one finds that the relevant measure of importance is much closer to the standard measure of share (i.e., not capitalized) than to the K&S measure. Since the shares can be placed at below 1/4, one can conclude that, for the United States, a 10% decrease in the flow of bequests would be unlikely to decrease wealth by more than 2.5%, and could well have an even smaller effect.

The only other country for which one can find some information seems to be the United Kingdom. The share of inherited wealth there appears to be, again, close to 1/5.

But how can one possibly reconcile the fact that the decumulation of wealth after retirement occurs rather slowly with the assertion that the share of inherited wealth is no more than 25%? Actually, this apparent puzzle can be readily clarified by means of two considerations. The first is to remember that one of the several ways by which we reached the above figure for the share relies precisely on estimating the flow of bequests from the observed holding of wealth by age; so, by construction, there cannot be any contradiction between the two observations.

The second and more fundamental substantive consideration is that, from the fact that bequeathed wealth is not much lower than the peak accumulation, one cannot conclude that most of the wealth ever accu-mulated is finally bequeathed. To see this, one need only realize that if one fixes the path of wealth from peak, around age 65, to death, there is still an infinity of possible paths from, say, age 20 to 65, and each of these paths implies a different amount of aggregate wealth. The quicker the average path approaches the peak value, the larger will be the wealth and hence the life cycle component. It can be shown that the observed path of wealth implies a much larger aggregate wealth than would correspond to the path chosen by a consumer scheduling to accumulate the observed average terminal amount of wealth while ensuring for himself the highest feasible (constant growth) consumption path.

Sources of Bequeathed Wealth: The Precautionary Motive
What accounts for the observed flow of bequests? One can distinguish two main motives, which may also interact. The first is the precautionary

motive arising from the uncertainty of the time of death. Indeed, in view of the practical impossibility of having negative net worth, people tend to die with some wealth, unless they can manage to put all their retirement reserves into life annuities. However, it is a well-known fact that annuity contracts, other than in the form of group insurance through pension systems, are extremely rare. Why this should be so is a subject of considerable current interest and debate (see, e.g., Friedman and Warshawsky, 1985a,b). Undoubtedly, "adverse selection," causing an unfavorable payout, and the fact that some utility may be derived from bequests (Masson, 1984)—see below—are an important part of the answer. In the absence of annuities, the wealth left behind will reflect risk aversion and the cost of running out of wealth (besides the utility of bequests).

This point has been elaborated in particular by Davies (1981) (see also Hubbard, 1984), who has shown that, for plausible parameters of the utility function, including a low intertemporal elasticity of substitution, the extent to which uncertainty of life depresses the propensity to consume increases with age. As a result, "Uncertain life time could provide the major element in a complete explanation of the slow decumulation of the retired" (relative to what would be implied by a standard LCH model).

Bequests originating from the precautionary motive fit quite naturally in the LCH framework since they are determined by the utility of consumption and, furthermore, the surviving wealth must tend, on the average, to be proportional to life resources.

The Bequest Motive in the LCH
The second source of inherited wealth is the bequest motive. Contrary to a common perception, there is no intrinsic inconsistency between a significant amount of bequests induced by a bequest motive and the LCH view of the world—in particular, implications 1–5.

First, it is obvious that no inconsistency arises if planned bequests are, on average, proportional to life resources. However, this possibility is uninteresting. The most casual observation suggests that the planning and leaving of bequests is concentrated in the upper strata of the distribution of life resources, by which we now mean the sum of (discounted) lifetime labor income and bequests received. This observation suggests the following hypothesis, first proposed in MB-A (pp. 173–174):

BI. The share of its resources that a household earmarks, on the average, for bequests is a (nondecreasing) stable function of the size of its life resources *relative* to the average level of resources of its age cohort.

We might expect the share to be close to zero until we reach the top percentiles of the distribution of resources, and then to rise rapidly with income.

One can readily demonstrate (cf. Modigliani, 1975) that this assumption assures that propositions 1–5 will continue to hold at least as long as

BII. The frequency distribution of the ratio of life resources to mean life resources for each age group is also stable in time.

Indeed, under these conditions, if income is constant, wealth will also tend to be constant and, therefore, saving to be zero, even in the presence of bequests. To see this, note first that BI ensures that bequests left (BL) are a fraction, say γ, of life resources, $BL = \gamma(\hat{Y} + BR)$, where BR is bequests received. BII in turn insures that γ is constant in time (and presumably less than one). Next, note that life savings, LS, is given by

$$LS = BL - BR = \gamma\hat{Y} - (1 - \gamma)\,BR. \tag{5}$$

Thus, LS increases with Y and decreases with BR, and is zero if $BR = [\gamma/(1 - \gamma)]\,\hat{Y}$. But this last condition must hold in long run equilibrium since, if BR is smaller, then there will be positive saving that will increase BR and reduce LS toward zero; and vice versa if BR is larger.

This generalization of the basic model has a number of implications, a few of which may be noted here.

i. The age patterns in figure 1.1 for a stationary society are modified, as bequests raise the average wealth path by a constant, equal to BR, beginning at the age at which bequests are received. The new path remains parallel to the old so that at death it has height $BL = BR$.

ii. If labor income is growing at some constant rate, then average BR will tend to grow at this same rate and so will BL, but BL will exceed BR by a factor $e^{\rho T}$, where T is the average age gap between donor and recipient. Thus, with positive growth, and then only, the existence of bequests involves life saving, on top of hump saving. Alternatively, bequests result in a higher wealth-income ratio, depending on γ, and, hence, a higher saving ratio, to an extent that is proportional to ρ.

iii. The share of life resources left as bequests could be an increasing function of the household's resources *relative* to the resources of his cohort. This, in turn, implies that at any age, the saving-income and wealth-income ratios for individual families could be an increasing function of *relative* (not absolute) income.

This last proposition, which is clearly inconsistent with PIH, is supported by a good deal of empirical evidence, from Brady and Friedman (1947) to Mayer (1972). As for the first part of (iii), and the underlying assumption BI, it receives strong support from a recent test by Menchik and David (1983). In this imaginative contribution, the authors have assembled, from probate records, a large body of data on individual bequests that they have matched with income data from tax returns. Their sample covers persons born since 1880 (including a few before) and deceased between 1947 and 1978. They find striking evidence (a) that bequests depend on the position of the household's life resources in the distribution of life resources of *its cohort*, that (b) they are small for people whose estimated life resources fall below the 80th percentile in that distribution, but (c) that beyond the 80th percentile, they rise rapidly with (permanent) income.

The Quantitative Importance of the Bequest Motive

It would be interesting to have some idea of how important is the role of the pure bequest motive—as distinguished from the precautionary one—in the accumulation of wealth. It should be apparent, in fact, that if one could conclude that it accounts for a very large fraction of total wealth, then the LCH and hump saving would lose considerable interest as an explanation of private accumulation. Unfortunately, at present, we know very little on this score, and it is not even clear that we will even be able to acquire reliable knowledge. There is nonetheless a certain amount of evidence suggesting that the true bequest motive affects a rather small number of households located mostly in the highest income and wealth brackets.

The best known evidence is that coming from surveys conducted in the 1960s. In a 1962 survey (Projector and Weiss 1964), only 3% of the respondents gave as a reason for saving, "To provide an estate for the family." However, the proportion rises with wealth, reaching 1/3 for the top class (1/2 million 1963 dollars and over). Similar, though somewhat less extreme, results are reported for a Brookings study (Barlow et al., 1966). Thus, the bequest motive seems to be limited to the highest economic classes.

This hypothesis is supported by the finding of Menchik and David that for (and only for) the top 20%, bequests rise proportionately faster than total resources, something that presumably cannot be explained by the precautionary motive. Actually, another very recent study (Hurd, 1986) yields results that are even more negative about the importance of bequests. It starts from the reasonable hypothesis that if the true bequest motive is an important source of terminal wealth, then retired households with living children should have more wealth and should save more (dissave less) than childless ones. It is found that in fact those with children have *less* wealth and, by and large, *dissave* the same fraction of wealth. The first result, as pointed out earlier, is fully consistent with the standard no-bequest LCH, because of the "cost" of children; but for this reason the rest may be biased. But the second result is indeed hard to reconcile with a significant bequest motive.

Considering that the overall share of inherited wealth can be placed below 1/5, we seem safe in concluding that the overwhelming proportion of wealth existing at a given time is the result of life cycle accumulation, including in it a portion reflecting the bequest arising from the precautionary motive.

Aside from this quantitative evaluation, it is important to note that the model generalized to allow for bequests of all sources still satisfies propositions 1–5. On the other hand, proposition 6 must be generalized to allow for several forces, discussed in this section, that could affect the equilibrium wealth-income ratio. These include the age structure not accounted for by steady state population growth, the rate of return on wealth, and the household access to credit, as well as the strength of the bequest motive. Another potentially important variable is social security, though its systematic effect on saving has so far proven elusive, a failure not convincingly accounted for by its having two offsetting effects on private saving (cf. section 2.3). Pursuing the above implications opens up a vast area of research that so far has been barely scratched.

3   Policy Implications

Limitations of space make it impossible to pursue a systematic analysis of policy issues for which the LCH has implications that are significantly different from those derivable by the standard Keynesian consumption function or refinements thereof. I shall, however, list some of the major areas of applications with a brief statement of the LCH implications.

3.1   Short-Run Stabilization Policy

The Monetary Mechanism
The fact that wealth enters importantly in the short-run consumption function means that monetary policy can affect aggregate demand not only through the traditional channel of investment but also through the market value of assets and consumption (see Modigliani, 1971).

Transitory Income Taxes
Attempts at restraining (or stimulating) demand through transitory income taxes (or rebates) can be expected to have small effects on consumption and to lower (raise) saving because consumption depends on life resources, which are little affected by a transitory tax change (empirically supported) (see the literature cited in Modigliani and Steindel, 1977, and Modigliani and Sterling, 1985).

3.2   Long-Run Propositions

Consumption Taxes
A progressive tax on consumption is more equitable than one on current income because it more nearly taxes permanent income (quite apart from its incentive effects on saving.)

Short- and Long-Run Effects of Deficit Financing
Expenditures financed by deficit tend to be paid by future generations; those financed by taxes are paid by the current generation. The conclusion rests on the proposition that private saving, being controlled by life cycle considerations, should be (nearly) independent of the government budget stance (Modigliani and Sterling, 1985), and therefore private wealth should be independent of the national debt (Modigliani, 1984). It follows that the national debt tends to crowd out an equal amount of private capital at a social cost equal to the return on the lost capital (which is also approximately equal to the government interest bill).

This conclusion stands in sharp contrast to that advocated by the so-called Ricardian Equivalence Proposition (Barro, 1974), which holds that whenever the government runs a deficit, the private sector will save more in order to offset the unfavorable effect of the deficit on future generations.

Of course, to the extent that the government deficit is used to finance productive investments, future generations also receive the benefit of the expenditure, and letting them pay for it through deficit financing may be consistent with intergenerational equity.

In an open economy, the investment crowding out effect may be attenuated through the inflow of foreign capital, attracted by the higher interest that results from the smaller availability of investable funds. However, the burden on future generations is roughly unchanged because of the interest to be paid on the foreign debt.

Finally, if there is slack in the economy, debt-financed government expenditures may not crowd out investment, at least if accompanied by an accommodating monetary policy, but may, instead, raise income and saving. In this case, the deficit is beneficial, as was held by the early Keynesians; however, the debt will have a crowding out effect once the economy returns to full employment. LCH suggests that to avoid this outcome, a good case can be made for a so-called cyclically balanced budget.

References

Ackley. G., "The Wealth-Saving Relationship," *Journal of Political Economy*, April 1951.

Ando, A., "The Savings of Japanese Households: A Micro Study Based on Data from the National Survey of Family Income and Expenditure, 1974 and 1979," Economic Planning Agency, Government of Japan, 1985.

Ando, A., and A. Kennickell, "How Much (or Little) Life Cycle Is There in Micro Data? Cases of U.S. and Japan," this volume.

Ando, A., E. G. Brown, J. Kareken, and R. M. Solow, "Lags in Fiscal and Monetary Policy," in *Stabilization Policies*, prepared for the Commission on Money and Credit, Prentice-Hall, 1963.

Avery, R. B., G. E. Elliehausen, G. B. Canner, and T. A. Gustafson, "Survey of Consumer Finances, 1983: A Second Report," *Federal Reserve Bulletin, 70,* 1984.

Barlow, R., H. E. Brazer, and J. N. Morgan, *Economic Behavior of the Affluent*, Washington: The Brookings Institute, 1966

Barro, R. J., "Are Government Bonds Net Wealth?" *Journal of Political Economy, 82,* 1974.

Bentzel, R., "Nagra Synpunkter pa Sparandets Dynamik," in *Festskrift Tillagnad Halvar Sundberg* (Uppsala Universitetes Arsskrift 1959:9) Uppsala, 1959.

Blinder, A., R. Gordon, and D. Wise, "Social Security, Bequests and the Life Cycle Theory of Saving: Cross-Sectional Tests," in F. Modigliani and R. Hemming, eds., *The Determinants of National Saving and Wealth*, St. Martins Press, New York, 1983, pp. 89–122.

Boskin, M., and M. Hurd, "The Effect of Social Security on Early Retirement, *Journal of Public Economics, 10,* 1978.

Brady, D. S., and R. D. Friedman, "Savings and the Income Distribution," *Studies in Income and Wealth, 9,* National Bureau of Economic Research, New York, 1947.

Brown, T. M., "Habit Persistence and Lags in Consumer Behavior," *Econometrica, 20,* 1952.

Davies, J. B., "Uncertain Lifetime, Consumption, and Dissaving in Retirement," *Journal of Political Economy*, 89, 1981.

Diamond, P. A., and J. A. Hausman, "Individual Retirement and Savings Behavior," *Journal of Public Economics*, 23, 1985.

Duesenberry, James S., *Income, Saving and the Theory of Consumer Behavior*, Harvard University Press, Cambridge, MA, 1949.

Feldstein, M., "Social Security, Induced Retirement, and Aggregate Accumulation," *Journal of Political Economy*, 82, 1974.

Feldstein, M., "Social Security and Private Savings: International Evidence in an Extended Life-Cycle Model," in M. Feldstein and R. Inman, eds., *The Economics of Public Services*, Macmillan, London, 1977.

Fisher, F., and R. Brown, "Negro-White Savings Differentials and the Modigliani-Brumberg Hypothesis," *Review of Economics and Statistics*, February 1958.

Fisher, I., *The Theory of Interest*, Macmillan, New York, 1930.

Fisher, J., "The Economics of an Aging Population, A Study in Income, Spending and Savings Patterns of Consumer Units in Different Age Groups, 1935–36, 1945 and 1949," unpublished dissertation, Columbia University, New York, 1950.

Friedman, Benjamin M., and Mark Warshawsky, "The Cost of Annuities: Implications for Saving Behavior and Bequests," National Bureau of Economic Research Working Paper #1682, August 1985.

Friedman, Benjamin M., and Mark Warshawsky, "Annuity Prices and Saving Behavior in the United States," National Bureau of Economic Research Working Paper #1683, June 1985.

Friedman, M., *A Theory of the Consumption Function*, Princeton University Press, Princeton, 1957.

Goldsmith, R. W., *A Study of Saving in the United States*, Princeton University Press, Princeton, 1956.

Hamburger, W., "Consumption and Wealth," unpublished dissertation, University of Chicago, Chicago, 1951.

Harrod, R. F., *Towards a Dynamic Economics*, London, 1948.

Houthakker, H. S., "An International Comparison of Personal Saving," *Bulletin of the International Statistical Institute*, 38, 1961.

Houthakker, H. S., "On Some Determinants of Saving in Developed and Under-developed Countries," in *Problems in Economic Development*, E. A. G. Robinson, ed., Macmillan, London, 1965.

Hubbard, R. Glenn, "'Precautionary' Saving Revisited: Social Security, Individual

Welfare, and the Capital Stock," National Bureau of Economic Research Working Paper #1430, August 1984.

Hurd, Michael D., "Savings and Bequests," National Bureau of Economic Research Working Paper #1826, January 1986.

Kennickell, A., "An Investigation of Life Cycle Savings Behavior in the United States", unpublished dissertation, University of Pennsylvania, Philadelphia, 1984.

Keynes, J. M., *General Theory of Employment, Interest and Money*, Harcourt, Brace, New York, 1936.

King, M. A., and L.-D. L. Dicks-Mireaux, "Asset Holdings and the Life-Cycle," *Economic Journal, 92*, 1982.

Kotlikoff, L. J., and L. Summers, "The Role of Intergenerational Transfers in Aggregate Capital Accumulation," *Journal of Political Economy, 89*, 1981.

Kotlikoff, L. J., A. Spivak, and L. Summers, "The Adequacy of Savings," *American Economic Review, 72*, 1982.

Kuznets, S., *National Income: A Summary of Findings*, National Bureau of Economic Research, New York, 1946.

Leff, N., "Dependency Rates and Saving Rates," *American Economic Review, 59*, 1969.

Lydall, H., "The Life Cycle in Income, Saving and Asset Ownership," *Econometrica, 23*, 1955.

Masson, Andre, "A Cohort Analysis of Wealth-Age profiles generated by a Simulation Model: France (1949–1975)," *Economic Journal, 96*, 1986, March.

Mayer, T., *Permanent Income, Wealth and Consumption*, University of California Press, 1972.

Menchik, P. L., and David, M., "Income Distribution, Lifetime Savings, and Bequests," *American Economic Review, 73*, 1983.

Mirer, T. W., "The Wealth-Age Relationship among the Aged," *American Economic Review, 69*, 1979.

Modigliani, F., "Fluctuations in the Saving-Income Ratio: A Problem in Economic Forecasting," *Studies in Income and Wealth, 11*, National Bureau of Economic Research, New York, 1949.

Modigliani, Franco, "The Life Cycle Hypothesis of Saving and Inter-Country Differences in the Saving Ratio," in W. A. Eltis et al., eds., *Induction, Growth and Trade: Essays in Honor of Sir Roy Harrod*, London: Clarendon Press, 1970.

Modigliani, F., "Monetary Policy and Consumption: Linkages via Interest Rate and Wealth Effects in the FMP Model," in *Consumer Spending and Monetary Policy: The Linkages*, Conference Series No. 5, Federal Reserve Bank of Boston, Boston, 1971.

Modigliani, F., "The Life Cycle Hypothesis of Saving Twenty Years Later," in M. Parkin, ed., *Contemporary Issues in Economics*, Manchester University Press, 1975.

Modigliani, F., "The Economics of Public Deficits," paper presented at Conference in memory of Abba Lerner, Tel Aviv University, Israel, May 28–31, 1984. Proceedings forthcoming.

Modigliani, F., "Measuring the Contribution of Intergenerational Transfers to Total Wealth: Conceptual Issues and Empirical Findings," paper presented at Modeling the Accumulation and Distribution of Personal Wealth seminar, Paris, France, September 10–11, 1985. Proceedings forthcoming.

Modigliani, F., and A. Ando, "Tests of the Life Cycle Hypothesis of Savings: Comments and Suggestions," *Bulletin of the Oxford University Institute of Statistics*, 1957.

Modigliani, F., and A. Ando, "The 'Permanent Income' and the 'Life Cycle' Hypothesis of Saving Behavior: Comparison and Tests," in *Consumption and Saving*, Vol. 2, Wharton School of Finance and Commerce, University of Pennsylvania, 1960.

Modigliani, F., and A. Ando, "The 'Life Cycle' Hypothesis of Saving: Aggregate Implications and Tests," *American Economic Review*, 53, 1963.

Modigliani, F., and R. Brumberg, "Utility Analysis and the Consumption Function: An Interpretation of Cross-Section Data," in K. Kurihara, ed., *Post-Keynesian Economics*, Rutgers University Press, New Brunswick, 1954.

Modigliani, F., and R. Brumberg, "Utility Analysis and Aggregate Consumption Functions: An Attempt at Integration," in A. Abel, ed., *Collected Papers of Franco Modigliani*, Vol. 2, MIT Press, Cambridge, MA, 1979.

Modigliani, F., and C. Steindel, "Is a Tax Rebate an Effective Tool for Stabilization Policy?" *Brookings Papers on Economics Activity*, 1977:1.

Modigliani, F., and A. Sterling, "Determinants of Private Saving with Special Reference to the Role of Social Security—Cross-Country Tests," in F. Modigliani and R. Hemming, eds., *The Determinants of National Saving and Wealth*, St. Martins Press, New York, 1983, pp. 24–55.

Modigliani, F., and A. Sterling, "Government Debt, Government Spending, and Private Sector Behavior: A Comment," 1985. Forthcoming in *American Economic Review*.

Modigliani, F., A. Mason, and A. Sterling, "Effect of Fiscal Policy on Saving: Evidence from an International Cross-Section," paper in progress.

Munnell, A., *The Effect of Social Security on Personal Saving*, Ballinger Press, Cambridge, MA, 1974.

Neisser, H. P. "The Economics of a Stationary Population," *Social Research*, 1944.

Projector, D., *Survey of Changes in Family Finances*, Board of Governors of the Federal Reserve System, Washington, 1968.

Projector, D., and G. Weiss, *Survey of Financial Characteristics of Consumers*, The Board of Governors of the Federal Reserve, Washington, 1964.

Reid, M. G., "The Relation of the Within-Group Permanent Component of Income to the Income Elasticity of Expenditure," unpublished paper.

Ricci, U., "L'offerta del Risparmio," Part I, *Giornale degli Economisti*, 1926; Part II, ibid., 1926; "Ancora Sull'Offerta del Risparmio," ibid., 1927.

Royal Commission on the Distribution of Income and Wealth, *Report No. 5, Third Report on the Standing Reference*, HMSO, London, 1977.

Shefrin, H. M., and R. Thaler, "Life Cycle vs. Self-Control Theories of Saving: A Look at the Evidence," unpublished paper, 1985.

Shiba, Tsunemasa, "The Personal Savings Functions of Urban Worker Household in Japan," *Review of Economics and Statistics*, 61, 1979.

Shorrocks, A. F., "The Age-Wealth Relationship: A Cross-Section and Cohort Analysis," *Review of Economics and Statistics*, 57, 1975.

Tobin, James, "Life Cycle Saving and Balanced Growth," in Fellner, et al., *Ten Economic Studies in the Tradition of Irving Fisher*, J. Wiley, New York, 1967.

2 The 1985 Nobel Prize in Economics

Paul A. Samuelson

Franco Modigliani of the Massachusetts Institute of Technology was awarded the seventeenth Nobel Prize in economics. This choice was widely applauded since Modigliani has been a versatile and deep contributor to modern economics for 40 years.

Two countries can take pride in his being honored: Italy, from which he fled as a young victim of Mussolini's racial persecutions and whose postwar policy problems he has attentively researched; and the United States, where he received his Ph.D. training (at the "University in Exile," the New School for Social Research) and where he has held many university chairs.

More than 40 years ago, when Modigliani was only 25, he wrote a seminal article setting Model-T Keynesianism on its modern evolutionary path and probing its microfoundations in rigid, nonmarket-clearing prices (1944). Although neither this paper nor his 1963 classic (1963), which set the pattern for today's post-Keynesian eclecticism, were mentioned in the citation of the Swedish Royal Academy of Science, they form the basis for the Federal Reserve Board—MIT—Penn forecasting and policy model that has long been useful in framing Federal Reserve monetary policy. As an MIT colleague documented at a September 1985 conference at Martha's Vineyard attended by scholars from all over the world to honor Modigliani, the best state of the macroeconomic art in these days after "monetarism" and "the new classical economics" of the rational expectationists calls for a paradigm that is a natural evolution from those 1944 and 1963 classics (Fischer, 1987).

Franco Modigliani shares one characteristic with his older countryman, Enrico Fermi. Fermi, also a refugee from Mussolini's Italy, was a doubly great physicist. In addition to being a great theorist, Fermi had the rare quality of being a brilliant experimentalist. Modigliani is recognized as an

Reprinted from *Science*, Vol. 231, pp. 1399–1401, 27 March 1986.

outstanding economic theorist. At the same time he insists on measuring empirical behavior patterns econometrically, refusing others all the pleasures of quantitative testing of his own novel hypotheses. Before he had ever heard of Karl Popper, Modigliani was already practicing the advice that a scholar should be his own most stringent critic. It is good for science; it is good for self-protection; besides, it is good fun.

In a field known for its voluble talkers, Modigliani is one of the fastest— quick off the mark in the short sprints, but ahead of the pack also for the long jog. Stealing a line from Sydney Smith's conversation with Thomas Babington Macaulay, I used to utter the mock complaint, "Franco, when I am dead you will be sorry you never heard the sound of my voice." Actually, as we both know, this is quite untrue. Economists from all over the world, and not least young scholars from Italy, bring their problems to Franco Modigliani. He is slow to digest the issues because he insists on fundamental understanding at every stage of the examination, avoiding facile handling. (Once, referring to a world-famous scholar, Modigliani said to me, quite guilelessly, unselfconsciously, and truthfully, "He's *deep*—like me.") Although known to be a lover of argument, Modigliani is also known as one who never argues for victory, but rather for truth. That is why, at 67, he remains a Mecca for both young and established researchers.

1   The Life-Cycle Saving Model

Modigliani has many brainchildren to his credit. All of a scholar's children are equal, but in my view the jewel in the Modigliani crown is his life-cycle hypothesis of saving, developed in collaboration with Richard Brumberg, a scholar who died young (Modigliani and Brumberg, 1954). The Royal Academy of Sciences agreed and mentioned it first in their official citation announcing the award.

I believe it to be the best single explainer, across time and space, of saving and investing behaviors and their responsiveness to various policy programs. From its deceptive simplicity, novel and testable expectations emerge. Here is how it goes.

Most of us will live beyond our prime earning years. So we must save when in our prime to accumulate the assets on which we will live in retirement. In the purest life-cycle model, when the end comes we'll die broke.

Simple stuff? They give prizes, you will ask, for that? Yes, so simple as to be fundamental. And the insights gained are far from simple or obvious. Suppose population ceased to grow (as in Denmark or the Germanies).

Suppose productivity improvements that raise real incomes virtually cease (as happened from 1973 to 1980 over much of the globe). A life-cycle system without growth involves zero net saving and investment: saving of the young is canceled by dissaving of the old. Modigliani gets us to focus on the right questions. Growing nations save much, stagnating nations save little—a different hypothesis from "rich people save much, poor people little."

Science says: Let them who can be clever. What counts is which clever theory fits and predicts the observable facts. On this score Modigliani wins hands down. Early Americans, though poor, saved much; we affluent moderns save little. The first-growing Japanese and Germans save much; the French and Italians, allegedly so romantic and carefree, have high saving rates between those of Japan and the United States.

An inexact science like economics benefits enormously from theoretical models that are themselves only partially accurate. Ten physiologists could make their reputations disproving aspects of Claude Bernard's seminal theories. Fifty economists win fame by finding exceptions to Modigliani's life-cycle paradigm. Leading that pack is Franco Modigliani himself. (Not knowing when we will die, we leave bequests willy-nilly. Some classes do dance to the bourgeois drumbeat and plan for their posterity's economic needs.)

2 Indifference of Leveraging

Modigliani has contributed both to the macroeconomics of business cycles and inflation and to the microeconomics of relative prices and rational decision-making. The 1985 award explicitly cited a second line of his work, that dealing with "efficient-market" analysis and leading to the 1958 Modigliani-Miller theorem concerning the neutrality of corporate leveraging (Modigliani and Miller, 1958).

Some companies float bonds as well as stocks; some eschew debt and any such "leveraging." The conventional wisdom before 1958 was that, depending on the growth prospects and intrinsic variability of your industry and product line, your corporation should ideally borrow a certain optimal fraction of its total capital needs. The canny board of directors that achieves this golden leveraging ratio lifts, so to speak by its own bootstraps, the total market value of its owners' shares. The lazy or stupid management, which either stays zero leveraged or overleverages, loses prospective wealth and, in a cruel competitive world, may in the long run be forced out of office.

Merton Miller and Franco Modigliani argued otherwise. "Chicken legs and breasts can be separately packaged at the supermarket: the values of each such package must add up closely to the value of whole chickens. Otherwise consumers can do their own packaging." Similarly, Modigliani and Miller showed that firm A, with much debt and its entailed riskiness of common-stock earnings, cannot command a premium from risk-tolerant investors. Why not? Those investors can buy a zero-debt company on borrowed funds (margin purchases or collateral loans at the bank) and can produce with no premium that same attractive pattern of leveraged high-mean-return-cum-high-volatility. Similarly, no firm can win a premium by having a clean debt-free balance sheet. Private investors can put half their assets in leveraged stocks while keeping the other half in safe overnight deposits: that way they duplicate for themselves (premium free) whatever the clean balance sheet can produce. Conclusion: to a first approximation, total value to the owners of a company is invariant, independent of the degree of leverage, because investors can do for themselves, or undo for themselves, whatever leveraging can accomplish.

More important than deductive syllogizing is empirical testing, which showed that the alleged advantages of optimal leveraging could not be factually identified. Also important are deviations from the theory's axioms, such as recognition of how bankruptcy events can alter the simplicity and sweep of the proposition. Gratifying are corollaries, such as the 1961 Miller-Modigliani theorem that the percentage payment of earnings as dividends will not affect a stock's valuation.

We live in an age of accelerated corporate borrowing. This explosion in leveraging is in accord with the Modigliani-Miller theory: taxes aside, leveraging is neutral; inasmuch as deductability of debt interest from corporate taxation is patently favorable to borrowing, the 1960–1986 trend toward debt confirms the Modigliani-Miller analysis. We are left, though, with the puzzle: why do firms pay dividends to taxpaying shareholders? Why not buy back shares more than corporations actually do?

3   Self-Falsifying Prophecy?

Although a critic of the new Lucas-Sargent school of rational expectationism, Modigliani is himself a founder of rational expectationism. (For a sketch of competing paradigms in modern macroeconomics—post-Keynesian eclecticism, monetarism, and the new classical rational expectationism—see Samuelson and Nordhaus, 1985, part 3.) In a 1954 tour de force, written with Emile Grunberg, he contributed a solution to the old problem of whether correct prediction is a self-contradictory impossibility (Grunberg and Modigliani, 1954).

Here is how the late Oskar Morgenstern put the issue in a 1928 publication that led ultimately to his collaboration with John von Neumann on *The Theory of Games and Economic Behavior* (von Neumann and Morgenstern, 1944). The diabolical Professor Moriarty pursues the incomparable Sherlock Holmes. Holmes boards in London the Dover train that makes an intermediate stop at Canterbury. Moriarty can just catch his prey in Dover if he flies a geodesic to there; however, if the quarry anticipates that fate and gets off in Canterbury, the gambit will fail and Moriarty will rue that he did not aim for Canterbury and victory there. We seem to be in the regression, What does A think B thinks A is thinking ...?, and so forth, seemingly endlessly. Morgenstern concluded that perfect prediction is impossible, since knowing it must alter it.

Now the white knights Grunberg and Modigliani come to the rescue of the logical possibility of perfect prediction. Here is how they would treat the case of a never-published Gallup poll that can correctly predict the fraction of votes, x, that Ike will get while Adlai gets $1 - x$. Provided no one is apprised of this datum, the election will (by hypothesis) yield an actual outcome fraction that equals the predicted fraction: $x' = x$. No Morgenstern problem yet. Suppose now that the Gallup fact of x is announced to the electorate. Then there may be a bandwagon effect: when $x > 1/2$ is announced, impressionable voters shift over to the front runner Ike and the result is actual $x' >$ predicted x. In this case, no correct prediction by candor is possible. Or, suppose there is an "underdog" effect, which is the reverse of a bandwagon effect: now when x is announced greater than $1/2$, some voters pity Adlai and the shift of their votes makes actual $x' <$ predicted x. Again, candor destroys omniscience.

Grunberg-Modigliani (1954) cut the Holmes-Moriarty knot thus. Stipulate that there is a knowable law (never mind *how* it is knowable), which specifies what actual x' will be for each pair of poll-finding x and *reported-finding* y:

$x' =$ known continuous function of $(y; x)$

$$= f(y; x); \quad 0 \leq [x\,y, f(y; x)] \leq 1.$$

Then they conclude, "Whatever the x finding that occurs, there is always a calculable y report that will be a self-fulfilling prophecy with actual $x' =$ published-prediction y."

The proof is trivial, a one-dimensional application of L. E. J. Brouwer's

1912 fixed-point theorem. (Doubters can try to move from a square's left wall to its right wall, never taking pencil off paper, and avoiding ever touching the square's diagonal.)

As the authors stress, the continuity assumption is basic to the demonstration. Thus, suppose that the variables (x, y, x') must be rational numbers (as literally they must be if the electorate is finite in number). The above square then is replaced by a lattice of nails lined up in the same number of rows and columns.

Can we tie a long red string around a specified nail in each column, and end up with a path for the string made up of line segments—a path that traverses from the first left-hand column to the last right column, without ever touching any nail in the diagonal of the lattice? Of course we can; and in a stupendous number of ways. Indeed if we knot our string around each column's nail selected at random, the odds are better than one-third that the resulting x will never equal the reported y [the exact probability being almost exactly $e^{-1} = (2.718\ldots)^{-1}$]. The 1928 Morgenstern point thus can still be a worry.

All this relates to rational expectationism, à la John Muth and others, as follows. A rational-expectation equilibrium time-profile of economic variables must be such that, if everyone were apprised of it, they would together all recreate exactly that profile. Hail to the Carnegie-Mellon workshops of the 1950s where Herbert Simon, John Nash, Abraham Charnes, William Cooper, John Muth, Charles Holt, Albert Ando, and Franco Modigliani made intellectual history with the perceptive support of Dean George Leland Bach.

4 Ad Hominem Matters

Hitler and Mussolini enriched American science. Along with Einstein, Weyl, Bethe, Ernst Mayr, von Neumann, and so many others in the natural sciences, they presented us with such economists as Joseph Schumpeter, Wassily Leontief, Jacob Marschak, Gottfried Haberler, and Abraham Wald. Modigliani, by his youth, was at the end of this illustrious migration. By good luck, Jacob Marschak and Hans Neisser at the New School enabled him to land on his feet running. Great universities—Chicago, Illinois, Carnegie-Mellon, Northwestern, MIT—recognized his merits and he repaid their perspicuity. Every scholarly honor came his way, and fittingly early—presidencies of the American Economic Association, the Econometric Society, the American Finance Society, and so forth. Not only have governments benefited from his wisdom, but in addition he has helped universities and academies recognize undervaluations in Wall Street.

Still, there is one remarkable feature in Modigliani's scholarly profile. No lone scholar he; instead, dozens of his most famous contributions have been with joint authors, bearing such bylines as Modigliani-Ando, Modigliani-Brumberg, Modigliani-Grunberg, Modigliani-Miller, Modigliani-Samuelson, Modigliani-Drèze, and Modigliani-Papedemos. No one doubts Franco Modigliani's autonomous originality; all envy his ability to raise his own productivity and that of others by intense and joyful collaboration.

References

Abel, A., ed., *The Collected Papers of Franco Modigliani* (MIT Press, Cambridge, MA, 1980).

Fischer, S., in *Macroeconomics and Finance: Essays in Honor of Franco Modigliani*, R. Dornbusch and S. Fischer, eds. (MIT Press, Cambridge, MA, 1987).

Grunberg, E., and F. Modigliani, *J. Pol. Econ.* 62, 465 (1954); reprinted in Abel (1980).

Miller, M. H., and F. Modigliani, *J. Business* 34, 411 (1961); reprinted in Abel (1980).

Modigliani, F., *Econometrica* 12, 45 (1944); reprinted in Abel (1980).

Modigliani, F., *Rev. Econ. Stat.* 45, 79 (1963); reprinted in Abel (1980).

Modigliani, F., and R. Brumberg, in *Post Keynesian Economics*, K. K. Kurihara, ed. (Rutgers University Press, New Brunswick, NJ, 1954), pp. 388–436; reprinted, along with other publications by Modigliani, and by Albert Ando and Franco Modigliani, on the life-cycle model, in Abel (1980).

Modigliani, F., and M. H. Miller, *Am. Econ. Rev.* 48, 261 (1958); reprinted in Abel (1980).

Samuelson, P. A., and W. D. Nordhaus, Economics (McGraw-Hill, New York, 1985).

Von Neumann, J., and O. Morgenstern, *The Theory of Games and Economic Behavior* (Princeton University Press, Princeton, 1944). Pp. 176–178 describe the Holmes-Moriarty problem, referred to in earlier work by Morgenstern.

3

The Informational
Content of Dividends

Merton H. Miller

1 Introduction

In our 1961 article on "Dividend Policy, Growth and the Valuation of Shares," Franco Modigliani and I invoked the "informational content of dividends" as a way of reconciling the basic theory of dividends developed in the article with some seemingly contradictory, stylized facts. We had shown that in a world of well-functioning capital markets, a firm's dividend policy was essentially an exercise in financial packaging. The payout ratio chosen by the firm governed the division of its shareholders' returns between cash dividends and capital gains; and it governed the division of the firm's financing between internal and external sources of funds. But, to a first approximation at least, the payout policy would have no effect on the value of the shares. That value would reflect only the underlying real, economic factors—the stream of future cash flows from the firm's present assets and future growth opportunities, adjusted for the additional investment of real resources in the future to initiate and sustain those flows.

But if dividends are a "mere financial detail," as we put it, why are announcements of dividends increases typically followed by stock price increases, sometimes spectacularly so? And why are dividend cuts or eliminations often followed by price falls, sometimes even more spectacular?

These questions held a special poignancy for us after a disconcerting incident during our search for a convenient data base for testing the then newly developed M and M propositions. I happened to be lecturing on our

I acknowledge with thanks criticisms of an earlier draft by many present and former colleagues, especially Nai-fu Chen, Dosoung Choi, George Constantinides, Douglas Diamond, Ron Dye, Eugene Fama, Wayne Ferson, Sanford Grossman, Robert Holthausen, Gur Huberman, Kose John, Allan Kleidon, Marc Reinganum, Myron Scholes, Lester Telser and Theo Vermaelen. Helpful suggestions were made also by my commentator, Stewart Myers, and by Stanley Fischer.

dividend irrelevance proposition to the research department of a large Wall Street brokerage firm in December 1958 at the very moment when the American Telephone and Telegraph Corp. announced a stock split and an increase in the $9.00 annual dividend it had maintained for the previous 30 years. When trading (and my lecture on dividend irrelevance) was resumed a half-hour later, AT&T had jumped in price by over 10%!

The reconciliation in terms of information effects of dividends offered in my talk—and greeted, needless to say, with some derision—was developed in greater detail in the 1961 published version. Our model, we pointed out, was a full-information model that assumed everything relevant to valuation known by the firm's managers was known to the investing public. Eventually, perhaps so. But at the time of the dividend announcement, perhaps not. Because higher dividends are associated with higher earnings, investors may interpret an announced increase in dividends as a sign of improved prospects for the firm's earnings. And it is to these improved real earnings prospects rather than to the dividend increase per se that the market is responding.

Our proposed explanation has motivated a stream of empirical research papers over the last 25 years seeking to establish more systematically whether and what information was being conveyed by the dividend beyond that in other announcements by the firm; and, at a more theoretical level, why and how the firm's managers choose dividends as the vehicle for conveying that information.

I will not attempt to review that stream of literature here. The list is too long and many of the issues in controversy have yet to be satisfactorily resolved. Instead, I propose to pursue one, more narrowly focused theme raised in a number of recent papers, namely, that dividends, thanks to their informational content, can (and do) serve, at least in part, as *signals* in the technical sense of that term. Signaling in that sense is among the key concepts in the exciting and rapidly growing field that has come to be called "information economics," but obviously, it was not a lead that Franco Modigliani and I could have pursued in the late 1950s when we were puzzling over the problems raised by announcement effects: formal signaling theory wasn't even invented by Michael Spence until 10 or 12 years later!

The term signaling, of course, was and still is used, in connection with dividends in a looser, more heuristic way. The notion of signaling in general, and dividend signaling in particular, is so intuitively appealing that it is all too easy to overlook the very stringent conditions for a sustainable signaling equilibrium in the strict sense to emerge. What I propose to do here is essentially to go over those conditions in detail, to check their consistency with existing models of dividend decisions and valuation on the one hand and, on the other, with the established empirical regularities about dividends and the market's response to them. As we shall see, the conditions for a signaling equilibrium can be matched up with some existing dividend decision and valuation models, though not without imposing additional and somewhat arbitrary structure on the problem. Whether these signaling models do describe the role of dividends in conveying information to the market is harder to say.

2   The Conditions for a Signaling Equilibrium

The potential for signaling arises whenever the sellers of a commodity know more about its quality than do the buyers. Unable to distinguish differences in quality, the buyers offer a price that reflects only their perception of average quality (leading to what has been dubbed, for some reason, a "pooled" equilibrium). Sellers who know their product to be at the highest end of the quality spectrum thus have an incentive to distinguish themselves from the common herd by informing the market of their superiority. If they can find a way to "signal" their high quality and if their signal is believed, they will command a higher price. With the cream of the pool thus skimmed off, the pooled price for the remainder falls and the sellers with the highest remaining quality rank now have the greatest incentive to signal; and so on, until in the limit, everyone's true quality is known and priced accordingly, giving rise to what has been called a "separating" equilibrium.[1]

The sufficient conditions for such a separating equilibrium, specified originally by Spence, have been generalized and compactly summarized in a recent paper by John Riley, "Information Equilibrium" (1979). I will take up Riley's conditions one by one but in a somewhat different order and in a more intuitive way designed to highlight their significance in the specific context of dividend signaling.

2.1   The Costs of Dividend Signaling

To be believable, a signal must be costly—a notion long recognized in the folk wisdom that "talk is cheap"—and increasingly so, to discourage fakers. The cost, however, need not be deliberate waste as, say, in the potlatch ceremonies of the Kwakiutl Indians, whose chiefs signaled their wealth by burning their blankets. And indeed it would be hard to take signaling models seriously if they could be driven only by self-inflicted wounds of this kind. Where, after all, are the Kwakiutl's today?[2] But as Riley reminds us, cost in economics is opportunity cost; and cost in that sense will be incurred whenever the desire to signal leads the decision maker to adopt policies differing from those that would have been optimal in a full-information world where all the cards were on the table. The cost of signaling is thus the cost of departing from an otherwise best strategy— still wasteful, of course, but less violative of an economists' sensibilities than the pure potlatch models.[3]

The Cost of Signaling in an M and M World

Endogenizing the costs of signaling in that way as a departure from the full-information optimum may make signaling more palatable, but it clearly creates problems for anyone attempting to graft signaling onto the M and M dividend model. In an M and M world, there *is* no optimal dividend!

The nature of the difficulty as well as some of the possible routes around it can be illustrated with a simple, stylized, two-period, no-tax, Fisherian model of the firm adapted from Miller and Rock (1985).

The firm was founded in period 0 (the past) with an investment of I_0 by the original shareholders in a production process whose output is the sum of a deterministic component $F_0(I_0)$ and a random component $\tilde{\varepsilon}_1$ of known distribution. The sum of the two constitutes the firm's earnings, $\tilde{X}_1$, whose value is known by the firm's managers at the start of period 1 (the present). The managers in turn must allocate these earnings between dividends D_1 and investment I_1, raising any shortfall of funds B_1 by selling securities. The funds invested yield an output $F(I_1)$ plus another random increment $\tilde{\varepsilon}_2$ and the sum of the two, $\tilde{X}_2$, constitutes the firm's liquidating value in period 2 (the future).

In an M and M, no-tax, perfect-market world, investors place equal weight on a dollar of the dividends and a dollar of capital gains, and no transaction costs are incurred either by investors or by the firm when securities are bought or sold. Assuming also, for simplicity, universal risk neutrality, the cum dividend value of the firm, after the announcement of X_1, B_1, and I_1, and the declaration of D_1 can be written as

$$V_1 = D_1 + \frac{1}{1+i}[F(I_1) + E(\tilde{\varepsilon}_2)] - B_1, \tag{1}$$

where i is the appropriate one-period discount rate.[4]

The firms's managers choose values of D_1, B_1, and I_1 to maximize V_1 subject to the budget or "sources and uses" constraint

$$X_1 + B_1 = D_1 + I_1, \tag{2}$$

or equivalently

$$X_1 - I_1 = D_1 - B_1. \tag{3}$$

Substituting from (3) into (1) yields the familiar net cash-flow form of the valuation equation,

$$V_1 = X_1 - I_1 + \frac{1}{1+i}[F(I_1) + E(\tilde{\varepsilon}_2)], \tag{4}$$

and the M and M conclusion that, with full information and perfect markets, the value of the firm depends solely on the underlying real economic magnitudes X_1, I_1, $F(I_1)$, and $E(\tilde{\varepsilon}_2)$, and not at all on the purely financial flows D_1 and B_1.[5]

Clearly, then, if the cost of signaling is to be the deviation of actual dividends from their full-information optimum, one or more of the underlying assumptions must first be replaced. But which one or ones is by no means clear.

Some Possible Routes for Introducing a Cost to Dividend Signaling

Allowing for a Tax Penalty on Dividends Relative to Capital Gains   A natural place to start the search for ways to break the M and M indeterminancy is the basic M and M assumption that a dollar in current dividends is the same as a dollar in current capital gains. Certainly that is not the position of the Internal Revenue Code. Dividends (beyond some trivial threshold amount) are treated as ordinary income under the personal income tax, whereas capital gains are never taxed at higher rates than ordinary income and typically taxed at much lower rates. The rate differential is not uniform, can be reduced below its statutory range by certain sheltering and laundering devices (see Miller-Scholes, 1978), and for corporate shareholders is reversed. But there need be nothing obviously violative of common sense in looking to unnecessary taxes paid as a possible cost of signaling with dividends. Two recent papers on dividend signaling by Bhattacharya (1979) and John-Williams (1985) have done so. The tax cost plays essentially the same role in both papers, but since John-Williams specifically relate the features of their model to the Riley conditions here being reviewed, the John-Williams formulation will be taken as the exemplar of its class.

Appealing as the tax cost may be as a place to start, difficulties with the approach arise as soon as it comes to identifying the full-information or nonsignaling optimum against which the tax costs of dividend signals are to be measured. If one retains all the other essential M and M assumptions, as John-Williams do, the firm retains the ability to transform dividends to capital gains costlessly by share repurchase. Hence the assumed tax penalty on dividends relative to capital gains makes their full-information optimal level of dividends zero. Any dividends, in other words, would thus be paid by firms *only* because they were costly signals. Dividends would be a pure potlatch.

Potlatches are unsatisfactory explanations of any important class of long-enduring economic institutions such as dividends, and purely tax-induced ones particularly so. The dividend policies we observe for firms today, after all, differ little from those followed before the present income tax existed and from those in other countries with substantially different tax systems. Still, the John-Williams exercise can serve at least as a useful reminder that credible dividend signaling models must, in principle, be general enough to encompass the full panoply of tax regimes, and that such credible models are unlikely to be attainable without imposing costs or other restrictions on a firm's ability to transmute dividends and capital gains.

A Generalized M and M Dividend Model

In our M and M paper, we abstracted from costs of buying or selling securities so as to focus more sharply on the first-order determinants of firm value. To this end, we invoked the standard economic distinction between production and exchange opportunities—the essense of the former being their use of real resources and their being subject to the technological constraint of diminishing returns. The latter, by contrast, are essentially "paper" operations, transferring claims to existing commodities and consuming directly amounts of real resources that are small relative to those in productive transformations. So small, in fact, that to a first approximation they can be neglected entirely.

But when attention shifts from first-order points about valuation to second-order points, such as dividend signaling, the sharp and complete separation between the real and financial opportunities can and should be relaxed to capture additional empirically relevant detail. For the dividend signaling problem this means recognizing that transactions in securities cannot in fact be effected without commitment of real resources, and hence that there will be costs to changing the firm's supply of dividends just as for any other commodity or service the firm supplies.

Consider, for example, the dividend decision problem of a firm when the market, as in an M and M world, places equal weight on dividends and capital gains, but in which, unlike the M and M world, transactions in securities by the firm are not costless. Then, for firms with ample internal funds, i.e., with $X_1 > I_1^*$, the minimum cost solution is the "residual policy" $D_1^* = X_1 - I_1^*$ and $B_1 = 0$; and for firms with shortfalls of funds, $I_1^* \geq X_1$, it is $D_1^* = 0$ and $B_1 = X_1 - I_1^{**}$ (where the second star is added as a reminder that the investment level is not quite the Fisherian optimum, but a lower level that reflects the cost of raising the outside funds).

We thus now have one point on a firm's *supply curve for dividends*, given its earnings X_1, viz., the point where the supply price of dividends, defined as the market's valuation of a dollar of dividends relative to a dollar of capital gains, is unity. To trace out the rest of the supply curve, imagine first that the supply price of dividends relative to capital gains were greater than unity (perhaps, say, reflecting the transaction cost savings in supporting personal consumption from dividend receipts rather than from sales of shares). Then clearly, for the cash-rich firms the optimal response to the higher relative price of dividends would be to supply more of them. The funds to support the higher payments could be drawn either from transactions in securities, from cutbacks in the real investment budget, or most likely from both. Since both are costly, an optimum can be expected here as elsewhere to involve equalization at the margin. As for the cash-poor firms, paying no dividends when dividends and capital gains were valued equally, some will still find it optimal to remain in that state. But for others, the higher assumed premium on dividends may be enough to induce them to begin supplying dividends even though they are supporting substantial investment programs and relying heavily on outside financing.

At higher and higher values for the relative price of dividends the quantity of dividends supplied will continue to expand and additional and increasingly costly sources of financing will be tapped to support the flow. More frequent resort to costly flotations will be required and further paring of capital budgets will take its toll on the firm's competitive position. The supply curve of dividends, in sum, is likely to be increasingly inelastic as the price of dividends rises.

The firm's supply curve of dividends can be traced out in the other direction as well. Suppose that the relative price of dividends were less than that of capital gains, as might be the case, say, if a tax penalty on dividends or the costs of reinvesting dividends overweighed the liquidity advantages of cash dividend receipts. Then the cash-rich firms would clearly have an incentive to cut their dividends below the residual level of $D_1^* = X_1 - I_1^*$ optimal in the equal-weights case. And, again, they have a variety of real and financial alternatives to effect that cut, ranging from taking on lower return capital investments, to accumulating larger than efficient quantities of liquid financial assets, to the repurchasing of the firm's outstanding bonds and shares—either directly on the open market with attendant transaction costs, or by formal, above-market tender offers with dilution costs for the nontendering shareholders. All are costly and likely to become increasingly so as the cutback of dividends continues.[6]

In sum, then, the standard, full-information M and M valuation model can be generalized to admit an optimal, nonzero dividend payout for at least some firms even in a world with tax advantages to capital gains. Hence, for those firms paying dividends, there will indeed be an endogenous cost of signaling with dividends, and it will have two components: the profitable real investment opportunities foregone and the costs incurred in financial transactions to provide the funds for the additional dividend payments.

As is often the case, however, solving one problem creates others. The trouble is that there now may be too many potential signals in the model—B_1 and I_1 as well as D_1. The current technology of signaling models can handle only one signal at a time except in very special circumstances; and for present purposes that one must clearly be D_1. The most direct way to concentrate attention on this variable is perhaps just to impose the timing assumption that D_1 is declared before the firm's decision values for B_1 and I_1 are announced to outside investors. A simpler, but cruder approach is that of Miller and Rock, who assume simultaneous announcement of D_1 and B_1 (if any). They can thus assimilate D_1 and B_1 into a single variable, the net dividend $(D_1 - B_1)$, leaving I_1 as the only unobserved decision variable. Their approach sacrifices much interesting detail about financing decisions, but does retain, thanks to the I_1 term, the important qualitative properties of an endogenous cost of dividend signaling and at a considerable saving in model complexity.

2.2   The Benefits of Dividend Signaling

Who Are the Beneficiaries of Signaling?
That there must be a benefit to dividend signaling seems almost too obvious to require comment. Yet, as will become clear, some of the most difficult and still largely unresolved problems in defining a dividend signaling equilibrium arise in trying to pin down precisely what the benefits are and to whom they accrue. It is not enough merely to say that the "dividend decision maker" has private information, not yet known to the market,

which, if credibly disclosed, could raise the share price above its pooled equilibrium value. A higher share price, after all, despite its pleasant connotations, is not an economic end in itself. The higher price benefits only someone selling the shares or someone whose wealth will be in some other way permanently enhanced by the rise. Otherwise, why bother to incur the costs of signaling?

Identifying the presumed seller-beneficiaries of the dividend signal is, in a deeper sense, really the problem of defining an appropriate objective function for a *firm* under conditions of asymmetric information between its insiders and outsiders. Appropriate here refers not to functional form in the econometric sense: the essential properties of the function needed to sustain a signaling equilibrium are clear enough. Appropriate means rather conforming to the requirement of the basic economic paradigm that the objective functions of entities such as firms be grounded ultimately in utility maximization by the individuals who commit resources to them.

That requirement in the standard, finance theory of the firm is satisfied by the familiar criterion: maximize the value of the shares held by the current owners. With full-information and perfect and complete capital markets, decisions by the firm reflecting that criterion can indeed be shown to be in the best interests of all the owners, despite differences in their time and state preferences and regardless of whether they intend to buy, to hold, or to sell their shares at that market value. But when the full-information assumption is dropped to allow the firm's decision makers to be better informed than outside investors, the criterion and its rationale lose force. There is no longer a single, unique value for the shares on which all interests converge. In fact, the signaling problem arises precisely because outside investors view the shares differently from the firm's owners and their agents. And with no unique value for the firm, even the current shareholders need not agree as to the best course of action. Those planning to sell out may opt for policies, such as costly signaling, that run counter to the interests of those planning to retain their shares. How are the firm's managers to reconcile these potential conflicts of interest among the firm's owners?

The Firm as a Seller of Securities   One way, invoked in a number of recent papers on signaling in finance finesses the issue of possible internal conflict by making the decision problem that creates the motive for signaling one of selling shares by the firm to outsiders. If so, *all* the current shareholders can be presumed to have a common interest in obtaining the best price for the shares, or at least a better price than obtainable in the pooling equilibrium. This is the approach of Leland and Pyle (1977) in their model of signaling and initial public offerings, and of Harris and Raviv (1984) in their paper on signaling and the forced conversion of securities convertible into common stock. John and Williams (1985) adopt the same tactic in their dividend signaling model, but there are problems with the approach in that context. It would make most sense when applied to the initiation of dividends by firms undertaking their initial public offering. Indeed that was, for long, the supposed *locus classicus* of dividend signaling. The leading underwriting firms were said to insist on an initiation of an increase in regular dividends as a condition for sponsoring the issue. But if the concern is with the possibility of dividend signaling by well-established firms already on a regular dividend-paying basis, the relevance of the issue price criterion becomes much harder to establish. Common stock flotation, after all, is a fairly rare event in the life of most firms. Even if the term equity financing is interpreted broadly to include any publicly floated security junior to riskless debt, such transactions differ substantially in frequency from that of dividend payments by established firms. True, routine financing such as bank loans or flotations of commercial paper does go on more or less continuously, but those security issues are monitored directly by the lenders (and often collateralized) so that it is hard to see any major role for dividend signaling in the pricing of securities of that kind.[7]

Perhaps the steady stream of dividend payments by the firm over long periods with no outside equity financing is, in part, at least simply a way of keeping the financing window open for future public flotations should they ever become necessary, by signaling that the firm's finances are under control. There may well be a good deal of truth in this traditional argument for dividends, but it would be dividend signaling in the looser sense of that term rather than the Riley information equilibrium of concern here.

The Shareholders as Sellers   To find a wealth motive for dividend signaling by established firms, without invoking external financing, Miller and Rock look to the sales of shares not by the firm itself, but by its individual shareholders. Transactions by individuals, after all, are a daily occurrence for most listed companies, and there is even some evidence that transactions do speed up in and around dividend declaration days (see, e.g, Grundy, 1985, and Lakonishok and Vermaelen, 1984).

The advantage of the approach is that it suggests a relatively simple objective function for the firm of the form

$$W = kV_1^m + (1 - k)V_1^d, \tag{5}$$

where V_1^m is the value of the firm as seen by the outside market, V_1^d is the value of the firm as seen by the firm's directors, and k is the fraction of the firm's shares sold on personal account by the firm's stockholders. With kV_1^m as the source of the benefits of dividend signaling and $(1 - k)V_1^d$ as the source of the costs of signaling along the lines described in the previous section, all the required elements for the signaling trade-off are then neatly in place.

A function such as (5) solves the immediate problem of getting a maximand with the right properties for a signaling equilibrium, but leaves the link back to individual utilities unspecified.[8] It is imposed, not derived. Invoking standard portfolio rebalancing arguments can reduce the arbitrariness somewhat by endogenizing the ks. But, there is still no compelling reason to believe that this function, for all its plausibility, would in fact be chosen either by the firm's original organizers or by the shareholders in place at the time of the dividend decision.

On the other hand, one can be too fastidious in these matters. The problem of what might be called the "unanchored objective function for the firm" arises not because something is peculiar about dividends or dividend signaling, but because the assumptions of complete information and perfect costless markets have been dropped. Drop those assumptions and the firm takes on some of the characteristics of a government (or a family) in which differing interests must sometimes be reconciled and compromised in the course of reaching the organization's broader goals. No completely general method of modeling this process yet exists (see Drèze, 1985), but at least in some contexts and for some problems it has been found effective to represent the organization's objectives as a "social welfare function," in the sense of a somehow appropriately weighted average of the utilities of its constituent members. Perhaps social welfare function analogs like (5) can perform the same service at the level of the firm.

Management Compensation and Management Shares   Still another approach to anchoring the objective function in utility maximization would be to make the interests of the firm's managers the driving force behind the firm's decisions. The terms kV_1^m and $(1 - k)V_1^d$, or their equivalents, might then be interpreted as parts of the executive compensation package that depend, respectively, on "immediate short-run performance" and "long-run return." Additional cost penalties on dividend performance could be incorporated if needed as in Kalay (1980), which is based in turn on the incentive-signaling model of Ross (1977). Such approaches, however, merely push one stage deeper the fundamental difficulties arising from the differences in stockholder interests. The question still remains why the firm's stockholders, given their own interests, agreed to choose that particular compensation package.

Nor are the difficulties escaped by endowing management with shares and assuming their interests to be aligned thereby with those of the owners. If the managers retain the power to buy and sell shares, their decisions to alter their holdings will become informative, perhaps even more so than their dividend decision. We are back then to multiple signals, a problem for which, as noted earlier, general results have yet to be developed.

We may conclude this survey of the presumed benefits from dividend signaling by noting that a number of more or less plausible possibilities exist, none of them completely satisfactory on all counts. Before speculating further about their relative merits, however, it may pay first to pin down more precisely what message the dividend signal might be conveying.

2.3   The Attribute to Be Signaled

The valuation formula (4) is a function of the market's perception of four firm-specific variables—X_1, I_1, $F(I_1)$, and $E(\tilde{\varepsilon}_2)$—any one of which, in principle, might serve as the unobserved attribute that the dividend is to signal.

The investment terms I_1 and $F(I_1)$ can probably be eliminated as candidates for the information to be signaled by dividends even though recent research has shown that announcements of changes in capital spending programs can have a measurable impact on prices (see McConnell and Muscarella, 1984). The trouble is that the signs are wrong. Unexpectedly large, profitable new uses for internal funds would be reason for *cutting* dividends, if anything; and the market is hardly likely to interpret such cuts as good news. The more promising candidates for the attribute signaled would seem to be the firm's current and future earnings.

Of these it is natural to look first to the firm's expected future earnings prospects, $E(\tilde{X}_2)$, and especially of its random component, $E(\tilde{\varepsilon}_2)$, which seems to epitomize so directly the commonsense notion of "inside information." And, that is certainly very much the notion Franco Modigliani and I had in mind when we introduced the concept of the informational content of dividends. It is also the approach taken in the dividend signaling models of Bhattacharya (1979) and John-Williams (1985). There are, however, at least two serious difficulties in identifying this forward peek at earnings as the key to dividend signaling.

Current Dividends and Future Earnings

First, attempts to establish empirically an informational content of dividends of this kind have not been strikingly successful, to say the least. As far back as the early 1970s, Watts (1973) had shown that once past earnings, X_1, are known, the marginal contribution of D_1 to forecasts of future earnings X_2 is negligible. Gonedes (1978) found the same to be true for forecasts of future rates of return on the shares. Time series of dividends both at the aggregate level (see Lintner, 1956) and at the individual company level (see Fama-Babiak, 1968) suggest strongly that dividends are better described as lagging earnings than as leading earnings. More recent studies, using very refined techniques (e.g., Kormendi, Leftwich, and Lipe, and 1984; Marsh and Merton, 1986) have found evidence that may well be consistent with a modest amount of marginal future-looking content to dividends, but even so, hardly enough to make a convincing case for dividend signaling.[9]

There are problems at the theoretical level as well. Even if the firm wanted to convey some unsuspected good news about future earnings prospects, why do it by raising current dividends? There is certainly no direct linkage in (4) that associates higher current dividends with higher expected future earnings, and hence no reason for outside investors to draw that inference. That is why Bhattacharya (1979) and John-Williams (1985) have to impose an exogenous cost on dividends; otherwise the market would not realize it was being signaled! That the market, once so alerted, interprets the dividend signal as news about future earnings in their models is by default, rather than by necessity; everything else of relevance to the firm's value is assumed already known before the dividend was declared.[10]

Current Dividends and Current Earnings

Some of these difficulties with dividends as signals of future earnings can be avoided by making the connection between them a bit more roundabout. There is, after all, a great deal of persistence in corporate earnings. Hence, a dividend that conveys information about X_1, the current state of the business, would also inevitably convey information about X_2, its future prospects. This is the route chosen in the Miller-Rock signaling model.

They assume that the conditional expectation of the random component of future earnings can be represented as the autoregression

$$E(\tilde{\varepsilon}_2|\varepsilon_1) = \gamma\varepsilon_1, \tag{6}$$

where γ, the "persistence parameter," may range from 1.0 (implying the first-period shock is "permanent") to 0 (implying the shock is "transitory") to possibly even values less than 0 (implying a likely reversal). The (net) dividend decision in the Miller-Rock model is the modified "residual" policy discussed earlier. Thus, the announced (net) dividend D_1, added to the market's (rational) expectation of the firm's optimal real investment, I_1^*, can combine to reveal X_1 and ε_1, should any uncertainty about them still remain for outside investors at the time of the dividend declaration. The inferred value for ε_1, mediating through the persistence parameter γ, then leads to an updated and improved forecast of future earnings.

Under this approach, dividend announcement effects (and hence potential dividend signals) can readily be reconciled with the findings of Watts and Gonedes that dividends have little marginal predictive power for future earnings *after* current earnings have become known. Signaling by dividends, moreover, is more credible in this framework where the dividend and the attribute signaled are linked by an explicit accounting identity, than in models relying entirely on a serendipitous mutual acceptance of an otherwise unmotivated action.

If dividends are indeed conveying information mainly about ε_1—that part of current earnings, if any, not fully known to the market at the time of the dividend declaration—then the price variability surrounding dividend announcements should be expected to be somewhat smaller on average than for earnings announcements. (For some confirmatory evidence at the micro level, see Patell and Wolfson, 1984, and, less directly, at the macro level, see Kleidon, 1983.)[11] The dividend announcement effect is certainly not negligible, however, even in the presence of nearby earnings announcements. Aharony and Swary (1980), for example, report an average absolute share price response to quarterly dividend changes on the order of 1%.[12] Somewhat larger effects (on the order of 3% or so) are found by Asquith and Mullins (1983) for firms initiating dividends or resuming dividend payments after a long hiatus. And larger effects yet have been found for firms eliminating dividends (see Pettit, 1972).

Dividends and the Persistence Parameter
Still another, and in some way, the most intuitively appealing, candidate for the attribute being signaled is the persistence parameter γ. The scenario would call for a firm with an increase in earnings believed to be *permanent* (i.e., the firm believes $\gamma = 1$ or perhaps even somewhat greater than one) to signal that permanence by raising its dividend to its new equilibrium value. Should it believe, on the other hand, that the increase in earnings is a mere transitory windfall ($\gamma = 0$), then it would hold its dividend at its previous value as a sign that its long-run prospects are really unchanged. Appro-

priate partway adjustments of dividends for values of γ between 0 and 1 would also be natural in this context and might even provide a rationalization for the otherwise somewhat mysterious "speed of adjustment" coefficient in the familiar Lintner model of dividend smoothing.

There are, alas, two major difficulties with this interpretation. (I say "alas," because Franco Modigliani and I relied heavily on what amounted essentially to this "permanent earnings" model of dividends in our own empirical work on valuation (see especially Miller and Modigliani, 1966). First, until very recently, at least, researchers have had little success in disentangling the permanent from the transitory components of corporate earnings and hence in being able to demonstrate convincingly that dividends do indeed respond to the former, but not the latter. The time series of earnings are still too short for confident use with present-day econometric technology at the individual company level; and there have as yet been no counterparts to the ingenious cross-sectional tests on special samples that played so key a role in establishing the credibility of the permanent income-life cycle theories of consumption. There are a few signs, however, that the tide may perhaps be beginning to turn. The recent study by Kormendi, Leftwich, and Lipe (1984) presents evidence suggestive of a link between the persistence properties of earnings, the smoothing of dividends, and the responsiveness of share prices to unexpected changes in earnings and dividends.[13] Marsh and Merton (1986) find, at least for aggregate data, that lagged share prices may be the long-sought effective proxy for permanent earnings in models of dividend supply. These are certainly promising leads, but at the moment one must concede in all fairness that the permanent earnings model of dividends remains merely a plausible conjecture.

It is a conjecture, moreover, that has still to find an accepted anchorage in the theory of the firm. The permanent income-life cycle models of consumption have such an anchorage, of course, in the Fisherian model of resource allocation over time by utility-maximizing households. Consumption smoothing over time emerges naturally in that model from the interation of irregular incomes, convex tastes, and linear opportunities in perfect capital markets. But the critical convexity that would produce smoothing by households even (if not actually, especially) in perfect capital markets is lacking when we turn to value-maximizing firms in perfect capital markets.

To get dividend smoothing as an optimal policy for firms it will thus be necessary at the very least to weaken the perfect capital market assumption. By allowing explicitly for transaction costs for dealings in securities by the firm (and its shareholders), dividend smoothing might well emerge as a joint, cost-minimizing strategy. Sticky response patterns of an analogous kind have been found, after all, in transactions cost-driven models of optimal management of cash and liquid asset balances (see Constantinides, 1976, and also Miller and Orr, 1966). Still, I cannot help voicing this nagging thought: If the difficulties aren't insurmountable along this route, why has it taken the more than 30 years since Lintner's paper for someone to find the way through?

2.4   Other Conditions for a Separating Signaling Equilibrium

Costs, benefits, and a well-defined attribute are the main requirements for a signaling equilibrium in which dividends might credibly convey information otherwise unobservable about the firm's real value. Completing the list of Riley's conditions are three requirements of a more technical nature. First, to make false signaling a losing proposition the cost-benefit ratio of dividend signaling must be assumed to rise as the signal increases. Second, to ensure an unambiguous reverse inference from any and every observed dividend to the unobserved attribute, the cost and benefit functions of the dividend must not have discontinuities or multiple crossings. And finally, as in any other fixed-point problem the range of values of the attribute to be inferred from the dividend must not be unbounded. Under some circumstances, as shown by John and Williams, an upper bound on the attribute may become superfluous, but the lower bound is critical and has an additional important role to play as well, as we shall see.[14]

If the six conditions taken together are met, then there can emerge an equilibrium of mutually consistent and self-fulfilling conjectures in which the market believes it understands the firm's dividend policy, the firm believes the market understands it, and both are right. The trouble is that here, as elsewhere in "noncooperative games," there will, in general, be more than one policy (in principle even an infinite number of policies) that might be sustainable in that sense if they were somehow stumbled upon simultaneously by the firm and the market. For the notion of dividend signaling to have any practical value, therefore, there must be some clue in the context that breaks the indeterminacy and focuses the attention of all the participants on one particular solution.

And that is where the lower bound on the attribute can become decisive. As long as firms, whatever may be the precise form of their objective functions, try at least to avoid all unnecessary waste, then a firm whose realization is at the lower bound will not signal (i.e., it will set dividends to their full-information solution value, which may or may not be zero).

Whether it signals or not, the firm knows it cannot expect to avoid disclosing its position at the low end of the totem pole, as the Kwakiutls might put it. Incurring any costs for futile signaling would thus clearly be wasteful. If, therefore, the market accepts this "no unnecessary waste" principle as guiding the firm's behavior—and that is certainly a position that economists, at least, can feel comfortable with—one point on the focal reaction function will have been identified. From there attention shifts to a firm with the next higher realization of the attribute. That firm, unlike its downstream neighbor, will find it profitable to incur some signaling cost, but no more than necessary to distance itself from the firm just below it. Similarly in turn for the firm just above it and so on in similar steps until a complete separating equilibrium has been achieved.

3 Dividends, Information, and Signaling: An Appraisal

Model structures using basically standard components can thus be constructed to meet the stringent conditions for a consistent, dividend signaling equilibrium. They do, however, demand of their academic users a somewhat more than usual "willingness to suspend disbelief." The maximizing calculations to be performed by the firm in some of the models are of a complexity that would make Herbert Simon smile; and the thorough understanding by outside observers of the firm's inner workings and motives presumed in all of the models would lead him to laugh out loud.

Finance specialists might still be willing, of course, to endure the ridicule if convinced that the models, for all their seeming artificiality, could successfully account for empirical phenomena beyond the reach of existing models. The prospects on that score would seem to be mixed.

If the phenomenon requiring explanation is to be the perennial "Why do firms pay dividends?" the answer is almost certainly that signaling cannot account for it. But the question itself is at fault. The widespread impression that the optimal level of dividends for all firms would necessarily be zero in a world with tax penalties on dividends is based, as we have seen, on an inadequate model of dividend supply.

A more relevant way to put the question would be whether signaling can account for at least the feeling on the part of many close observers of the dividend behavior of firms, dating back to the pioneering investigations of John Lintner (1956), that many firms do seem to pay out more in dividends than either their managers or outside academic observers can convincingly explain. Here, the answer would be, quite possibly. But proving it will not be easy since, among other things, it is by no means clear how to establish the base for comparison, that is, how to determine what the dividends would have been in the absence of signaling.

There remains, of course, the empirical phenomenon that provided the initial motivation for this paper, the response of share prices to dividend announcements. Here, the chances of establishing a satisfactory signaling explanation may be somewhat better. Certainly signaling is not the only explanation for these price effects. They can arise, in principle, even in a symmetric-information world, as Miller and Rock show. But the very presence of price effects on dividend announcements does serve subtly to shift the burden of proof. The price responses to dividend announcements are evidence that the potential for signaling—the motive and opportunity, as it were—is already in place. If, therefore, signaling does not occur, it can be only because some lower cost (i.e., less dissipative), but still incentive-compatible and time-consistent route has been found for communicating the information in the dividend. The challenge becomes thus to explain why the price jump we see *is not* signaling; and that may be even harder to explain than why it is.

Notes

1. Mixed equilibria with pooling over some ranges and separation over others are also possible, but will not be considered here.

2. My colleague Lester Telser suspects that they now probably own oil wells and compete for status by flaring off the gas.

3. Signaling models in which the signalers incur costs in equilibrium are said to be "dissipative"—a term borrowed from electrical engineering and not particularly descriptive in this context. The economics literature also contains references to so-called "nondissipative signaling models" (see Bhattacharya, 1980), but they are of a somewhat different genre from the models here considered and probably should have been given a different name.

4. Here and throughout I abstract from all leverage-related risks and costs of the kind involved in the other M and M proposition.

5. Although no optimal dividend exists in this formulation, there is an optimal investment level, I_1^*, at which the marginal internal rate of return on real investment (minus unity), $F'(I_1^*) - 1$, equals the capital market rate of discount, i.

6. It may perhaps be worth noting explicitly that buying Treasury bills is not a costless alternative to dividends. The cost comes not primarily from the direct transaction costs, which are admittedly small, but from the low yield such treasury securities have, precisely because their low transaction costs make them such liquid repositories for temporarily idle balances. A firm piling up cash in bills to avoid

paying dividends is thus paying for more liquidity than it needs, a policy just as wasteful, in its own way, as overinvesting in lower-yield real assets. The interest on any funds withheld from the shareholders and put into idle Treasuries will, of course, be subject to an unnecessary corporate income tax, a fact not likely to be lost on institutional and corporate holders of the shares (and especially potential holders like T. Boone Pickens or Carl Icahn!). The major tax and nontax costs of corporate hoarding as an alternative to paying dividends are described at some length in Miller (in press).

7. On the other hand, officials of Continental Illinois maintained that their refusal to cut or eliminate the bank's dividend while the crisis was building around it was to avoid sending a panic signal ("pulling the red handle" as they put it) that might, in turn, have led to massive withdrawals by depositors and refusals of outside lenders to renew maturing short-term loans. A case at least as compelling can be made, however, for the opposite proposition that the cash drains from their dividend bravado, in the face of what were clearly serious difficulties, had an even greater adverse effect on the confidence of the outside lenders.

8. The linearity of (5) is also a restriction, though probably unnecessary. But when swallowing camels, why strain at gnats? For an insightful discussion, though from a somewhat different perspective from that taken here, of the problems of defining a utility-grounded objective function for the firm when the Fisher conditions do not apply see Drèze (1985).

9. Some marginal information content of dividends when both dividends and earnings are announced simultaneously is reported for Australian data in Brown, Finn, and Hancock (1977). For a similar study of US firms see Kane, Lee, and Marcus (1984).

10. Even without an objective reason, of course, nothing stops investors from interpreting higher dividends as a portent of higher earnings, or stops manage-ment from conforming to those anticipations, thus leading perhaps to mutually reinforcing, self-fulfilling prophecies of the kind associated with a signaling equilib-rium. That such a delicately poised equilibrium could be maintained for so many years across so wide a range of economies may well, however, strike observers as highly improbable. But here, as elsewhere in information economics and game theory, it is impossible to rule it out a priori.

11. Kleidon, unlike Patell and Wolfson, is concerned not with "announcement effects" per se, but with the correlation between current price changes of the Standard and Poor's Index and future changes in aggregate earnings and divi-dends. For recent years, at least, he finds price changes more strongly correlated with future earnings than with dividends, though the reverse seems to have been the case for the era 1926–1950.

12. They find roughly the same effect whether the dividend precedes or follows the firm's earnings announcement, which might seem to conflict with the interpre-tation here of ε_1 as the information content. But the present model is intended as merely one link in a much longer chain. Except for strictly synchronous announce-

ments, every dividend would thus precede the next earnings announcement and follow the last one just as the left foot follows and leads the right foot in walking.

13. See also Kane, Lee, and Marcus (1984), who find somewhat stronger price responses to the unanticipated components of dividend and earnings announcements when both components are in the same direction, which would be one implication of the permanent earnings model, though probably of some other competing hypotheses as well.

14. As a historical aside, it is worth pointing out that the necessity of continuity and boundedness for an information equilibrium, as well as the fixed-point problem analogy, were noted by Grunberg and Modigliani in their paper (1954) on the accuracy of published forecasts, a paper that is among the early, if not actually the earliest, formal treatment of an information equilibrium.

References

Aharony, Joseph, and Itzhak Swary, "Quarterly Dividend and Earnings Announcements and Stockholder Returns: An Empirical Analysis," *Journal of Finance* 35, No. 1 (1980).

Asquith, Paul, and David Mullins, Jr., "The Impact of Initiating Dividend Payments On Shareholders' Wealth," *Journal of Business* 56 (January 1983).

Bhattacharya, Sudipto, "Imperfect Information, Dividend Policy and the 'Bird in the Hand' Fallacy," *Bell Journal of Economics* 10, No. 1 (Spring 1979), 259–270.

Bhattacharya, Sudipto, "Signalling Structures and Dividend Policy," *Quarterly Journal of Economics* 95, No. 1 (August 1980), 1–24.

Brown, Philip, Frank J. Finn, and Philip Hancock, "Dividend Changes, Earnings Reports and Share Prices: Some Australian Findings," *Australian Journal of Management* (1977), 127–147.

Constantinides, George, "Stochastic Cash Management with Fixed and Proportional Transaction Costs," *Management Science*, 22, No. 12 (August 1976), 1320–1331.

Drèze, Jacques H., "(Uncertainty and) the Firm in General Equilibrium Theory," *The Economic Journal*, 95 (Supplement: Conference Papers), 1–20, 1985.

Fama, Eugene, and Harvey Babiak, "Dividend Policy: An Empirical Analysis," *American Statistical Assn. Journal* 53 (December 1968).

Gonedes, Nicholas J., "Corporate Signalling External Accounting, and Capital Market Equilibrium: Evidence on Dividends, Income and Extraordinary Items," *Journal of Accounting Research* 16, No. 1 (1978).

Grunberg, Emile, and Franco Modigliani, "The Predictability of Social Events," *Journal of Political Economy* 62, No 6 (December 1954), 465–478.

Grundy, Bruce, "Trading Volume and Stock Returns around Ex Dividend Days," University of Chicago, Graduate School of Business, February 1985, Mimeo.

Harris, Milton, and Artur Raviv, "A Sequential Signalling Model of Convertible Debt Call Policy," Department of Finance, J. L. Kellogg Graduate School of Management, Revised, February 1984. Mimeo.

John, Kose, and Joseph Williams, "Dividends, Dilution and Taxes: A Signalling Equilibrium," *Journal of Finance* 40, No. 4 (September 1985), 1053–1070.

Kalay, Avner, "Signalling, Information Content and the Reluctance to Cut Dividends," *Journal of Financial and Quantitative Analysis* 15, No. 4 (November 1980), 855–863.

Kane, Alex, Young Ki Lee, and Alan Marcus, "Earnings and Dividend Announcements: Is There a Corroboration Effect," *Journal of Finance* 39, No. 4 (September 1984), 1091–1099.

Kleidon, Allan W., "Stock Prices as Rational Forecasters of Future Cash Flows," Ph.D. dissertation, Graduate School of Business, University of Chicago, December 1983.

Kormendi, Roger, Richard Leftwich, and Robert Lipe, "Earnings Innovations, Earnings, Persistence and Rational Firm Valuation," University of Chicago, August 1984. Mimeo.

Lakonishok, Josef, and Theo Vermaelen, "Tax-Induced Trading around Ex-Dividend Days," Tel-Aviv University, Preliminary, July 1984. Mimeo.

Leland, Hayne, and David Pyle, "Information Asymmetries, Financial Structure and Financial Intermediation," *Journal of Finance* 32, No. 4 (May 1977), 371–387.

Lintner, John, "The Distribution of Incomes of Corporations among Dividends, Retained Earnings and Taxes," *American Economic Review* 46 (May 1956).

McConnell, John, and Chris J. Muscarella, "Corporate Capital Expenditure Decisions and the Market Value of the Firm," Purdue University, Fourth Revision, August 1984. Mimeo.

Marsh, Terry, and Robert C. Merton, "Dividend Behavior for the Aggregate Stock Market," Sloan School, MIT, 1986. Mimeo.

Miller, Merton H., "Behavioral Rationality in Finance: The Case of Dividends," *Journal of Business* (in press).

Miller, Merton H., and Franco Modigliani, "Dividend Policy, Growth and the Valuation of Shares," *Journal of Business* 34, No. 4 (1961).

Miller, Merton H., and Franco Modigliani, "Some Estimates of the Cost of Capital to the Electric Utility Industry, 1954–57," *American Economic Review* 56 (June 1966), 333–391.

Miller, Merton H., and Daniel Orr, "A Model of the Demand for Money by Firms," *Quarterly Journal of Economics* 80 (1966), 413–435.

Miller, Merton H., and Kevin Rock, "Dividend Policy under Asymmetric Information," *Journal of Finance* 40, No. 4 (September 1985), 1031–1051.

Miller, Merton H., and Myron S. Scholes, "Dividends and Taxes," *Journal of Financial Economics* 6, No. 2 (December 1978), 333–364.

Patell, James M., and Mark H. Wolfson, "The Intraday Speed of Adjustment of Stock Prices to Earnings and Dividend Announcements," *Journal of Financial Economics* 13, No. 2 (June 1984), 222–252.

Pettit, Richardson, "Dividend Announcements, Security Performance and Capital Market Efficiency," *Journal of Finance* 27, No. 4 (1972).

Riley, John, "Informational Equilibrium," *Econometrica* 47, No. 2 (March 1979), 331–359.

Ross, Stephen, "The Determination of Financial Structure: The Incentive-Signalling Approach," *Bell Journal of Economics* 8, No. 1 (Spring 1977), 23–40.

Spence, Michael, "Job Market Signalling," *Quarterly Journal of Economics* 87, No. 3 (August 1973); 355–379.

Watts, Ross, "The Information Content of Dividends," *Journal of Business* 46, No. 2 (1973).

Comments on "The Informational Content of Dividends"

Stewart C. Myers

It is an honor to comment on an extremely lucid paper by one of the justly famous Ms at a conference honoring the other justly famous M. They are the fathers of modern corporate finance.

I appreciate their influence every time I think of their trademark. If my colleague Robert Merton and I collaborated on a paper, no one would be allowed to refer to us as MM. I do sometimes aspire to a lowercase m, or perhaps an m', since much of my work is derived from theirs.

In this paper, Miller reasserts the original MM insight that dividend payments convey information about current and future earnings. For me that insight first struck home in the late 1960s when I assisted in security analysis of an Italian company with absolutely impenetrable accounts. The company had reported steadily increasing earnings for several years— a fine record—but had never changed its cash dividend. There was no apparent acceleration of capital investment, repayment of debt, or other unusual financing transactions. We decided to assume that *true* earnings equaled cash dividends until the company did something to convince us otherwise. A cash dividend increase would have made us more enthusiastic about the stock.

This example is perhaps extreme, but consistent with the signaling model of dividends presented by Miller in this paper and in his related work with Kevin Rock. Since these two papers' formal models are similar, the following comments are directed to both papers.

The key to the Miller and Miller-Rock models is that dividend primarily signal true *current* earnings, which investors cannot observe fully, either because earnings are not announced at the same time, or because of the fog of accounting. Current earnings are important because they convey information about future earnings, and because current stock price responds to them.

Because investors begin with less information than managers, stock price is not constrained to "intrinsic value." Potential differences between price and value are important to the fraction of the firm's stockholders that will sell out before the next dividend and earnings announcements. As a result, firms pay more dividends than they should in order to help departing stockholders. Nevertheless, differences in firms' equilibrium dividend payouts reveal true earnings, so that the stock price responses to dividend announcements end up being fully rational.

Although this model is extremely insightful and satisfying, it has an important weakness. Define "net cash surplus" as the net flow of cash from the firm to money and capital markets. If Miller had instructed his word processor to replace "dividend" with "net cash surplus" throughout his paper, his model and much of his discussion would still make sense. Miller of course, recognizes this, but I would like to develop the point.

Think of five channels through which the firm may raise or distribute cash. It can raise cash by (1) issuing debt or (2) equity securities; it can distribute cash by (3) a cash dividend, (4) repurchasing shares, or (5) paying off debt securities. (I keep normal debt service in the background because that is not usually discretionary and therefore would not serve as a signal.) The net cash surplus, the net of all five flows, could serve as the signal in Miller's model. A dividend payout would convey information about the net cash surplus, as would cash payments or receipts through the other four channels, but only the surplus would reveal current earnings.

This reinterpreted model is not so easy to square with empirical observation. First, cash movements along different channels seem to have different effects. For example, Eckbo and Shyam-Sunder have found that stock price falls, on average, at debt issue announcements. However, the average decline is roughly an order to magnitude less than the average decline on stock issue announcements (compare, for example, Asquith and Mullins's results).

Second, dividends seem more stable over time than the net cash surplus or flows along the other four individual channels. Why do firms not smooth share repurchases and let dividends fluctuate instead?[1] Better still, why not smooth the net cash surplus?

Third, why in this reinterpreted model would a firm pay excessive dividends—more than the optimal amount given the frictions discussed in section 2.1 of Miller's paper—and issue securities at roughly the same time? If the net surplus is the true signal, then the firm should cut out the excess dividend and reduce the amount of securities issued in order to reduce issue costs.

These questions are not intended to shoot down Miller's paper or the

Miller-Rock model, but to pose a constructive question: If the firm can choose from a variety of ways to distribute cash to investors, what is it that gives cash paid out as dividends special clout? My own inclination is to search for a model combining agency theory, as in Easterbrook's recent paper, and the signaling approach Miller expounds so well in this volume. If such a model exists, the odds are that one or both of the Ms will beat the rest of us to it.

Note

1. A share repurchase program with all the trappings of dividend policy might be challenged by the Internal Revenue Service as a de facto dividend payout policy designed to avoid taxes. However, public firms have repurchased shares year in and year out without challenge.

References

Asquith, Paul, and David W. Mullins, "Equity Issues and Offering Dilution." *Journal of Financial Economics* 15, No. 1/2 (1986).

Easterbrook, Frank H., "Two Agency-Cost Explanations of Dividends." *American Economic Review* 74, No. 4 (1984).

Eckbo, B. Espen, "Valuation Effects of Corporate Debt Offerings." *Journal of Financial Economics* 15, No. 1/2 (1986).

Miller, Merton H. and Kevin Rock, "Dividend Policy under Asymmetric Information." *Journal of Finance* 40, No. 4 (1985).

Shyam-Sunder, Lakshmi, "The Stock Price Effects of risky Versus Safe Debt." Sloan School of Management, Working Paper, MIT (February 1985).

4

Conventional Valuation and the Term Structure of Interest Rates

Robert J. Shiller

1 Introduction

It is plausible that prices of long-term bonds and other long-term assets might be substantially influenced by simple rules of thumb of investors. Here, I wish to consider the possibility that investors may tend to price long-term bonds by the rule that their yield to maturity should be equal to their recent memories of the level of short-term interest rates plus a constant "risk premium." Such a rule can be expressed more formally by saying that the long rate is a simple weighted average with weights that decline into the past (declining because of human memory decay) of short rates, plus a constant term. Such a distributed lag valuation rule may become a matter of convention: investors may feel that prices have generally behaved in accordance with such a rule, and they may thus feel that prices are "not out of line" when the pricing rule is followed.

It is also plausible that prices of long-term bonds are influenced by changing perceptions unrelated to any such mechanistic rule of thumb. Changing attitudes, fashions, public confidence, or beliefs would plausibly account also for some unpredictable drift in long-term interest rates. One possible interpretation of the error term in the distributed lag regression of long rates on short rates is that it represents such changing perceptions.

Together, the conventional valuation rule and the unpredictable drift notions might be regarded as Keynesian. Keynes said at one point that the long-term interest rate is "a highly psychological phenomenon," and at another that it is "highly conventional .... its actual value is largely governed by the prevailing view as to what its value is expected to be."[1]

I am indebted to John Y. Campbell, Stanley Fischer, and William D. Nordhaus for helpful comments. Sam Ouliaris provided research assistance. This research was sponsored by the United States National Science Foundation under grant SES-8408565. This paper is part of the NBER's program of research on financial markets and monetary economics.

The literature on efficient markets is widely interpreted as providing evidence contrary to this conventional-psychological view. If people are guided exclusively by convention or by changing fashions or attitudes, then it seems likely that they should create "profit opportunities" for others not blinded by convention. The general impression in the profession from the large literature testing for market efficiency is that such profit opportunities do not exist. Ironically, this general impression persists even though there is no agreement about *which* efficient markets model is supported by the data.

The Rational Expectations theory of the term structure of interest rates with constant risk premium is the form of the efficient markets models most widely cited with regard to interest rates. By this theory, if the long rate is well-described as a distributed lag on short rates, it is because the distributed lag is implied by the expectations model given the stochastic properties of short rate. If there is an error term in the distributed lag regression, it is because investors have information about the future course of interest rates that is not contained in past interest rates. The theory is a useful starting point from which to describe the behavior of interest rates.[2] Departures from the theory are usually referred to in terms of time variation of risk premiums, and showing how the expectations theory fails might also be described as describing the behavior through time of the risk premium. The expectations theory with constant risk premium has had its ups and downs when tested with data. Sutch (1968), Modigliani and Shiller (1973), and Sargent (1979) have claimed evidence supportive of the theory. Later, however, it was claimed that the theory could be rejected (Shiller, 1979, Hansen and Sargent, 1981). I then claimed that long-term interest rates appear to be too volatile to be in accordance with such simple expectations theories. Yet the evidence for the claimed excess volatility of long-term interest rates was itself criticized by Flavin (1983, 1984b) and others. Moreover, it was claimed by Campbell and Shiller (1984) and Mankiw and Summers (1984) that recent US long-term interest rates do not seem to overreact to short-term interest rates.

This paper will attempt to straighten out some of these apparently conflicting claims, as well as to point to directions for alternatives to rational expectations models. The simple linearized expectations model will be described and compared with the data. New in this paper are estimates of the Modigliani-Sutch equations, characterizing in simple terms how long and short rates are related, for a number of sample periods and two countries. This gives us a better picture of the robustness of the relation, and enables us to view it under different monetary policy regimes. Some notions of "overreaction" of long-term interest rates to short rates will be studied, and estimates and standard deviations of the extent of overreaction or underreaction will be presented for the various sample periods. This puts on a surer footing some comparisons made by Sutch (1968) and Modigliani and Shiller (1973). Finally, an attempt will be made here to determine whether the behavior of the component of the long rate that is a distributed lag on short rates or the component of long rate unrelated to lagged short rates might be considered the reason that the slope of the term structure gives wrong signals as to the course of future interest rates.

2 Description of the Historical Relation between Long and Short Rates

It is important first to clarify in what sense the long rate is actually described by the sort of distributed lag on short rates that is suggested by the notion of a conventional valuation rule mentioned above. Modigliani and Sutch (1966) were the first to show that the long-term interest rate might well be described as a simple distributed lag on short-term interest rates, or, in terms of the annual data used in this paper,[3]

$$R_t^{(n)} = \sum_{i=0}^{4} \beta_i^{(n)} R_{t-i}^{(1)} + C^{(n)} + u_t^{(n)}, \tag{1}$$

where $R_t^{(n)}$ is the n-period rate (yield to maturity in percent on n-period coupon bonds) at time t,[4] $R_t^{(1)}$ is the one-period rate at time t, C is a constant term, and u_t is an error term uncorrelated with current and lagged short rates. In their estimates of the quarterly analogue of (1), they imposed an "Almon" fourth-order-polynomial distributed lag on all coefficients except the first, which was unconstrained. In their estimates for 1952 first quarter to 1961 fourth quarter, the estimate of β_0 was 0.32, and the sum of all the coefficients β_i, $i = 0, \ldots, 16$ was 0.99, or virtually one. The pattern of distributed lag coefficients after β_0 was hump shaped, with comparatively small values for interest rates corresponding to lags of less than a year or more than three years, and the largest values for lags of about two years.

Modigliani and Sutch interpreted this distributed lag as representing the combined effect of two different expectations mechanisms for future short-term interest rates. A regressive expectations mechanism would make expected future short rates a moving average (with positive weights that decline exponentially with increasing lag) of current and lagged short rates. An extrapolative expectations mechanism would make the expected change in short-term interest rates a moving average with positive weights (that decline with lag) of current and lagged *changes* in short-term interest rates. The combination of both mechanisms might produce, they argued, the pattern of distributed lag coefficients that they found in their estimates. They did not refer to "rational expectations" (actually they referred to Keynes, 1936) in motivating these mechanisms, so it seems that they were at that time referring to habits of thought or conventions people use to formulate expectations.

The original Modigliani-Sutch relation was expanded further by Modigliani and Shiller (1973) to allow for a separate effect of real interest rates and of inflation on long-term interest rates. This two-distributed-lag equation was incorporated as the basic term structure equation in the MIT-Penn-SSRC Econometric Model of the United States. The out-of-sample performance of this equation has been good (see Shiller, Campbell, and Schoenholtz, 1983).

Estimates of equation (1) for data sets other than those used by Modigliani and Sutch appear in table 4.1. The various sample periods used here were chosen with the idea of looking separately at various monetary policy regimes (see appendix) in two countries, the United States and the United Kingdom. There is a very substantial amount of data used here that is out of the sample used by Modigliani and Sutch (1966). Here, the estimates are produced by ordinary least squares, without the Almon constraint. With these annual data, the multicollinearity that necessitated a procedure like the Almon is less of a problem.

While these estimates do not show evidence of the extrapolative expectations hypothesized by Modigliani and Sutch,[5] it does appear indeed that for widely different sample periods and for two different countries there is some consistency in the pattern of response of long rates to short rates. In all cases, the estimated coefficients β_i are positive. In all cases the distributed lag has an exponential appearance, gradually tailing off. In several estimates, the last coefficient β_4 is larger than the rest, suggesting that the last coefficient is proxying for omitted further lags.

There are, however, some differences in response patterns across sample periods. The more recent data sets show a much higher R^2 than do the predepression data sets, which represented gold-standard monetary regimes. The predepression data for the United Kingdom, where the dependent variable is the British Consol yield, are conspicuously different in that the sum of the β_i is less than .5, rather than over 1.00 as is the case with the US data sets.

One might note that the Durbin-Watson statistic in these regressions is

Table 4.1
Regressing the long rate on current and lagged short rates[a]

Data set Country	Sample period	Constant (standard error)	Lag (i)	Coefficient of short rate $\hat{\beta}_i$	(Standard error)	R^2 Sum of coefficients lags 0–4 R'^2	Durbin-Watson SER
1	1956–	0.793	0	0.380	(0.063)	0.970	1.269
	1984	(0.271)	1	0.243	(0.095)		
US			2	0.130	(0.111)	1.026	0.600
			3	0.171	(0.111)		
			4	0.102	(0.087)	0.893	
1	1956–	0.121	0	0.305	(0.077)	0.963	0.873
	1978	(0.297)	1	0.256	(0.079)		
US			2	0.282	(0.082)	1.183	0.410
			3	0.180	(0.082)		
			4	0.160	(0.077)	0.919	
2	1960–	1.954	0	0.427	(0.127)	0.747	0.274
	1984	(1.110)	1	0.193	(0.151)		
UK			2	0.170	(0.147)	0.856	1.677
			3	0.008	(0.151)		
			4	0.058	(0.129)	0.580	
3	1861–	−0.248	0	0.304	(0.068)	0.852	0.549
	1930	(0.301)	1	0.253	(0.074)		
US			2	0.191	(0.067)	1.030	0.570
			3	0.052	(0.069)		
			4	0.231	(0.062)	0.664	
4	1828–	1.502	0	0.168	(0.047)	0.417	0.167
	1930	(0.225)	1	0.092	(0.055)		
UK			2	0.092	(0.056)	0.524	0.479
			3	0.046	(0.056)		
			4	0.126	(0.048)	0.803	

a. See appendix for source of data. All distributed lags were estimated with ordinary least squares. R'^2 is the R^2 in a regression with the long rate minus the current short rate as the dependent variable, and the same independent variables.

uniformly low, meaning that we ought not to trust the t-statistics from the regression. Phillips and Pippenger (1979) seized upon this fact to criticize Modigliani and Sutch (1966) and Modigliani and Shiller (1973). They found that with their quarterly US data from 1955 to 1971, if one first-differences the data, both long and short rates, and runs a similar regression, the coefficients of lagged short rates are significant at the 1% level only if corporate yields are used. They reported that the lagged interest rates were not significant at the 5% level if treasury yields were used. However, their results with the treasury data still show a distributed lag pattern that was similar to that estimated with corporate yields. In all of the regressions shown in table 4.1, the coefficient β_1 of the short rate lagged a year is significant at the 5% level whether a Cochrane-Orcutt serial correlation was used or whether the data were first differenced prior to running an ordinary least-squares regression. Similarly, coefficient β_2 was significant at the 5% level in half of these regressions.[6]

The original Modigliani-Sutch relation can also be interpreted in terms of the spread between the long interest rate and the short rate. Subtracting the current short rate from both sides of the Modigliani-Sutch equation, one finds that the spread depends negatively on the current short rate and positively on a distributed lag of short rates. The R^2 in this transformed regression is usually quite high (see the R'^2 shown in table 4.1). Thus, the spread shows a distinct tendency to be negative when the current short rate is below a sort of average of lagged short rates and to be positive when the current short rate is above the average of lagged short rates. The sum of the coefficients in the transformed regression is often about zero, indicating that the *level* of short interest rates has little effect on the spread. If we added a constant to all of the short rates over the last 5 years, the prediction for the spread would be nearly unchanged.

The changes across sample periods in the relation of long rates to short rates documented in table 4.1 might be justified in terms of the rational expectations theory of the term structure if the time series properties of short rates had changed appropriately across sample periods. Whether the distributed lag coefficients like those in table 4.1 are consistent with the rational expectations theory of the term structure has been the subject of discussion for some time, starting with Richard Sutch's Ph.D. dissertation (1968), and my own Ph.D. dissertation (1972), and then with Modigliani and Shiller (1973), Sargent (1979), Hansen and Sargent (1981), and others. However, these authors did not investigate whether broad changes in the time series properties of the short rate across sample periods could account for the changes in the relation between the long rate and the short rate.

3 The Linearized Expectations Theory of the Term Structure of Interest Rates

A linearized version of the expectations theory of the term structure of interest rates for coupon bonds was presented in Shiller (1972) and Modigliani and Shiller (1973) and developed further in Shiller (1979), Shiller, Campbell, and Schoenholtz (1983), and Campbell and Shiller (1984). The underlying assumption of this linearized expectations theory is that long-term interest rates (yields to maturity) on coupon bonds not far from par can be written as a weighted average of expected future short-term interest rates with *more weight* on the interest rates *less far in the future*. In the extreme case of a consol, whose maturity is infinite, the long rate is a weighted average of all future short-term rates, with weights that decline geometrically into the future. The conventional assumption in the literature testing the expectations theory of the term structure had been that the long-rate is an *unweighted* average of expected future short rates. This conventional assumption is really appropriate as an approximation only for relatively short-term bonds, and could of course not be used to study consols, which are part of the data for this paper.

It is helpful to write the expectations theory of the term structure with the help of the concept of *duration* (Macaulay, 1938). The duration of a bond is a discount-factor-times-payment-weighted average of all the times to payments of a bond. It is supposed to give a better measure of how long-term a bond is than does the time to maturity. The formula gives less weight to the coupons and principal, which occur far into the future because these contribute relatively less to price today, as they are heavily discounted. For par coupon bonds whose yield to maturity in percent is r, Macaulay's duration is

$$D_n = (1 - g^n)/(1 - g), \tag{2}$$

where $g = 1/(1 + r)$ and where n is the number of periods to maturity of the bond.[7] Thus, the duration of a consol ($n = \infty$) is not infinite but equals $(1 + r)/r$. The duration of very long-term bonds is just less than $(1 + r)/r$. For example, if $r = 5\%$, then a consol has a duration of 20 years and a 25-year bond has a duration of 15 years. Indeed, we would expect its price or yield to resemble somewhat those of consols.

The linearized expectations theory of the term structure of interest rates is then

$$R_t^{(n)} = (1/D_n) \sum_{j=0}^{n-1} (D_{j+1} - D_j) E_t R_{t+j}^{(1)} + \Phi_n, \tag{3}$$

where E_t denotes expectation conditional on all information publicly available at time t. Φ_n is a risk or liquidity premium, which is assumed constant through time.[8] In this formula, each future one-period rate is given weight corresponding to the contribution to total duration of the time period to which it applies. Since time periods further into the future have less contribution to duration, the short rates corresponding to these time periods will be given less weight. Equation (3) can be motivated in a number of ways. One is by linearizing the present value formula for coupons and principal [discounted by $E_t R_t^{(1)}, E_t R_t^{(n)}, \ldots$] around r.

Accompanying the model are various expressions for linearized holding period yields and forward rates, so that (except for the constants Φ_n) all expected linearized holding period yields equal the spot rate of the corresponding maturity and all linearized forward rates equal the corresponding expected spot rates (see Shiller, Campbell, and Schoenholtz, 1983, where the accuracy of the linearizations was also studied). These linearizations allows us to interpret the expectations model in various ways, without encountering the "Jensen's inequality" problems emphasized by Cox, Ingersoll, and Ross (1981), problems that are for the most part inconsequential. For our purposes here, we need only the linearized one-period holding yield on n-period bonds:

$$h_t^{(n)} = R_t^{(n)} + (D_n - 1)(R_t^{(n)} - R_{t+1}^{(n-1)}). \tag{4}$$

This formula is a linearization around r of the one-period holding return on an n-period bond in terms of $R_t^{(n)}$, $R_{t+1}^{(n-1)}$, and the coupon. The one-period holding return is the return from buying an n-period bond at time t, receiving its coupon between t and $t + 1$, and selling the bond at time $t + 1$, when it is an $(n - 1)$-period bond. The model (3) implies that $E_t h_t^n = R_t^{(1)}$ plus a constant, or, conversely, the latter (subject to a terminal condition) implies the model (3). When maturities are distant as with the long bonds in this paper, there is no significant distinction between the yield $R_{t+1}^{(n)}$ and $R_{t+1}^{(n-1)}$. With consols, the two are of course identical. In each application of the formula (4) in this paper, a single long-term bond yield will be used for both $R^{(n)}$ and $R^{(n-1)}$.

4   Implied Behavior of the Long Rate for Various Subperiods

Let us consider an autoregressive forecasting equation for the short-term (one-period) interest rate $R_t^{(1)}$:

$$R_t^{(1)} = \sum_{i=1}^{5} \alpha_i R_{t-i}^{(1)} + C + u_t, \tag{5}$$

where u_t is an error term that is serially uncorrelated and uncorrelated with $R_{t-i}^{(1)}$, $i > 0$, and C is a constant term. Table 4.2 shows results from estimation of this fifth-order autoregressive model for the short-term interest rate for each of the data sets.

If this is indeed the optimal forecasting equation that is based on 5 lagged values, and no other information is available that will help forecasting, then by the expectations model the long-term interest rate $R_t^{(n)}$ will be explained perfectly (that is, with no error) as a distributed lag, depending on $R_{t-i}^{(1)}$, $i = 0, \ldots, 4$:

$$R_t^{(n)} = \sum_{i=0}^{4} \mu_i^{(n)} R_{t-i}^{(1)} + C. \tag{6}$$

The coefficients μ_i, $i = 0, \ldots, 4$, in the distributed lag and the constant term C can be derived from those in equation (5) using (3) and the "chain principle of forecasting." These coefficients are related to those in (5) by

$$0 = D_n \mu_i - (D_n - 1)(\mu_{i+1} + \mu_0 \alpha_{i+1}) - I(i), \qquad i = 0, \ldots, 4, \tag{7}$$

where $I(i) = 1$ if $i = 0$ and is zero otherwise, and $\mu_5 = 0$. If we replaced $R_t^{(n)}$ with $\sum \mu_i R_{t-i}^{(1)}$ and $R_{t+1}^{(n-1)}$ with $\sum \mu_i R_{t-i+1}^{(1)}$ in formula (4) for the holding yield, then $h_t^n - R_t^{(1)}$ would be uncorrelated with each of the current and five lagged short rates.

Of course, the assumption that market forecasts of future interest rates equal autoregressive forecasts is quite restrictive, and could easily be rejected since long-term interest rates cannot be explained perfectly by a distributed lag on short-term interest rates. However, if long rates are set in accordance with (3) with *more* information than is contained in the history of short rates, then it follows that a theoretical regression of long rates on a distributed lag of short rates will show μ_i as the coefficient of r_{t-i}, $i = 0, \ldots, 4$.

One can thus evaluate the expectations model (3) by estimating the autoregression (5) for the one-period rate and then solving the system of equations (7) for the weights μ_i, $i = 0, \ldots, 4$, and comparing these with the estimates of β_i, $i = 0, \ldots, 4$. Except for sampling error, the two must be the same. Such estimates of μ_i, $i = 0, \ldots, 4$, for the data sets of this paper appear in table 4.3 alongside the estimates of β_i.

At the first level of approximation, the rational expectations model of the term structure would appear to be supported by these results. As pointed out before for one sample in Modigliani and Shiller (1973), there is a gross similarity between the μ_i and the β_i, $i = 0, \ldots, 4$.

We may say, however, that except for the very recent data sets, data

Table 4.2
Regressing the short rate on lagged short rates[a]

Data set Country	Sample period	Constant (standard error)	Lag	Coefficient of short rate	(Standard error)	$\bar{R}^2$ Sum of co-efficients lags 1–5	Durbin-Watson SER
1	1957–	0.416	1	1.089	(0.213)	0.695	2.126
	1984	(0.960)	2	−0.616	(0.340)		
US			3	0.217	(0.370)	1.057	1.957
			4	0.052	(0.367)		
			5	0.315	(0.315)		
1	1957–	1.338	1	0.516	(0.267)	0.542	1.921
	1979	(1.031)	2	−0.369	(0.274)		
US			3	0.051	(0.286)	0.868	1.421
			4	0.419	(0.284)		
			5	0.251	(0.267)		
2	1961–	0.351	1	0.714	(0.161)	0.733	2.349
	1984	(1.506)	2	−0.678	(0.200)		
UK			3	0.735	(0.199)	1.106	2.112
			4	−0.689	(0.204)		
			5	1.024	(0.225)		
3	1862–	0.907	1	0.482	(0.127)	0.481	1.956
	1931	(0.568)	2	−0.007	(0.139)		
US			3	0.269	(0.127)	0.813	1.075
			4	0.080	(0.130)		
			5	−0.011	(0.118)		
4	1829–	1.807	1	0.564	(0.102)	0.221	1.992
	1931	(0.491)	2	−0.215	(0.119)		
UK			3	0.184	(0.122)	0.479	1.045
			4	−0.055	(0.121)		
			5	0.001	(0.105)		

a. See appendix for source of data. All distributed lags were estimated with ordinary least squares.

Table 4.3
Actual and theoretical reactions of long rates to short rates

Data set Country	Sample period	Lag (i)	Actual $\hat{\beta}_i$ from table 4.1	Theoretical $\hat{\mu}_i$ from (7) and table 4.2	Theoretical μ'_i from (7) and first-difference autoregression
1	1956–	0	0.380	0.823	0.541
	1984	1	0.243	0.086	−0.074
		2	0.130	0.415	0.247
US		3	0.171	0.266	0.152
		4	0.102	0.242	0.136
1	1956–	0	0.305	0.220	0.352
	1978	1	0.256	0.051	0.104
		2	0.282	0.136	0.235
US		3	0.148	0.134	0.223
		4	0.160	0.052	0.085
2	1960–	0	0.427	0.479	0.334
	1984	1	0.193	0.090	0.044
UK		2	0.170	0.423	0.269
		3	0.008	0.110	0.061
		4	0.058	0.450	0.292
3	1861–	0	0.304	0.235	0.512
	1930	1	0.253	0.067	0.203
		2	0.191	0.073	0.209
US		3	0.052	0.015	0.063
		4	0.231	0.015	0.012
4	1828–	0	0.168	0.062	0.507
	1930	1	0.092	−0.005	0.129
		2	0.092	0.008	0.217
UK		3	0.046	−0.003	0.071
		4	0.126	0.000	0.076

set number one when estimated through 1983 and data set number 2, the long-term interest rate appear to overreact to short-term interest rates; i.e., μ_i tends to be less than the corresponding β_i, $i = 0, \ldots, 4$.

There is, however, reason to suspect that this procedure may be biased toward finding overreaction, at least in some of the sample periods. In both the recent US and UK regressions the sum of the coefficients of the lagged interest rates in table 4.2 is about one, suggesting that the characteristic equation corresponding to the autoregression may have a root equal to one. It is well established that in the case of a simple autoregression, with one lag only, if the coefficient α_1 equals 1.00, the ordinary least squares estimate of it will be biased downward. In this case, there is a bias in the method toward finding spurious overreaction.[9] There do not appear to be Monte Carlo results that would tell us the extent of the bias for the fifth-order autoregression used here.

Those who studied whether the μ_i equal the β_i dealt with this problem generally by imposing a unit root and estimating the forecasting equation for short-term interest rates in first-differenced form. The unit root was assumed in Modigliani and Shiller (1973) and Campbell and Shiller (1984).[10] Sutch (1968) did not assume a unit root, but he proceeded the other way, computing α_i, $i = 1, \ldots, 5$, from (7) and comparing these with the estimates of α_i from an autoregression. His procedure appeared to have an effect on these comparisons similar to that of assuming the unit root.

The problem of assuming the unit root is that it forces the μ_i to sum to one. Imposing the unit root thus assumes the conclusion that there is no overreaction as defined here. It remains possible, however, that some other sort of overreaction might be revealed with this procedure. In Campbell and Shiller (1984) overreaction was defined so that the β_i showed relatively too much weight on the current short rate relative to short rates lagged more periods.

As a way of exploring this possibility, the autoregressive equations for the short rate in table 4.2 were reestimated subject to the constraint that $\sum \alpha_i = 1$; i.e., a fourth-order autoregressive model for the first difference of the short rate was estimated. Using (7) with μ_i' in place of μ_i, the coefficients μ_i', $i = 0, \ldots, 4$, were computed, and these also appear in table 4.3. Of course, we no longer find that there is overreaction as defined above since the $\sum \mu_i' = 1$ by construction. It probably makes sense to look at these estimated μ_i' only for the twentieth-century data, where short rates seem to show evidence of nonstationarity. Here, the long rate appears to under-react to the current short rate (confirming results in Campbell and Shiller, 1984) and to put relatively too much weight on the past.

None of these methods readily allows for any formal testing of the model. We can look to see whether the estimated coefficients $\hat{\beta}_i$ are similar in appearance to the implied coefficients μ_i, $i = 0, \ldots, 4$, in table 4.3, but we cannot tell directly whether the difference is statistically significant. This shortcoming of the procedure was rectified by Sargent (1979), who showed how a likelihood ratio test can test the cross-equation restrictions that were examined, subject of course to his imposition of the unit root.

Fortunately, it is easy to run such a test in the present context. One can merely regress the excess return $h_t^n - R_t^{(1)}$ on current and lagged short rates. That is, one estimates the model

$$h_t^{(n)} - R_t^{(1)} = \sum_{i=0}^{4} f_i^{(n)} R_{t-i}^{(1)} + u_t, \tag{8}$$

where f_i, $i = 0, \ldots, 4$, are coefficients and u_t is an error term uncorrelated with $R_{t-i}^{(1)}$, $i = 0, \ldots, 4$. By model (3) all coefficients f_i, $i = 0, \ldots, 4$, should be zero (the short rates are in the public information set at time t) and moreover the error terms are serially uncorrelated.[11] As a test of model (3), we may perform significance tests with the estimated values of f_i, $i = 0$, $\ldots, 4$. These tests may be regarded as "forward-filtered tests" as defined by Hayashi and Sims (1983) of model (3). Such tests are much simpler to perform than the tests Sargent (1979) and Hansen and Sargent (1981) performed, tests that they described as involving complicated nonlinear cross-equation restrictions. Their tests were much more complicated because they in effect assumed that they had data on $R_{t+1}^{(n)}$ but not on $R_{t+1}^{(n-1)}$. They did not use consol data or make the approximation that these are the same as was done here. For their relatively short maturities, such a distinction may be more important.

The excess return regressions are shown in table 4.4. The significance levels at which the expectations hypotheses can be rejected by an F-test vary from .01 for data set 3 to .26 for data set 2. There does seem to be some evidence against the expectations model here, although not always impressive evidence judged from the standpoint of conventional significance levels. There seems to be a pattern for the coefficients. Except for data set 1 when estimated through 1983, the sum of the coefficients f_i, $i = 0, \ldots, 4$, is positive. Moreover, for each data set the coefficient of the current short rate is negative, and the sum of the lagged coefficients is positive. This pattern of coefficients is crudely consistent [given the estimates of equation (1)] with the notion that the excess return is explained by the spread between the long rate and the short rate, as will be discussed below.

The results of the above regression can be interpreted in terms of an overreaction or underreaction of long rates to short rates. Call $j_i^{(n)} = \beta_i^{(n)} - \mu_i^{(n)}$. Thus, j_i is the amount by which the long rate "overreacts" to $R_{t-i}^{(1)}$. Then it can be shown that, assuming the error term u_t in (1) is uncorrelated with all current and lagged $R_t^{(1)}$, the following relation holds:

$$f_i = D_n j_1 - (D_n - 1)(j_{i+1} + j_0 \alpha_{i+1}), \qquad i = 0, 1, 2, 3, 4. \tag{9}$$

If we substitute (9) into (8) and consider this and equation (5) as a two-equation system in the 12 parameters α_i, $i = 1, \ldots, 5$, j_i, $i = 0, \ldots, 4$, and constant terms, then we can derive joint estimates of the parameters and their standard errors using nonlinear multivariate regression (seemingly unrelated regression). Under the null hypothesis, equation (3), and under the assumption that the autoregression was not truncated too early, the

Table 4.4
Regressing the linearized excess return $h_t - R_t^{(1)}$ on current and lagged short rates[a]

Data set Country	Sample period Assumed duration	Constant (standard error)	Lag (i)	Coefficient of short rate $\hat{f}_i$	(Standard error)	$\bar{R}^2$ Sum of coefficients lags 1–4 F	Durbin-Watson SER Probability $> F$
1	1956–	−0.892	0	−3.976	(1.459)	0.217	2.952
	1983	(6.571)	1	4.617	(2.332)		
			2	−1.882	(2.535)	3.467	13.403
US	15		3	2.892	(2.512)		
			4	−2.160	(1.967)	2.493	0.062
1	1956–	−4.277	0	−1.635	(1.358)	0.121	2.279
	1978	(5.236)	1	1.735	(1.393)		
			2	1.187	(1.455)	1.911	7.219
US	15		3	−0.250	(1.440)		
			4	−0.761	(1.358)	1.607	0.212
2	1960–	10.809	0	−1.249	(1.083)	0.086	2.320
	1983	(10.155)	1	2.518	(1.350)		
			2	−0.215	(1.339)	2.246	14.232
UK	12		3	1.484	(1.372)		
			4	−1.541	(1.516)	1.432	0.260
3	1861–	−3.500	0	−1.270	(0.650)	0.142	2.150
	1930	(2.897)	1	1.151	(0.708)		
			2	1.229	(0.645)	2.063	5.480
US	15		3	−1.247	(0.666)		
			4	0.930	(0.600)	3.279	0.011
4	1828–	−1.094	0	−1.111	(0.448)	0.052	1.521
	1930	(2.154)	1	1.172	(0.524)		
			2	−0.047	(0.536)	1.305	4.586
UK	30		3	−0.321	(0.533)		
			4	0.501	(0.459)	2.124	0.068

a. See appendix for source of data. All distributed lags were estimated with ordinary least squares. Durations are approximately from (2) using the sample mean for the long rate, $n = 25$ for US data, $n = \infty$ for UK data.

error term in each equation is serially uncorrelated. The error terms will still be serially uncorrelated in both equations under an alternative hypothesis that makes the long rate equal to that given by (3) plus $\sum j_i r_{t-i}$. Of particular interest are the "overreaction" coefficients j_i, $i = 0, \ldots, 4$, and these are shown in table 4.5. These were computed without constraining the sum of the α_i to be one.

In other words, the j_i, $i = 0, \ldots, 4$, in table 4.5 were computed so that if one "corrected" the long rate $R_t^{(n)}$ by subtracting $\sum j_i R_{t-i}^{(1)}$ from it, and if one then computed the excess return $h_t^{(n)} - R_t^{(1)}$ using the corrected $R_t^{(n)}$ and $R_{t+1}^{(n)}$ in place of the actual values, then this excess return would be perfectly uncorrelated in the sample with each of $R_{t-i}^{(1)}$, $i = 0, \ldots, 4$.[12]

The pattern of coefficients forecasting excess returns in table 4.4 can be interpreted in terms of the j_i, $i = 0, \ldots, 4$. It follows from (9) that $f_0 = (D_n - (D_n - 1)\alpha_1)j_0 - (D_n - 1)j_1$, or, roughly speaking, $f_0 = D_n(j_0/2 - j_1)$. The negative first coefficient in each of the equations forecasting excess returns is thus due to the overreaction of the long rate to the lagged short rate $R_{t-1}^{(1)}$ (j_1 is always positive in table 4.5) and in the recent US data, underreaction to the current short rate (j_0 is negative).

It should be noted that the standard errors of the estimated j_i here may not be trustworthy. One factor not accounted for here is that while the error terms under the null are each serially uncorrelated, the assumption that cross correlations are zero at other than zero lag does not follow from the model. And of course, any assumption about error terms under the alternative hypothesis is lacking in motivation. Moreover, there is also the above-mentioned problem concerning applicability of asymptotic distribution theory.

The estimated forecasting equations for the short rate in table 4.2 always have a negative value at one lag, and this tends to produce a small value of μ_1 compared to adjacent values of μ_i. In other words, there ought to be the extrapolative expectations hypothesized by Modigliani and Sutch (1966), and the absence of evidence for it in table 4.1 here stands in contradiction of the rational expectations model.

5   Another Characterization of the Failure of the Expectations Model

One might say that the simplest and most fundamental implication of the rational expectations theory of the term structure is that relatively upward sloping term structures (where the long rate is greater than the short rate by more than the usual term premium) ought to portend a subsequent

Table 4.5
Discrepancies between actual and theoretical reactions of long rates to short rates.[a]

Data set Country	Sample period	Lag (i)	Discrepancy $\hat{f}_i$ from system estimation	(Standard error of Discrepancy)	Actual $\hat{\beta}_i$ from table 4.1	Theoretical $\hat{\mu}_i$ from $\hat{f}_i$ and $\hat{\beta}_i$
1	1956–	0	−0.203	(0.336)	0.380	0.583
	1983	1	0.280	(0.122)	0.243	−0.037
		2	−0.147	(0.219)	0.130	0.277
US		3	0.017	(0.174)	0.171	0.154
		4	−0.180	(0.165)	0.102	0.282
1	1956–	0	−0.080	(0.203)	0.305	0.385
	1978	1	0.092	(0.098)	0.256	0.164
		2	−0.048	(0.151)	0.282	0.330
US		3	−0.121	(0.137)	0.148	0.269
		4	−0.072	(0.090)	0.160	0.232
2	1960–	0	0.462	(0.169)	0.427	−0.035
	1983	1	0.287	(0.066)	0.193	−0.094
UK		2	0.398	(0.178)	0.170	−0.228
		3	0.113	(0.068)	0.008	−0.105
		4	0.307	(0.183)	0.058	−0.249
3	1861–	0	0.133	(0.096)	0.304	0.171
	1930	1	0.169	(0.055)	0.253	0.084
		2	0.100	(0.056)	0.191	0.091
US		3	−0.016	(0.039)	0.052	0.068
		4	0.061	(0.034)	0.231	0.170
4	1828–	0	0.008	(0.034)	0.168	0.160
	1930	1	0.042	(0.016)	0.092	0.050
		2	0.005	(0.021)	0.092	0.087
UK		3	0.005	(0.015)	0.046	0.041
		4	0.017	(0.014)	0.126	0.109

a. For data sets 1 and 2 the $\Sigma\alpha_i$ was constrained to one (i.e., the forecasting regression used to compute the μ_i was based on first differences of the short rate), while for data sets 3 and 4 the $\Sigma\alpha_i$ was unconstrained.

increase in interest rates. Relatively downward sloping term structures (where the long rate is less than the short rate plus the usual term premium) ought to portend subsequent decreases in interest rates. Expectations model (3) allows us to say this more formally. If the excess return $h_t - r_t^{(1)}$ is to be uncorrelated with the spread $R_t^{(1)} - R_t^{(1)}$, then a regression of $R_{t+1}^{(n)} - R_t^{(n)}$ on the spread $R_t^{(n)} - R_t^{(n)}$ should yield a positive slope coefficient, equal to $1/(D_n - 1)$.[13] It is easy to see why the correct formulation must look like this. Let us suppose to simplify the argument that the term premium Φ_n in model (3) is zero, so that expected returns on both long and short debt must be the same, and suppose that the bond is a consol. If the long rate is above the short rate, there must be a capital loss to offset the higher current yield on long bonds, if the high yield is not to indicate a relatively higher expected return on the long bond. A capital loss of course means a rise in long-term interest rates.

It was Franco Modigliani who first pointed out to me that the fact is just the opposite: when long-term interest rates are above short rates the long-term interest rate shows a tendency to decline subsequently rather than rise. Thus, when long rates are relatively high there tends to be a subsequent capital gain on long bonds that further augments their higher current yield. As far as I can tell, this fact had not been documented before.[14]

I showed evidence for this fact for a number of sample periods (Shiller, 1979) and the fact was further confirmed in Shiller, Campbell, and Schoenholtz (1983), Campbell and Shiller (1984), and Mankiw and Summers (1984). Table 4.6 shows the regressions for the data sets used in this paper. The t-statistics presented in table 4.6 are not the usual t-statistics but are for the null hypothesis that the coefficient of the spread is $1/(D_n - 1)$.

This perverse behavior of the term structure relative to the expectations hypothesis could be due to the way the long rate responds to the short rate, as estimated in table 4.1, or it could be due to noise in the long-rate series that is unrelated to the history of short rates. To decide which, the spread $R_t^{(n)} - R_t^{(1)}$ was decomposed into two components: that corresponding to the fitted value in the regressions of table 4.1 and the residuals of table 4.1. Regressions of excess returns on these two variables appear in table 4.7. We see that both variables play some role. The coefficients of the fitted spread greater than one indicate that the pattern of reaction of long rates to short rates is part of the reason the shape of the term structure gives wrong signals as to the future course of interest rates.

Mankiw and Summers (1984) looked at regressions of changes in long rates on the long-short spread for evidence for a different notion of over-

Table 4.6
Regression the change in the long-term interest rate ($R_{t+1}^{(n)} - R_t^{(n)}$) on the spread between the long rate and the short rate ($R_t^{(n)} - R_t^{(1)}$)

Data set Country	Sample period	Constant (standard error)	Coefficient of spread (standard error)	$\bar{R}^2$ T^a	Durbin-Watson SER
1 US	1956– 1983	0.459 (0.180)	−0.293 (0.107)	0.193 −3.406*	2.439 0.917
1 US	1956– 1978	0.357 (0.120)	−0.128 (0.084)	0.055 −2.374*	2.057 0.501
2 UK	1960– 1983	0.209 (0.280)	−0.049 (0.119)	−0.038 1.175	1.850 1.342
3 US	1861– 1930	−0.067 (0.045)	−0.133 (0.048)	0.088 −4.519*	2.233 0.378
4 UK	1828– 1930	0.010 (0.004)	0.004 (0.016)	−0.009 −2.418*	1.480 0.160

*Significant at 5% level.
a. T-statistic for hypothesis that coefficient equals $1/1(D_n - 1)$. See appendix for source of data.

Table 4.7
Regressing the excess return of long bonds over the short rate on the fitted value of the long-short spread and residual from the regression of table 1[a]

Data set Country	Sample period	Constant (standard error)	Coefficient of fitted value (standard error)	Coefficient of residual (standard error)	$\bar{R}^2$ F	Durbin-Watson SER
1 US	1956– 1983	−6.380 (2.567)	3.661 (1.303)	8.502 (4.537)	0.269 5.977*	2.114 12.943
1 US	1956– 1978	−4.843 (1.727)	2.563 (1.252)	5.336 (4.211)	0.147 2.898	1.913 7.112
2 UK	1960– 1983	−2.323 (3.178)	1.604 (1.814)	1.446 (2.124)	−0.031 0.658	1.863 15.112
3 US	1861– 1930	0.928 (0.635)	2.494 (0.829)	3.590 (1.166)	0.193 9.264*	2.167 5.313
4 UK	1828– 1930	−0.287 (0.465)	0.940 (0.490)	0.694 (0.988)	0.021 2.084	1.489 4.662

*Significant at the 1% level.
a. See appendix for source of data.

reaction. For them, overreaction occurs if long-term bonds are priced in accordance with (3) but with too short a duration, i.e. with a duration less than implied by the actual maturities and average levels of interest rates. They pointed out that this sort of overreaction could never explain the wrong sign of coefficient of the spread variable in regressions like those in table 4.6.

In contrast, the wrong sign of the coefficient of the spread variable could instead be due to the exponential decay pattern in the distributed lag regressions (1) of the long rate on the short rate, a pattern that puts too much weight on the short rate lagged once (j_1 in table 4.5 is always positive) and, for recent US data, too little weight on the current short rate (j_0 is negative). In those cases where $\sum \beta_i \approx 1$ the spread variable tends to be high when short rates are low relative to their average level over the preceding few years. If long rates were to tend to increase subsequently, as the expectations model would predict, then given the fact that long rates tend to behave like a moving average of short rates, it would have to be the case that the short rate tends to increase substantially at such a time. In fact it does not.

An extreme caricature for all but data set 4 would be that the long-term interest rate is a moving average of the short rate with exponentially decaying weights that sum to one:

$$R_t^{(n)} = (1 - h) \sum_{i=0}^{\infty} h^i R_{t-i}^{(1)}, \qquad 0 < h < 1.$$

If this is the case, then the change in the long rate $R_{t+1}^{(n)} - R_t^{(n)}$ equals $(1 - h)(R_{t+1}^{(1)} - R_t^{(m)})$. For this to be positively correlated with the yield spread $R_t^{(n)} - R_t^{(1)}$, it would have to be the case that when the short rate is below the long rate (or equivalently below its recent average value as defined by the moving average), it would have to tend to be above it the following year. In fact, the short rate is more persistent than that and tends to stay on the same side of the long rate. The caricature would be more realistic if we added a transient error term (representing an exogenous drift of long rates unrelated to short rates) to the above equation, another factor that would tend to make for a wrong sign in the regression of the change in the long rate on the spread.

6   The Volatility of Long-Term Interest Rates

It was shown in Shiller (1979) that model (3) for $n = \infty$ implies that, for a given variance of h_t, there is a lower bound to the possible variance of $R_t^{(1)}$.

Table 4.8
Sample standard deviations of actual and fitted linearized holding-period returns and variance inequality[a]

Data set Country	Sample period	$\sigma(h)$ $\sigma(h)/\sqrt{D_n(g^2)}$	$\sigma(hf)$ $\sigma(hf)/\sqrt{(D_n(g^2)}$	$\sigma(R^{(i)})$
1 US	1956– 1983	14.942 5.738	12.569 4.827	3.563
1 US	1956– 1978	7.683 2.950	6.822 2.620	1.796
2 UK	1960– 1983	15.714 6.710	14.252 6.085	3.623
3 US	1861– 1930	6.105 2.345	6.681 2.566	1.497
4 UK	1828– 1930	4.469 1.227	6.476 1.778	1.184

a. h is defined as in expression (4) in text, while hf is as in expression (4) but with the fitted values of equation (1) as estimated in table 4.1 in place of $R_t^{(m)}$ and $R_{t+1}^{(n-1)}$. The inequality (10) in the text implies that $\sigma(h)/\sqrt{(D_n(g^2)}$ be less than $\sigma(R^{(1)})$, if model (3) is valid and sample standard deviations equal population standard deviations. Duration D_n is as shown in table 4.3. See appendix for source of data.

A high variance of h_t can only be justified if there is enough variation in short-term interest rates themselves.[15] The variance inequality was extended formally to the finite-n case in Shiller (1981a). In the present notation this is

$$\text{var}(R^{(1)}) \geq \text{var}(h^{(m)})/D_n(g^2), \tag{10}$$

where $D_n(g^2) = (1 - g^{2n})/(1 - g^2)$. When sample variances were substituted into (10), the inequality was found generally to be violated for g in the relevant range, as is verified for all of the data sets of this paper (table 4.8). Rejection of the expectations model for violation of this inequality was criticized by Flavin (1983, 1984b) and others on the grounds that small sample properties of the estimates of these variances may be unreliable. This criticism of the use of this inequality is certainly valid, especially with regard to more recent interest rate data that seem more likely to show nonstationarity. The violation of the variance equalities only show, as I originally noted, that the variability of changes in long-term interest rates can only be reconciled with the expectations theory if the anticipated variance of short rates was much higher than the historical variance. This is true as well for the nineteenth-century data.

My concern here is merely to judge which component of the long rate accounts for the violation of this inequality in the data sets used here. Table

4.8 also shows standard deviations for the various data sets in this paper of the excess return computed not from the actual $R_t^{(n)}$ and $R_{t+1}^{(n)}$ but using the fitted values of the regressions of table 4.1. Clearly the fitted values violate the inequalities too.

7 Conclusion and Summary

This paper began with the plausible notion that a conventional valuation rule for the pricing of long-term bonds causes their yields to behave as a sort of moving average of lagged short rates. If people are relying on their memories to price bonds, then it is plausible that they would blur the past, and that the distributed lag would have a simple form, such as the roughly exponential decay form estimated here. Whether this is an "overreaction" or "underreaction" would depend on the stochastic properties of the short-term interest rate.

Although no formal statistical testing of this simple notion was done here, the results here may be interpreted as suggesting that the notion by itself does not give a better description of the data than does the rational expectations model of the term structure, but may help provide an interpretation for some of the failures of the rational expectations model.

The rational expectations model appears in a rough sense to be supported by the results in this paper. The reaction of long-term interest rates to short-term interest rates is not grotesquely different from that predicted by the rational expectations model (See table 4.3 or 4.5). Moreover, with the predepression UK series, the short rate appeared quickly mean-reverting and the duration of the consol was much longer than with the other series studied. Indeed the consol yield showed much less reaction to short rates than did long yields in other periods.

The rational expectations theory of the term structure is also seem to be sharply contradicted in certain senses by these data. A distributed lag of short rates alone appears to predict excess returns (table 4.4), and the slope of the term structure generally gives wrong signals as to the future course of interest rates (table 4.6).

These anomalies might be interpreted as reflecting a tendency for the response pattern of long rates to short rates to deviate from the optimal pattern in the direction of the conventional valuation formula noted above. The greater similarity across subperiods of the actual response pattern of long rates to short rates than the optimal response patterns, as well as the comparative simplicity of the actual response pattern, seems to account for some of the anomalies. Thus long rates showed a tendency to overreact to the current short-term interest rates in the early historical series, and to underreact in the latest US series, when the monetary regime was very different. The actual distributed lag pattern of long rates on short rates is too smooth in all sample periods, omitting the "notch" in the lag pattern at one lag.

Appendix: Data Sources

Data set 1: 1948–1984. The long-term interest rate for the United States is Moody's Aaa Corporate Bond Yield Average for January, from Moody's Investor Service, *Bond Survey*. The short-term interest rate is the bond-equivalent yield on 6-month (150–179 day prior to November 1979) commercial paper rate for January, from the Board of Governors of the Federal Reserve System of the United States, as reported in the *Federal Reserve Bulletin*. January figures are monthly averages of daily figures. Bond equivalent yield is computed by the transformation $r = D/(1 - D/200)$, where D is the rate on a discount basis.

Data set 2: 1956–1984. The long-term interest rate for the United Kingdom is the flat yield on $2\frac{1}{2}\%$ British Consols Observations, taken on the last Friday of March. The short-term interest rate is the 3-month local authorities temporary loan rate for the last Friday of the March starting in 1961 and for the last Saturday of the March before that, as reported in the *Bank of England Statistical Abstract*, No. 1 (1970), table 29, and subsequent issues of the *Bank of England Quarterly Bulletin*.

Data set 3: 1857–1930, Macaulay (1938). The long-term interest rate is the unadjusted index number for January of yields of American Railroad Bonds. The short-term interest rate is the January commercial paper rate in New York City: for 1857–1923, "choice 60–90 day two name paper"; 1924–1930, "4 to 6 month prime double and single name paper." These data are in columns three and five of Macaulay's table 10, pp. A142–A160.

Data set 4: 1828–1930. The long-term interest rate is the annual average of 3% British Consols through 1888 and on $2\frac{1}{2}\%$ government annuities starting in 1889 (Homer, 1963, table 19, column 2, and table 57, column 2). The short rate is, for 1824–1844, Overend and Gurney's annual average of first class 3-month bill rates and, after 1844, the annual average rates (averaging maximum and minimum) for 3-month bank bills, both from Mitchell and Deane (1962, p. 460). This data set was data set number 6 in Shiller (1979).

Notes

1. *General Theory*, pp. 202–203. This possibility may also call to mind the literature on multiple rational expectations equilibrium—for example, Cass and Shell (1983). But here it will not be assumed that rules of thumb are strictly rational.

2. There are actually a number of variants of this theory with similar implications for data. They will be unified in a linearized model below.

3. In this paper, with its annual data I shall estimate distributed lags that include the current and four lagged values, approximately the same total lag length as Modigliani and Sutch (1966) used with their quarterly data. Throughout this paper the term "short rate" and "one-period rate" will be used interchangeably, though in the data sets the short rates are not exactly one-year rates.

4. Superfluous parentheses in superscripts are to indicate that the superscript is not to be interpreted as an exponent. In what follows, the (n) superscript will be omitted on coefficients and error terms except when necessary for clarity.

5. That is, β_1 is not negative or small relative to the adjacent coefficients. This may be due in part to the choice of annual rather than quarterly data.

6. Ordinary least squares rather than Cochrane-Orcutt results were presented in table 4.1 because the former allows us to make an argument in the context of a rational expectations model that the expected values of the coefficients are unaffected by omission in the regression of information in the market information set.

7. The rate r is expressed as a proportion per period, while interest rates in the data used in the tables are in percent per annum.

8. We might call Φ_n a "rolling risk premium" since it relates to the difference between the long rate and a rolling-over of short rates. This will distinguish it from the holding period risk premiums or forward rate risk premiums with which it is often confused. See Campbell and Shiller (1984).

9. A similar point was raised by Mankiw and Shapiro (1985) regarding Flavin's (1984a) observation that consumption appears to overreact to income.

10. Sargent (1979) and Hansen and Sargent (1981) also imposed the unit root in their rather different procedures.

11. The t-test here may be unreliable in small samples, of course. A simple example will illustrate why this may be a problem. Suppose that the short rate is a first-order autoregressive process with autoregressive coefficient h just under one, and the long rate is equal to the short rate times $(1 - g)/(1 - hg)$. If (8) were run truncating the distributed lag at zero, then in finite samples f_0 would tend to be negative, falsely suggesting that long rates tend to overreact to short rates.

12. In the final column of table 4.5 are estimates of what the distributed lag of long rates on short rates *should* have looked like in table 4.1. These estimates are just

$\mu_i = \beta_i - j_i$. When these are compared with estimates derived from the α_i in table 4.2 using equations (7), in table 4.3, the estimated μ_i, $i = 0, \ldots, 4$, look reasonably similar except for data set number 2. Any differences between these two estimates of μ_i, $i = 0, \ldots, 4$, can come only from a nonzero correlation of the residual in the estimated equation 1 with $R_{t-5}^{(1)}$ when the sample is shifted one period. Such a correlation would mean, essentially, that the distributed lag was truncated too early.

13. As before, technically the dependent variable should be $R_{t+1}^{(n-1)} - R_t^{(n)}$.

14. This observation was made by Macaulay (1938, p. 33), who, however, did not document it or emphasize it.

15. Analogous variance inequalities were also used to evaluate the model that corporate stock prices equal the present value at a constant discount rate of expected future dividends (Shiller, 1981b, and LeRoy and Porter, 1981).

References

Campbell, John Y., "Bond and Stock Returns in a Simple Exchange Model," National Bureau of Economic Research Working Paper No. 1509, November 1984.

Campbell, John Y., and Robert J. Shiller, "A Simple Account of the Behavior of Long-Term Interest Rates," *American Economic Review Papers and Proceedings*, 74(2), May 1984, 44–48.

Cass, David A., and Karl Shell, "Do Sunspots Matter?" *Journal of Political Economy*, 91, April 1983, 193–227.

Cox, John C., John Ingersoll, Jr., and Stephen A. Ross, "A Reexamination of Traditional Hypotheses about the Term Structure of Interest Rates," *Journal of Finance*, 36, 1981, 769–799.

Cox, John C., John Ingersoll, Jr., and Stephen A. Ross, "An Intertemporal General Equilibrium Model of Asset Prices," *Econometrica*, 53(2), March 1985a, 363–384.

Cox, John C., John Ingersoll, Jr., and Stephen A. Ross, "A Theory of the Term Structure of Interest Rates," *Econometrica*, 53(2), March 1985b, 385–408.

Fama, Eugene F., "The Information in the Term Structure," *Journal of Financial Economics*, 13, 1984, 509–528.

Flavin, Marjorie, "Excess Volatility in the Financial Markets: A Reassessment of the Empirical Evidence," *Journal of Political Economy*, 91, 1983, 929–996

Flavin, Marjorie, "Excess Sensitivity of Consumption to Current Income: Liquidity Constraints or Myopia?" NBER Working Paper #1341, May 1984a.

Flavin, Marjorie, "Time Series Evidence on the Expectations Hypothesis of the Term Structure," Carnegie-Rochester Conference Series on Public Policy, Vol. 20, Spring 1984b, pp. 211–238.

Hansen, Lars Peter, and Thomas J. Sargent, "Exact Linear Rational Expectations Models: Specification and Estimation," Staff Report, Federal Reserve Bank of Minneapolis, 1981.

Hayashi, Fumio, and Christopher Sims, "Nearly Efficient Estimation of Time Series Models with Predetermined, but Not Exogenous, Instruments," *Econometrica*, 51, May 1983, pp. 783−798.

Homer, Sidney, *A History of Interest Rates*, New Brunswick NJ, Rutgers University Press, 1963.

Huizinga, John, and Frederic S. Mishkin, "The Measurement of Ex-Ante Real Interest Rates on Assets with Different Risk Characteristics," unpublished paper, Graduate School of Business, University of Chicago, 1984.

Kane, Edward J., "Nested Tests of Alternative Term Structure Theories," *Review of Economics and Statistics*, 65(1), February 1983, 115−123.

Keynes, John M., *The General Theory of Employment, Interest and Money*, Harbinger, 1964 (1936).

LeRoy, Stephen F., and Richard D. Porter, "The Present Value Relation: Tests Based on Implied Variance Bounds," *Econometrica*, 49(3), May 1981, 555−574.

Lutz, Frederick A., "The Structure of Interest Rates," *Quarterly Journal of Economics*, 55, November 1940, 635−663.

Macaulay, Frederick, *Some Theoretical Problems Suggested by the Movements of Interest Rates, Stock Prices and Bond Yields in the United States Since 1856*, New York, National Bureau of Economic Research, 1938.

Mankiw, N. Gregory, and Matthew D. Shapiro, "Trends, Random Walks, and the Permanent Income Hypothesis," forthcoming, *Journal of Monetary Economics*, 1985.

Mankiw, N. Gregory, and Lawrence H. Summers, "Do Long-Term Interest Rates Overreact to Short-Term Interest Rates?" *Brookings Papers on Economic Activity*, 1, 1984, 223−248.

McCulloch, J. Huston, "Measuring the Term Structure of Interest Rates," *Journal of Business*, 64, December 1973, 19−31.

McCulloch, J. Huston, "The Tax Adjusted Yield Curve," *Journal of Finance*, 30(3), June 1975, 811−830.

Mitchell, Brian R., and Phyllis Deane, *Abstract of British Historical Statistics*, Cambridg University Press, Cambridge, 1962.

Modigliani, Franco, and Robert J. Shiller, "Inflation, Rational Expectations, and the Term Structure of Interest Rates," *Economica*, February 1973, 12−43.

Modigliani, Franco, and Richard Sutch, "Innovations in Interest Rate Policy," *American Economic Review*, May 1966.

Modigliani, Franco, and Richard Sutch, "Debt Management and the Term Structure of Interest Rates: An Analysis of Recent Experience," *Journal of Political Economy*, August 1967.

Phillips, Llad, and John Pippenger, "The Term Structure of Interest Rates in the MPS Model: Reality or Illusion?" *Journal of Money, Credit and Banking*, 11, May 1979, 151–164.

Richard, F. Scott, "An Arbitrage Model of the Term Structure of Interest Rates," *Journal of Financial Economics*, 6, 1978, 33–57.

Sargent, Thomas J., "A Note on the Estimation of the Rational Expectations Model of the Term Structure," *Journal of Monetary Economics*, 5, January 1979, 133–143.

Shiller, Robert J., "Rational Expectations and the Structure of Interest Rates," unpublished Ph.D. dissertation, MIT, 1972.

Shiller, Robert J., "The Volatility of Long-Term Interest Rates and Expectations Models of the Term Structure," *Journal of Political Economy*, 87(6), December 1979, 1190–1199.

Shiller, Robert J., "Alternative Tests of Rational Expectations Models: The Case of the Term Structure," *Journal of Econometrics*, 16, 1981a, 17–87.

Shiller, Robert J., "Do Stock Prices Move too Much to be Justified by Subsequent Changes in Dividends?" *American Economic Review*, 71(3), 1981b, 421–436.

Shiller, Robert J., and Pierre Perron, "Testing the Random Walk Hypothesis: Power versus Frequency of Observation," *Economic Letters*, 1985.

Shiller, Robert J., John Y. Campbell and Kermit L. Schoenholtz, "Forward Rates and Future Policy: Interpreting the Term Structure of Interest Rates," *Brookings Papers on Economic Activity*, pp. 173–217, 1-1983.

Summers, Lawrence H, "Do We Really Know That Markets Are Efficient?" NBER Working Paper, 1982.

Sutch, Richard, "Expectations, Risk and the Term Structure of Interest Rates," unpublished Ph.D. dissertation, MIT, 1968.

Vasicek, Oldrich, "An Equilibrium Characterization of the Term Structure," *Journal of Financial Economics*, 6, 1978, 33–57.

Comments on "Conventional Valuation and the Term Structure of Interest Rates"

Franco Modigliani

In this paper Shiller touches on a subject particularly dear to my heart, and he does it in the masterly fashion that is common to many of his contributions, even though the news he brings me is a rather mixed bag.

The aim is to test how well the term structure of interest rates can be accounted for by the rational expectation model and, to the extent that this theory appears to fail, to examine whether that failure can be explained by other models. The principal alternative considered is what Shiller labels "conventional valuation," a rather nondescriptive expression by which he really means some form of adaptive expectations plus "perceptions unrelated to any such rule of thumb."

The quest begins with table 4.1 which presents estimates of the coefficients of "Modigliani-Sutch equations." (1966, 1967), for periods other than those originally covered and for the United Kingdom as well as the United States. One is immediately struck by the fact that the coefficients of the distributed lags look rather different from those reported in Modigliani-Sutch or in Modigliani-Shiller (1973): everywhere, and especially for the earlier periods. The leading coefficient is substantially smaller, while the second coefficient is relatively large. It is clear, however, that the difference must be explained, in good measure, by the use of annual instead of quarterly data. Thus, the smaller value of the first coefficient presumably reflects the effect of averaging the high spike of the first quarter with the very small or negative value of the second quarter; similarly, the second coefficient corresponds to the average of those of quarters −4 to −7, which are much higher than that of quarter −1. Indeed, it is not even clear that the coefficient of the second *year* should show a dip.

A second likely source of noncomparability with the Shiller-Modigliani coefficients is that Shiller neglects the possible effects of inflation by not allowing for the possibility that expectation of the real rate and of inflation might be generated by a different distributed lag. It is a pity that throughout his paper he has failed to allow for this possibility, for it is precisely in the years after 1971 that inflation reached its highest value and its greatest volatility. Hence, taking inflation explicitly into account could conceivably have an appreciable effect on the results and their interpretation.

The next question is how the coefficients of table 4.1 relate to those implied by the theory of rational expectation cum stable risk premium. To answer this question, Shiller first reports his elegant reformulation of the expectation theory in terms of the concept of duration. To derive from this the weighting structure on past short rates implied by the rational expectation hypothesis, he estimates and reports for each sample in table 4.2 the actual regression of the short rate on previous short rates. The distributed lags all clearly exhibit a family resemblance, notably in the high first-period coefficient and the negative and sometimes quite large second-period coefficient, suggesting a strong extrapolative behavior of the short-term rate. However, this tendency, as measured say by the difference between the first and second coefficients, tends to be more marked in the more recent period, especially in the two samples that extend to 1984, something that can probably be attributed to the far greater persistence of inflation since the sixties (cf. Barsky, 1985).

One is also struck by the great variability of the coefficients, even within the same country and for periods that overlap to a substantial extent—cf. the two regressions 1. For instance, one cannot fail to be disquieted by the large difference in the pattern of the μ_is estimated for the United States for 1956–1984 versus 1956–1978. Of course these differences become less impressive if one allows for the rather large standard errors that characterize all the coefficients. But, then one is led to wonder how much significance to attach to the difference in the shape of the rational expectation coefficients, μ_is, reported in table 4.3.

Yet, Shiller uses those patterns as providing some evidence that "long-term interest rates tend to overreact to short-term interest rates" because the sum of the β_is tends to exceed the sum of the μ_is. In reality, the former sum exceeds the latter in but three cases, while in the remaining two it is very substantially smaller. By contrast, in two of the three cases where the β_is exceed the μ_is, the difference is modest—.2 to .3—and one may well wonder whether it is in fact significant. At the same time, the tendency for the weighting structure to be more extrapolative in the more recent period, which includes the 1980s, can be traced also in the β_is, though in rather attenuated form. On the negative side, one must acknowledge that the difference between the first two coefficients is uniformly smaller for the β_is than for the μ_is.

Fortunately, Shiller is able to carry out an ingenious test (table 4.4) for the significance of the difference between the actual and rational expectation lag distributions, without going through the tedious process of computing standard errors for the μ_is. I would interpret the results of this test as indicating that the rational expectation theory is not too bad an approximation to the long-term rate after all. The deviation of the holding yield from the short rate exhibits a very low correlation with lagged short-term rates, and only in the case of the seventy observations in the United States sample terminating in 1930 is the R^2 (.14) significant at the roughly 1% level (while in none of the remaining four cases is it significant at the 5% level). For the corresponding long United Kingdom sample, the R^2 is only .05. On the whole, these results suggest that the hypothesis that there is little unexploited information in the lagged short rates is well supported. On the other hand, as Shiller notes, the pattern of the coefficients is systematic across samples, with the leading coefficient always negative and the sum of the remaining coefficients positive. This pattern foreshadows the more dramatic failure of the rational expectation model, which is exhibited in table 4.6.

That failure, which has been attracting attention for some time now, consists in the fact that the rational expectation prediction that a positive spread between the long and the short rates should be followed, on the average, by a higher long rate is not supported by the data. Table 4.6 provides impressive evidence of this failure by reporting the result of correlating the change in the long rate with the spread. In 4 of the 5 samples, including the long United States pre-1930 sample, the correlation is actually negative. While the negative coefficients are generally not very significant, it is shown that they are in all cases significantly different (at the 5% level at least) from the value implied by the rational expectation model.

This result has always struck me as surprising because it implies that investors could make money by the simple strategy of holding whatever instrument has the higher rate and selling (or shorting) the instrument with the lower rate. (If there is a stable positive risk premium, then one should get into the long instrument only when the spread exceeds the premium.) Obviously, if such a strategy were widely followed, the phenomenon would disappear.

Now why would the market fail to take advantage of this strategy? The only answer that I can think of is that the amount to be gained by it is puny compared with the cost of the transaction and with the risk to be assumed when the strategy calls for going into longs. The plausibility of this explanation is supported by the observation that the R^2s in table 4.6 are uniformly low, though this only means that one cannot count on earning appreciably more than the difference between the two rates. To really throw light on this apparent case of glaring failure to pursue a money-making strategy, someone would have to work out how much money could actually be made by following the strategy and what is the variance of the outcomes (and maybe the covariance with the market).

Shiller does not pursue this line, but instead turns his attention to exploring what type of "nonrational" expectation formation—i.e., one failing to exploit the information contained in past short rates—could account for the observed phenomenon. He first shows that if expectations were roughly adaptive, then the change in the long rate would likely be negatively correlated with the spread, as we actually observe. And, he further suggests that the computed β_is are roughly consistent with adaptive expectations, in that, with but one modest exception, the weights decline monotonically (aside from the last coefficient, whose increase could reflect truncation). However, I have some question about this interpretation since, as already noted, the weights of an annual regression are strongly biased in the direction of producing a declining pattern of weights; I would, therefore, hesitate to accept Shiller's suggestion until I have seen the results of quarterly regressions, including the price component, at least for the regressions terminating in 1984. Certainly the quarterly coefficients reported in our 1973 paper do not much resemble exponentially declining weights.

Still, I would provisionally agree with Shiller's conclusion that his tests in several regards provide support for the hypothesis that the expectations are roughly rational and that the failures might be attributed to the fact that the actual expectations reflect elements of rationality as well as adaptive features. But, I remain puzzled by the failure of the market to exploit the opportunity to increase returns by following this naive rule: Hold that maturity that offers the highest interest rate!

References

Barsky, Robert, "Three Interest Rate Paradoxes," MIT Ph.D. Thesis, 1985.

Modigliani, Franco, and Robert Shiller, "Inflation, Rational Expectations and the Term Structure of Interest Rates," *Economica*, February 1973.

5

On the Current State of the Stock Market Rationality Hypothesis

Robert C. Merton

1 Introduction

The foundation for valuation in modern financial economics is the rational market hypothesis. It implies that the market price of a security is equal to the expectation of the present value of the future cash flows available for distribution to that security where the quality of the information embedded in that expectation is high relative to the information available to the individual participants in the market. As has been discussed at length elsewhere,[1] the question whether this hypothesis is a good approximation to the behavior of real-world financial markets has major substantive implications for both financial and general economic theory and practice.

The rational market hypothesis provides a flexible framework for valuation. It can, for example, accommodate models where discount rates are stochastic over time and statistically dependent on future cash flows. It can also accommodate nonhomogeneity in information and transactions costs among individual market participants. The theory is not, however, a tautology. It is not consistent with models or empirical facts that imply that either stock prices depend in an important way on factors other than the fundamentals underlying future cash flows and discount rates, or that the quality of information reflected in stock prices is sufficiently poor that investors can systematically identify significant differences between stock price and fundamental value.

Although the subject of much controversy at its inception more than two decades ago, the rational market hypothesis now permeates virtually every part of finance theory. It has even become widely accepted as the "rule" (to which one must prove the exception) for finance practice on Wall Street, LaSalle Street, and in courtrooms and corporate headquarters. However, recent developments in economic theory and empirical work have again cast doubts on the validity of the hypothesis. Representing one view, Summers (1985) sees much of the renewed controversy as little more than a case of financial economists and general economists engaging in a partisan diversion of intellectual effort over methodological questions instead of focusing on sound research on major substantive questions.[2] He sees this development as only hastening an apparent secular trend toward inefficient disjunction between the fields of finance and economics on subjects of conjoint research interest. Perhaps that is so. But I must confess to having quite the opposite view on these same research efforts with regard to both their substance and their presumed dysfunctional effects on the fields of finance and economics. However, to pursue this issue further would only be an exercise in self-refutation. Thus, it suffices to say that whether market rationality is viewed as a "hot topic" or as merely a "topic with too much heat," an analysis of the current state of research on this issue would appear timely—especially so on this occasion honoring Franco Modigliani, past president of both the American Economic Association and the American Finance Association and prime counterexample to the Summers doctrine.

This paper focuses on the central economic question underlying the issue of stock market rationality: Do real-world capital markets and financial intermediaries, as a practical matter, provide a good approximation to those ideal-world counterparts that are necessary for efficient investor risk bearing and efficient allocation of physical investment? Although satisfaction of the rational market hypothesis is surely not sufficient to ensure efficient allocations, its broad-based rejection is almost certainly sufficient to rule out efficient allocations.[3]

From this perspective on the issue, it matters little whether or not real-world dealers and deal makers can "scalp" investors and issuers as long as their profits are a small fraction of aggregate transactions in important and well-established markets. Similarly, it matters little for this issue whether, as suggested by Van Horne (1985), promoters often make large-percentage profits during the transient period of time between the inception of a new financial product (or market) and the widespread acceptance (or rejection) of the product by investors and issuers.

In evaluating market rationality as it bears on economic efficiency, it matters very much whether stock prices generally can be shown to depend in an important way on factors other than fundamentals. It also matters very much whether it can be shown that either academic economists or practitioners systematically provide better forecasts of fundamental values than stock prices do. Thus, this analysis focuses on empirical work on aggregate stock price behavior, and especially the new volatility test methodologies, which appear to provide evidence of this very sort.

Although these empirical findings have had the most immediate effect in reviving the controversy over stock market rationality, some of the emerging developments in theory may prove, in the longer run, to be more important in resolving the controversy. Before proceeding with the analysis of empirical work, therefore, I pause briefly to comment on two of the more promising candidates to supersede the rational market theory.

Grounded in the sociological behavioral theory of the self-fulfilling prophecy, the theory of rational expectations speculative bubbles[4] in effect provides a theoretical foundation for answering the "If you are so smart, why aren't you rich?" question underlying the rational market argument that fullyrecognized, sizable, and persistent deviations between market price and fundamental value must necessarily provide "excess profit" opportunities for either investors or issuers. As we know, however, from the work of Tirole (1982), the interesting conditions under which such rational bubble equilibria can exist are still to be determined. In particular, if the theory is to be applied to the aggregate stock market in realistic fashion, then it must accommodate both "positive" and "negative" bubbles in a rational expectations framework. Such application would seem to require a satisfactory process to explain both the limits on share repurchase by firms when prices are persistently below marginal production cost and the limits on the creation of new firms with "instant profits" for the promoters in periods when general stock market prices significantly exceed that marginal cost.

Although few economists would posit irrational behavior as the foundation of their models, many, of course, do not subscribe to the sort of "super-rational" behavior implied by the rational expectations theory (with or without bubbles). Based on the pioneering work of Kahneman and Tversky (1979, 1982), the theory of cognitive misperceptions (by which I mean the observed set of systematic "errors" in individual decision making under uncertainty) may become a base from which economic theory formally incorporates nonrational (or as some economists have described it, "quasi-rational") behavior.

As discussed in Arrow (1982), the empirical findings of such systematic misperceptions in repeated laboratory experiments appear sound, and there would also appear to be many test cases within economics. In terms of the current state of empirical evidence in both cognitive psychology and financial economics, it would seem somewhat premature, however, to conclude that cognitive misperceptions are an important determinant of aggregate stock market behavior. Specifically, the same sharp empirical findings of cognitive misperceptions have not (at least to my knowledge) been shown to apply to individual decision making *when the individual is permitted to interact with others (as a group) in analyzing an important decision and when the group is repeatedly called upon to make similar types of important decisions. But, this is, of course, exactly the environment in which professional investors make their stock market decisions.*

If professional investors are not materially affected by these cognitive misperceptions, then it would seem that either competition among professional investors would lead to stock prices that do not reflect the cognitive errors of other types of investors, or professional investors should earn substantial excess returns by exploiting the deviations in price from fundamental value. Unlike the theory of rational expectations bubbles with its self-fulfilling prophecy, there is no a priori reason in this theory to believe that investment strategies designed to exploit significant deviations of price from fundamental value will not be successful. However, as shown in the following section, rather robust evidence indicates that professional investors do not earn substantial excess returns.

These two theories, along with Shiller's (1984) theory of fads, explicitly incorporate in an important way positive theories of behavior derived from other social sciences. In doing so, they depart significantly from the "traditional" approach of mainstream *modern* economic theory: namely, to derive the positive theories of "how we do behave" almost exclusively from normative economic theories of "how we should behave." Whether these theories throw light on the specific issue of aggregate stock market rationality, it will surely be interesting to follow the impact on economic theory generally from these attempts to bring economics "back into line" with the rest of the social sciences.

2   Empirical Studies of Stock Market Rationality

In his seminal 1965 paper proving the martingale property of rationally determined speculative price changes, Paul Samuelson was careful to warn readers against interpreting conclusions drawn from his model about markets as empirical statements: "You never get something for nothing. From a nonempirical base of axioms, you never get empirical results. Deductive analysis cannot determine whether the empirical properties of the stochastic model I posit come close to resembling the empirical determinants of today's real-world markets" (p. 42). One can hardly disagree that the question whether stock market rationality remains a part of economic theory should be decided empirically. There is, however, a complication: we have no statute of limitations for rejecting a theory. To the extent that one assumes the advancement of knowledge, it is the fate of all theory to be encompassed, superseded, or outright rejected in the long run. Nevertheless, at any moment, one must choose: either to continue to use the theory or to discard it. It is with this choice in mind that I examine the empirical evidence to date on stock market rationality.

As economists have cause to know well, the "long run" in economic behavior can indeed be long. Having already sustained itself for at least twenty years,[5] the rational market theory exemplifies this same fact—here in the history of economic science instead of in the history of economic behavior. The longevity of the theory can surely not be attributed to neglect on the part of economists bent on putting it to empirical test. I have not made any formal comparisons, but I suspect that over these twenty years, few, if any, maintained hypotheses in economic theory have received as much empirical attention as the rational market hypothesis. Indeed, there have probably been *too many* such tests. Although it is likely that this claim could be supported on the grounds of optimal resource allocation alone, the case is made here solely on statistical grounds. In preparation for this and other matters that bear on the testing of market rationality, I briefly review the history of these tests.

2.1   Early Tests of Stock Market Returns

About the time that Samuelson's fundamental paper appeared in print, what has since become the Chicago Center for Research in Security Pricing completed the construction of a file of prices and related data on all New York Stock Exchange-listed stocks from 1926 to 1965. This file has been periodically updated and expanded to include other exchanges so that there are now available almost sixty years of monthly data and more than twenty years of daily data on thousands of stocks. In addition, Robert Shiller of Yale has created a return file for the aggregate stock market with data going back to 1872.

There had been some earlier empirical studies of the randomness of speculative price changes, but the availability of a large-scale, easily accessible data base caused a flurry of such studies beginning in the mid-1960s. From simple runs and serial correlation tests to sophisticated filtering and spectral analysis, the results were virtually uniform in finding no significant serial dependencies in stock returns. The few cases of significant serial correlation were small in magnitude and short-lived (disappearing over a matter of a few days), and they could largely be explained by specialist activities for individual stocks or "non-contemporaneous trading effects" for portfolios of stocks. These findings were, of course, consistent with the Samuelson martingale property as a necessary condition for rationally determined prices.

Financial researchers at this time were aware of the possibility that a significant part of this randomness could be from random "animal spirits," which would cause prices to deviate from fundamental values. There was, however, a widespread belief that the empirical evidence did not support this alternative to market rationality. The foundation for this belief was the assumption that even with animal spirits, in the long run, stock prices will converge in the statistical equilibrium sense to their fundamental values. From this assumption, it follows that deviations from fundamental values will, by necessity, induce serial dependences in stock returns.[6] If such deviations were significant, then these dependences should be detectable as, for example, systematic patterns in the long-wave frequencies of the spectral analysis of stock returns. Moreover, there had been empirical studies of "relative strength" portfolio strategies that should do well if the market "underreacts" to information and of "relative weakness" (contrary opinion) portfolio strategies that should do well if the market tends to "overreact" to information. Neither of these produced significant results.[7] Working along similar lines were the studies of stocks that appear on the most active trading list or that had moved up or down by unusually large amounts, designed to look for evidence of under- or overreaction. Once again, no significant findings. Thus, it appeared at the time that the empirical evidence not only gave support to Samuelson's necessary condition for rationally determined prices, but also failed to lend support to the alternative hypothesis of random animal spirits.

As we know today from the work of Summers (1986) and others, many of these studies provided rather weak tests for detecting the types of generalized serial correlations that random animal spirits might generate, especially when the speed of reversion to fundamental values is slow. However, the concern in the 1960s was over another issue surrounding the power of these tests: the selective bias inherent in "secret models."

2.2   Tests of Professional Investor Performance

As the cynical version of the story goes, one could not lose by testing market rationality. If, indeed, significant empirical violations were found, one could earn gold, if not glory, by keeping this discovery private and developing portfolio strategies to be sold to professional money managers who would take advantage of these violations. If, instead, one found no significant violations, then this (financial) "failure" could be turned into academic success by publishing the results in the scientific journals. Thus, while each study performed might represent an unbiased test, the collection of such studies *published* were likely to be biased in favor of not rejecting market rationality. Unlike the more generally applicable claim for "quality" bias that studies that are consistent with the accepted theory are subject to less scrutiny by reviewers than ones that purport to reject it, the potential for material effects from "profit-induced" biases is probably specialized within economic analyses to studies of speculative prices.

One need not, however, accept this cynical characterization of academic financial researchers to arrive at much the same conclusion. The portfolio strategies tested by academics were usually simple and always mechanical; therefore, the fact that they yielded no evidence of significant profit opportunities is perhaps no great surprise. However, real-world professional investors with significant resources might well have important information sources and sophisticated models (be they of fundamentals or market psychology) that are used to beat the market systematically. As this version of the story goes, *if only* the academics could gain access to these proprietary models, they would quickly be able to reject the rational market hypothesis. Unfortunately, one assumes that few successful professional investors are likely to reveal their hypothetically profitable models, and thereby risk losing their source of income, simply to refute publicly the rationally determined price hypothesis of economists (which by hypothesis they have, of course, already determined privately to be false). Thus, it would seem that the possibility of proprietary models would, at least, significantly weaken, and in all likelihood, bias, the academic tests of market rationality.

Concern over the "secret model" problem led to the next wave of empirical tests for which the pioneering study of the mutual fund industry by Jensen (1968) serves as a prototype. The basic assumptions underlying these tests hold that if such models exist, then professional investors have them, and if they have them, then the results should show themselves in superior performance (at least, before expenses charged to investors) of the funds they managed. Tracking the performance of 115 investment companies over the period 1945–1964, Jensen found no significant evidence of superior performance for the fund industry as a whole. Later work by Jensen and others also found no evidence that individual investment companies within the industry had superior performance. That is, it was found that for any fund which had outperformed the naive market strategy of investing in the past, the odds of the same fund doing so in the future were essentially fifty-fifty. Similar studies subsequently made of the performance of other professional investor groups (e.g., insurance company equity funds, bank trust departments) came to much the same results. Moreover, as I have indicated in my preliminary remarks, these findings have remained robust to date.[8]

To be sure, the variances of the returns on these managed portfolios are sufficiently large that although the point estimates of the excess returns in these studies support the null hypothesis of no superior performance, they cannot reject the alternative null hypothesis that the managers do provide sufficient performance to earn the 25−100 basis points they charge. This fact may be important to the economics of the money management industry, but is inconsequential for the broader question of market rationality as a good approximation to the real-world stock market. That is, the undiscovered existence of proprietary models is not likely to provide an important explanation for the rational market hypothesis having remained unrejected for so long a time.

2.3   Anomalous Evidence on Stock Market Rationality

During the period of the 1960s and early 1970s, the overwhelming majority of empirical findings continued to support the market rationality theory (cf. Fama, 1970). Indeed, editors of both finance and broader economic journals, quite understandably, became increasingly reluctant to allot scarce journal space to yet another test that did not reject market rationality. Despite the mountain of accumulated evidence in support of the hypothesis, there were a relatively few of the empirical studies conducted during this period that did not seem to fit the rational market model. For example, low-price-to-earnings-ratio stocks seem systematically to earn higher average returns (even after correcting for risk differences) than high-price-to-earnings-ratio stocks. This "PE effect," later renamed the "small stock effect" after it was shown to be more closely associated with firm size than PE ratios, still remains a puzzle. Some other anomalies were the finding of various seasonal regularities such as the "January effect" and "the-day-of-the-week effect," and still another is the behavior of stock returns after a stock split. As the number of such puzzles gradually accumulated, the apparently closed gate on the empirical issue of market rationality began to reopen. Indeed, by 1978, even the *Journal of Financial Economics* (with its well-known editorial view in support of market rationality) devoted the entire June–September issue to a symposium on anomalous evidence bearing on market efficiency.

During this period, there were a number of empirical findings in the general economics literature that also cast doubt on the hypothesis of market rationality. Time series calculations of Tobin's Q appeared to suggest that stock market prices were too high at times while much too low at others, to be explained by economic fundamentals alone. Modigliani and Cohn (1979) presented a theory and empirical evidence that stock prices were irrationally low during the 1970s because investors failed to take correct account of the radically increased levels of the inflation rate in assessing expected future corporate profits and the rate at which they should be discounted.

Collectively these findings raised questions about the validity of stock market rationality, but they were hardly definitive. Some were found to be significant in one time period, but not in another. Others, such as Long's (1978) study on the market valuation of cash dividends, focused on a small sample of obscure securities. Virtually all shared the common element of testing a joint hypothesis with other important and unproven assumptions in addition to stock market rationality. There is, for example, the common joint hypothesis of stock market rationality *and* prices that are formed according to (one or another tax version of) the Capital Asset Pricing Model. Thus, at most, these tests rejected a hypothesis including stock market rationality but also other assumptions that, on a priori grounds, could reasonably be argued as less likely to obtain than market rationality.

During the past five years, a series of tests based upon the volatility of stock prices has produced seemingly new evidence of market non-rationality that some consider relatively immune to these criticisms of the earlier apparent rejections. One group of these tests pioneered by LeRoy and Porter (1981) and Shiller (1981) has focused on the volatility of aggregate stock market price relative to either aggregate earnings or dividends over long time periods (in the case of the former for the postwar period, and in the latter since before the turn of the century). Their findings have been interpreted as confirming the long-felt-but-unproved belief among some economists that stock prices are far more volatile than could ever be justified on fundamental evaluations alone.

A second group of tests examines the short-run volatility of stock price changes from one trading day to the next. It was known in the 1960s that the measured variance rate on stock returns is significantly lower over short time periods including weekends and holidays when the market is closed than over the same-length time periods when the market is open every day. The "rational" explanation given for this "seasonal" observation on volatility held that with businesses and many government activities closed, less new information is produced on these nontrading days than on trading days when they are open. However, using a period in the 1960s when the stock market was closed on every Wednesday, French and Roll (1984) show that the previously identified lower stock return volatility over short time periods that include a nontrading day applied to the Wednesday closings as well. Because nonspeculative market activities were generally open on these Wednesdays, the earlier presumed explanation was thus plainly inadequate. It would appear that market trading itself seems to cause increased volatility in market prices, and some interpret this finding as evidence against market prices being based on fundamentals alone.[9]

2.4   *Ex Ante* and *Ex Post* Predictions of the Theory

Explaining why rationally determined speculative price changes would exhibit the martingale property even though the underlying economic variables upon which these prices are formed may have considerable serial dependences, Samuelson (1965, p. 44) writes, "We would expect people in the market place, in pursuit of avid and intelligent self-interest, to take account of those elements of future events that in a probability sense may be discerned to be casting their shadows before them." The empirical evidence to date has been remarkably robust in finding no important cases of either lagged variables explaining stock price returns or of real-world investors (who make their decisions without benefit of even a peek into the future) being able to beat the market. This impressive success in confirming the *ex ante* component of the theory's prophecy has not, however, been matched in confirming its *ex post* component: namely, one should be able to find current or future economic events related to the fundamentals that, on average, explain current and past changes in stock prices.

As has been discussed elsewhere (cf. Fama, 1981; Fischer and Merton, 1984; Marsh and Merton, 1983, 1985), the change in aggregate stock prices is an important leading indicator of macro economic activity. Indeed, it is the best single predictor of future changes in business fixed investment, earnings, and dividends. Moreover, the forecast errors in the realization of future earnings changes are significantly correlated with the then-contemporaneous changes in stock prices. Nevertheless, although the writers for the popular financial press try hard, they often cannot identify the specific economic events that are important enough to cause the aggregate value of the stock market to change by as much as 2% in a single day.

At the micro level, the accounting and finance literatures are populated with studies of the behavior of individual stock prices, on, before, and after, the date of some potentially important event such as an earnings or tender offer announcement. These "event" studies lend some support to the *ex post* component of market rationality by showing that stock price changes predict many such events, respond quickly and in an unbiased fashion to surprises, and do not respond to seemingly important events that, in fact, should be affect the fundamentals (e.g., "cosmetic" changes in accounting earnings that have no impact on current or future cash flows). However, some of these studies (cf. Ohlson and Penman, 1985, who find that stock price return volatility appears to increase significantly after a stock split) provide conflicting evidence that indicates that stock prices may be affected by factors other than fundamentals.

Just as the strong empirical support for the *ex ante* component of market rationality has moved the focus of theoretical research from models of differential information to models of rational expectations bubbles, animal spirits, and fads, so the relative lack of closure on the *ex post* component seems to be the driving force behind the methodological focus of current empirical tests of the hypothesis. Finance specialists seem to favor short-term volatility or event studies, while general economists favor long-term studies, but both appear to agree that the statistical properties of volatility tests make them the most promising approach for rejecting the hypothesis of aggregate stock market rationality. The bulk of the formal analysis in this paper is focused on the long-term volatility tests, leaving for another occasion the examination of the event-study approach. Before undertaking that task, I digress to comment on a few, perhaps prosaic, but nevertheless important issues that frame the testing of this hypothesis.

2.5   Some Methodological Problems in Testing the Theory

As we all know, what the stock market actually did from 1872 to 1985 is an enumerable fact. As such, those numbers do not change even as the number of tests of the rational market hypothesis on these same data continues to grow. As we also know, the standard test statistics used in these studies do not reflect that fact. While, of course, the same comment could be made about virtually every area of economic model testing (cf. Leamer, 1983), it perhaps warrants more than usual attention in this case because of the unusually large number of studies, the large number of observations in the data set, and the magnitudes of unexplained volatility in stock prices.

As a case study of the problem, let us consider the regression study of the hypothesis that the expected real rate of return on the market is a constant, which is discussed in the Summers (1985) article. He writes, "Simple regression of real ex post stock returns on lagged dividend yields find that the null hypothesis that the real ex ante rate is constant can be rejected at almost any confidence level" (p. 635). Although hardly a proponent of this null hypothesis in either theory or practice (cf. Merton, 1973, 1980), I would nevertheless argue that in making his statement for apparently clear rejection, Summers does not take account of the number of regressions, *collectively*, researchers have run of stock returns on various contemporaneous and lagged variables. That some adjustment for this fact could have material implications for the strength of his conclusion is readily apparent from the negligible R^2 or explanatory power of these lagged yields. While one could perhaps argue on a priori grounds that dividend yield is a reasonable surrogate variable for expected return, I can report that much the same statistical significance results obtain (on the same data set, of course) if one regresses returns on the reciprocal of current stock price alone, omitting the dividend series altogether.[10]

If knowledge is to advance, we must seek out the exceptions, the puzzles, the unexplained residuals and attempt to explain them. But, before problem solution must come problem identification. Thus, economists place a premium on the discovery of puzzles, which in the context at hand amounts to finding apparent rejections of a widely accepted theory of stock market behavior. All of this fits well with what the cognitive psychologists tell us is our natural individual predilection to focus, often disproportionately so, on the unusual. As I have hinted earlier, this emphasis on the unusual has been institutionalized by responsible and knowledgeable journal editors who understandably look more favorably upon empirical studies that find anomalous evidence with respect to a widely accepted theory than upon studies that merely serve to confirm that theory yet again. This focus, both individually and institutionally, together with little control over the number of tests performed, creates a fertile environment for both unintended selection bias and for attaching greater significance to otherwise unbiased estimates than is justified.

To clarify the point, consider this parable on the testing of coin-flipping abilities. Some three thousand students have taken my finance courses over the years, and suppose that each had been asked to keep flipping a coin until tails comes up. At the end of the experiment, the winner, call her A, is the person with the longest string of heads. Assuming no talent, the probability is greater than a half that A will have flipped 12 or more straight heads. As the story goes, there is a widely believed theory that no one has coin-flipping ability, and, hence, a researcher is collecting data to investigate this hypothesis. Because one would not expect everyone to have coin-flipping ability, he is not surprised to find that a number of tests failed to reject the null hypothesis. Upon hearing of A's feat (but not of the entire environment in which she achieved it), the researcher comes to MIT where I certify that she did, indeed, flip 12 straight heads. Upon computing that the probability of such an event occurring by chance alone is 2^{-12}, or .00025, the researcher concludes that the widely believed theory of no coin-flipping ability can be rejected at almost any confidence level.

Transformed to the context of tests of stock market rationality, what empirical conclusion about the theory can be reached if we are told of a certified discovery of a particular money manager who outperformed the market in each and every year for twelve years? Even if the individual researcher can further certify that the discovery of this apparently gifted manager was by a random drawing, the significance of the finding cannot be easily assessed. We know that the population size of (past and present) money managers is quite large. We also know that the number of re-searchers (past and present) studying professional money management performance is not small. However, as indicated, for quite legitimate individual and institutional reasons, results that simply confirm the "norm" (of no significant performance capability) tend not to be reported. Thus, the number of such random drawings undertaken *collectively* by researchers is unknown, and this makes the assessment of significance rather difficult.

As we surely could do in the case of A's purported coin-flipping talent, we might try to resolve this problem by testing the money manager's talent "out of sample." Because of survivorship bias, this cannot be done easily with data from years prior to the money manager's run. If the run is still current, then we must wait many years to accumulate the new data needed to test the hypothesis properly.

The problem of assessing significance becomes, therefore, especially acute for testing theories of stock market behavior where very long observation periods (e.g., fifty to one hundred years) are required. One such class of examples is theories where price and fundamental value deviate substantially and where it is further posited that the speed of convergence of price to value is slow.

If, as is not unusual (cf. Shiller, 1984), a theory is formulated as a possible solution for an empirical puzzle previously found in the data, then the construction of a proper significance test of the theory on these same data becomes quite subtle.

Consider, for example, the following sequence of empirical studies and theories, which followed the finding in the early 1970s, that low-price-to-earnings-ratio stocks seem significantly to outperform high-price-to-earnings-ratio stocks when performance is adjusted for risk according to the Capital Asset Pricing Model. Because there was already theory and evidence to suggest that the CAPM was inadequate to explain all the cross-sectional differentials in average security returns and because price-to-earnings ratios are not statistically independent of other firm characteristics (e.g., industry, dividend yield, financial and business risks), early explanations of the puzzle centered on additional dimensions of risk as in the arbitrage pricing and intertemporal capital asset pricing theories and on the tax effects from the mix of the pretax returns between dividends and capital gains. Further empirical analysis of the same data suggested that the aberration was more closely related to the size of the firm than to price-to-earnings ratios, although this claim is still subject to some dispute. Although firm size is also not statistically independent of other firm characteristics, this finding added the prospect of market segmentation or "tiering" to the original list of possible explanations for the puzzle.

Still further empirical analysis of the same data found a "seasonal" effect in stock returns that appeared to produce systematically larger returns on the market in the month of January. Closer inspection of these data pinpointed the source in place and time to be smaller firms in the early part of January. Moreover, by combining these two studies, it seems that the original PE/small-firm puzzle is almost entirely the result of stock price behavior in January. This result shifted the emphasis of theoretical explanation from risk factors and segmentation to "temporary" depressions in prices caused by year-end tax-loss sales of stocks that have already declined in price.

In the growing list of theoretical explanations of this puzzle (followed by tests on the same data set), perhaps the most recent entry is the "over-reaction behavioral theory" of DeBondt and Thaler (1985) which implies that a "contrary opinion" portfolio strategy will outperform the market. It is particularly noteworthy because it also represents an early attempt at a formal test of cognitive misperceptions theories as applied to the general stock market.[11] To test their theory, they construct two portfolios (each containing 35 stocks): one contains extreme winners based on past returns and the other extreme losers. They find that in a series of nonoverlapping three-year holding periods, the "winners," on average, underperformed the market by 1.7% per year and the "losers" overperformed the market by 6.5% per year. The difference between the two, 8.2% per year, was judged to be significant with a *t*-statistic of 2.20.

Do the empirical findings of DeBondt and Thaler, using over a half-century of data, really provide significant evidence for their theory? Is it reasonable to use the standard *t*-statistic as a valid measure of significance when the test is conducted on the same data used by many earlier studies whose results influenced the choice of theory to be tested? As it happens in this particular case, the former substantive question can be answered without addressing the latter methodological one. That is, Franco Modigliani is fond of the saying, "If, for a large number of observations, you have to consult the tables to determine whether or not your *t*-statistic is significant, then it is not significant." This expressed concern over the delicate issue of balancing type I and type II errors would seem to apply here. Moreover, consider the additional findings of the study as described by the authors (p. 799): "First, the overreaction effect is asymmetric; it is much larger for losers than for winners. Secondly, consistent with previous work on the turn-of-the-year effect and seasonality, most of the excess returns are realized in January." As the authors later put it. (p. 804), "Several aspects of the results remain without adequate explanation." It is at this moment difficult to see a clear theoretical explanation for overreaction being asymmetric and, even more so, for the excesses tending to be corrected at the same time each year.

Suppose, however, that the authors had found no such unexplained anomalies with respect to their theory and a larger *t*-statistic. Would their test, considered in methodological terms, have fulfilled their expressed goal? Namely, "... our goal is to test whether the overreaction hypothesis is *predictive* [their emphasis]. In other words, whether it does more for us than merely to explain, ex post, the P/E effect or Shiller's results on asset price dispersion" (p. 795). When a theory is formulated as an explanation of a known empirical puzzle and then tested on the same data from which the puzzle arose, it would appear that the distinction between "prediction" and "ex post explanation" can be quite subtle.

These same concerns, of course, apply equally to the many empirical studies that do not reject market rationality. The early tests of serial dependences in stock returns that used the newly created data bases in the 1960s may have been sufficiently independent to satisfy the assumptions underlying the standard test statistics. It is, however, difficult to believe in the same level of independence for the practically countless subsequent runs used to test closely related hypotheses on the same data.

Although there is no obvious solution to these methodological problems in testing the rational market hypothesis, it does not follow that the controversies associated with the hypothesis cannot be empirically resolved. It does follow, however, that the reported statistical significance of the evidence, both for and against the hypothesis, is likely to overstate—perhaps, considerably so—the proper degree of precision to be attached to these findings. As noted at the outset, although common to all areas of economic hypothesis testing, these methodological problems appear to be especially acute in the testing of market rationality. Thus, it would seem that in evaluating the evidence on this matter, "more-than-usual" care should be exercised in examining the substantive economic assumptions and statistical methodologies used to present the evidence. In this spirit, I try my hand at examining the recent volatility tests of aggregate stock market rationality.

2.6   Volatility Tests of Stock Market Rationality

Having already expressed my views on the LeRoy and Porter (1981) and Shiller (1981) variance bound studies as tests of stock market rationality,[12] I provide only a brief summary of those views as background for the discussion of more recent volatility tests that have evolved from their work.

In formulating his variance bound tests, Shiller (1981) makes three basic economic assumptions: (S.1) stock prices reflect investor beliefs, which are rational expectations of future dividends; (S.2) the real expected rate of return on the stock market is constant over time; (S.3) aggregate real dividends on the stock market can be described by a finite-variance stationary stochastic process with a deterministic exponential growth rate. From these assumptions, Shiller derives two variance bound relations: the first is that the variance of real and detrended stock prices is bounded above by the variance of real and detrended "perfect-foresight" stock prices constructed by discounting ex post the realized stream of dividends at the estimated average expected rate of return on the stock market. The second is that the variance of the innovations (or unanticipated changes) in stock prices is bounded from above by the product of the variance of dividends and a constant that parametrically depends on the long-run or statistical equilibrium expected dividend-to-price ratio. Using 109 years of data, Shiller found that the sample statistics violated by a very large margin both of his variance bounds on stock price behavior. Although he did not derive the sampling properties of his estimates, Shiller argued that the magnitude of the violations together with the long observation period make sampling error an unlikely candidate to explain these violations. Nevertheless, subsequent simulations by Flavin (1983) and Kleidon (1983a,b) have shown that sampling error, and, in addition, sample bias, could be important factors.

Some economists interpret the Shiller findings as strong evidence against the theory that stock prices are based upon fundamentals alone. Others, most recently Summers (1985) and Marsh and Merton (1986), are more careful in noting that even if the results are "true" rejections, then they reject the joint hypothesis (S.1), (S.2), and (S.3), which need not, of course, imply rejection of (S.1).[13] As noted earlier in this section, there are a priori economic reasons as well as empirical evidence leading us to reject the hypothesis (S.2) that the expected real rate is constant. While these are perhaps sufficient to reconcile the test findings with market rationality, some economists (including Shiller, 1981, 1982) have presented analyses suggesting that fluctuations in the expected real rate might have to be "unreasonably large" to make this accommodation.

If (S.2) were modified to permit the expected real rate to follow a stochastic but stationary process, then, together with (S.3), detrended rational stock prices must follow a stationary process. The prototype processes for stock prices and dividends used by both finance academics and practitioners are not stationary, and this raises a priori questions about assumption (S.3). Kleidon (1983a,b) reports time series evidence against stationarity for both stock prices and dividends, and, using simulations, shows that Shiller's findings can occur for nonstationary dividend processes and rationally determined stock prices.

Marsh and Merton (1986) show that if the stationarity assumption is replaced by a Lintner-like dividend model where the dividend is a positive distributed lag of past stock prices, then the inequality in Shiller's first variance bounds test is exactly reversed. Thus, for any given time series of stock prices, this variance bound will always be violated by one or the other assumption about the dividend process. Hence, they conclude that the bound is wholly unreliable as a test of stock market rationality. They further show that for this class of dividend processes, there is no easily identified bound between the variance of dividends and the variance of stock price innovations.

Judging from these studies, the amount of light that these variance bounds tests can shed on the issue of market rationality seems to depend critically on the way in which we model the uncertainty surrounding future economic fundamentals. That is, if the underlying economic fundamentals are such that the levels of rationally determined, real (and detrended) stock prices can be described by a stationary process, then they have power. If, instead, it is the percentage change in stock prices that is better described by a stationary process, then they have no power. This observation was surely one of the important driving forces in the development of the "second-generation" volatility tests beginning with West (1983, 1984) and represented most recently by Mankiw, Romer, and Shapiro (1985). Although closely related to the original Shiller-LeRoy-Porter formulations, these tests appear to be far more robust because they do not require the stationarity assumption. Since the Mankiw, Romer, and Shapiro (MRS) study is the most recent version of these tests, the analysis here focuses on it.

As with the original Shiller variance bound test, which derived an inequality between the variance of rational stock prices $\{P(t)\}$ and the variance of ex post, perfect-foresight stock prices $\{P^*(t)\}$, MRS also use these series, together with a time series of "naive forecast" stock prices $\{P^0(t)\}$, to test the following derived bounds [p. 679, (11') and (12')]:

$$E_0[P^*(t) - P^0(t)]^2 \geq E_0[P^*(t) - P(t)]^2 \tag{1}$$

and

$$E_0[P^*(t) - P^0(t)]^2 \geq E_0[P(t) - P^0(t)]^2, \tag{2}$$

where E_0 denotes the expectation operator, conditional on initial conditions at $t = 0$. Although MRS do retain what has been called here Shiller's assumptions (S.1) and (S.2), they do not make the stationarity assumption (S.3). Hence, this conditioning of the expectations is necessary to make sense of (1) and (2) when the series are not stationary processes.

To test the bounds (1) and (2), they form the test statistics [p. 683, (16), (17)],

$$S_1 = \frac{1}{T}\sum_{t=1}^{T}[P^*(t) - P^0(t)]^2 - \frac{1}{T}\sum_{t=1}^{T}[P^*(t) - P(t)]^2 \tag{3}$$

and

$$S_2 = \frac{1}{T}\sum_{t=1}^{T}[P^*(t) - P^0(t)]^2 - \frac{1}{T}\sum_{t=1}^{T}[P(t) - P^0(t)]^2, \tag{4}$$

and show that $E[S_1] \geq 0$ and $E[S_2] \geq 0$. With the same data set used by Shiller (1981) but now extended to run from 1872 to 1983, and a "naive forecast" $\{P^0(t)\}$ based on the current dividend, MRS find that these second moment inequalities are substantially violated by the point estimates of both (3) and (4).

The MRS analysis appears to address all the cited criticisms of the first-generation volatility tests with two exceptions, both of which they point out (p. 686): the assumption of a constant discount rate and the statistical significance of their estimates. Since the former has already been discussed in the literature on the first-generation tests, I examine only the latter here.

As with the original Shiller analysis, it is understandable that MRS did not examine the significance issue formally. After all, it is no easy task to derive the necessary mathematical relations for general processes. In the Shiller case, the assumption of stationarity for the underlying processes make somewhat credible the heuristic argument that with a 109-year observation period, the sample statistic is not likely to differ from its expected value by the large magnitudes necessary to void his apparent rejection. Such creditability does not, however, extend to nonstationary processes. Because the extension to include nonstationary processes is the most important contribution of the MRS and other second-generation volatility tests, it is appropriate to examine the sampling properties of their statistics in such an environment.

As noted, deriving these properties in general is no easy task. Thus, I focus here on a simple example that fits their conditions and is easy to solve for the sampling properties.

Suppose there is a rationally priced stock that we know as of today ($t = 0$) will not pay a dividend until at least time T in the future. Suppose (as is often assumed in representative finance models) the dynamics for stock price in real terms, $P(t)$, follows a geometric Brownian motion, which we can describe by the Itô stochastic differential equation:

$$\frac{dP}{P} = r\,dt + \sigma\,dZ, \tag{5}$$

where r is the required expected real return on the stock; σ^2 is the instantaneous variance rate; and dZ is a Weiner process. r and σ^2 are positive constants.

Suppose further that we decide to perform an MRS type experiment using price data from today until year T in the future. Since none of us knows today what stock prices will be in the future, it is clear that the test statistic is conditional only on the current price, $P(0) = P_0$, and the date at which we end the test, T.

By the MRS definition, the ex post perfect-foresight stock price series,

$\{P^*(t)\}$, will be constructed according to the rule

$$dP^*(t) = rP^*(t)\,dt \tag{6}$$

with the further terminal or boundary condition that

$$P^*(T) = P(T). \tag{7}$$

From (6) and (7), it follows immediately that

$$P^*(t) = e^{-r(T-t)}P(T). \tag{8}$$

From the posited dynamics (5), we can represent the random variable for the stock price at time t in the future, conditional on $P(0) = P_0$, by

$$P(t) = P_0 \exp[\mu t + \sigma Z(t)], \tag{9}$$

where $\mu \equiv (r - \sigma^2/2)$ and $Z(t) = \int_0^t dZ(s)$ is a normally distributed random variable with the properties that

$$E_0[Z(t)] = 0,$$

$$E_0[Z(t)Z(s)] = \min(s, t). \tag{9a}$$

It follows from (9) and (9a) that $(0 \le t \le T)$

$$E_0[P(t)] = P_0 e^{rt} \tag{10a}$$

and

$$E_0[P^2(t)] = P_0^2 \exp[(2r + \sigma^2)t]. \tag{10b}$$

It follows from (8), (10a), and (10b) that

$$E_0[P^*(t)] = P_0 e^{rt} \tag{11a}$$

and

$$E_0\{[P^*(t)]^2\} = P_0^2 \exp[2rt + \sigma^2 T]. \tag{11b}$$

By comparison of (10) with (11), we see that the conditional expectation of the "forecast," $P(t)$, is equal to the conditional expectation of the "realization," $P^*(t)$, and the conditional noncentral second moment of the forecast is always less than the corresponding second moment of the realization. This verifies in this model the fundamental principle underlying both the first- and second-generation volatility tests, the principle that rational forecasts should exhibit less volatility than the realizations.

For analytic convenience, suppose that in performing this test, we choose our "naive forecast," $P^0(t)$, equal to zero for all t (which is acceptable within the MRS methodology). In this case, the MRS volatility bound statistic (3) can be rewritten as

$$E_0(X_1) \geq E_0(X_3) \tag{12}$$

and the MRS volatility bound statistic (4) can be rewritten as

$$E_0(X_1) \geq E_0(X_2), \tag{13}$$

where

$$X_1 \equiv \frac{1}{T} \int_0^T [P^*(t)]^2 \, dt,$$

$$X_2 \equiv \frac{1}{T} \int_0^T [P(t)]^2 \, dt, \tag{14}$$

$$X_3 \equiv X_1 + X_2 - \frac{2}{T} \int_0^T P^*(t)P(t) \, dt.$$

with the MRS $S_1 = X_1 - X_3$ and the MRS $S_2 = X_1 - X_2$.

Substituting from (8) and (9) and computing the conditional expectations, we have that

$$E_0[S_1] = E_0[X_1 - X_3]$$
$$= (P_0)^2 [e^{(2r+\sigma^2)T} - 1]/[2r + \sigma^2]T \tag{15}$$

and

$$E_0[S_2] = E_0[X_1 - X_2]$$
$$= \frac{(P_0)^2 e^{\sigma^2 T}}{2r(2r + \sigma^2)T} [\sigma^2(e^{2rT} - 1) - 2r(1 - e^{-\sigma^2 T})]. \tag{16}$$

By inspection of (15) and (16), we confirm the MRS inequalities $E_0[S_1] \geq 0$ and $E_0[S_2] \geq 0$, and moreover, we see that for $\sigma^2 > 0$, they are strict inequalities whose magnitudes grow without bound as the observation period T becomes large. Unfortunately, the standard deviations of both statistics also grow without bound as the observation period becomes large, and moreover, the rates of growth are at a larger exponential rate than the expected values. Hence, for large T, virtually any realized sample values for S_1 and S_2 are consistent with the ex ante inequalities (12) and (13).

In noting the upward trend in their series and the prospect for hetero-skedasticity, MRS (pp. 685–686) attempt to correct for this possible inefficiency by weighting each observation by the inverse of the market price of the stock. However, such a scaling of the data does not rectify the sampling problem. For example, using their scheme, the new statistic S_2', replacing S_2 in (16), can be written as

$$S_2' = \frac{1}{T} \int_0^T \{[P^*(t)]/P(t)\}^2 \, dt - \frac{1}{T} \int_0^T [P(t)/P(t)]^2 \, dt. \tag{17}$$

Again computing expectations, we have

$$E_0[S_2'] = [e^{\sigma^2 T} - 1]/\sigma^2 T - 1, \tag{18}$$

which is positive and growing in magnitude without bound. Again, the standard deviation of S_2' also grows at a larger exponential rate than $E_0[S_2']$.

Because $E_0(S_1) \geq 0$ and $E_0(S_2) \geq 0$, it follows that $E_0(X_3)/E_0(X_1) \leq 1$ and $E_0(X_2)/E_0(X_1) \leq 1$. A perhaps tempting alternative method for testing the inequalities (12) and (13) would be to use the ratios X_3/X_1 and X_2/X_1 instead of the differences S_1 and S_2. However, as we now show, unless the real discount rate is considerably larger than the volatility parameter σ^2, the ex ante expected values of both these ratios produce exactly the reverse of the inequalities for the ratios of their individual expectations.

Define the statistics $Q_1 \equiv X_3/X_1$ and $Q_2 \equiv X_2/X_1$. By substituting from (8), (9), and (14), we can write the expressions for Q_1 and Q_2 as

$$Q_1 = 1 + Q_2 - 4r \left\{ \int_0^T \exp[-(r + \mu)(T - t) \right.$$
$$\left. - \sigma[Z(T) - Z(t)]] \, dt \right\} \Big/ [1 - e^{-2rT}] \tag{19}$$

and

$$Q_2 = 2r \left\{ \int_0^T \exp[-2\mu(T - t) - 2\sigma[Z(T) - Z(t)]] \, dt \right\} \Big/ [1 - e^{-2rT}]. \tag{20}$$

Taking expectations and integrating (20), we have

$$E_0[Q_2] = 2r[1 - e^{-(2r - 3\sigma^2)T}]/\{(2r - 3\sigma^2)[1 - e^{-2rT}]\}. \tag{21}$$

By inspection of (21), if $2r > 3\sigma^2$, then $E_0[Q_2] \to 2r/[2r - 3\sigma^2] > 1$ as T gets large. If $0 < r \leq 3\sigma^2$, then $E_0[Q_2] \to \infty$ as T gets large. Thus, for large T, the expectation of the ratio X_2/X_1 satisfies exactly the reverse of the inequality satisfied by the ratio of their expectations $E_0[X_2]/E_0[X_1]$, and this is the case for all positive parameter values r and σ^2.

Taking expectations in (19) and substituting from (21), we have

$$E_0[Q_1] = 1 + 2r \left\{ \frac{[1 - e^{-(2r-3\sigma^2)T}]}{(2r - 3\sigma^2)} - \frac{2[1 - e^{-(2r-\sigma^2)T}]}{(2r - \sigma^2)} \right\} \Bigg/ [1 - e^{-2rT}]. \quad (22)$$

From (22), if $0 < 2r \leq 3\sigma^2$, then $E_0[Q_1] \to \infty$ as T gets large. For $2r > 3\sigma^2$ and large T, we have that $E_0[Q_1] \to 1 + 2r(5\sigma^2 - 2r)/(2r - 3\sigma^2)(2r - \sigma^2)$ which only becomes less than one if $2r > 5\sigma^2$. As described in Merton (1980, p. 353, table 4.8), the average monthly variance rate on the market between 1926 and 1978 was estimated to be 0.003467, which amounts to a $\sigma^2 = 0.0416$ in annual units. Hence, an expected annual real rate of return on the market of the order of 10% would be required to make $E_0[Q_1]$ satisfy the inequality $E_0[Q_1] < 1$. Thus, in addition to being indicative of the sampling problems, the expectation of these ratios are largely consistent with the empirical evidence reported by MRS.

The choice of $P^0(t) \equiv 0$ as the "naive forecast" in this example does not explain these findings. If, for example, we chose $P^0(t) = P_0 e^{rt}$, the "true" conditional expected value for both $P(t)$ and $P^*(t)$, the large T results will remain essentially unchanged because the ratios of second central and noncentral moments tend to one for both $P(t)$ and $P^*(t)$. Indeed, in this case, the MRS inequality just reduces to the original Shiller variance bound defined here in terms of conditional variances and using the "true" ex ante expected values for $P^*(t)$ and $P(t)$. For much the same reason, the selection of almost any naive forecast whose volatility is considerably less than that of stock price is unlikely to change these results. As shown by example in the appendix, the asymptotic distributions for S_1 and S_2 need not converge even if the naive forecast is unbiased and follows a nonstationary process quite similar to the one posited for stock prices.

The example presented here assumes that the underlying stock pays no interim dividends, and therefore one might wonder whether perhaps this polar case is also pathological with respect to the MRS analysis. Although unable to solve fully the dividend-paying case analytically, I offer the following analysis to suggest that the fundamental sampling problems identified by this example will not be significantly changed.

The MRS analysis appears to be impeccable with respect to bias (i.e., the expected value conditions on their inequalities). The problem is that the standard deviation of their estimate for the noncentral second moments grows at an exponential rate greater than the growth of the expected value of the estimate. Thus, the important characteristic to examine is the relation between the second moment and the square root of the fourth moment of future stock prices. Suppose that the dividend paid is a constant proportion ρ of the current stock price. The noncentral second moment of $P(T)$, given $P(0)$, can be written as $[P(0)]^2 \exp[2(r - \rho + \sigma^2/2)T]$. The square root of the noncentral fourth moment of $P(T)$ can be written as $[P(0)]^2 \cdot \exp[(2(r - \rho) + 3\sigma^2)T]$. Thus, as long as $2r + \sigma^2 > 2\rho$, the expected second-moment estimate grows exponentially. However, the ratio of the expected value of the estimate to its standard deviation will, for large T, always decline according to $\exp[-2\sigma^2 T]$, independently of the payout ratio, ρ. Because the MRS estimates involve simple averages of sums (or integrals) of squared stock prices, it thus seems unlikely that the sampling properties of the estimators for large T will be significantly affected by appending dividends to the model. To the extent that dividend changes are more sticky than proportional to stock price changes (which as an empirical matter, they seem to be),[14] the model presented here becomes an even better approximation.

In this light and given that Shiller (1981) had already found enormous empirical violations of the central second-moment bounds between actual stock prices and ex post perfect-foresight prices, it is not altogether surprising to find that the measured noncentral second moments of these same two series also exhibit large violations when estimated on the same data set. In that sense, the Mankiw-Romer-Shapiro study provides no important new empirical findings about the magnitudes of stock market volatility. Nevertheless, their study (together with the West, 1984, analysis) is central to the controversy over the rational market hypothesis because of its claim to rule out the interpretation of Shiller's empirical findings as simply a rejection of the assumption of a stationary process for dividends and stock prices. As shown here, this claim remains to be proved.

3   Conclusion

In summary, I believe that when the heat of the controversy dissipates, there will be general agreement that the rejection or acceptance of the rational market hypothesis as a good approximation to real-world stock market behavior will turn on how we model uncertainty. If, in fact, the levels of expected real corporate economic earnings, dividends, and discount rates in the future are, *ex ante*, well-approximated by a long average of the past levels (plus perhaps a largely deterministic trend), then it is difficult to believe that observed volatilities of stock prices, in both the long and not-so-long runs, are based primarily on economic fundamentals. This assertion can be confirmed by simulations using economic models of the nonfinancial sector with stationary processes for the levels of outputs generating the uncertainty.

Thus, if the well-informed view among economists and investors in the 1930–1934 period was that corporate profits and dividends for *existing*[15] stockholders would return in the reasonably near future to their historical average levels (plus say a 6% trend), then market prices in that period were not based upon fundamentals. If this were the view, then it is surely difficult to explain on a rational basis why the average standard deviation of stock returns during this period was almost three times the corresponding average for the forty-eight other years between 1926 and 1978 (cf. Merton, 1980, pp. 353–354). If once again in the 1962–1966 period, the informed view was that required expected returns and the levels and growth rates of real profits in the future would be the same as in the long past, then stock prices were (ex ante) too high.[16]

If, as is the standard assumption in finance, the facts are that the future levels of expected real corporate economic earnings, dividends, and discount rates are better approximated by nonstationary stochastic processes, then even the seemingly extreme observations from these periods do not violate the rational market hypothesis.

In light of the empirical evidence on the nonstationarity issue, a pronouncement at this moment that the rational market theory should be discarded from the economic paradigm can, at best, be described as "premature." However, no matter which way the issue is ultimately resolved, the resolution itself promises to identify fruitful new research paths for both the finance specialists and the general economist. Just as the break-throughs of more than two decades ago by Lintner, Markowitz, Miller, Modigliani, Samuelson, Sharpe, and Tobin dramatically changed every aspect of both finance theory and practice, so the rejection of market rationality together with the development of the new theory to supersede it would, once again, cause a complete revision of the field. If, however, the rationality hypothesis is sustained, then instead of asking the question "Why are stock prices so much more volatile than (measured) consumption, dividends, and replacement costs?" perhaps general economists will begin to ask questions like "Why do (measured) consumption, dividends, and replacement costs exhibit so little volatility when compared with rational stock prices?" With this reversed perspective may come the development of refined theories of consumer behavior (based upon intertemporally dependent preferences, adjustment costs for consumption, the nontradability of human capital, and cognitive misperceptions) that will explain the sluggish changes in aggregate consumption relative to permanent income. They may also see new ways of examining the question of sticky prices that has long been an important issue in the analysis of the business cycle.

Because rational speculative prices cannot be sticky, comparisons of the volatilities of such prices with nonspeculative prices may provide a useful yardstick for measuring the stickiness of nonspeculative prices and their impact on aggregate economic activity.

Appendix

In the text, it was shown that if rational stock prices follow a geometric Brownian motion and if the naive forecast $P^0(t) = 0$, then the MRS sample statistics, S_1 and S_2, will have asymptotic distributions whose dispersions are growing at an exponential rate greater than their expected values. As noted, the choice of a naive forecast that follows a stationary process with an exponential trend does not change this conclusion about the asymptotic distributions. Using the model of the text, we now show that selection of a naive forecast variable that is both unbiased and follows a nonstationary process very much like the rational stock price need not alter this conclusion. Thus, it would appear that conditions under which the MRS statistics will exhibit proper distributional properties for long observation periods are quite sensitive to the choice of the naive forecast variable and, therefore, are not robust.

Suppose that the naive forecast is given by $P^0(t) = \lambda(t)P(t)$, where $\{\lambda(t)\}$ are independently and identically distributed positive random variables with

$$E[\lambda(t)] = 1,$$
$$\text{var}[\lambda(t)] = \delta^2,$$
$$E[\lambda^3(t)] = m_3, \tag{A.1}$$
$$E[\lambda^4(t)] = m_4.$$

$\lambda(t)$ describes the "noise" component of the naive forecast relative to the optimal forecast, which by assumption is the stock price, $P(t)$. It is further assumed that the noise is independent of all stock prices [i.e., $\lambda(t)$ and $P(s)$ are independent for all t and s]. Therefore, $E[P^0(t)|P(t)] = P(t)$, and hence, $P^0(t)$ is an unbiased forecast. Because, moreover, the $\{\lambda(t)\}$ follow a stationary process, the nonstationary part of the process describing the naive forecast is perfectly correlated with the optimal forecast, $P(t)$.

Substituting for $P^0(T)$ in (3) and rearranging terms, we can write the continuous-time form for the MRS statistics S_1 as

$$S_1 = \frac{1}{T} \int_0^T P(t)[2[1 - \lambda(t)]P^*(t) - [1 - \lambda^2(t)]P(t)]\,dt. \tag{A.2}$$

From (A.1) and (A.2), we can write the expectation of S_1 conditional on the sample path $\{P(t)\}$, $\overline{S}_1$, as

$$\overline{S}_1 = \frac{\delta^2}{T} \int_0^T [P(t)]^2\,dt, \tag{A.3}$$

because $\lambda(t)$ is independent of both $\{P(t)\}$ and $\{P^*(t)\}$. Note: $\overline{S}_1$ does not depend on the sample path of $P^*(t)$. From (A.3) and (10.b), we have

$$E_0[S_1] = \delta^2 P_0^2 [e^{(2r+\sigma^2)T} - 1]/[(2r + \sigma^2)T], \qquad (A.4)$$

which satisfies the MRS strict inequality $E_0[S_1] > 0$ provided the naive forecast is not optimal (i.e., $\delta^2 > 0$).

Define the random variable $Y_1 \equiv [S_1 - \bar{S}_1]^2$. From (A.2) and (A.3), we write Y_1 as

$$Y_1 = \frac{1}{T^2} \int_0^T \int_0^T P(t)P(s)[2[1 - \lambda(t)]P^*(t) - [1 + \delta^2 - \lambda^2(t)]P(t)] \\ \cdot [2[1 - \lambda(s)]P^*(s) - [1 + \delta^2 - \lambda^2(s)]P(s)] \, ds \, dt. \qquad (A.5)$$

Because $\lambda(t)$ is independent of $\lambda(s)$ for $t \neq s$, we have from (A.1) and (A.5) that the expectation of Y_1, conditional on the sample path $\{P(t)\}$, $\bar{Y}_1$, can be written as

$$\bar{Y}_1 = \frac{1}{T^2} \int_0^T P^2(t)[4\delta^2[P^*(t)]^2 + 4[1 + \delta^2 - m_3]P(t)P^*(t) \\ + [m_4 - (1 + \delta^2)^2]P^2(t)] \, dt. \qquad (A.6)$$

Note that the integrand of (A.6) is always positive. From (8) and (9), we have, for $k = 2, 3, 4,$

$$E_0\{[P(t)]^k[P^*(t)]^{4-k}\} = [P_0 e^{rt}]^4 \exp[6\sigma^2 T + \frac{\sigma^2}{2}k(k - 7)(T - t)]. \qquad (A.7)$$

Taking expectations in (A.6) and substituting from (A.7), we have that $E_0[Y_1] = E_0[\bar{Y}_1]$ grows exponentially as

$$E_0[Y_1] \sim \exp[(4r + 6\sigma^2)T]/T^2. \qquad (A.8)$$

Therefore, the standard deviation of the MRS sample statistics S_1 given by $\sqrt{E_0[Y_1]}$ grows exponentially according to $\exp[(2r + 3\sigma^2)T]/T$. By inspection of (A.4), we have that the ratio of $E_0[S_1]$ to $\sqrt{E_0[Y_1]}$ declines exponentially at the rate $(-2\sigma^2 T)$. Thus, for large T, virtually any sample result for S_1 is consistent with the population condition $E_0[S_1] > 0$. By a similar analysis, the reader can verify that the same result obtains for the MRS statistic S_2.

In contrasting their tests with the earlier Shiller (1981) analysis, MRS (1985, p. 683) point out that their statistics do not require detrending "... because the 'naive forecast' P_t^0 can grow as dividends grow ...." On p. 684, they further their case for robustness by noting "... that the naive forecast need not be efficient in any sense." The naive forecast analyzed here does not seem to be pathological with respect to the conditions they set forth. Thus, it would appear that the naive forecasts necessary to provide proper asymptotic distributional properties for their statistics are anything but naive.

Notes

1. See Fischer and Merton (1984), Marsh and Merton (1983, 1986), and Merton (1983).

2. As may come as a great surprise to those financial economists who regularly publish papers on capital budgeting problems, earnings estimation, financing decisions, and dividend policy, Summers (1985, p. 634) finds it rather "... unfortunate that financial economists remain so reluctant to accept any research relating asset prices and fundamental values." In making this remark, perhaps Summers has in mind those financial economists who might select the closing price on the New York Stock Exchange of a ketchup company's common stock as a better estimate of that firm's fundamental value than an estimate provided by a general economist who computes a present value based on a linear regression model 1 of the supply and demand for ketchup; autoregressive forecasts of future costs of tomatoes, wages, prices of ketchup substitutes, and consumer incomes; and a "reasonable" discount rate.

3. As is well known, even with well-functioning (although not complete) markets and rational, well-informed consumer-investors, the competitive market solution may not be a pareto optimum, and thus, market rationality is not a sufficient condition for efficiency. Using the neoclassical model with overlapping generations, Tirole (1985) has shown that financial security prices that deviate from fundamentals can lead to better allocations than "rational" prices. However, I would argue that those cases in which stock prices both deviate substantially from fundamental values *and* lead to a pareto optimum allocation of investment are, at best, rare.

4 On the self-fulfilling prophecy, see R. K. Merton, (1948). On the rational expectations speculative bubble theory, see Blanchard (1979), Blanchard and Watson (1982), Tirole (1982), and Van Horne (1985).

5. This assumes as a "base date" the publication of Samuelson's 1965 paper, which first set forth the theory in rigorous form. There was, of course, the oral publication of his ideas for at least fifteen years before 1965, as well as many studies of speculative prices and their random properties, extending back as far as the early 1900s.

6. See, for example, the model analyzed in Merton (1971, pp. 403–406), which examines price behavior and optimal portfolio selection when instantaneous stock price changes are random, but the level of stock price regresses toward a "normal price level" with a trend.

7. As will be discussed, the recent study by DeBondt and Thaler (1985) presents evidence that seemingly contradicts these earlier findings.

8. Jensen (1968) found that the average "excess return" per year (including management expenses) across all funds in his sample and all the years from 1945 to 1964, was -1.1%, and 66% of the funds had negative average excess returns. When expenses were excluded, the corresponding statistics were -0.4% per year and 48%. As reported in a recent Business Week article (February 4, 1985, pp. 58–59), based on the industry standard data from SEI Funds Evaluation Services, 74% of managed equity portfolios underperformed the Standard & Poor's 500 Index in 1984; 68% underperformed for the period 1982–1984; 55% underperformed for 1980–1984; and 56% underperformed for 1975–1984.

9. To the extent that stock market prices themselves are an important source of information for investors in calibrating and evaluating other data used to make their assessments of the fundamentals, the original argument that systematically less information is produced on days when the market is closed can be extended to include the Wednesday closings.

10. See Marsh and Merton (1985). Miller and Scholes (1982) find the same result for individual stock returns.

11. As perhaps some indication of the tentative nature of the evidence drawn to support behavioral theories of the stock market, we have, on the one hand, DeBondt and Thaler concluding that investors make cognitive mistakes that result in the underpricing of stocks that have declined (losers) and overpricing of stocks that have risen (winners) and, on the other, Shefrin and Statman (1985) concluding that the evidence supports (different) cognitive mistakes that cause investors to sell their winners "too early" and hold on to their losers "too long." It would seem, therefore, that even a "rational" investor, fully cognizant of his natural tendency to make these mistakes, would, nevertheless, find himself "convicted" by his actions of one or the other cognitive failures.

12. As junior author of Marsh and Merton (1983, 1986).

13. More precisely, Summers (1985, p. 635) refers to the joint hypothesis involving what has been called here "(S.1) and (S.2)." I do not know whether his failure to note the stationarity condition (S.3) as well was intended or not.

14. See Marsh and Merton (1985).

15. Some investors in 1930–1934 may have believed that there was a significantly changed probability of broad-based nationalization of industry than in the past. Given the substantially increased levels of business and financial leverage, there were perhaps others who saw a different prospect for widespread bankruptices than was the case in the past.

16. There were, however, some economists and professional investors who apparently believed that the government had finally found both the will and the means to avoid major macroeconomic disruptions from high unemployment, erratic growth rates, and unstable inflation. Their best guesses for the future may have been formulated with less weight on the distant past.

References

Arrow, K. J., 1982, "Risk Perception in Psychology and Economics," *Economic Inquiry* 20 (January), 1–9.

Blanchard, O., 1979, "Speculative Bubbles, Crashes, and Rational Expectations," *Economic Letters* 3, 387–389.

Blanchard, O., and M. W. Watson, 1982, "Bubbles, Rational Expectations, and Financial Markets," in *Crises in the Economic and Financial Structure*, P. Wachtel (ed.), Lexington Books, pp. 295–315.

DeBondt, W. F. M., and R. Thaler, 1985, "Does the Stock Market Overreact?" *Journal of Finance* 40(3) (July), 793−805.

Fama, E., 1970, "Efficient Capital Markets: A Review of Theory and Empirical Work," *Journal of Finance* 25 (May), 383−417.

Fama, E., 1981, "Stock Returns, Real Activity, Inflation and Money," *American Economic Review*, 71, 545−565.

Fischer, S., and R. C. Merton, 1984, "Macroeconomics and Finance: The Role of the Stock Market," in *Essays on Macroeconomic Implications of Financial and Labor Markets and Political Processes*, K. Brunner and A. H. Meltzer (eds.), Carnegie-Rochester Conference Series on Public Policy, Vol. 21 (Autumn), pp. 57−108.

Flavin, M. A., 1983, "Excess Volatility in the Financial Markets: A Reassessment of the Empirical Evidence," *Journal of Political Economy* 91 (December), 929−956.

French, K., and R. Roll, 1984, "Is Trading Self-Generating?" unpublished paper, Graduate School of Business, University of Chicago (February).

Jensen, M. C., 1968, "The Performance of the Mutual Funds in the Period 1945−1964," *Journal of Finance* 23 (May), 384−416.

Kahneman, D. and A. Tversky, 1979, "Prospect Theory: An Analysis of Decision under Risk," *Econometrica* 47 (March), 263−291.

Kahneman, D. and A. Tversky, 1982, "Intuitive Prediction: Biases and Corrective Procedures," in *Judgement under Uncertainty: Heuristics and Biases*, D. Kahneman, P. Slovic, and A. Tversky (eds.), Cambridge University Press.

Kleidon, A. W., 1983a, "Variance Bounds Tests and Stock Price Valuation Models," working paper, Graduate School of Business, Stanford University (January).

Kleidon, A. W., 1983b, "Bias in Small Sample Tests of Stock Price Rationality," unpublished, University of Chicago.

Leamer, E. E., 1983, "Let's Take the Con Out of Econometrics," *American Economic Review* 73(1), 31−43.

LeRoy, S. F., and R. D. Porter, 1981, "The Present-Value Relation: Tests Based on Implied Variance Bounds," *Econometrica* 49(3), 555−574.

Long, Jr., J. B., 1978, "The Market Valuation of Cash Dividends: A Case to Consider," *Journal of Financial Economics* 6(2/3) (June/September), 235−264.

Mankiw, N. G., D. Romer, and M. D. Shapiro, 1985, "An Unbiased Reexamination of Stock Market Volatility," *Journal of Finance* XL(3) (July), 677−687.

Marsh, T. A., and R. C. Merton, 1983, "Aggregate Dividend Behavior and Its Implications for Tests of Stock Market Rationality," working paper No. 1475−83, Sloan School of Management, MIT (September).

Marsh, T. A., and R. C. Merton, 1985, "Dividend Behavior for the Aggregate

Stock Market," working paper No. 1670–85, Sloan School of Management, MIT (May).

Marsh, T. A., and R. C. Merton, 1986, "Dividend Variability and Variance Bounds Tests for the Rationality of Stock Market Prices," *American Economic Review.* 76(3) (June), 483–498.

Merton, R. C., 1971, "Optimum Consumption and Portfolio Rules in a Continuous Time Model," *Journal of Economic Theory* 3 (December), 373–413.

Merton, R. C., 1973, "An Intertemporal Capital Asset Pricing Model," *Econometrica* 41 (September), 867–887.

Merton, R. C., 1980, "On Estimating the Expected Return on the Market: An Exploratory Investigation," *Journal of Financial Economics* 8, 323–361.

Merton, R. C., 1983, "Financial Economics," in *Paul Samuelson and Modern Economic Theory*, E. C. Brown and R. M. Solow (eds.), McGraw-Hill, pp. 105–138.

Merton, R. K., 1948, "The Self-Fulfilling Prophecy," *Antioch Review* (Summer), 193–210.

Miller, M. H., and M. S. Scholes, 1982, "Dividends and Taxes: Some Empirical Evidence," *Journal of Political Economy* (90), 1118–1142.

Modigliani, F., and R. Cohn, 1979, "Inflation, Rational Valuation and the Market," *Financial Analysts Journal* (March–April), 3–23.

Ohlson, J. A., and S. H. Penman, 1985, "Volatility Increases Subsequent to Stock Splits: An Empirical Abberation," *Journal of Financial Economics* 14(2) (June), 251–266.

Samuelson, P. A., 1965, "Proof That Properly Anticipated Prices Fluctuate Randomly," *Industrial Management Review* 6 (Spring), 41–49.

Shefrin, H., and M. Statman, 1985, "The Disposition to Sell Winners Too Early and Ride Losers Too Long: Theory and Evidence," *Journal of Finance* 40(3) (July), 777–790.

Shiller, R. J., 1981, "Do Stock Prices Move Too Much to be Justified by Subsequent Changes in Dividends?" *American Economic Review* 71 (June), 421–436.

Shiller, R. J., 1982, "Consumption, Asset Markets, and Macroeconomic Fluctuations," *Carnegie-Rochester Conference on Public Policy* 17, 203–250.

Shiller, R. J., 1984, "Stock Prices and Social Dynamics," *Brookings Papers on Economic Activity* 2, 457–498.

Summers, L. H., 1982, "Do We Really Know That Financial Markets are Efficient?" National Bureau of Economic Research, working paper No. 994 (September).

Summers, L. H., 1985, "On Economics and Finance," *Journal of Finance* XL(3) (July), 633–635.

Summers, L. H., 1986, "Does the Stock Market Rationally Reflect Fundamental Values?" *Journal of Finance* 41(3) (July), 591–600.

Tirole, J., 1982, "On the Possibility of Speculation Under Rational Expectations," *Econometrica* 59 (September), 1163–1181.

Tirole, J., 1985, "Asset Bubbles and Overlapping Generations," *Econometrica* 53(5) (September), 1071–1100.

Van Horne, J. C., 1985, "On Financial Innovations and Excesses," *Journal of Finance* XL(3) (July), 621–631.

West, K. D., 1983, "A Variance Bounds Test of the Linear-Quadratic Inventory Model," in *Inventory Models and Backlog Costs: An Empirical Investigation*, unpublished Ph.D. dissertation, Massachusetts Institute of Technology (May).

West, K. D., 1984, "Speculative Bubbles and Stock Price Volatility," Financial Research Center, Memorandum No. 54, Princeton University (December).

Comments on "On the Current State of the Stock Market Rationality Hypothesis"

James Tobin

Recognizing Franco Modigliani's signal contributions to the theory of finance and to financial economics, Robert Merton has honored this celebration by an important paper reviewing findings and controversies to date on the rationality of the stock market. He is, of course, a leading contributor to this literature; it is good to have his considered appraisal of the current state of play. I, an amateur in the field, learned a great deal from his paper, as will, I am sure, all who read it.

As a commentator, however, my amateur status is a disadvantage and, I am afraid, unfair to the author. Merton's paper is about the current state of a proposition on which there is a vast and highly technical ingrown literature. I confirmed my unfamiliarity with it by picking up the issue of the *Journal of Finance* where Larry Summers's lament on the economics/finance gulf appears. Merton is worried about that gulf too; early in this paper it becomes clear that Summers's irreverent piece hit him in a sensitive spot. Summers's note sounded like fun, and it was, especially the part about ketchup economics.[1] As I leafed through the other pages of the *Journal* I could see that my case was hopeless. In all fairness I should also confess that I cannot read *Econometrica* either.

There is one difference I do think I understand between us general economists and finance specialists. We struggle and mine data to detect effects that are significant; confirmation of our theories depends on rejecting hypotheses that our favorite explanatory variables have no effect. That is hard, and even if one appears to succeed, five other guys will find fifteen reasons why your significant regression is spurious. We have to give the finance fraternity credit. They invented games where you win when you lose. That is, you win if you cannot reject the null hypothesis. And so they have run up for the market rationality team the enviable winning streak Merton recounts. And if by chance anyone comes up with some variables that seem significant—Januaries or Wednesdays or P/E ratios or small stocks, to recall sources of anomalies acknowledged by Merton—then you can invoke the secondary defenses of statistical skepticism. (Of the anomalies, by the way, the closed-Wednesday effect seems the most telling because it suggests that trading per se creates volatility.)

The clinching tactic of this strategy is the statute of limitations decreed by Merton. Once his team has piled up a "mountain of accumulated evidence in support of the [market rationality] hypothesis," he declares closure on further research on the grounds that the degrees of freedom in the data have been collectively exhausted.

Why do many economists refuse to be convinced by twenty years of successful empirical testing? One reason is that they do not think that adding up pages and pages of tests of low power adds up to power.

I am willing to believe, nevertheless, that you cannot find a simple formula relating stock prices to generally available past statistics that will make money. That is not sufficient to convince me that stock prices are rational estimates of fundamental values, the present values of the future incomes to which the shares are titles. If there have been twenty years of finance literature reporting successful tests of that second proposition, Merton does not tell us about them. And it is that proposition, not the you-can't-make-money proposition, that is needed to justify any claim that the stock market gives the right signals for efficient allocation of risk and investment.

As Merton says, the LeRoy-Porter and Shiller volatility tests are pointed right at the crucial question. That is why they sent the finance profession scrambling. As I understand it, we should expect fundamental-rational prices to be less volatile than the earnings or dividend streams they supposedly reflect. That they turn out to be more volatile, therefore, is a superstrong negative finding. My guess is that it will be reinforced, not diluted, if actual observations of risk-free rates are substituted for the assumed constant discount rate used in the tests.[2]

I suspect that most macroeconomists were gratified but not surprised by the findings of excess volatility, because it accorded with their prior beliefs. Why? Because it is hard for us to imagine any macroeconomic news within a week's or a month's time that could alter one's view of the whole macroeconomic future as much as stock prices frequently move in a day or a week. Suppose you took the medium-term macroforecasts of professionals, including those employed in Wall Street firms. Their volatility is surely much less than that of stock market averages.

I do have a modest complaint about these tests. I should think earnings are better than dividends. Earnings presage future dividends, especially for growth stocks, and this is especially important for tests that have to be cut off at an arbitrary data. However, if earnings are used, then stock prices need to be adjusted for the retention of earnings, to simulate what would have happened if the capital had instead been raised by issuing new shares. In other words, try to keep constant the quantity of capital that a "share" represents. Still better, investigate the volatility of q, a ratio that has some economic meaning, as the shares whose only constancy over time is the name of the corporation do not. And the q ratio would be free of the perils of nonstationarity.

Arguments about the dividends "process" could be avoided by using earnings. Merton and Marsh tried to reverse Shiller by postulating a relation of dividends to lagged stock values such that dividends are in effect averaging stock prices rather than the opposite. That model of dividends does not carry conviction to me. Merton characterized the model as "Lintner-like," but I did not see Lintner in it. As I recall Lintner's model, he related dividends to earnings current and lagged and to past dividends. The idea was that managers and directors have a target payout ratio, but they do not like to lower the dividend and try to avoid raising it so much that they might have to reduce it later.

Merton says that average stock price is the leading indicator best predicting investment, earnings, and dividends. I do not know what to make of a race among single predictors. It is more relevant that the stock market is not as good a forecaster as the consensus of macroeconometric models. Paul Samuelson used to be fond of saying that the stock market called ten of the last five recessions. Anyway the finding of which Merton boasts does not necessarily support the alleged fundamental rationality of the market. Maybe instead the real economy suffers from the stock market's failures. Maybe the same "animal spirits" that drive the market infect investment decisions. The apparently exaggerated procyclical sensitivity of fixed investment has long been a disquieting puzzle.

Some observers of corporate management on business school faculties have been alarmed by the shortness of managers' horizons. No matter where he is or what he is doing, I am told, the CEO of General Electric gets a note telling the price of his company's stock an instant after market closing every day. Should we be happly if CEOs are judged by what happened to their companies' stock prices during their watches? Yes, if we could be sure the market is rationally appraising *long-run* prospects. No, if the market's horizons are no longer than the managers'.

Merton is comforted by evidence that the market is not fooled by cosmetic accounting gimmicks, those that do not reflect fundamentals.

Nevertheless managers seem to go for such gimmicks, sometimes even when they damage the fundamentals. The continued preference of many corporations for FIFO inventory accounting, even though LIFO would save them taxes, is attributed to the paper accounting losses that would be shown at the time of change.

Are the managers acting on behalf of the shareowners? If not, signals from the stock market, however rational, will be distorted in transmission to business decisions of real economic import. If managers are pursuing divergent aims of their own, does the market perceive that and devalue the shares accordingly? If it does, do the directors get the message and act on it? Concerns like these used to be dismissed as the deviant grumblings of institutionalists and lawyers, from Berle and Means to Galbraith. Now that theorists of finance and economics have discovered the "principal/agent" problem, these concerns are respectable in the same circles that assert stock market rationality. Are the two lines of inquiry consistent? I am not sure.

To many economists, to me at least, the takeover epidemic is bad news, not for the reasons that provoke defensive managers and the press and the politicians, but because it indicates that in the absence of takeover bids the market was not fundamental-rational. Although Merton says that the market rationality hypothesis is accepted throughout Wall Street and LaSalle Street, I notice that those firms are spending a lot of very profitable time estimating fundamental values differing from prevailing market prices. Why had the market not reached those values already?

One of my graduate students had occasion, in the course of her dissertation, to estimate some qs for oil companies. They were well below 1 even on very conservative valuations of oil in the ground. She or I might hold a few shares of those stocks for decades and find the qs still low. But a Boone Pickens could deploy enough funds to move the price by taking control or threatening to do so, and still profit. Is he the chosen instrument of God's work? Are take over dramas the enforcers of long-run rationality?

Merton mentions two other arbitrage mechanisms, share repurchases when qs are low, and promotion of new firms when qs are high. These responses do occur, but they appear to be weak and slow. As Merton says, it is a challenge to understand why.

My vision of the stock market is very different from that of finance theorists and indeed from that of many theorists in my own profession. I see the participants as diverse in many dimensions: Few of them, I suspect, are risk-neutral, as the finance theory assumes. Most are risk-averse, some are risk-loving. They also differ in their access to information and their ability to use it, in their expectations of macro and micro futures, in the costs and frequencies of their transactions, in their wealth and their access to credit, and in the personal circumstances relevant to their portfolio strategies. The marginal investors whose decisions make the market are not identical from day to day or year to year.

I do not see why there are any transactions in markets modeled on the assumption that the players are all alike or that a representative participant always makes the market. In that model news would move prices without transactions. In fact, the volume of transactions is breathtaking; the turn-overs of institutional investors are very high; and the holding periods of individuals vary enormously. I suspect there is a lot of short-term speculative trading going on, as in the Keynesian beauty contest; the Wednesday effect is consistent with that suspicion. I wonder what the finance theorists' explanation of transactions volume is.

Merton notes that Franco and his partner Cohn advanced a provocative hypothesis about the apparent failure of the stock market to come up to fundamental values in the 1970s. I thought one of the most convincing and disturbing features of their findings was the corroborative evidence that "experts" on the Street did not understand about inflation and interest. They were discounting real returns by nominal rates.

Notes

1. The serious point of the satirical analogy is the question whether financial markets can be successfully analyzed in isolation from the rest of the economy. Merton's answer is that the stock market's valuation of a ketchup company is a better estimate of its fundamental value than a group of econometricians could obtain from statistical demand, cost, and production functions, etc. I doubt that Summers will be shaken by this riposte. As for me, I thought that if the stock market is rational in this fundamental sense, it would be because the investors who matter for prices are precisely those econometricians or their equivalent, or persons who retain them.

2. Much of Merton's paper is devoted to criticism of the latest entry in volatility research, the paper of Mankiw, Romer, and Shapiro. I cannot enter this technical controversy. I am assured by my colleague Shapiro that MRS's follow-up paper will absorb the criticisms without damage to the conclusions.

6 Aggregate Savings in the Presence of Private and Social Insurance

Andrew B. Abel

1 Introduction

Over the last decade there has been a lively debate over the effects of social security on consumption and capital accumulation. This debate has distinguished between a pay-as-you-go social security system and a fully funded social security system. A balanced-budget pay-as-you-go system levies taxes on young consumers and uses the tax revenue to pay the social security benefits of old consumers. In a standard overlapping generations model in which consumers have no bequest motive (e.g., Diamond, 1965), the saving of young consumers is reduced both by the tax they pay when they are young and by the benefit they receive when they are old. Thus, the private (and national) capital stock is reduced by the introduction of pay-as-you-go social security (see Feldstein, 1974). However, if consumers obtain utility from the utility of their heirs, as well as from their own consumption, then the introduction of pay-as-you-go social security will not affect consumption or private capital accumulation; as shown by Barro (1974), consumers will adjust their bequests in order to offset the lump-sum intergenerational transfers imposed by the social security system.

In contrast to pay-as-you-go social security, the introduction of fully funded social security has no effect on consumption or the national capital stock, regardless of whether or not consumers have bequest motives. The reason for the irrelevance of fully funded social security is that the implicit rate of return on social security is the same as the rate of return on private wealth. Consumers will offset an increase in social security taxes

Previous drafts of this paper were circulated under the title "The Effects of Social Security in the Presence of Perfect Annuity Markets." I thank Olivier Blanchard, Greg Duffee, Stanley Fischer, Nobu Kiyotaki, Franco Modigliani, and participants in the Summer Institute of the National Bureau of Economic Research for helpful comments. I also thank the National Science Foundation for financial support.

and benefits by reducing private saving while maintaining unchanged consumption.

In order for fully funded social security to affect consumption and the national capital stock, the rate of return on social security must differ from the rate of return on privately traded assets. If consumers have random dates of death, then a social security system that taxes young consumers and gives benefits only to consumers who survive to old age has the characteristics of an annuity. The gross rate of return on this publicly provided nontradable annuity will exceed the rate of return on private assets that are not contingent on survival. If there is no private annuity market, and if consumers have no bequest motive, then the introduction of fully funded social security reduces the steady state national capital stock and narrows the distribution of wealth (see Abel, 1985a). However, if there were a competitive annuity market, then the rate of return on private annuities would equal the rate of return on social security, and hence social security would have no effect.

The possibility for fully funded social security to have an effect on the consumption and portfolio decisions in the presence of a competitive annuity market arises when we introduce heterogeneous ex ante mortality probabilities. If, as in actual practice, the social security system does not discriminate across individuals in a cohort according to the probability of death, then social security has real effects under two alternative information structures. First, if annuity companies know the ex ante mortality probability of each individual, then a competitive annuity market will provide annuities with different rates of return to consumers with different mortality probabilities. Clearly, in such a case, some individuals must face different rates of return on private annuities and on social security. In general, the consumption and investment decisions of these people will be affected by changes in social security. Alternatively, if an individual's ex ante mortality probability is private information observable only by that individual, then heterogeneity introduces adverse selection into the private annuity market. However, the social security system is immune to the problem of adverse selection because of the compulsory nature of social security taxes and benefits. Again, for at least some consumers, the rate of return on social security differs from that on private annuities, so that the consumption and portfolio decisions of these people are affected by changes in the level of social security. In this paper, I assume the first structure of information i.e., public information; in a companion paper (Abel, 1985b) I make the alternative assumption of private information.

In order to analyze the effects of social security on steady state welfare, it is not sufficient to determine the effect on the steady state capital stock, especially in an economy with heterogeneous consumers. The effects on the aggregate capital stock and aggregate welfare can be in opposite directions for two reasons: first, well-known Golden Rule considerations imply that aggregate consumption and the aggregate capital stock can move in opposite directions; second, and more important, it will be shown that social security narrows the steady state cross-sectional distribution of consumption, which tends to increase average steady state welfare.

Much of the existing literature on uncertain lifetimes examines the consumption and portfolio behavior of an individual, taking as given any wealth received by the individual in the form of bequests.[1] In the next two sections of this paper, I also analyze the individual consumer's decision problem. In section 2, I state and solve the consumption and portfolio decision problem of a consumer who lives for either one period or two periods and who can hold his wealth in the form of riskless bonds and actuarially fair annuities. As a step toward analyzing the aggregate behavior of heterogeneous consumers, I show in section 3 that consumption and bequests are increasing functions of expected lifetime wealth. In addition, for a given value of expected lifetime wealth, consumption and bequests are increasing functions of the probability of dying young.

After examining individual behavior, I then analyze steady state behavior allowing for the endogenous adjustment of bequests using an extension to uncertain lifetimes of the Modigliani-Brumberg (1954)–Samuelson (1958)–Diamond (1965) overlapping generations model. Previously, Abel (1985a,b), Eckstein, Eichenbaum, and Peled (1985), and Sheshinski and Weiss (1981) have examined uncertain lifetimes in an overlapping generations framework. Sheshinski and Weiss (1981) assumed that all consumers in a given cohort have identical ex post mortality experiences, whereas Abel (1985a,b) and Eckstein, Eichenbaum, and Peled (1985) allow for consumers with the same ex ante mortality probabilities to have different mortality experiences ex post. By allowing ex post mortality experiences to differ, these models generate intracohort variation in bequests and have implications for the intergenerational transmission of inequality. In this paper, I allow for different ex post mortality experiences, but the presence of *actuarially fair* annuities eliminates the intracohort variation in bequests received and left by members of a given cohort with identical ex ante mortality probabilities.[2]

In section 4, I analyze steady state consumption and bequest behavior and present sufficient conditions for the existence of a unique steady state. Then I demonstrate that the steady state values of consumption and bequests are higher for families with a high probability of dying young. In addition, I show that fully funded social security narrows the steady state intracohort distributions of consumption and bequests. In section 5, I restrict the analysis to homothetic utility functions and show that fully funded social security reduces steady state aggregate bequests and steady state aggregate consumption of young consumers. The steady state aggregate private capital stock is crowded out by a degree greater than, equal to, or less than one-for-one depending on whether the steady state consumption of young consumers is less than, greater than, or equal to the inheritances received. Then in section 6, I show that if the utility function is sufficiently concave (more concave than logarithmic utility), then average steady state welfare is increased by the introduction of fully funded social security.

2   Consumption and Portfolio Behavior of an Individual

In this section we analyze the consumption and portfolio behavior of an individual consumer who does not know when he will die. We show that if the consumer can buy actuarially fair annuities, and if the utility from leaving a bequest is independent of the consumer's date of death, then the consumer will leave the same bequest whether he dies young or old. Furthermore, as shown by Sheshinski and Weiss (1981), the consumer will hold riskless bonds to provide for his bequests and will hold annuities to provide for consumption when old.

Consider consumers with the following life-cycle of events: At birth, each consumer receives an initial inheritance I from his parent. During the first period of his life the consumer earns a fixed labor income Y, pays a social security tax ($T < Y$), and consumes an amount c_1. At the end of the first period, the consumer selects a portfolio to carry his wealth, $I + Y - T - c_1$, to the next period. There are two assets: an actuarially fair annuity and a riskless bond. One unit of output invested in the annuity yields A units of output to the consumer if the consumer survives to the second period; if the consumer dies after one period, his estate receives nothing from the annuity. Let Q denote the number of units of output that the consumer invests in an annuity. The consumer invests the remainder of his wealth $I + Y - T - c_1 - Q$ in a riskless bond that pays a gross rate of return R to the consumer if he survives, or to his estate if he dies after one period.

At the beginning of the second period, the consumer gives birth to $G \geq 1$ children. There is a probability p that the consumer dies at the beginning of the second period after giving birth to G heirs. If the consumer dies at the beginning of the second period, each of his heirs receives a bequest B^D/G, where B^D is equal to the consumer's riskless bonds with accrued interest,

$$B^D = (I + Y - T - c_1 - Q)R. \tag{1}$$

If the consumer survives in the second period, he receives a social security payment S ($S \geq 0$) in addition to the principal and interest on his portfolio of bonds and annuities. The consumer then consumes an amount c_2 and gives the remainder of wealth, B^S, to this heirs, where

$$B^S = (I + Y - T - c_1 - Q)R + QA + S - c_2. \tag{2}$$

This total bequest, B^S, is divided equally among the consumer's G children.

At the end of the second period, the consumer dies. Because we have assumed that the consumer does not live beyond the second period, all uncertainty is resolved at the beginning of the second period. Therefore, the bequest, B^S, can be given to the consumer's heirs at the beginning of the second period, i.e., at the beginning of the first period of his heirs' lives. Thus, we can assume, as stated above, that all inheritances are received at birth.[3]

The consumer's utility function is assumed to be additively separable. In particular, the utility function is specified as

$$U(c_1) + (1 - p)\delta U(c_2) + p\delta V(B^D) + (1 - p)\delta V(B^S), \tag{3}$$

where $\delta > 0$ is the one-period discount factor, $U(\ )$ is the utility index of the consumer's own consumption, and $V(\ )$ is the index of utility derived from leaving a bequest. We assume that $U(\ )$ and $V(\ )$ are strictly concave and satisfy the Inada conditions $\lim_{c \to 0} U'(c) = \infty = \lim_{B \to 0} V'(B)$ and $\lim_{c \to \infty} U'(c) = 0 = \lim_{B \to \infty} V'(B)$.

The utility function in (3) can be viewed simply as the expected value of utility, where the only uncertain element is the consumer's date of death. Since the utility function is a function of the bequest left to the consumer's heirs, it is an example of what Yaari (1965) has called a "Marshall utility function."[4,5]

The consumer's optimization problem is to maximize (3) subject to (1) and (2). Substituting (1) and (2) into (3) and then differentiating with respect to c_1, c_2, and Q, respectively, yields

$$U'(c_1) = \delta R[pV'(B^D) + (1 - p)V'(B^S)], \tag{4a}$$

$$U'(c_2) = V'(B^S), \tag{4b}$$

$$pRV'(B^D) = (1 - p)(A - R)V'(B^S). \tag{4c}$$

We now assume that annuities are actuarially fair, which implies that

$$R = (1 - p)A. \tag{5}$$

That is, the expected return on an annuity is equal to the return on a riskless bond. Substituting (5) into (4c) yields

$$V'(B^D) = V'(B^S). \tag{6}$$

The strict concavity of $V(\ )$ then implies that $B^D = B^S$. Let $B = B^D = B^S$ denote the optimal level of bequests. Since $B^S = B^D$, it follows immediately from equations (1) and (2) that

$$c_2 = QA + S. \tag{7}$$

Thus, in the presence of a market for actuarially fair annuities, annuities are used to provide for second-period consumption and riskless bonds are used to provide for bequests, as shown by Sheshinski and Weiss (1981). The interpretation of (7) that second-period consumption is equal to the payoffs from annuities recognizes that the social security payment S is contingent on survival and thus is appropriately viewed as an annuity. It is clear from (7) that if the social security benefit S is less than second-period consumption c_2, the consumer will hold a positive amount of annuities. Alternatively, if S is greater than c_2, then the consumer would want a negative position in annuities. If actuarially fair life insurance (which pays a gross rate of return R/p to the consumer's estate if he dies young and pays zero if he dies old) is available, then the consumer can, by holding life insurance and bonds,[6] achieve the same payoff structure as provided by a negative holding of annuities.

3   The Effects of Changes in the Probability of Death and Changes in Wealth

In this section we calculate the effects of variation in the probability of death and variation in expected lifetime wealth on consumption and portfolio decisions. We shall show that consumption at each age and bequests are increasing functions of the expected present value of lifetime wealth. Also, for a given level of expected lifetime wealth, consumption at each age and the amount of bequests are increasing in p. These results will be useful in later sections when we aggregate over consumers with different probabilities of dying.

The income expansion path is easily derived from (4a,b) and (6):

$$U'(c_1) = \delta R V'(B) = \delta R U'(c_2). \tag{8}$$

The strict concavity of $U(\ )$ and $V(\ )$ implies that $dc_2/dc_1 > 0$ and $dB/dc_1 > 0$ along the income expansion path. Furthermore, because consumers can buy actuarially fair annuities, the income expansion path is independent of p.

The choice of c_1, c_2, and B is constrained by a lifetime budget constraint. Using (1), (2), (5), and the fact that $B = B^S = B^D$, the lifetime budget constraint can be written as[7]

$$c_1 + (1 - p)R^{-1}c_2 + R^{-1}B = W, \tag{9}$$

where $W \equiv I + Y - T + (1 - p)R^{-1}S$. According to (9), the expected present value of lifetime purchases (of consumption and of bequests) is equal to expected lifetime wealth. The optimal values of c_1, c_2, and B are determined by the intersection of the income expansion path in (8) and the lifetime budget constraint in (9).

Given the fixed value of R, the optimal values of c_1, c_2, and B can each be expressed as functions of W and p. Clearly, c_1, c_2, and B are each increasing functions of W. As for the effect of an increase in p, note that if some bundle (c_1, c_2, B) satisfies (9), then an increase in p holding W constant will make the relevant expected present value of purchases on the left-hand side of (9) smaller than W. Hence, c_1, c_2, and B will all be increased along the expansion path until the budget line (9) is satisfied. Therefore, we have

$$c_i = c_i(W, p); \qquad \frac{\partial c_i}{\partial W} > 0, \quad \frac{\partial c_i}{\partial p} > 0; \qquad i = 1, 2, \tag{10a}$$

$$B = B(W, p); \qquad \frac{\partial B}{\partial W} > 0, \quad \frac{\partial B}{\partial p} > 0. \tag{10b}$$

We have shown that the *partial* effect of an increase in p, holding W constant, is to increase c_1, c_2, and B. However, since $W = I + Y - T + (1 - p)R^{-1}S$, an increase in p will, if $S > 0$, decrease W and tend to offset the increases in c_1, c_2, and W. Of course, if $S = 0$, then this offsetting effect is absent. In general, the total effect of an increase in p is to increase (decrease) c_1, c_2, and B if S is less (greater) than c_2. If $S = c_2$, then the consumer holds no private annuities or life insurance and the optimal values of c_1, c_2, and B are invariant with respect to p.

In addition to determining the qualitative effect of W on B as above, it will be useful to calculate the magnitude of this effect. Totally differentiating the lifetime budget constraint (9) with respect to c_1, c_2, B, and W yields

$$dc_1 + (1 - p)R^{-1}dc_2 + R^{-1}dB = dW. \tag{11}$$

Logarithmically differentiating the income expansion path (8) yields

$$\frac{\sigma_U(c_1)}{c_1} dc_1 = \frac{\sigma_V(B)}{B} dB, \tag{12a}$$

$$\frac{\sigma_U(c_2)}{c_2} dc_2 = \frac{\sigma_V(B)}{B} dB, \tag{12b}$$

where $\sigma_U(c) \equiv -cU''(c)/U'(c) > 0$ is the coefficient of relative risk aversion for the utility index $U(\ )$ and $\sigma_V(B) \equiv -BV''(B)/V'(B) > 0$ is the coefficient of relative risk aversion of $V(\ )$. Substituting (12a,b) into (11) yields

$$\frac{\partial B}{\partial W} = \frac{1}{\Phi(p, c_1, c_2, B)} > 0, \tag{13a}$$

where

$$\Phi(p, c_1, c_2, B) = \frac{\sigma_V(B)}{\sigma_U(c_1)} \frac{c_1}{B} + (1 - p)R^{-1} \frac{\sigma_V(B)}{\sigma_U(c_2)} \frac{c_2}{B} + R^{-1}. \tag{13b}$$

4   The Steady State Cross-Sectional Distributions of Consumption and Bequests

In this section we demonstrate that if $R \leq G$, then there exists a unique positive steady state level of bequests. It is well-known from the Golden Rule literature that $R < G$ characterizes a dynamically inefficient steady state, and hence we would also like to analyze steady state behavior under the alternative assumption that $R > G$. However, if $R > G$, then the existence of a positive steady state level of bequests depends on the parameters of the utility function as well as on R and G; we defer discussion of the existence of a positive steady state level of bequests with $R > G$ until section 5 where we restrict attention to homothetic utility. However, before restricting the utility function to be homothetic, we are able to show in this section that the introduction of fully funded social security narrows the steady state distributions of consumption and bequests.

In previous sections we derived the optimal consumption and portfolio behavior of an individual with probability p of dying after one period. Henceforth, we assume that all descendents of an individual face the same probability p as the individual. However, we allow for heterogeneity of p across members of the same cohort and we index consumers by their probability of dying after one period. We shall say that a consumer is a type p consumer if his probability of an early death is equal to p. In order to rule out a known date of death, we assume that $0 < p < 1$. Let $H(p)$ be the fraction of consumers in each cohort who have a probability of early death less than or equal to p. Let $\bar{p}$ be the population average probability of early death, so that $\bar{p} = \int_0^1 p \, dH(p)$. In order to rule out aggregate uncertainty, we assume that a fraction p of type p consumers does indeed die early. Thus $\bar{p}$ is the fraction of consumers of each cohort who dies early.

Since each consumer has G children, the assumption that a consumer's bequest is divided equally among his heirs implies that $I_t = B_{t-1}/G$. (The consumer born in period t receives an inheritance I_t and leaves a total bequest B_t.) Using (10b), it follows that the sequence of bequests in a family with a given probability of dying, p, evolves according to the first-order nonlinear difference equation

$$B_t = B((B_{t-1}/G) + Y - T + A^{-1}S, p). \tag{14}$$

A steady state level of bequests, B^*, must satisfy the difference equation (14) with $B_{t-1} = B_t = B^*$. Below we specify a simple sufficient condition for the existence of a unique positive steady state level of bequests.

Proposition 1 If $R \leq G$, then there exists a unique steady state level of bequests $B^* > 0$.

Proof Existence: Since $\lim_{B \to 0} V'(B) = \infty$, the optimal bequest is positive if $(B_{t-1}/G) + Y - T + A^{-1}S > 0$. Therefore, since $Y - T + A^{-1}S > 0$, if $B_{t-1} = 0$, then $B_t > B_{t-1}$. Observe from (9) that, setting $I_t = B_{t-1}/G$, we have

$$c_{1,t} + (1-p)R^{-1}c_{2,t} + R^{-1}B_t = (B_{t-1}/G) + Y - T + A^{-1}S, \tag{15}$$

where $c_{i,t}$ is the consumption of a consumer of age i born in period t. Using (15), we obtain

$$\begin{aligned} B_{t-1} - B_t = (1 - R/G)B_{t-1} + Rc_{1,t} + (1-p)c_{2,t} \\ - R(Y - T + A^{-1}S). \end{aligned} \tag{16}$$

Since $\lim_{B \to \infty} V'(B) = 0$ and $U'(c) > 0$ for finite c, it follows that $Rc_{1,t} + (1-p)c_{2,t}$ exceeds $R(Y - T + A^{-1}S)$ for sufficiently large B_{t-1}. Therefore, for large enough B_{t-1}, the right-hand side of (16) is positive and hence $B_t < B_{t-1}$. Since $B_t = B((B_{t-1}/G) + Y - T + A^{-1}S, p)$ is a continuous function, there exists some $B^* > 0$ such that $B^* = B(B^*/G + Y - T + A^{-1}S, p)$.

Uniqueness: It suffices to show that $dB_t/dB_{t-1} < 1$ at any positive steady state level of bequests. It follows from (13a) and (14) that

$$\frac{dB_t}{dB_{t-1}} = \frac{1}{G\Phi(p, c_1, c_2, B)}. \tag{17}$$

It follows from (13b) that $G\Phi(p, c_1, c_2, B) > GR^{-1}$, so that if $G \geq R$, then $G\Phi(p, c_1, c_2, B) > 1$.   Q.E.D.

To establish the existence of a unique steady state when $R > G$ we need some additional restrictions on the utility function. We postpone the analysis of this case until section 5, when we introduce homothetic utility. The following useful proposition allows us to characterize the steady state cross-sectional distributions of consumption and bequests. Note that it does not require $R \leq G$.

Proposition 2   If there exists a unique positive steady state level of bequests, then $\partial B/\partial W < G$ when evaluated in the steady state.

Proof   Since $\lim_{B \to 0} V'(B) = \infty$, it follows that if $B_{t-1} = 0$, then $B_t > B_{t-1} = 0$. In addition, the existence of a unique positive steady state, $B_t = B_{t-1} = B^*$, implies that

$$B((B_{t-1}/G) + Y - T + A^{-1}S, p) - B_{t-1} \gtreqless 0 \qquad \text{as} \qquad B_{t-1} \lesseqgtr B^*. \tag{18}$$

The proposition follows immediately from (18).   Q.E.D.

We can now compare the steady state behavior of families with different probabilities of dying young. We begin by comparing bequests. Let $B^*(p)$ denote the steady state level of bequests for a type p family.

Proposition 3   If there exists a unique $B^*(p) > 0$ for every p, and if the social security payment $S \geq 0$ is sufficiently small, then $dB^*(p)/dp > 0$.

Proof   Observe from (14) that B^* satisfies

$$B^* = B((B^*/G) + Y - T + (1 - p)R^{-1}S, p). \tag{19}$$

Totally differentiating (19) with respect to B^* and p yields

$$\left(1 - G^{-1}\frac{\partial B}{\partial W}\right)dB^* = \left(\frac{\partial B}{\partial p} - R^{-1}S\frac{\partial B}{\partial W}\right)dp. \tag{20}$$

The existence of a unique positive steady state level of bequests implies that $G^{-1}(\partial B/\partial W) = dB_t/dB_{t-1} < 1$ when evaluated at B^* (proposition 2). Therefore, the coefficient of dB^* in (20) is positive. Recall from (10b) that $\partial B/\partial p > 0$, so that for small enough S, the coefficient of dp is also positive. Therefore $dB^*/dp > 0$.   Q.E.D.

One may be tempted to explain proposition 3 by arguing that an increase in p is an increase in the frequency with which people die young leaving large bequests. However, we have shown that with a market for actuarially fair annuities, consumers leave the same bequest whether they die after one period or after two periods. The explanation for proposition 3 is that, provided S is small, an increase in p reduces the expected present value of expenditures on the left side of the budget constraint (9) for given values of c_1, c_2, and B. Provided that $S \geq 0$ is small (in particular, if $S < c_2$), the reduction in expected expenditure exceeds the reduction in expected lifetime wealth on the right-hand side of (9), thereby permitting the consumer to increase c_1, c_2, and B. This reasoning suggests the following Corollary.

Corollary 1 If there exists a unique positive steady state level of bequests and if the social security payment $S \geq 0$ is sufficiently small, then $dc_i/dp > 0$, $i = 1, 2$.

Proof Observe that for $i = 1, 2$, $c_i^* = c_i((B^*/G) + Y - T + (1 - p)R^{-1}S, p)$,

$$\frac{\partial c_i}{\partial W} > 0, \quad \frac{\partial c_i}{\partial p} > 0, \quad \text{and} \quad \frac{dB^*}{dp} > 0. \qquad \text{Q.E.D.}$$

We now consider a fully funded social security system. In such a system, the total benefits to a cohort are equal to the return on the system's investment of that cohort's contribution. We shall limit our attention to a social security system that does not discriminate on the basis of an individual's probability of dying early.[8] Therefore, in an actuarially fair system, the taxes and benefits satisfy

$$RT = (1 - \bar{p})S. \qquad (21)$$

It follows from (5) and (21) that the expected net present value of social security benefits for a type p consumer is

$$-T + A^{-1}S = -T\frac{p - \bar{p}}{1 - \bar{p}}. \qquad (22)$$

According to (22), the introduction of fully funded social security increases the expected lifetime wealth of consumers with a low p (less than $\bar{p}$) and decreases the expected lifetime wealth of consumers with a high p (greater than $\bar{p}$). The effects on the steady state distributions of consumption and bequests are given by the following proposition.

Proposition 4   Suppose that there exists a unique positive steady state level of bequests for families of every type p. Then, provided that $S \geq 0$ is small, an increase in fully funded social security, $R\,dT = (1 - \bar{p})\,dS > 0$, will narrow the steady state cross-sectional distributions of c_1, c_2, and B^*.

Proof   Substituting (22) into (19) yields

$$B^*(p) = B\left((B^*(p)/G) + Y - \frac{p - \bar{p}}{1 - \bar{p}}\,T, p\right). \tag{23}$$

Applying the implicit function theorem to (23) yields

$$\frac{dB^*(p)}{dT} = \frac{-\partial B/\partial W}{1 - G^{-1}(\partial B/\partial W)} \cdot \frac{p - \bar{p}}{1 - \bar{p}}. \tag{24}$$

Since $0 < G^{-1}(\partial B/\partial W) < 1$, the coefficient of $(p - \bar{p})$ in (24) is negative, so that $dB^*(p)/dT \lessgtr 0$ as $p \gtrless \bar{p}$. Thus $B^*(\bar{p})$ is invariant with respect to T. Since $dB^*(p)/dp > 0$ (proposition 3), it follows that an increase in T causes $B^*(p)$ to move toward $B^*(\bar{p})$.

Let $c_i^*(p)$ be the steady state level of c_i for type p consumers. It follows from (9), (10a), and (22) that

$$c_i^*(p) = c_i\left((B^*(p)/G) + Y - \frac{p - \bar{p}}{1 - \bar{p}}\,T, p\right). \tag{25}$$

Differentiating (25) with respect to T yields

$$\frac{dc_i^*(p)}{dT} = \left(G^{-1}\frac{dB^*(p)}{dT} - \frac{p - \bar{p}}{1 - \bar{p}}\right)\frac{\partial c_i}{\partial W}. \tag{26}$$

Now substitute (24) into (26) to obtain

$$\frac{dc_i^*(p)}{dT} = \frac{-\partial c_i/\partial W}{1 - G^{-1}(\partial B/\partial W)}\frac{p - \bar{p}}{1 - \bar{p}}. \tag{27}$$

Since $\partial c_i/\partial W > 0$ and $G^{-1}(\partial B/\partial W) < 1$, the coefficient of $(p - \bar{p})$ in (27) is negative. Therefore $dc_i^*/dT \lessgtr 0$ as $p \gtrless \bar{p}$. Hence $c_i^*(\bar{p})$ is invariant with respect to T. Since $dc_i^*(p)/dp > 0$ (corollary 1), it follows that an increase in T causes $c_i^*(p)$ to move toward $c_i^*(\bar{p})$.   Q.E.D.

The intuition underlying proposition 4 is quite straightforward. For consumers with a low probability of dying early, the annuity offered by social security system has a rate of return, $R/(1 - \bar{p})$, that exceeds the rate of return available from private annuity companies $R/(1 - p)$. Thus an increase in social security effectively raises the wealth of the consumers with $p < \bar{p}$. Hence these consumers increase consumption and bequests. As for consumers with $p > \bar{p}$, an increase in social security forces them to hold annuities with a lower rate of return than on annuities in the private market; for these consumers, an increase in T effectively lowers wealth and leads to a reduction in bequests and consumption. Finally observe that for consumers with $p = \bar{p}$, an increase in social security has no effect since these consumers can undo the effects of an increase in social security by reducing their holdings of private annuities.

In Abel (1985a) it was also shown that an increase in the level of actuarially fair social security will narrow the steady state distributions of bequests and consumption. It is worth noting how proposition 4 differs from the result in Abel (1985a). In the previous paper, there are no annuity markets, no bequest motive, and no heterogeneity of ex ante mortality probabilities. In the model presented there, all bequests are "accidental"; bequests are equal to the wealth of consumers who die after one period. The introduction of social security reduces the need to save for retirement consumption and thus reduces the size of accidental bequests. Since all intracohort variation is due to intracohort variation in bequests, the reduction in all positive bequests reduces intracohort variation. However, in the current paper with actuarially fair annuities, consumers with the same wealth and the same ex ante mortality probabilities leave the same bequest whether they die young or old. Thus, for consumers with a given p, there is no intracohort variation in bequests or consumption. The intracohort variation is across consumers with different ex ante mortality probabilities. To the extent that the social security system forces all people to hold a particular asset in their portfolios, it reduces the intracohort variation in portfolios and hence in bequests and consumption.

5 The Effects of Social Security on Steady State Aggregate Capital and Consumption

Much of the literature on the effects of social security has focused on its effects on the long-run aggregate capital stock. Presumably the reason for examining the effects on the capital stock is that if the long-run capital stock is below the Golden Rule capital stock, then if social security reduces the long-run aggregate capital stock, it will also reduce long-run aggregate consumption. The implication of the reduction in aggregate consumption is evidently that aggregate welfare is reduced. We argue in this section and the next section that, for two reasons, the emphasis on the long-run capital stock is misplaced if one is actually interested in social welfare. First, as is well-known from the Golden Rule literature, the long-run aggregate capital stock and long-run aggregate consumption can move in opposite directions in response to social security. Second, and more important, with heterogeneous consumers, it can happen that aggregate consumption is reduced but aggregate welfare is increased by social security. This apparent contradiction can be explained by observing that social security narrows the distribution of consumption.

We restrict our attention henceforth to the case of homothetic utility as in Hakansson (1969), Fischer (1973), and Richard (1975). There are two reasons for restricting the utility function to be homothetic. First we can present necessary and sufficient conditions for the existence of a unique steady state that do not require $R \leq G$. Second, homothetic utility implies linear decision rules, which are easily aggregated.

Suppose that $U(c)$ and $V(B)$ are characterized by constant and equal coefficients of relative risk aversion σ:

$$U(c) = \frac{c^{1-\sigma} - 1}{1 - \sigma}, \tag{28a}$$

$$V(B) = \lambda \frac{B^{1-\sigma} - 1}{1 - \sigma}. \tag{28b}$$

Note that $U(\ )$ and $V(\ )$ are each strictly concave and satisfy the Inada conditions. Therefore, propositions 1–4 apply to this specification of the utility function.

Homothetic utility is particularly convenient because it implies that the income expansion path is a ray through the origin. Using (28a,b) the income expansion path in (8) can be expressed as

$$c_1 = \theta_1 B, \qquad \text{where} \quad \theta_1 = (\delta \lambda R)^{-1/\sigma}, \tag{29a}$$

$$c_2 = \theta_2 B, \qquad \text{where} \quad \theta_2 = \lambda^{-1/\sigma}. \tag{29b}$$

Substituting (29a,b) into the lifetime budget constraint (9) yields

$$B(p) = \frac{1}{\phi(p)} (I + Y - T + A^{-1} S), \tag{30a}$$

where

$$\phi(p) \equiv \theta_1 + (1 - p)R^{-1}\theta_2 + R^{-1}. \tag{30b}$$

It follows from (13b) and (29a,b) that $\phi(p)$ in (30b) is simply $\Phi(p, c_1, c_2, B)$ evaluated under the assumption of homothetic utility. In this case, $\Phi(p, c_1, c_2, B)$ is independent of c_1, c_2, and B and is simply a decreasing function of p. Recall from the proof of proposition 1 that the steady state will be unique if $G\Phi > 1$. The analogous result for homothetic utility is given below.

Proposition 5 Suppose that $U(\ )$ and $V(\ )$ have equal constant degrees of relative risk aversion as specified in (28a,b). There will be a unique positive steady state level of bequests, $B^*(p)$, if and only if $G\phi(p) > 1$, where $\phi(p)$ is defined in (30b).

Proof Setting I equal to B/G in (30a) yields

$$B^*(p) = \frac{G}{G\phi(p) - 1}(Y - T + A^{-1}S), \tag{31}$$

which immediately proves the proposition.   Q.E.D.

Corollary 2 If $\delta\lambda R \leq 1$, then there exists a unique steady state level of bequests.

Proof If $\delta R\lambda \leq 1$, then $\theta_1 \equiv (\delta R\lambda)^{-1/\sigma} \geq 1$. Therefore $\phi > 1$ and $G\phi > 1$. Q.E.D.

In the remainder of this section we analyze the effects of changes in fully funded social security on various aggregate magnitudes in the steady state. We adopt the notational convention of using two asterisks to denote the average value of a variable in the steady state. For example, $B^{**} \equiv \int_0^1 B^*(p)\, dH(p)$. We shall demonstrate below that an increase in fully funded social security decreases aggregate bequests and aggregate consumption of young consumers in the steady state. The steady state national capital stock will be increased or decreased depending on whether consumption of the young is greater or less than the inheritance they receive. Whether aggregate consumption in the steady state increases or decreases depends on whether the interest rate exceeds the growth rate as well as whether the consumption of the young is greater or less than the inheritance they receive.

5.1 Steady State Bequests

To examine the effects of fully funded social security on steady state bequests, substitute (22) into (31) and integrate over all types p to obtain

$$B^{**} = \int_0^1 \frac{G}{G\phi(p) - 1}\left[Y - \frac{p - \bar{p}}{1 - \bar{p}}T\right]dH(p). \tag{32}$$

It is evident from (32) that an increase in T redistributes resources away from consumers with $p > \bar{p}$ toward consumers with $p < \bar{p}$. Since $G/[G\phi(p) - 1]$, the ratio of steady state bequests to noninheritance income, is increasing in p, the redistribution of resources is from consumers with a high value of $G/[G\phi(p) - 1]$ to consumers with a low value of this factor; hence B^{**} declines.

Proposition 6[9,10] Suppose that $U(\ )$ and $V(\ )$ have equal constant relative risk aversion as specified in (28a,b) and that $G\phi(p) > 1$ for all p in the support of $H(p)$. Then an increase in fully funded social security reduces aggregates bequests in the steady state, B^{**}.

5.2 Steady State Consumption

Now we examine the effects on aggregate consumption of consumers of each age. The steady state aggregate (per capita) consumption of the young cohort is $c_1^{**} \equiv \int_0^1 c_1^*(p)\,dH(p)$. Since the ratio of c_1 to B is θ_1 for all consumers, it follows immediately that

$$c_1^{**} = \theta_1 B^{**}. \tag{33}$$

Equation (33) and proposition 6 lead to

Proposition 7   Under the assumptions of proposition 6, an increase in fully funded social security reduces the aggregate consumption of the young.

   Although social security unambiguously reduces the steady state consumption of the young, it can either reduce, raise, or leave unchanged the steady state aggregate consumption of the old cohort. To understand why the effect on the consumption of the old is ambiguous, recall that, in the long run, social security raises both the first-period and second-period consumption of consumers with $p < \bar{p}$ and reduces the first-period and second-period consumption of consumers with $p > \bar{p}$. Consumers with $p < \bar{p}$ represent a larger share of the old generation than of the young generation because of their higher survival rates. Thus, even though average first-period consumption is unambiguously reduced in the long run, it is possible for average second-period consumption to be increased in the long run.

Let c_2^{**} denote the steady state consumption (per capita) of the old generation and observe that

$$c_2^{**} = \int_0^1 (1 - p)G^{-1}c_2^*(p)\,dH(p). \tag{34}$$

The factor $(1 - p)G^{-1}$ reflects the facts that (a) only a fraction $(1 - p)$ of type p consumers survives, and (b) each cohort is only G^{-1} times as large as the succeeding cohort. Substituting (22) into (31), and using (29b) and (31), equation (34) may be rewritten as

$$c_2^{**} = \int_0^1 \frac{(1 - p)\theta_2}{G\phi(p) - 1}\left[Y - \frac{p - \bar{p}}{1 - \bar{p}}T\right]dH(p). \tag{35}$$

The factor $(1 - p)\theta_2/[G\phi(p) - 1]$, which is the ratio of consumption of old consumers to bequests, can be rewritten using (30b) is

$$\frac{(1 - p)\theta_2}{G\phi(p) - 1} = \left[1 + \frac{1 - (\theta_1 + R^{-1})G}{G\phi(p) - 1}\right]\frac{R}{G}. \tag{36}$$

It is clear from (36) that the factor $(1 - p)\theta_2/[G\phi(p) - 1]$ is decreasing in p if and only if $(\theta_1 + R^{-1})G > 1$. Therefore, since social security transfers resources from high-p consumers to low-p consumers, the redistribution is from consumers with a low value of the factor $(1 - p)\theta_2/[G\phi(p) - 1]$ to consumers with a high value of this factor if and only if $(\theta_1 + R^{-1})G > 1$. Therefore we have

Proposition 8[11]   Suppose that $U(\ )$ and $V(\ )$ have equal constant coefficients of relative risk aversion as specified in (28a,b) and that $G\phi(p) > 1$ for all p in the support of $H(p)$. Then for an increase in fully funded social security,

$$\frac{dc_2^{**}}{dT} \gtreqless 0 \quad \text{as} \quad G(\theta_1 + R^{-1}) \gtreqless 1. \tag{37}$$

5.3   The Steady State Capital Stock

Let $K^*(p)$ be the steady state capital stock of type p consumers and $K^{**} \equiv \int_0^1 K^*(p)\,dH(p)$ be the aggregate steady state private capital stock.

We shall measure K^{**} at the end-of-period, that is, before interest is accrued. At the end of a period, all privately owned capital is held by young consumers; the surviving old consumers have already consumed c_2 and have already given the remaining wealth to their heirs. Thus, the private capital stock is equal to inheritances received by the young, I^{**}, plus net labor income, $Y - T$, minus first-period consumption, so that

$$K^{**} = I^{**} + Y - T - c_1^{**}. \tag{38}$$

Since $I^{**} = B^{**}/G$ and $c_1^{**} = \theta_1 B^{**}$, equation (38) can be rewritten as

$$K^{**} = Y - T + (G^{-1} - \theta_1)B^{**}. \tag{39}$$

Equation (39) and Proposition (6) imply

Proposition 9   Suppose that $U(\ )$ and $V(\ )$ have equal constant relative risk aversion as specified in (28a,b) and that $G\phi(p) > 1$ for all p in the support of $H(p)$. Then the effect on the long-run aggregate private capital stock of an increase in fully funded social security is

$$\frac{dK^{**}}{dT} \gtreqless -1 \quad \text{as} \quad \theta_1 \gtreqless G^{-1}. \tag{40}$$

In a fully funded social security system, the long-run aggregate national capital stock, K_N^{**}, is equal to $K^{**} + T$, the sum of aggregate private capital K^{**} and the government capital stock. Therefore, the following corollary to proposition 9 is obvious.

Corollary 3   If the assumptions of proposition 9 hold, then under fully funded social security

$$\frac{dK_N^{**}}{dT} \gtreqless 0 \quad \text{as} \quad \theta_1 \gtreqless G^{-1}. \tag{41}$$

To interpret the condition in (40) and (41), observe that since $c_1^{**} = \theta_1 B^{**}$ and $B^{**} = GI^{**}$, we have $c_1^{**} = G\theta_1 I^{**}$. That is, in comparing steady states, $G\theta_1$ is the response of consumption of young consumers to changes in the inheritances they receive. The introduction of fully funded social security reduces B^{**} and hence reduces I^{**} and c_1^{**}. If $G\theta_1$ is less than 1, the reduction in first-period consumption is smaller than the reduction in inheritances and the national capital stock falls. Alternatively, if $G\theta_1$ is greater than 1, the reduction in c_1^{**} exceeds the reduction in inheritances and the national capital stock rises.

It is useful at this point to present the aggregate resource constraint of the economy. In the steady state, the aggregate disposable resources of the private sector are given by $Y + (R/G)K^{**} + (1 - \bar{p})S/G - T$, where $Y - T$ is the net labor income of the young, $(R/G)K^{**}$ is the per capita gross income accruing to privately held capital carried over from the previous period, and $(1 - \bar{p})S/G$ is the per capita social security income of the old. The private sector uses these resources for consumption $c^{**} \equiv c_1^{**} + c_2^{**}$ and (gross) capital accumulation K^{**}. Equating $c^{**} + K^{**}$ with total disposable resources yields

$$c^{**} = Y - T + (1 - \bar{p})S/G + (R/G - 1)K^{**}. \tag{42}$$

Using condition (21) for fully funded social security, we obtain

$$c^{**} = Y + (R/G - 1)(K^{**} + T). \tag{43}$$

Equation (43) displays the well-known result from the Golden Rule literature that an increase in the steady state national capital stock leads to an increase, decrease, or no change in aggregate consumption depending on whether the net rate of return to capital is greater than, less than, or equal to the population growth rate.

Equation (43) and corollary 3 imply the following:

Corollary 4 Suppose that the assumptions of proposition 9 hold. Then, under fully funded social security

$$\frac{dc^{**}}{dT} \gtreqless 0 \qquad \text{as} \qquad [\theta_1 - G^{-1}][R - G] \gtreqless 0. \tag{44}$$

The condition in (44) has a simple interpretation.[12] The direction of the effect of social security on the national capital stock is given by the sign of $\theta_1 - G^{-1}$ (corollary 3). The direction of the effect of a change in the capital stock on aggregate consumption is given by the sign of $R - G$, as is well known from the Golden Rule literature.

Propositions 6–9 and their corollaries describe the conditions under which various aggregate magnitudes either increase or decrease in response to an increase in fully funded social security. Only bequests and consumption of the young have unambiguous responses to social security. The effects on consumption of the old, aggregate consumption, and the national capital stock are summarized in figure 6.1. If a steady state exists, then the directions of the effects of social security on c_2^{**}, c^{**}, and K_N^{**} depend only on $\theta_1 \equiv (\delta \lambda R)^{-1/\sigma}$ and on R; the existence of a steady state depends on $\theta_2 \equiv \lambda^{-1/\sigma}$ and p_{max} (the largest value of p in the population) as well.

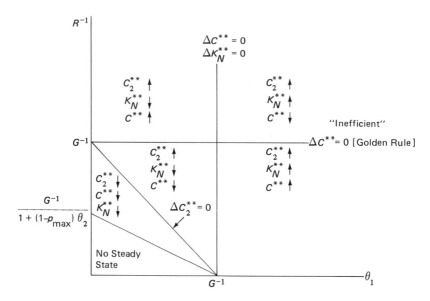

Figure 6.1
Effects of $R\,dt = (1 - \bar{p})\,dS > 0 : \Omega^{**}\!\uparrow$ if $\sigma \geq 1$; $c_1^{**}\!\downarrow$.

It is not obvious how one might best choose an estimate for the crucial parameter θ_1 in the two-period lifetime model presented above. However, I shall offer a casual guess without pretending it is anything more than a guess. As is clear from proposition 9 and its corollaries (corollaries 3 and 4), the critical value of θ_1 is G^{-1}. Recalling that $\theta_1 G$ is the steady state ratio of aggregate consumption of the young to aggregate inheritances received at birth, a reasonable guess is that the bequest motive is sufficiently weak so that this ratio is greater than one, which implies that $\theta_1 > G^{-1}$.[13] In addition, it appears that the marginal product of capital is greater than the population growth rate, so that $R^{-1} < G^{-1}$. As is clear from figure 6.1, these two guesses imply that the national capital stock, consumption of the old, and aggregate consumption are all increased by fully funded social security, whereas aggregate bequests and aggregate consumption of the young are decreased.

6   Steady State Welfare

In this section, we examine the effect of an increase in social security on the steady state level of aggregate welfare. Our measure of aggregate welfare is simply the sum of the individual utilities of all consumers in a given cohort. We demonstrate that if consumers are sufficiently risk-averse, then the introduction of social security will increase steady state aggregate welfare.

Let $\Omega(p)$ be the maximized value of the individual utility function (3) subject to the constraints in (1) and (2). Restricting $U(\ )$ and $V(\ )$ to have equal constant relative risk aversion as in (28a,b), we can use the income expansion path in (29a,b) to obtain

$$\Omega(p) = \frac{\theta_1^{-\sigma}}{1 - \sigma} \phi(p)[B(p)]^{1-\sigma} - \frac{\gamma(p)}{1 - \sigma}, \tag{45}$$

where $\gamma(p) \equiv 1 + \delta(1 - p + \lambda)$.

Let $\Omega^*(p)$ be the steady state value of $\Omega(p)$. It is clear from (45) that for a given p steady state welfare $\Omega^*(p)$ is an increasing function of the steady state bequest $B^*(p)$. Therefore, in view of proposition 4, an increase in fully funded social security increases steady state utility for consumers with $p < \bar{p}$ and reduces steady state utility for consumers with $p > \bar{p}$.

To examine to effects of social security on social welfare, we of course need to specify a social welfare function. We use a utilitarian social welfare function, which is the sum of the utility of all consumers in a given cohort. The steady state level of social welfare Ω^{**} is $\Omega^{**} \equiv \int_0^1 \Omega^*(p)\,dH(p)$, so that evaluating (45) in the steady state, we have

$$\Omega^{**} = \frac{\theta_1^{-\sigma}}{1 - \sigma} \int_0^1 \phi(p)[B^*(p)]^{1-\sigma}\,dH(p) - \frac{\gamma(\bar{p})}{1 - \sigma}. \tag{46}$$

We shall limit our attention to the introduction of a small amount of social security into an economy without social security. Substituting (31) into (46), differentiating with respect to T, and evaluating the derivative of $T = 0$ yield

$$\left.\frac{d\Omega^{**}}{dT}\right|_{T=0} = \frac{(\theta_1 Y)^{-\sigma}}{1 - \bar{p}} \int_0^1 J(p)(p - \bar{p})\,dH(p), \tag{47a}$$

where

$$J(p) = -\phi(p)\left[\frac{G}{G\phi(p) - 1}\right]^{1-\sigma}. \tag{47b}$$

We now state and prove

Proposition 10   Suppose that $U(\ )$ and $V(\ )$ have equal and constant relative risk aversion as specified in (28a,b) and that $G\phi(p) > 1$ for all p in the support of $H(p)$. Then if $G\phi(p) > 1/\sigma$, the introduction of actuarially fair social security increases steady state welfare.

Proof   From (47a) and the lemma in note 9, it is clear that

$$\frac{d\Omega^{**}}{dT}\bigg|_{T=0} > 0$$

if $J'(p) > 0$ for all p in the support of $H(p)$. Differentiating (47b) with respect to p and simplifying yield

$$J'(p) = -\phi'(p)\left[\frac{G}{G\phi(p)-1}\right]^{1-\sigma}\left[\frac{\sigma G\phi(p)-1}{G\phi(p)-1}\right]. \tag{48}$$

Since $\phi'(p) < 0$ and $G\phi(p) - 1 > 0$, it is clear that if $\sigma G\phi(p) - 1 > 0$, then $J'(p) > 0$.   Q.E.D.

Corollary 5   Suppose that $G\phi(p) > 1$ for all p in the support of $H(p)$ and that $\sigma \geq 1$. Then the introduction of actuarially fair social security increases steady state social welfare.

We have shown that the introduction of actuarially fair social security can reduce steady state aggregate consumption, but, if the CRRA utility functions $U(\ )$ and $V(\ )$ display at least as much risk aversion as the logarithmic utility function, it increases steady state social welfare. Although a reduction in aggregate consumption may seem, at first, to be inconsistent with an increase in social welfare, these results are easily reconciled by the observation that social security reduces the variation in bequests and consumption (proposition 4). If the individual utility functions are sufficiently risk averse, the welfare-improving effects of reduced variance outweigh the welfare-reducing effects of reduced aggregate consumption.

Corollary 5 indicates that if the coefficient of relative risk-aversion is greater than or equal to one, then the welfare-improving effects of reduced variance are strong enough to raise social welfare. Alternatively, if the coefficient of relative risk aversion is sufficiently small, then the introduction of social security will reduce steady state welfare. A sufficient condition is given in the following corollary.

Corollary 6   Suppose that $1 < G\phi(p) < 1/\sigma$ for all p in the support of $H(p)$. Then the introduction of fully funded social security reduces steady state welfare.

7   Conclusion

The social security system essentially forces all workers to hold an annuity in their portfolios. If the rate of return on this annuity is equal to the rate of return on the private annuities that a consumer holds, then the consumer can offset the effects of social security simply by reducing his holding of private annuities. However, if the rate of return on social security differs from the rate available to the consumer in the private annuity market, then changes in the level of social security will, in general, force the consumer to change his consumption and/or portfolio behavior. Thus, in a world in which consumers all face the same rate of return on social security but face different rates of return on private annuities, changes in social security will affect the behavior of at least some individuals.

In this paper, we have assumed that each consumer can buy private annuities at an actuarially fair rate of return. After presenting sufficient conditions for the existence of a unique steady state equilibrium, we then established that increased social security narrows the steady state distributions of bequests and consumption. We showed that fully funded social security will crowd out steady state private wealth by more than, less than, or exactly one-for-one depending on whether steady state consumption of the young is less than, greater than, or equal to steady state inheritance received by the young. We also established simple conditions that determine whether steady state aggregate consumption rises, falls, or remains unchanged. Finally, we showed that if individual utility functions are sufficiently risk-averse, then fully funded social security increases steady state social welfare because it reduces inequality; however, if individual utility functions display very little risk-aversion, then social welfare is reduced by social security.

Notes

1. See, for example, Yaari (1965), Hakansson (1969), Fischer (1973), Richard (1975), Barro and Friedman (1977), Levhari and Mirman (1977) and Kotlikoff and Spivak (1981). Kotlikoff and Spivak (1981) analyze the role of the family in providing annuities but stop short of a general equilibrium model in which the distribution of bequests is determined endogenously.

2. If there are annuities and if consumers derive some utility from leaving bequests, then in general there will be intracohort variation in bequests received and left by members of the same cohort with identical ex ante mortality probabilities (see Abel, 1985b). Only if the rate of return on annuities is actuarially fair will there be

no intracohort variation in bequests by consumers who can live either one period or two periods.

3. We are using the term "inheritance" to refer to a transfer received from one's parent, regardless of whether the parent is alive.

4. We follow Yaari (1965), Hakansson (1969), Fischer (1973), and Richard (1975) in specifying utility as a function of the size of the bequest left to one's heirs. An alternative formulation that gives rise to a bequest motive is to specify utility as a function of the utility of one's heirs' as in Barro (1974).

5. More generally we might specify the utility of bequests as a function $\tilde{V}(B, G)$, where B is the size of the total bequests and each child receives B/G. However, since G is assumed to be fixed exogenously, we can write the utility of bequests simply as a function of B.

6. Fischer (1973) derived conditions under which there will be a positive demand for life insurance. The two-period version of Fischer's utility function is

$$u(c_1) + (1 - p)\delta u(c_2) + p\delta\lambda^D u(B^D) + (1 - p)\delta\lambda^S u(B^S). \tag{N.1}$$

Substituting (1) and (2) into (N.1) and differentiating with respect to c_2 and Q yields

$$c_2 = (\lambda^S)^{-1/\sigma}B^S, \tag{N.2}$$

$$B^D = (\lambda^S/\lambda^D)^{-1/\sigma}B^S, \tag{N.3}$$

where we used the actuarial fairness condition (5) to derive (N.3). Combining (1) and (2) yields

$$QA = B^S + c_2 - B^D - S. \tag{N.4}$$

Substituting (N.2) and (N.3) into (N.4) yields

$$QA = \{1 + (\lambda^S)^{-1/\sigma} - (\lambda^S/\lambda^D)^{-1/\sigma}\}B^S - S. \tag{N.5}$$

If QA is positive, then the demand for annuities will be positive, and if QA is negative, the demand for life insurance wil be positive. If $S = 0$, the demand for life insurance will be positive if and only if the term in curly brackets is negative, i.e., if and only if $(\lambda^D)^{1/\sigma} > 1 + (\lambda^S)^{1/\sigma}$.

7. More specifically, multiply equation (1) by p and equation (2) by $(1 - p)$ and add the resulting equations together. Using the fact that $B^S = B^D = B$ allows us to recognize that $pB^D + (1 - p)B^S = B$. Equation (9) is then easily derived.

8. We have assumed that private annuity companies can observe the p of each individual. We are not assuming that the government cannot observe each individual's p; rather, we are assuming, in accordance with actual practice, that the government chooses not to discriminate on the basis of p.

9. In proving this proposition and subsequent propositions more formally, the following lemma is useful.

Lemma   Let $\bar{p} \equiv \int_0^1 p \, dH(p)$. If $f(p)$ is a strictly increasing function of p, then $\int_0^1 f(p)(p - \bar{p}) \, dH(p) \geq 0$, with strict inequality if the distribution of p is not degenerate.

Proof   Observe that

$$\int_0^1 f(p)(p - \bar{p}) \, dH(p) = \int_0^{\bar{p}} f(p)(p - \bar{p}) \, dH(p) + \int_{\bar{p}}^1 f(p)(p - \bar{p}) \, dH(p)$$

$$\geq \int_0^{\bar{p}} f(\bar{p})(p - \bar{p}) \, dH(p) + \int_{\bar{p}}^1 f(\bar{p})(p - \bar{p}) \, dH(p)$$

$$= f(\bar{p}) \int_0^1 (p - \bar{p}) \, dH(p) = 0,$$

where the inequality follows from the fact that $f(p)$ is strictly increasing.   Q.E.D.

10. To prove this proposition formally, differentiate (32) with respect to T to obtain

$$\frac{dB^{**}}{dT} = \frac{-G}{1 - \bar{p}} \int_0^1 [G\phi(p) - 1]^{-1} (p - \bar{p}) \, dH(p),$$

which is negative in view of the lemma in note 9 and the fact that $[G\phi(p) - 1]^{-1}$ is increasing in p.

11. To prove this proposition more formally, differentiate (35) to obtain

$$\frac{dc_2^{**}}{dT} = \frac{\theta_2}{1 - \bar{p}} \int_0^1 D(p)(p - \bar{p}) \, dH(p),$$

where

$$D(p) = \frac{-(1 - p)}{G\phi(p) - 1}.$$

It follows immediately from the lemma in note 9 that if $D(p)$ is monotonic, then dc_2^{**}/dT will have the same sign as $D'(p)$. Differentiating $D(p)$ with respect to p and using the definition of $\phi(p)$ in (30b) yield

$$D'(p) = \frac{G(\theta_1 + R^{-1}) - 1}{(G\phi - 1)^2},$$

which proves the proposition.

12. An alternative, but perhaps more direct, derivation of (44) is to observe from (29) that

$$c^{**} = \int_0^1 [\theta_1 + (1 - p)G^{-1}\theta_2] B^*(p) \, dH(p). \tag{N. 6}$$

Differentiating (N. 6) with respect to T yields

$$\frac{dc^{**}}{dT} = \frac{G}{1 - \bar{p}} \int_0^1 F(p)(p - \bar{p}) \, dH(p),$$

where $F(p) = -[G\phi(p) - 1]^{-1}[\theta_1 + (1 - p)G^{-1}\theta_2]$. Using the lemma, dc^{**}/dT has the same sign as $F'(p)$ if $F(p)$ is monotonic. Differentiating $F(p)$ yields

$$F'(p) = \frac{\theta_2}{R(G\phi - 1)^2}(\theta_1 - G^{-1})(R - G),$$

which proves (44).

13. On the other hand, Kotlikoff and Summers (1981) claim that 80% of private household wealth is inherited wealth and hence that the bequest motive is strong.

References

Abel, Andrew B., "Precautionary Saving and Accidental Bequests," *American Economic Review*, 75, 4 (September 1985a), 777–791.

Abel, Andrew B., "Capital Accumulation with Adverse Selection and Uncertain Lifetimes," National Bureau of Economic Research Working Paper No. 1664, 1985b, forthcoming in *Econometrica*.

Barro, Robert J., "Are Government Bonds Net Wealth?" *Journal of Political Economy* 82, 6 (November/December 1974), 1095–1117.

Barro, Robert J., "Reply to Feldstein and Buchanan," *Journal of Political Economy* 84 (April 1976), 343–349.

Barro, Robert, and James W. Friedman, "On Uncertain Lifetimes," *Journal of Political Economy* 85 (August 1977), 843–849.

Diamond, Peter A., "National Debt in a Neoclassical Growth Model," *American Economic Review* 55 (December 1965), 1126–1150.

Eckstein, Zvi, Martin S. Eichenbaum, and Dan Peled, "The Distribution of Wealth and Welfare in the Presence of Incomplete Annuity Markets," *Quarterly Journal of Economics*, 100 (August 1985), 789–806.

Feldstein, Martin S., "Social Security, Induced Retirement, and Aggregate Capital Accumulation," *Journal of Political Economy*, 82 (September/October 1974), 905–926.

Feldstein, Martin S., "Perceived Wealth in Bonds and Social Security: A Comment," *Journal of Political Economy* 84 (April 1976), 331–333.

Fischer, Stanley, "A Life Cycle Model of Life Insurance Purchases," *International Economic Review*, 14 (February 1973), 132–152.

Hakansson, Nils H., "Optimal Consumption and Investment Strategies under Risk, an Uncertain Lifetime, and Insurance," *International Economic Review* (October 1969), 443–466.

Kotlikoff, Laurence J., and Avia Spivak, "The Family as an Incomplete Annuities Market," *Journal of Political Economy*, 89 (April 1981), 372–391.

Kotlikoff, Laurence J., and Lawrence Summers, "The Role of Intergenerational Transfers in Aggregate Capital Accumulation," *Journal of Political* Economy, 89 (August 1981), 706–732.

Levhari, David, and Leonard Mirman, "Savings and Consumption with an Uncertain Horizon," *Journal of Political Economy*, 85 (April 1977), 265–281.

Modigliani, Franco, and Richard Brumberg, "Utility Analysis and Aggregate Consumption Functions: An Attempt at Integration," mimeo, 1954.

Richard, Scott F., "Optimal Consumption, Portfolio and Life Insurance Rules for an Uncertain Lived Individual in a Continuous Time Model," *Journal of Financial Economics*, 2 (1975), 187–203.

Samuelson, Paul A., "An Exact Consumption-Loan Model of Interest with or without the Social Contrivance of Money," *Journal of Political Economy* 66, 6 (December 1958), 467–482.

Sheshinski, Eytan, and Yoram Weiss, "Uncertainty and Optimal Social Security Systems," *The Quarterly Journal of Economics* 96 (May 1981), 189–206.

Yaari, Menachem E., "Uncertain Lifetimes, Life Insurance, and the Theory of the Consumer," *Review of Economic Studies* 32 (April 1965), 137–150.

7

How Much (or Little) Life Cycle Is There in Micro Data? The Cases of the United States and Japan

Albert Ando and Arthur B. Kennickell

1 Introduction

The "life cycle model" of saving has come of age, and today most analysis of intertemporal allocation of resources by households, both theoretical and empirical, seems to be conducted in the framework of some version of this theory. When a theory plays such a wide role in the analysis of a vitally important aspect of the economy, it is natural that the theory acquires more and more varied interpretations in the literature, as it is used by many investigators for many different purposes. Some interpretations may not even be recognizable to Franco Modigliani as related to the theory that he perceived some 35 years ago.

Aggregate time series data on consumption, income, and wealth, especially in the United States, appeared to be broadly consistent with a relatively narrow formulation of the hypothesis given by Modigliani and Brumberg (1954, 1979). Since the late 1960s, however, questions asked of the aggregate consumption function have become more complex and demanding. We want now to know, for example, how the aggregate saving income ratio would be affected by gradual shifts in the age structure of population. Following Feldstein (1974), the net effects of the larger scale of the social insurance programs on private saving have been closely

Views expressed here are those of the authors, and do not necessarily reflect those of the Board of Governors of the Federal Reserve System (on which A. B. Kennickell is Economist) or its staff. The US portion of this study was partially supported by the National Science Foundation and by the Subcommittee on Monetary Research, Social Science Research Council. The Japanese portion was conducted jointly with the staff members of the Economic Research Institute, Economic Planning Agency, Government of Japan. We wish to thank M. Yamashita and M. Yoshitomi of the Agency and senior officials of the Statistics Bureau, Prime Minister's Office, of their cooperation and assistance in carrying out this project. Finally, we are grateful to Franco Modigliani and Robert Solow for their comments on an earlier version of this paper.

studied. Effects of different forms of taxes and subsidies on savings, which are closely related to the sensitivity of savings to variations in the real rate of interest, are also critical to the eventual disposition of current debates on how to design a better tax and transfer system. We do not believe, however, that aggregate time series data contain enough information to answer these and other questions, which depend in a complex way on individual behavior and on the distribution of economic agents with respect to their relevant characteristics.

At the micro level, it has always been very difficult to confront the life cycle theory directly with data for a number of reasons, including the lack of information on the balance sheet status of individual households in most cross-section data, with a few exceptions. Taking advantage of the rapid accumulation of micro data on households not only in the United States but in other countries, we have been conducting a series of empirical analyses designed to check some features of the life cycle theory, with the emphasis on extracting from these data eventual implications for the aggregate consumption function.[1] Eventually, we would like to be able to characterize the savings behavior of individual countries a little better and in more detail than we are capable of at the present time, and also to arrive at a coherent explanation of international differences in the savings behavior.

Following King and Dicks-Mireaux, we have found a somewhat more informally descriptive characterization of the age profile of asset accumulation and decumulation to be more successful than attempts at estimating more formal optimizing models.[2] In this paper, we present a summary of results that we have obtained so far for the United States and for Japan.[3] Somewhat surprisingly, there appears to be only a partial support for the life cycle theory as traditionally perceived in Japan, and even less support in the United States. On the other hand, the behavior we do observe at the micro level seems consistent with the characteristics of aggregate data, thus suggesting that the power of aggregate data to distinguish between the life cycle theory and its alternatives appears to be even weaker than we had previously thought.

We begin with a brief review of older historical evidence in the United States. We then present very briefly some of our attempts to utilize more elegant and formal formulations in dealing with the US data, whose results were mostly disappointing. We conclude with less formal results, both for the United States and for Japan, which we believe are more informative for our purposes. In the process, the nature of sampling procedures generating most available micro data and potential biases introduced by them are shown to be critical, and we consider a number of alternative methods for dealing with them.

2 Historical Evidence

In this section, we review features of a series of cross-section data for the United States to see whether the observed pattern of asset accumulation by households conforms to the hump shape visualized in the life cycle theory.

The earliest published age-structured household saving data we know derive from the 1935–36 Consumer Purchases Survey (see Monroe et al., 1942). Tabulations of these data and the early Federal Reserve Board Surveys of Consumer Finances (see e.g., Federal Reserve *Bulletin*, 1947) were examined by Janet Fisher (1950, 1952), who concludes, "The data ... indicate not only that dissaving does not predominate among consumers in the oldest age group but also that members of this group save on average about as high a percentage of their income as consumers in the middle age groups and a higher percentage than consumers in the youngest age group. In addition, the proportion of those dissaving among consumer units in the oldest group tends to be relatively small in comparison with younger groups" (Fisher, 1952, p. 100).

One might justly question data gathered from the time of the Great Depression or immediately after World War II by means of relatively primitive sampling. In addition the definition of saving is a rather narrow one, excluding net accumulation of consumer durable stock from the saving flows.

Because of the awkwardness of the classifications in the published tabulations and the unavailability of a substantial body of the data in machine-readable form, we can say nothing further for these surveys. However, we do have access to magnetic tapes of a number of household surveys beginning around 1960, and we present the array of age-stratified statistics for them in table 7.1. Unfortunately, for some surveys we can compute net worth but not savings, while for others we can compute savings but not net worth. Furthermore, it is inevitable that there be a variety of definitions of savings and wealth in these profiles (see notes to table 7.1.). The intention has been in each case to construct the concept of net worth to be as close as possible to the aggregate definition used by the Flow of Funds accounts of the Board of Governors of the Federal Reserve System (and the same holds for the corresponding definition of savings). As a caution to the reader who might be tempted to attach too much significance to detailed movements of patterns presented here, we add, below the mean and

Table 7.1
Cross section age profile of saving or net worth, various surveys between 1960 and 1983[a]

Survey	Variable	Statistic	≤25	26–35	36–45	46–55	56–64	65–69	70–74	75–79	≥80
CES60	Number of observations		821	2580	3021	2764	2022	1009	736	454	311
	TS	μ	2388	3069	3220	3062	2462	1722	845	701	657
		median	1554	2145	2373	2003	1305	512	238	48	19
		σ	4497	6409	6637	6726	6289	6162	4765	4889	5960
	TSP	μ	2370	3089	3220	3045	2358	1197	225	357	299
		median	1560	2145	2386	2021	1258	351	134	1	0
		σ	4459	6417	6755	6841	6355	6330	4078	5049	6105
	TSPS	μ	2462	3257	3373	3139	2104	−1345	−2799	−2442	−2014
		median	1714	2453	2676	2233	1150	−1830	−2447	−2442	−2260
		σ	4586	6559	6953	7107	6736	7189	4619	5475	6302
SFCC	Number of observations										
	NW62	μ	1100	9484	17941	31234	28460	24288	23113	17601	25047
		median	203	1838	5603	10133	13406	11650	5610	7000	6640
		σ	3303	51082	67028	173528	56245	42264	56952	49096	72617
	S	μ	−128	1537	878	868	603	−277	587	−83	618
		median	75	619	577	550	342	150	21	0	0
		σ	4567	8845	6126	16859	6847	6464	2312	3683	3765
CES72	Number of observations		1028	1737	1571	1737	1348	676	538	385	346
	S1	μ	801	1765	1909	1875	1348	455	−104	56	−179
		median	372	711	793	702	273	−142	−199	−210	−229
		σ	2819	5712	6266	12158	6477	6449	3589	3252	3449

Age class

SALT	μ	642	1872	2436	3479	2359	864	286	243	392
	median	342	1375	1973	2048	1431	402	173	20	2
	σ	2801	4900	5908	24189	6541	6151	3849	3978	4220
S1P	μ	839	1856	2025	1966	1068	−528	−892	−516	−716
	median	399	805	901	760	149	−316	−309	−297	−302
	σ	2852	5731	6269	12200	6668	6707	4139	3492	3778
S1PS	μ	1067	2131	2254	2134	893	−2228	−2967	−2490	−2610
	median	617	1120	1272	1111	289	−2045	−2282	−2258	−2148
	σ	2894	5781	6367	12268	6937	7094	4390	3729	4000
CES73	Numbers of observations	1050	1966	1575	1707	1375	622	491	374	349
S1	μ	922	2027	2461	2387	1622	744	158	604	158
	median	454	908	1013	848	427	−126	−121	−180	−190
	σ	2913	7102	11244	10296	20156	6716	3962	4180	4558
SALT	μ	881	2308	2497	3605	2912	1311	582	967	939
	median	511	1736	2140	2240	1784	370	96	329	204
	σ	3904	6168	7397	12345	6995	5640	4291	4492	6309
S1P	μ	953	2108	2604	2455	1295	−165	−644	−143	−326
	median	467	991	1109	890	281	−272	−265	−293	−261
	σ	2930	7126	11260	10547	20190	6842	4294	4403	4913
S1PS	μ	1229	2471	2829	2637	1084	−2280	−3160	−2588	−2401
	median	719	1411	1529	1286	353	−2466	−2583	−3476	−2219
	σ	3010	7173	11341	10574	20279	79078	4592	4583	5077
HPS79	Number of observations	1019	1011	627	562	437	220	210	146	60
NW79	μ	17485	44850	74786	76195	86080	63516	62522	74240	34468
	median	4130	25050	42925	54537	44129	41032	32556	26993	13560
	σ	77302	75010	138079	124006	121097	94553	93203	220101	62407

Table 7.1 (continued)

Survey	Variable	Statistic	Age class								
			≤25	26–35	36–45	46–55	56–64	65–69	70–74	75–79	≥80
	NW79P	μ	23505	672267	106127	127184	107084	84659	80650	82083	35815
		median	4671	33974	62260	72800	58001	52740	43333	34936	15530
		σ	85243	10904	164300	185203	143044	107949	139704	222230	63121
	NW79PS	μ	20544	63609	107690	141887	139373	130097	112908	102168	39306
		median	6627	33837	68238	91029	90405	899483	81157	54747	16985
		σ	83248	105328	160682	183445	145717	119085	114437	223789	65894
SCF83	Number of observations		386	871	680	572	478	237	198	145	116
	NW83	μ	3619	14535	34273	71531	59794	70584	64628	38070	37289
		median	124	4011	16674	21099	27724	27001	20886	19547	10993
		σ	17464	34067	66900	374448	102629	135047	149085	64339	100913

a. All figures in this table are deflated by CPI and expressed in terms of 1972 dollars.

$CES60$: Consumer Expenditure Survey, 1960, Bureau of Labor Statistics, Department of Labor. TS: Net changes in financial and real assets including purchases of consumer durables and excluding depreciation and capital gains. TSP: TS plus employee contributions to private (including those for government employees) pension programs less benefit receipts. $TSPS$: TSP plus employee contributions to Oasi minus benefit receipts from Oasi. $SFCC$: Survey of Financial Characteristics of Consumers, 1962–63, Board of Governors of the Federal Reserve System. $NW62$: 1962 net wealth excluding consumer durables, private pension reserves, and net present value of social security program. S: Saving = 1963 net wealth minus 1962 net wealth. Both $NW62$ and S are weighted by weights constructed by Ian Novos (1984). $CES72$ and $CES73$: Consumer Expenditure Survey, 1972–73 Bureau of Labor Statistics, Department of Labor. $S1$: Directly measured change in net worth including consumer durables and excluding private pension and net social security wealth. $SALT$: Saving measured as income less consumption, defined as consistently as possible with $S1$. $S1P$: $S1$ plus employee contributions to private pension programs less benefit receipts. $S1PS$: $S1P$ plus employee contribution to Oasi less benefits from Oasi. $HPS79$: Household Pension Survey, President's Commission on Pension Policy, 1979. $NW79$: Net wealth including Keogh, IRA, and value of consumer durables stock but not pension or social security wealth. $NW79P$: $NW79$ plus the accumulated value of private pension programs. $NW79PS$: $NW79P$ plus the social security wealth. *SCF83*: Survey of Consumer Finance, 1983, Board of Governors of the Federal Reserve System. [Figures reported from this survey are based on a preliminary version of the data, which is still subject to editorial adjustments. In particular, we note (1) that the figure for the mean of age group 46–55 is distorted by the presence of a family with net worth of some $17 million carrying a larger weight than seems justifiable (see also note 5) and (2) that the reported value of pension fund reserves appears to be subject to serious doubts at the present time, although in principle the survey is supposed to contain this information; for this reason, we have not reported here values of net worth including the value of pension fund reserves for this survey.] *NW83*: Net worth in roughly the standard definition including the value of consumer durable stock but excluding value of pension programs and social security wealth.

median of each cell, the standard deviation for the cell, and the number of observations in the cell. The reader can see that the distribution of savings and of net worth in each cell is extremely diversified, and we need a very large number of observations in each cell before we can place any confidence in the mean value in each cell.

In looking at the age pattern of net worth, we must remember that these tables represent pattern observed over different age groups at one point in time, and we must at least adjust the pattern of net worth for the rate of growth of income per household in order to infer the possible patterns of net worth that a single family might follow over time. (See Shorrocks, 1975, and Kennickell, 1984.)[4]

Even with all these caveats, there is ample evidence in virtually every data set reviewed for the usual presumption of substantial savings and the resulting rising net worth income ratio for the preretirement years. On the other hand, evidence for the savings behavior after retirement age is, at best, quite mixed. Interpretation depends on the breadth of the definition of wealth. Three of them must be considered: the first excluding both the social security program and the private pension programs from net worth of the household, the second including the private pension programs but excluding the social security program (corresponding most closely to the definition used in the national income accounts), and the third including both. We choose not to deal explicitly with the third and broadest definition here, although we shall look at effects of the social security program on other forms of savings later in this essay.

In terms of the first, narrow definition of savings and net worth, there is very little indication that households dissave and reduce their net worth after retirement. We have data for net worth for *SFCC*, *HPS79*, and *SCF83*. They all show a mild decline in net worth as age rises, but not quite enough to overcome the adjustment for the growth of per capita income.[5] In terms of savings, data for *CES60* and *CES72–73* all show continued positive savings at old age. We must conclude, therefore, that in terms of this narrow definition there is very little evidence to support the proposition that consumers dissave after their retirement.

On the other hand, in terms of the second definition including savings through private pension funds (including government pension for its employees), there are some indications that dissaving occurs after the retirement. Pension programs have developed rather rapidly since the 1950s, and by 1980 it has become a major portion of personal savings. But in 1960, it was still a relatively small program (see table 7.14).

In terms of savings flows, we have at best information on employee contributions and benefits received, not on employer contributions or interest earned on reserves. For *CES60*, savings of groups after 65 are reduced when benefits from private pension programs are subtracted, but not enough to make the net savings of these groups negative. By 1972–73, however, savings by this broader definition is clearly negative for groups over 65, although not by very large amounts.

We do not have the necessary information in *SFCC* to construct net worth including the value of private pension programs. For *HPS79*, we can make an attempt to do so, and resulting figures are reported as *NW79P*. *NW79P* seems to accumulate much faster than *NW79*, then declines, barely enough to counter the growth adjustment (except for the age group 80 and over, which is not reliable and should be ignored). In principle, we should also be able to construct net worth including the value of pension fund reserves for *SCR83*. Unfortunately, this set of data is still partially under the editorial process, and the value of pension fund reserves is an aspect of data that cannot be utilized with confidence at this time.

On the basis of the pattern of savings generated by *CES72–73*, it seems reasonable to conclude that there is some dissaving after retirement, when benefits from private pension program is treated as dissaving. It is, however, puzzling that *CES60* does not show any dissaving. Since private pension programs were relatively small in 1960, we might have expected that older persons would have dissaved in terms of other assets. But we see no evidence for such behavior.

Obviously, interpretations of these simple tabulations are subject to substantial revision as various subsurface phenomena are explicitly introduced into our analysis. It seems to us that measurement error, while always a serious problem, would not be likely to bend in any distinct way for the elderly. One argument might be that systematic variations in micro characteristics, such as permanent income, family composition, and other socio demographic features of families, may mask the "true" life cycle behavior. This is an argument for taking these factors explicitly into account in formulating our model, and we present below results of our effort to move in this direction.

3 A Formal Representation of the Life Cycle Theory

The title of this section refers to an attempt to formulate the preference function of households explicitly and to estimate its parameters from data.[6] In this paper, data used are part of the survey data reviewed in the preceding section. There are a number of reasons why this type of formulation has gained in popularity in the literature of micro empirical studies of household behavior, of which two are most important.

It may be argued that the essence of the life cycle theory is not any particular pattern of assets accumulation, which is merely a consequence of the complex dynamic decision-making processes of households with a specific preference function, but is the rational, forward-looking behavior imputed to households. The original formulation of Modigliani and Brumberg (1954) began with a description of such an optimizing behavior. While this general proposition may be appealing, in order to make the theory operational as a basis of empirical study, it is, of course, necessary to restrict the admissible form of preferences functions. Almost all studies on this question assume that the utility function is time separable, and in most cases, it is assumed to be a slightly generalized version of the Yaari utility function (Yaari, 1977). If we could estimate the parameters of a preference function that turns out to be common among individual households and stable over time for each household, we should have gone a long way toward a complete description of the household savings behavior. This point was further reinforced by the influential paper of Lucas (1975), who emphasized possible difficulties of identifying parameters of a decision rule with parameters of the preference function, independent of constraints.

The second of the reasons is related to the nature of most available micro data on household behavior. They usually contain a vast amount of information about individual households, but definitions for many critical variables are often at variance with concepts used in economic theory, and their measurement is subject to substantial errors and biases. Under the circumstances, it is essential that the model in terms of which we attempt to characterize data be capable, to some degrees, of suppressing noise and irrelevant detail and allowing us to focus on the critical dimensions of data. A model of explicit forward-looking optimization, of which the life cycle model is a special case, is very powerful for this purpose. There are, however, some costs to be paid. We shall discuss them after we have presented the results of our attempts to estimate a particularly simple preference function.

The original formulation by Modigliani and Brumberg may be considered as a special case of the following optimization problem by household (see, for example, Yaari, 1977):

$$\max_{\{C_j\}_{j=t}^{T}} \sum_{j=t}^{T} \delta^{j-t} \frac{N_j(C_j/N_j)^{1-\gamma}}{1-\gamma} \tag{1}$$

subject to

$$\sum_{j=t}^{T} (Y_j - C_j)R_t^{j-t} + A_t = 0, \tag{2}$$

where $\{C_j\}$ is a temporal sequence of (aggregated) consumption goods, $\{Y_j\}$ is the parallel sequence of all income other than that generated by A (that is, labor income and receipts of all transfer payments, net of taxes), and $\{N_j\}$ is the path of effective household size. We assume that expected one period rates of discount, both the market one and the subjective one, will remain the same for all future periods although they may be different from each other, and denote them by R_t and δ_t, respectively. That is, $\delta_t = 1/(1 + \rho_t)$ and $R_t = 1/(1 + r_t)$, where ρ_t and r_t are (real) subjective and market one-period rates of interest expected to prevail from the period t on. T is the effective ending point of the family life, and γ is the inter-temporal elasticity of substitution. There is no uncertainty, and labor supply decisions are assumed to be either separable or exogenous. We shall comment on the question of less than perfect capital markets and liquidity constraints later on.

It is straightforward to show that the solution consumption sequence is given by

$$C_t = W_t \left[1 + \sum_{j=t+1}^{T} \frac{N_j}{N_t} \theta_t^{j-t} \right]^{-1}, \tag{3}$$

$$\theta_t = \left(\frac{\delta}{R_t} \right)^{1/\gamma} \cdot R_t \equiv \left(\frac{1 + r_t}{1 + \rho_t} \right)^{1/\gamma} \cdot \frac{1}{(1 + r_t)}, \tag{4}$$

$$A_t = A_{t-1}(1 + r_{t-1}) + Y_{t-1} - C_{t-1}, \tag{5}$$

$$W_t \equiv \sum_{j=t}^{T} Y_j R_t^{j-t} + A_t. \tag{6}$$

The expression inside the brackets in (3) is a discounted sum of future relative family sizes and does not depend on Y or C.

The informational demands for directly estimating micro consumption function (3) is very severe, since it involves the expected future streams of income, including benefits from social securities and private pension programs, and real discount rates for relevant future periods, in addition to current consumption, income, and the initial value of net worth. There is no data set that can supply such information directly, and it is unlikely that one may become available in the foreseeable future. We must therefore rely on careful imputations based on information that are contained in available data sets. We choose to use the Consumer Expenditure Survey (1972–73) as the basic data.[7]

We extend the parameterization of (1) to allow for the possibility of differential consumption out of the wealth stocks by rewriting (3) as

$$C_t = \frac{YL_t + \alpha_2 SSW_t + (1 - \alpha_1(1 + r)^{t-T})A_t}{\sum_{j=t}^{T}(N_j/N_t)\theta^{j-t}}. \tag{7}$$

YL should be understood as $\sum_{j=t}^{T} Y_j R_t^{j-t}$, except that it excludes social security benefits, which is separately introduced as SSW, and benefits from private pensions for which we have no information. As noted in note 7, all households having recorded flows to or from pension funds are excluded from the sample for this experiment. θ is given by equation (4), while α_1 should be thought of as representing the proportion of A not used for consumption during the life of the family.

A Davidon-Fletcher-Powell procedure was employed to estimate parameters α_1, α_2, and θ in the above function, and results are given in table 7.2a for the 1973 data (results for the 1972 data are virtually the same).

If we taken a stylized estimate of θ to be equal to unity, then from equation (4) we have

$$\gamma = \frac{\ln(1 + r_t) - \ln(1 + \rho_t)}{\ln(1 + r_t)}. \tag{8}$$

Under the reasonable assumption that r_t is positive, $\gamma \gtrless 0$ as $r \gtrless \rho$. There is no a priori reason why r must be larger than ρ. Many economists would probably say that ρ is likely to be larger than r. But if ρ is larger than r and therefore $\gamma < 0$, then the utility function is no longer concave, thus making our analysis meaningless.

One can argue in several ways that any number of assumptions underlying this model are not reasonable. For example, Mariger (1983), claiming that capital market constraints are important, estimated a similar model with endogenous constraints. We have employed his extension of the Kuhn-Tucker theorem to alter our likelihood function slightly and reestimated our model, allowing for the possibility of capital market constraints. The results are presented in table 7.6. The only significant change is that now the propensity to consume out of assets is lower and not significant.

To explore the dependence of this model on changes in underlying assumptions, we have expanded the parameterization further, particularly to include a naive "Keynesian" consumption function as a nested set of hypotheses. However, in every case we have examined, inclusion of additional variables caused the likelihood function to become so flat that no

Table 7.2
Estimates of parameters of equation (7) for various horizons[a]

	Survey Year: N: Horizon	Estimate	1973 815
a	To end of life	θ	1.00 (6.7E−3)
		α_1	.838 (.85)
		(α_2 constrained = 1)	
		θ	1.01 (8.2E−3)
		α_1	.09 (.51)
		α_2	.561 (.98)
b	Endogenous	θ	.992 (7.0E−3)
		α_1	1.00 (.40)
		(α_2 constrained = 1)	
		θ	.945 (6.5E−3)
		α_1	1.68E−5 (.46)
		α_2	1.00 (.45)

a. Figures given in parentheses are asymptotic standard errors.

parameter could be identified. Ultimately, attempts to estimate directly simple models like the one above do not seem to yield much information about the validity of the life cycle theory. Given the range of assumptions required for estimation, perhaps this should not be surprising.

We shall, therefore, review another implementation of the model, inspired by the well-known work of Hall and his followers. Starting again from the model given by equations (1) and (2), provided that capital market constraints are not binding, first-order conditions require each agent to satisfy, for any pair of periods,

$$C_t^{-\gamma}/\delta C_{t+\tau}^{-\gamma} = \frac{N_{t+\tau}}{N_t} \prod_{i=t}^{t+\tau-1} (1 + r_i).$$ (9)

For $\tau = 1$, we have

$$\ln(C_{t+1}) - \ln(C_t) = \frac{1}{\gamma}\ln(\delta) + \frac{1}{\gamma}\ln(1 + r_t) + \frac{1}{\gamma}\ln\frac{(N_{t+1})}{N_t}. \tag{10}$$

If, as is approximately the case, consumption is lognormally distributed in the population, then we can write

$$\ln\left(\sum_i C_t^i/HH_t\right) = HH_t^{-1}\sum_i \ln C_t^i - \ln(1 + \sigma_c^2/\mu_c^2), \tag{11}$$

where HH_t is the number of households at time t and σ_c^2 and μ_c are, respectively, the variance and mean of consumption. The ratio of σ_c^2/μ_c^2 has been approximately constant over recent history. If we consider the average variation in $\ln(N_{t+1}/N_t)$ to be negligible, we may then rewrite (10) in aggregate terms as

$$[\ln(\sum C_{t+1}^i) - \ln(\sum C_t^i) + \ln(HH_t/HH_{t+1})]$$
$$= \frac{1}{\gamma}(\ln\delta) + \frac{1}{\gamma}\ln(1 + r_t) + \text{constant}. \tag{12}$$

This formulation has the virtue that it does not involve information for the future expected stream of income and consumption needs (here represented by family size). It would have required observations at two points in time or more for each household, and since we do not have this luxury, we have estimated the aggregate formulation (12) by the ordinary least squares for various sample periods, using aggregate time series data on real personal consumption and the commercial paper rate adjusted for the inflation rate.[8] The coefficient of $\ln(1 + r_t)$ can be interpreted as an estimate of the reciprocal of γ, but the estimated constant corresponds to the sum of $(1/\gamma)(\ln\delta)$ and other constants due to the presence of the term $(1/\gamma)\ln(N_{t+1}/N_t)$ and the lognormal correction term $\ln(1 + \sigma_c^2/\mu_c^2)$, and it cannot be interpreted as representing any specific parameter. In some cases, we allowed for an additional trend term to check whether our estimates are sensitive to its presence. Finally, in order to guard against the possibility that the quarterly average of the actually observed rate of interest may not be the proper expected rate of interest that should be used in the estimation, we used four lagged values of the rate itself as instruments in estimation.

We report results using instrumental variables in table 7.3. When instruments were not used, none of estimated coefficients were significant. We see that in almost all cases, the estimated coefficient of $\ln(1 + r_t)$ is negative, implying that the value of γ itself is negative. As we noted

Table 7.3
Estimates of equation (12) from aggregate quarterly data, interest rate instrumented as four-period lag on itself[a]

Sample period	Constant	$1/\gamma$	Trend term	R^{**2}
1952:2–1983:2	.895E − 2	−.452		.05
	(3.8)	(2.5)		
	.833E − 2	−1.03	.111E − 3	.08
	(3.5)	(3.0)	(1.9)	
1952:2–1961:4	.201E − 1	−2.54		.11
	(2.4)	(2.1)		
	.213E − 1	−3.20	.131E − 3	.11
	(2.5)	(1.8)	(.5)	
1962:1–1972:4	.165E − 1	.971		.08
	(3.1)	(2.0)		
	.929E − 2	−1.96	.274E − 3	.13
	(1.3)	(2.3)	(1.4)	
1973:1–1983:2	.972E − 2	−.489		.04
	(1.4)	(1.3)		
	.239E − 1	−1.16	.419E − 3	.10
	(1.1)	(2.2)	(1.7)	

a. Figures given in parentheses are t-statistics.

before, however, the negative value of γ in turn implies that the utility function is not concave, rendering equations such as (12) meaningless.

While literature on this type of estimation since the mid-1970s contains a number of contributions that imply that labor supply and consumption demand are treated simultaneously, they usually contain sufficient assumptions to make them effectively separable, such as the appropriate separability properties of the utility function. The major exception is the recent contribution by Browning, Deaton, and Irish (1985). Using a somewhat different formulation of the demand function, known as the Frisch demand function, and taking advantage of the fact that the Lagrange multiplier associated with the budget constraint must be equal in all current and future periods at the optimum, they succeeded in deriving an eminently estimatable demand function in which consumption demand and labor supply are genuinely jointly determined. The paper is also noteworthy in that it treats a set of data generated by a series of surveys over time as generating, for each well-defined class of households, samples from a population that is itself a panel. Unfortunately, the result of their study is a resounding negative one in that a key symmetry condition on the effect of relative prices on labor supply and on commodity demand is violated.[9]

For the United States, we do not have data similar to the one used by Browning, Deaton, and Irish. However, we only need an additional assumption that all variables involved are approximately lognormally distributed in order to utilize aggregate data as well as means from any number of survey data sources. The assumption of lognormality cannot be rejected by some weak test, and we do not believe that it would cause serious biases in our estimates, although test results based on this assumption must be viewed with some skepticism. However reliable or unreliable they may be, our results completely parallel those of Browning, Deaton, and Irish, namely, that the critical symmetry condition is everywhere violated.

There is still another way of approaching models like equations (1) and (2). Looking at equations (3)–(6), it is clear that, by successive substitutions, we can reduce them to the relationship between Y and A. Taking advantage of this fact, Blinder, Gordon, and Wise (1981) looked at the pattern of net worth given age and a constructed measure of permanent income. Their effort did not yield very encouraging results. One possible cause of difficulty is that the value of net worth toward the end of the working life may be subject to exceptionally extensive noise.

We must conclude at this point that attempts to apply more formal models in explaining savings behavior of households have not been very encouraging, and our own effort in this direction has merely confirmed the general pattern observable in the literature.[10]

These negative results, however, do not necessarily have to be taken as indicating that households do not behave in accordance with the life cycle theory. They are not unambiguous evidence against even the simple optimizing model (1) and (2). The direct estimation of equations (3)–(6) or the implied relationship between the permanent income and wealth given age involve so many additional assumptions that the failure of the estimation may just as well be due to the failure of one or more of these additional assumptions as the failure of the basic hypothesis.

Formulations based directly on the Euler equation, such as equation (12) above and the formulation by Deaton, Irish, and Browning, have the advantage that they are usually not dependent on future expected values of variables, and hence, they appear to require less additional assumptions for their empirical implementation. But it is possible that they suffer from being focused on very fine details of the consumer behavior. The Euler equation states that the marginal rate of substitution between consumptions of any pair of periods must be carefully adjusted by households to satisfy the first-order conditions. It is easy to imagine that many households may have a rough notion of the pattern of consumption that they would like to follow over their lives, and if the actual pattern deviates substantially from the desired pattern, they would attempt to correct it, while they may not be very concerned with what they regard as relatively small, short-run deviations. When the change of consumption between two adjoining periods is analyzed, because the desired movement from one period to the next is likely to be small, actual movements of consumption may be dominated by random noises; yet households may consider these noises to be "small" and do not react to them significantly. If this description has any validity, the behavior of households over life may conform to some optimizing pattern approximately, and yet any test based on the Euler equation alone could fail decisively.

It does not seem to us plausible that difficulties that we have outlined will be overcome by generalizing the utility function to allow for non-separability over time. Such a generalization would make the estimation problem extremely complex and the interpretation of the estimated results more and more ambiguous. Euler equations under such a complex utility function would imply that households would be engaged in such complex and refined calculations in order to fine tune their decisions that the remarks we have recorded in the preceding paragraph would be even more applicable here.

These considerations lead us to the conclusion that it would be more fruitful, at least at the present time, to defer direct estimation of a preference function, and to inquire whether or not there exists a persistent pattern of asset accumulation and decumulation over the lifetime of a family, and if it does exist, what the factors influencing its detailed shapes are. This amounts to estimating decision rules followed by households, and Lucas (1975) has pointed out that there are dangers in proceeding in this manner, but advantages and disadvantages are by no means one-sided. Decisions by households can at least be observed directly, while the preference function will always remain an implicitly defined concept. This was the motivating consideration for Samuelson's reformulation of the demand theory in terms of revealed preference and the early investigations of integrability conditions. We also believe that the aggregation of decision rules over individual families is more likely to result in an aggregate behavioral function that preserves the basic characteristics of individual decision rules than the aggregation of individual preferences into an aggregate preference ordering.

In the remainder of this paper, therefore, we shall take our task to be a careful description of the pattern of assets accumulation and decumulation over lives of individual families as revealed in available micro data.

4   Problems of Sample Selection Bias

When the sampling procedure explicitly excludes some classes of the population from a survey, it is obvious that there is potential for sample selection biases, and analysts usually attempt to allow for them in their use of such samples. Even without such explicit exclusion criteria, however, it is possible to encounter serious sample selection biases, and we believe there are three possible sources of implicit sample selection biases when the standard survey data are used for a study of life cycle savings patterns.

First, it has long been suspected that the probability of survival at a given age is greater, the greater the income and wealth of the household. If this is so, and the sampling design selects all existing households at a given time with equal probability, then we face a sampling bias of unknown magnitude by relying exclusively on survey data in order to estimate the life cycle pattern of asset accumulation.

Earlier studies (see, e.g., Kitagawa and Hauser, 1973, and Mathis, 1969) have produced mixed results on the existence of strong socioeconomic mortality differentials. Using panel data from the National Longitudinal Survey of Mature Men (see Center for Human Resource Research, 1982) and a Cox type survival probability model, Kennickell (1984) has shown this effect to be surprisingly strong in the middle-age population of males. Unfortunately, we have not yet been able to integrate this estimated model formally into our saving models.

Second, by examining survey data and comparing the distribution of income and wealth with other sources of information on these distributions, such as the tabulations of federal income tax returns and estate tax returns, we are left with impression that these surveys, even ones like the Survey of Financial Characteristics of Consumers (see Projector, 1968), which are specifically designed to oversample the wealthy, tend to underrepresent the most wealthy families. Kennickell (1984) believes, from an examination of the estate tax data, that this group becomes even more wealthy with age. Since other members of the population appear to become somewhat poorer with age, their underrepresentation could create a bias in favor of the simple life cycle pattern of asset accumulation. Moreover, because wealth is heavily concentrated in the top few percent of the population (see, for example, Barlow, 1966), the bias may be quantitatively significant.

Third, the population from which these surveys are drawn is, generally, the pool of "independent" households. In any society, however, there are some families who have merged with other households, and individuals who are living in a variety of institutions. In particular, we would expect, among older individuals, those who have exhausted their own savings and are therefore poor to have greater probability of becoming merged or institutionalized. Kennickell (1984) confirms this general pattern by detailed examination of census data: the overwhelming majority of families younger than the normal retirement age live independently, and the proportion of such households containing related individuals other than a husband, a wife, and children is small, but beyond age 65, individuals have an increasing tendency to appear as subunits of younger households or as residents of institutions. If these families that are not living independently hold, on average, significantly less wealth than others of the same age, then we would face serious potential biases due to the absence of these families from the sample. In the next section, we shall report on some formal attempts to allow for these sampling biases using the US data.

In the case of Japan, this last source of sampling bias turns out to be much more important than in the United States, because Japanese workers retire much earlier than their American counterparts and most of them become merged with younger households after their retirement. We shall deal with this question extensively in a later section.

5   Results for the United States Based on a Less Formal Model

In this section we shall continue to work with the 1972–73 Consumer Expenditure Survey as our primary data source. We have considered in some detail a statistical model of the form

$$\frac{S_t^k}{PI_t^k} = \sum_{i=1}^{L} \sum_{j=1}^{M} \theta^{ij} a^i \frac{F^{kj}}{PI_t^k} + \sum_{h=1}^{N} \beta^h D^{kh} + l_t^k \tag{13}$$

θ^{ij} and β^h are parameters to be estimated, l_t^k is the error term, and

S_t^k = savings of the kth household in year t,

PI_t^k = "permanent" income of the kth household in year t,

a^i = equals one if the household belongs to the ith age class, and otherwise is zero,

F^{kj} = portfolio characteristics of the kth household,

D^{kh} = dummy variables representing the membership of the kth household in the group possessing the hth characteristic.

S is defined on an accrual basis, including net investment in houses and consumer durables.

Since $CES72-73$ purports to measure comprehensive income and expenditure flows as well as net change in the net worth of households, in principle we could speak indifferently of savings defined as net change in the asset-liability position or as income less consumption. In fact, as in most other data sets reporting on both of these two measures, the difference between these two measures could be substantial. While we can attempt to construct an optimally weighted average of the two (see Modigliani and Ando, 1960 and Kennickell, 1984), here we report two cases using each of two measures. Results are also given for savings defined both as including and excluding pension accumulation, but as noted in section 2, only employee contributions (not employer contributions) to and income received from pension plans are recorded in this survey.

PI is estimated as the predicted value of a two-stage process. In the first stage, current disposable income (defined in an accrual basis as far as possible) is regressed on a number of occupational and demographic characteristics. This regression is then used, under the assumption that the life pattern of earnings remains stable over time and that it is sufficiently similar among individuals of similar characteristics, to predict individuals' future earnings for the remainder of their working lives, and they are reduced to a present value at an annual rate. In the second stage, this value is used as an instrument along with other demographic characteristics in a regression explaining current net income flows, and the prediction of this regression is defined as PI. While one might question this particular definition of PI, results do not appear to vary greatly when the choice of the definition of PI is changed. This will not be the case with the Japanese data to be discussed in the next section.

The vector F includes net worth of the family including estimated market values of the principal residence and consumer durables (but not the value of unincorporated businesses and other real estates) (A), Net social security wealth (SSW), and the difference between current disposable income flow and $PI(\varepsilon)$.

The Ds include a set of dummies representing a selection of demographic characteristics. In addition, age dummies (a^i) are also included in D because we wished to allow for the possibility that the marginal propensity to save out of PI may vary with age. We also include two more dummies, indicating membership in the top and bottom quartiles of the wealth distribution within each age class, and another dummy indicating full retirement.

To limit effects of measurement error, we have excluded two groups—those for whom the discrepancy between the net change in the asset-liability position and income minus consumption is more than 70% of the latter, and households the occupation of whose head is reported as self-employed—since there are reasons to believe that their assets and income are especially subject to measurement errors.[11]

We have analyzed separately the group of households whose heads are aged less than 65 and those whose heads are 65 and over. Results are reported in tables 7.4 and 7.5 for the younger group and table 7.6 for the older group. In these tables, four sets of results corresponding to four definitions of savings (SISP, SALTP, SIS, and SALT, described in footnotes to tables) are given. First, we note that, because the dependent variable is the ratio of saving to PI, the marginal propensity to consume out of PI is represented by coefficients of pure age dummies. Almost any variation of the life cycle theory would imply that these coefficients should be positive, but their expected size and pattern over age are somewhat uncertain. Coefficients of any number of elements of Ds will contribute to the size of the marginal propensity. On average, we expect that coefficients of pure age dummies to be between .2 and .4, for most ages, and to become somewhat smaller for the retired group. Estimated coefficients in tables 7.4 and 7.5 are positive and significant, but they are somewhat smaller than expected. Ones in table 7.6 are rather erratic, but their erratic behavior by itself is not evidence either for or against the life cycle theory.

We expect the coefficient of W to be all negative, and its absolute value should increase with age. This pattern, combined with the fact that W increases with age, should result in negative savings for the group older than 65. We see from the tables that the coefficient of W is always negative, in accordance with the theoretical requirement, but its size is considerably less than expected, and it does not increase in its absolute size over age. In particular, the coefficient of W in table 7.6 is not large enough in absolute size to offset savings generated by the positive coefficients of PI. This is serious evidence against the life cycle theory, and corresponds to the lack of negative savings for older, presumably retired groups observed in table 7.1.

If we had observations on the value of private pension reserves, its coefficient would be roughly the same as that for net worth, provided that it is possible to handle the uncertainty associated with benefit defined programs satisfactorily. Since we do not have any direct data on the value of pension reserves, nor do we have enough information to estimate it, we have introduced instead a dummy variable (PEN) representing the membership of the family in the group with private pension programs, and interacted it with age dummies. Families in this group own, relative to

Table 7.4
Basic saving equation estimated by OLS, CES72–73, standard subsample 1973, household head aged less than 65[a]

Dependent variable	Variables interacted with age	Age interaction with independent variables at left					Other independent variables not interacted with age					
		≤25	26–35	36–45	46–55	56–64						
S1SP/PI	1	.1193 / 6.0	.1094 / 7.2	.2023 / 10.1	.2120 / 11.7	.1285 / 6.7	RACE	−.0613 / 5.3	SM	−.0598 / 4.2	SF	−.0512 / 5.2
	W/PI	.0307 / 1.6	−.0229 / 5.1	−.0567 / 7.6	−.0287 / 8.8	−.0091 / 5.2	CHLT18	−.0054 / 2.0	CHGE18	−.0126 / 1.8	OFAM	.0215 / 1.0
	SSW/PI	−.0117 / 1.1	.0210 / 3.2	−.0021 / .3	−.0099 / 2.2	.0073 / 2.0	NREL	−.0159 / .6	ELDERS	.0353 / .1	RETD	−.1936 / 8.7
	ε/PI	.1939 / 9.4	.4884 / 23.1	.3093 / 14.2	.2388 / 12.9	.1430 / 9.0	DPW1	−.0336 / 3.5	DPW4	.0487 / 4.9		
	PEN	.0910 / 2.9	.0441 / 2.5	.0502 / 2.7	−.0218 / 1.3	−.1649 / 8.8						
SALTP/PI	1	.2205 / 10.8	.2121 / 13.7	.3118 / 15.2	.3163 / 17.1	.3158 / 16.1	RACE	−.1008 / 8.5	SM	−.1285 / 8.8	SF	−.1376 / 3.6
	W/PI	−.0296 / 1.5	−.0130 / 2.9	−.0279 / 3.6	−.0257 / 7.7	−.0114 / 6.4	CHLT18	−.0166 / 5.9	CHGE18	.0226 / 3.1	OFAM	.0144 / .7
	SSW/PI	−.0098 / .9	.0093 / 1.4	−.0187 / 2.6	−.0062 / 1.3	.0013 / .4	NREL	−.0691 / 2.3	ELDERS	.5959 / 1.9	RETD	−.2919 / 12.8
	ε/PI	.5493 / 26.1	.6170 / 40.9	.5612 / 23.5	.5213 / 27.7	.4187 / 25.7	DPW1	.0386 / 3.9	DPW4	.0067 / .7		
	PEN	.0805 / 2.5	.0553 / 3.0	.0376 / 2.0	−.0003 / .0	−.01887 / 9.9						
S1S/PI	1	.1154 / 6.2	.1034 / 7.4	.1866 / 10.0	.2199 / 13.1	.1309 / 7.3	RACE	−.0601 / 5.6	SM	−.0595 / 4.5	SF	−.0351 / 5.8

W/PI	.0333	−.0222	−.0502	−.0295	−.0095	−.0049 CHLT18	−.0203 CHGE18	.0195 OFAM	
	1.9	5.4	7.2	9.8	5.8	1.9	3.1	1.0	
SSW/PI	−.0107	.0227	.0010	−.0131	.0038	−.0187 NREL	.0931 ELDERS	−.0592 RETD	
	1.1	3.7	.2	3.1	1.1	.7	.3	2.9	
ε/PI	.1882	.4849	.3022	.2489	.2382	−.0258 DPW1	.0478 DPW4		
	9.9	35.6	15.0	14.5	16.1	2.9	5.2		
PEN	.0562	.0047	.0175	−.0189	−.0152				
	1.9	.3	1.0	1.3	.9				

SALT/PI 1	.2167	.2062	.2961	.3242	.3174	−.0996 RACE	−.1281 SM	−.1395 SF	
	11.9	14.9	16.2	19.7	18.2	9.5	9.39	15.6	
W/PI	−.0271	−.0124	−.0213	−.0266	−.0118	−.0161 CHLT18	.0148 CHGE18	.0120 OFAM	
	1.6	3.1	3.1	9.0	7.4	6.5	2.3	.7	
SSW/PI	−.0088	.0110	−.0156	−.0093	−.0022	−.0718 NREL	.6506 ELDERS	−.1576 RETD	
	.9	1.8	2.4	2.2	.6	2.7	2.3	7.8	
ε/PI	.5436	.6144	.5141	.5331	.5139	.0464 DPW1			
	29.0	45.8	26.0	31.7	35.5	5.3			
PEN	.0485	.0159	.0049	.0025	−.0390	.0058 DPW4			
	1.6	1.0	.3	.2	2.3	.6			

a. Estimates are given above *t*-statistics.

Definition of variables for tables 7.4–7.6 and 7.8:

(A) one-zero dummy variables (in each case, variable = 1 if condition is true and = 0 otherwise):

SM: Head of household is a single male. *SF*: Head of household is a single female. *RACE*: Head of household is nonwhite. *RETD*: Head of household is reported as retired. *PEN*: Household has flows into or out of a private pension fund. *DPW1*: Household wealth is in the bottom quartile for its age class (as delimited below), wealth taken at its estimated mid year value. *DPW4*: Household wealth is in the top quartile for its age class (as delimited below), wealth taken at its estimated midyear value. *D1*: Head of household is age 25 or below. *D2*: Head of household is aged 26–35. *D3*: Head of household is aged 36–45. *D4*: Head of household is aged 46–55. *D5*: Head of household is aged 56–64. *D6*: Head of household is aged 65–69. *D7*: Head of household is aged 70–74. *D8*: Head of household is aged 75–79. *D9*: Head of household is aged 80 or over. *DRECP*: Household is receiving benefit from a pension program.

Table 7.4 (continued)

(B) discrete variables:

CHLT18: Number of children aged under 18. CHGE18: Number of children aged 18 or over. OFAM: Number of other (related) family members in household, weighted by weeks resident. NREL: Number of unrelated individuals living in household, weighted by weeks resident. ELDERS: Number of persons in household other than head/spouse aged 62 or over.

(C) continuous variables:

S1S: Direct measure of saving including changes in financial assets and net increase in consumer durables after depreciation of stock. SALT: Income minus consumption equivalent of S1S. S1SP: S1S plus household contributions to pensions minus pension income. SALTP: Income minus consumption equivalent of S1SP. INC: Cash flow measure of after tax income (including social security and pension incomes) plus service flows from house and durables. PI: Predicted value of regression of income as described in the text. ε: $INC - PI$. SSW: Net social security wealth as described in the text. W: Net wealth of household estimated as of beginning of survey year.

Table 7.5
Modified basic saving equation estimated by OLS, CES72–73, standard subsample 1973, household head aged less than 65[a]

Dependent variable	Variables interacted with age	Age interaction with independent variables at left					Other independent variables not interacted with age					
		≤25	26–35	36–45	46–55	56–64						
1973 S1SP/PI	1	.1183 6.0	.1052 7.1	.1930 9.8	.2156 12.1	.1119 6.0	RACE -.0631 5.6	SM -.0607 4.3	SF -.0513 5.3			
	W/PI	.0266 1.4	-.0236 5.4	-.0546 7.4	-.0291 9.1	-.0086 5.0	CHLT18 -.0052 1.9	CHGE18 -.0197 2.9	OFAM .0324 1.6			
	SSW/PI	-.0113 1.1	.0226 3.5	-.0011 .2	-.0112 2.5	.0096 2.7	NREL -.0155 .6	ELDERS .1457 .5	RETD -.1384 6.3			
	ε/PI	.1842 9.29	.4880 33.9	.3082 14.5	.2430 13.5	.1534 9.8	DPW1 -.0292 3.1	DPW4 .0518 5.4	DRECP -.3359 15.1			
	PEN	.1038 3.4	.0604 3.5	.0694 3.9	.0196 1.2	.0003 .0						
SALTP/PI	1	.250 10.7	.2053 13.6	.3019 15.1	.3217 17.8	.3005 15.8	RACE -.1030 9.0	SM -.1285 9.1	SF -.1382 14.1			
	W/PI	-.0492 2.5	-.0137 3.1	-.0253 3.4	-.0263 8.1	-.0110 6.3	CHLT18 -.0163 6.0	CHGE18 .0138 2.0	OFAM .0262 1.3			
	SSW/PI	-.0007 .1	.0121 1.9	-.0153 2.2	-.0074 1.7	.0033 .9	NREL -.0685 2.4	ELDERS .7208 2.4	RETD -.2303 10.3			
	ε/PI	.5631 28.0	.6164 42.3	.5200 24.1	.5264 28.8	.4341 27.5	DPW1 .0428 4.5	DPW4 .0098 1.0	DRECP -.3741 16.6			
	PEN	.0943 3.0	.0741 4.2	.0590 3.3	.0453 .1	-.0052 .2						

a. Estimates are given above t-statistics.

Table 7.6

Basic saving equation estimated by OLS, CES72–73, standard subsample 1973, household head aged 65 and over[a]

Dependent variable: Independent variables	SISP/PI	SALTP/PI	SIS/PI	SALT/PI
RACE	−.1947	−.3056	−.1546	−.0602
	3.4	7.1	3.2	2.5
SM	−.0686	−.1610	−.0852	−.0583
	1.4	4.3	2.0	2.8
SF	−.0250	−.1087	−.0244	−.0355
	.7	4.2	.8	2.4
CHLT18	.0261	.0237	.0007	.0025
	.5	.6	.0	.0
CHGE18	.0536	.0780	−.0217	.0340
	4.2	2.4	.6	1.9
OFAM	.0433	.0968	.0221	−.0032
	.6	1.8	.4	.1
NREL	.0282	.0406	−.0216	.0122
	.2	.4	.2	.2
ELDERS	−.2314	.3298	−.4386	.3435
	.2	.3	.4	.6
RETD	−.0120	−.0173	−.0402	−.0015
	.4	.7	1.4	.1
DPW1	−.0075	.0713	.0082	−.0048
	.2	2.4	.2	.3
DPW4	.1272	.0381	.0766	.0458
	2.7	1.1	2.0	2.4
D6	.5386	.4326	.5704	.0943
	7.3	7.9	9.2	3.1
D7	.0580	.1944	.1451	.0832
	.7	3.2	2.1	2.4
D8	−.1953	.0590	−.0078	−.0147
	1.9	.8	.1	.3
D9	.1645	.3471	.1676	.0345
	2.1	6.0	2.6	1.1
D6 W/PI*	−.0859	−.0437	−.0773	−.0163
	11.9	8.2	12.8	5.5
D7 W/PI*	−.0277	−.0259	−.0292	−.0152
	4.1	5.1	5.1	5.4
D8 W/PI*	−.0018	.0054	−.0079	−.0022
	.2	.7	.9	.5
D9 W/PI*	−.0061	−.0278	−.0012	−.0001
	1.2	7.1	.3	.0
D6 SSW/PI*	−.0242	−.0122	−.0401	−.0053
	2.1	1.4	4.1	1.1
D7 SSW/PI*	.0204	.0249	−.0034	−.0028
	1.5	2.4	.3	.5
D8 SSW/PI*	.0568	.0303	.0122	.0076
	2.8	2.0	.7	.9

Table 7.6 (continued)

Dependent variable: Independent variables	SISP/PI	SALTP/PI	SIS/PI	SALT/PI
D9 SSW/PI*	−.0298	−.0153	−.0625	−.0142
	1.4	1.0	3.5	1.6
D6 ε/PI*	.9085	.7427	.9638	.1687
	26.3	29.1	33.3	6.4
D7 ε/PI*	.1835	.4740	.3098	.1570
	3.1	10.9	6.3	2.0
D8 ε/PI*	−.1791	.1671	.1239	.0631
	2.3	2.9	1.9	2.0
D9 ε/PI*	.2586	.6080	.3614	.0945
	7.5	23.7	12.4	6.6
D6 PEN	−.4020	−.3221	−.1195	.0244
	7.5	8.1	2.7	1.1
D7 PEN	−.3262	−.3179	−.0196	.0115
	5.1	6.7	.4	.4
D8 PEN	−.2566	−.2691	−.0047	.0286
	3.0	4.8	.1	.9
D9 PEN	−.6699	−.4879	−.1801	−.0111
	8.2	8.0	2.6	.3
R**2	.4136	.5183	.5069	.1913

a. Estimates are given above t-statistics. Asterisk indicates normalization by same PI as dependent variables.

those not in this group, additional assets in the form of pension reserves and are provided with additional savings in the form of employer contributions to pension programs and interest earnings on reserves, neither of which has been recorded in our data for these families. The life cycle theory, therefore, would require that PEN must have a substantial negative effect on saving.

It is, therefore, quite disturbing to observe that the coefficient of PEN in table 7.4 is almost always positive, except for the age groups 46–55 and 56–64. These negative coefficients, however, appear to reflect a different empirical process. By the time the head of household is above 56, some individuals are retired and are receiving benefits from pension programs, and such benefits enter SISP and SALTP as negative contributions: the negative coefficient of PEN for this age group appears to be simply reflecting this mechanical fact. When SIS or SALT, neither of which includes benefits from pension programs, is used as the dependent variable, the coefficient of PEN for the age group 56–64 is still negative but completely insignificant. In table 7.5, we introduce one additional variable, DRECP, which is a one-zero dummy variable representing those receiving benefits from pension programs. This variable acquires a strong negative coefficient, and the coefficient of PEN now turns largely positive for age groups 46–55 and 56–64.

In table 7.6, for older households, the coefficient of PEN is strongly negative when the dependent variable is the savings including the benefit payments from pension programs. This is understandable. When the dependent variable does not include benefit payments, however, the coefficient of PEN is insignificant. On the whole, then, evidence is that the pattern of accumulation and decumulation of assets other than the private pension reserves is largely independent of whether the household belongs to a private pension program or not. We find this result somewhat implausible, but we could not detect any statistical bias or other mechanism responsible for this result if the true behavior of households were to be inconsistent with this evidence. To the extent that this finding reflects the behavior of households accurately, it must be considered as evidence inconsistent with the life cycle theory, even in its most flexible form.

Social security wealth (SSW) is imputed by us in accordance with the current law and our best estimates of the pattern of earnings by individuals in the family for those not yet receiving benefits, and based on actual benefits received for those who are already receiving benefits. One may argue that it is not quite the same type of wealth as other assets on which individuals can earn returns and which they can liquidate. Without going into detailed arguments, we believe that under any plausible assumptions about the nature of the social security wealth, if any form of the life cycle hypothesis is to be supported, the coefficient of this variable should be negative, and that its size should be between zero and the corresponding coefficient of other wealth.

The coefficient of SSW for younger households reported in table 7.4 is usually small, negative, and not often significant. For the older group reported in table 7.6, the situation appears to be the same. The evidence, taken at its face value, indicates that effects of social security wealth on private saving are quite uncertain, and likely to be quite small. This finding, however, must be taken with special caution. The imputation process involves many strong assumptions, and it is inevitable that SSW is estimated with substantial errors of measurement. At the same time, the true value of SSW among households does not vary a great deal. We have, therefore, a situation in which the variance of the error of measurement is likely to be very large relative to the variance of the true value of the variable, thus creating potentially serious biases in estimates of the coefficient of this variable.[12] The situation is further aggravated by the fact that *SSW* is strongly correlated with *PI* by construction.

The coefficient of ε is positive and significant in table 7.4, but it is much smaller when *SISP* or *SIS* rather than *SALTP* or *SALT* is used as the dependent variable. Conceptually, ε represents the pure transitory income, so that almost all of it should be saved if all variables are measured without error and if households behaved in accordance with the life cycle theory. Variables are, however, measured with errors. In addition, any measurement error in current income goes directly into the definition of *SALTP* and *SALT* as well as into ε, while it goes into *SISP* and *SIS* only indirectly. This explains the difference in two cases just observed. When *SALT* or *SALTP* is the dependent variable, the coefficient of ε is considerably larger than that of *PI*, but it is substantially smaller than unity. We interpret this result as providing a partial and weak support to one aspect of the life cycle theory, which is common with the permanent income hypothesis.

For the older group in table 7.6, the pattern of coefficient of ε is much more erratic. We believe that it is much more difficult to construct an estimate of *PI* for the retired persons than for currently working persons, because in most cases we do not know past occupational characteristics of the retired person in the survey. The division of current income between *PI* and ε is, therefore, likely to be subject to more serious error of measurement for older persons than for younger persons, making estimated coefficients of both variables less trustworthy.

The other demographic variables introduced in both tables 7.4 and 7.6 appears to acquire coefficients with more or less expected signs and orders of magnitude, and some of them are quite significant, suggesting that savings decisions by families are dependent on many factors other than the simple availability of resources and intertemporal preferences.

From the perspective of the life cycle theory, the most surprising finding so far is that households whose heads are more than 65 years old appear to continue saving on average. As we noted in section 4, however, there is a possibility that this finding is at least in part due to a sample selection bias. We know that a progressively larger proportion of individuals in an age group is being removed from the sample as they become older, because more and more of them become merged into younger households or become institutionalized and are no longer living independently, and therefore they are not subject to selection in a typical household survey. If this selection process is related to savings and asset accumulation behavior, then we have a potential source of the sample selection bias.[13] For example, persons with a lower level of assets may have higher probability of being removed from the population from which the sample is taken than persons with a higher level of assets, because independent living is no longer possible for the former.

Kennickell (1984) considered four methods of explicitly allowing for this possibility. Because the results obtained were not qualitatively sensitive to the technique chosen, we present here estimates using the more familiar Heckman (1976) correction. If one has a model of the form

$$Y = X\beta + \varepsilon, \tag{14}$$

where X and Y are variables, β is a parameter vector, and ε is a normal random term with unconditional mean of zero, then selection bias is said to be present when

$$E(\lambda) \equiv E[\varepsilon|X, Y, Z] \neq 0, \tag{15}$$

where Z is a (possibly null) vector of other characteristics. If one has some information on households that are selected and those that are not, then it is possible to estimate (15) consistently using a probit model of the selection process. The CES72−73 does not contain this information.

Fortunately, there exists a nearly contemporaneous survey, Demographic and Economic Characteristics of the Aged 1968 (see Wentworth and Motley, 1970), conducted by the Social Security Administration. The sample universe for this survey was virtually all order *individuals*, including persons living as subfamilies or living in institutions. Among the variables in this survey are many that overlap with the Consumer Expenditure Survey 1972−73. Using a subset of those variables, we have estimated the probit model given in table 7.7. Using these parameter estimates, we have constructed an estimate of λ for each observation in the Consumer Expenditure Survey. With that estimate as an additional variable, we recalculated our estimates of the parameters of the saving equation as shown in table 7.8 for the 1973 data.

The t-test of significance of the coefficient of λ is consistent test for sample selection bias (see Heckman, 1976, and Greene, 1981). Although in three of the four cases here we cannot reject sample selection bias, the other parameter estimates are very little changed. Kennickell (1984) found that this result was robust under a number of alternative choices of underlying probit models. Thus, the observation that older, retired persons do not seem to dissave contrary to the life cycle theory survives.[14]

Table 7.7
Probit estimation of probability of dependent living arrangements, Demographic and Economic Characteristics of the Aged 1968[a]

Model	N	Pseudo-R²	Constant	AVAGE	AVAGE2	SM	SF	RACE	NASSETS	NASSETS2	NINC	NINC2
1	4304	.2493	1.321 (.549)	-.096 (1.529)	.079 (1.961)	1.446 (11.235)	1.719 (14.742)	-.230 (3.437)	-.338 (11.462)	.210 (8.714)		
2	4304	.2358	1.721 (.721)	-.109 (1.761)	.088 (2.196)	1.501 (11.775)	1.728 (15.002)	-.177 (2.664)	-.150 (8.426)			
3	4304	.2260	2.559 (1.076)	-.132 (2.126)	.108 (2.695)	1.213 (13.188)	1.270 (14.664)	-.249 (3.769)	-.349 (12.066)	.221 (9.353)		
4	4304	.2102	3.025 (1.285)	-.147 (2.975)	.118 (2.975)	1.226 (13.481)	1.278 (14.941)	-.195 (2.987)	-.153 (8.724)			
5	4304	.2086	-3.950 (13.785)	.035 (10.139)		1.209 (13.328)	1.262 (14.776)	-.191 (2.914)	-.154 (8.788)			
6	4304	.2484	1.314 (.547)	-.096 (1.534)	.080 (1.967)	1.450 (11.269)	1.725 (14.816)	-.229 (3.422)	-.343 (11.744)	.217 (9.269)	-.568 (3.620)	.255 (.769)
7	4304	.2350	1.699 (.713)	-.110 (1.733)	.089 (2.216)	1.508 (11.837)	1.740 (15.123)	-.176 (2.653)	-.149 (8.439)		-.485 (3.534)	
8	4304	.2248	2.543 (1.070)	-.132 (2.130)	.108 (2.700)	1.219 (13.255)	1.279 (14.850)	-.247 (3.749)	-.354 (12.363)	.227 (9.894)	-.617 (9.894)	.279 (.879)

a. All individal components of money values are coded as min[actual value, 99999], this is, it is truncated at 99999.

Variable definitions:

*NASSETS: ASSETS/*median family income (median family income for 1968 was $7743—see Bureau of the Census, 1969). *NASSETS2: NASSETS* squared. *AVAGE:* For married respondents, the average age of respondent and spouse, for single persons, the age of the respondent. *AVAGE2: AVAGE* squared. *SM:* 1 if the respondent is a single male, 0 otherwise. *SF:* 1 if respondent is a single female, 0 otherwise. *RACE:* 1 if respondent is nonwhite, 0 otherwise. *NINC:* Before tax income including social security and pension benefits, divided by its median. *NINC2: NINC* squared.

Table 7.8
Basic saving equation estimated with Heckman correction, CES72–73, standard subsample 1973, household head aged 65 and over[a]

Dependent variable: Independent variables	SISP/PI	SALTP/PI	SIS/PI	SALT/PI
RACE	−.1973	−.3069	−.1571	−.2666
	3.4	6.9	3.2	7.0
SM	−.0041	−.1283	−.0231	−.1472
	.1	2.8	.5	3.6
SF	−.0357	−.0779	−.0341	−.0795
	.8	2.2	.9	2.4
CHLT18	.0261	.0237	.0008	.0016
	.5	.6	.0	.0
CHGE18	.0420	.0721	−.0329	.0029
	1.0	2.1	.9	.1
OFAM	.0324	.0913	.0116	.0705
	.4	1.6	.2	1.5
NREL	.0358	.0445	−.0143	−.0056
	.3	.4	.1	.1
ELDERS	−.1297	.3814	−.3408	.1702
	.1	.4	.3	.2
RETD	−.0130	−.0179	−.0392	−.0343
	.4	.7	1.4	1.6
DPW1	−.0243	.0628	−.0079	.0791
	.6	2.0	.2	3.0
DPW4	.2601	.1055	.2046	.0500
	4.6	2.4	4.2	1.3
D6	.5519	.4393	.5832	.4706
	7.2	7.3	8.8	8.9
D7	.0720	.2015	.1586	.2880
	.8	3.0	2.1	4.8
D8	−.1750	.0693	−.0118	−.2561
	1.6	.8	.1	3.5
D9	.1975	.3638	.1995	.3658
	2.4	5.6	2.8	6.4
D6 W/PI*	−.0883	−.0449	−.0795	−.0362
	12.5	8.3	13.2	7.9
D7 W/PI*	−.0304	−.0272	−.0318	−.0287
	4.5	5.3	5.5	6.5
D8 W/PI*	−.0055	.0035	−.0114	−.0024
	.5	.5	1.3	.4
D9 W/PI*	−.0085	−.0290	−.0035	−.0239
	1.6	7.3	.8	7.1
D6 SSW/PI*	−.0224	−.0113	−.0383	−.0272
	1.9	1.3	3.9	3.6
D7 SSW/PI*	.0205	.0249	−.0033	−.0011
	1.5	2.4	.3	.1
D8 SSW/PI*	.0554	.0296	.0108	−.0151
	2.7	1.9	.6	1.2

Table 7.8 (continued)

Dependent variable: Independent variables	SISP/PI	SALTP/PI	SIS/PI	SALT/PI
D9 SSW/PI*	−.0321	−.0165	−.0647	−.0491
	1.5	1.0	3.6	3.6
D6 ε/PI*	.9036	.7402	.9590	.7956
	26.7	28.7	33.4	36.2
D7 ε/PI*	.1748	.4695	.3014	.5961
	3.1	10.8	6.2	16.0
D8 ε/PI*	−.1795	.1668	.1235	.4699
	2.4	2.9	1.9	9.7
D9 ε/PI*	.2530	.6051	.3559	.7081
	7.3	22.9	12.1	31.5
D6 PEN	−.3988	−.3205	−.1164	.0382
	7.6	8.0	2.6	1.1
D7 PEN	−.3311	−.3204	−.0243	.0135
	5.2	6.7	.5	.3
D8 PEN	−.2520	−.2667	−.0002	−.0150
	3.4	4.7	.0	.3
D9 PEN	−.6706	−.4884	−.1810	−.0012
	8.4	8.1	2.7	.0
λ	−.0882	−.0477	−.0849	−.0415
	6.5	4.3	7.4	4.7

a. Estimates are given above t-statistics. Asterisk indicates normalization by same PI as dependent variables.

6   The Japanese Case

For Japan, data analyzed is a product of the National Survey of Family Income and Expenditure, a survey conducted every five years to construct weights for consumer price indices. It is a very large sample involving some 53,000 households, covering virtually all households in Japan except those primarily engaged in agriculture. A detailed evaluation of the quality of this data is given in Ando (1985). The quality of this data appears extremely high in most respects, with some notable exceptions.[15] The main problem appears to be that certain types of income and services provided in kind to households, such as medical services paid for by employers, by government programs, and by insurance, seem to be grossly underestimated. On the whole, both consumption and income are underestimated, but consumption more than income, and therefore savings is overestimated and the ratio of the variance of the measurement error to the true variance of the variable appears to be considerably higher for savings than for other variables. Among balance sheet items, we are missing data

Table 7.9A[a]

Means and quartiles of income, consumption, and assets, 1974, two-or-more-person families, other than workers, ¥10,000

Age class		All	<20	21–25	26–30	31–35	36–40	41–45	46–50	51–55	56–60	61–65	66–70	71–75	76–80	81–85	≥86
	Number of observations	14555.0	1.000	135.000	704.000	1400.00	2009.00	2039.00	1884.00	1591.00	1572.00	1418.00	927.00	553.00	228.00	79.00	15.00
2 YDM	MEAN OF YD	267.8	166.000	170.104	223.74	255.46	264.92	284.83	311.33	316.68	306.53	244.91	191.12	181.16	164.27	140.01	121.27
3 YD2	MEDIAN OF YD	211.0	166.000	156.000	185.50	201.00	215.00	224.00	252.50	248.00	235.00	191.50	136.00	125.00	102.50	55.00	12.00
4 YD1	Q1 OF YD	135.0	166.000	104.000	137.00	144.00	149.00	156.00	167.00	162.00	151.00	105.00	52.00	43.50	29.25	6.00	0.00
5 YD3	Q3 OF YD	331.0	166.000	195.000	267.00	293.50	316.50	346.00	378.00	381.00	386.00	317.25	270.00	241.50	248.75	215.00	134.00
6 YLDM	MEAN OF YLD	234.0	161.000	154.163	205.09	233.17	237.32	252.10	273.28	277.68	263.33	203.98	155.87	145.57	125.64	112.54	104.67
7 YLD2	MEDIAN OF YLD	187.0	161.000	142.000	173.50	185.00	193.00	198.00	223.00	217.00	202.00	156.00	102.00	92.00	77.00	37.00	0.00
8 YLD1	Q1 OF YLD	115.0	161.000	96.000	125.25	128.25	133.00	137.00	144.25	139.00	123.25	79.00	30.00	17.50	8.25	0.00	0.00
9 YLD3	Q3 OF YLD	288.0	161.000	173.000	239.75	263.75	284.00	304.00	329.75	334.00	328.75	270.25	222.00	204.00	198.50	179.00	106.00
10 ZLXM	MEAN OF ZLX	170.5	158.000	174.222	199.99	198.42	221.51	205.59	224.02	208.43	202.51	72.42	0.00	0.00	0.00	0.00	0.00
11 ZLX2	MEDIAN OF ZLX	188.0	158.000	183.000	196.00	185.00	201.00	187.00	203.00	194.00	186.00	0.00	0.00	0.00	0.00	0.00	0.00
12 ZLX1	Q1 OF ZLX	121.0	158.000	168.000	174.00	178.00	190.00	181.00	188.00	184.00	180.00	0.00	0.00	0.00	0.00	0.00	0.00
13 ZLX3	Q3 OF ZLX	206.0	158.000	188.000	207.00	196.00	231.00	211.00	237.00	215.00	206.00	184.00	0.00	0.00	0.00	0.00	0.00
14 ZLM	MEAN OF ZL	214.9	158.473	152.067	205.48	232.41	231.87	239.85	253.12	233.45	230.38	168.59	122.49	108.29	87.36	82.18	82.69
15 ZL2	MEDIAN OF ZL	173.9	158.473	135.787	173.24	182.10	186.77	188.72	206.22	197.73	181.10	132.92	79.00	60.40	50.95	25.82	0.00
16 ZL1	Q1 OF ZL	100.9	158.473	94.668	121.67	125.04	125.17	125.96	127.55	123.11	105.01	53.39	8.47	0.00	−1.45	−12.88	−18.25
17 ZL3	Q3 OF ZL	272.4	158.473	182.000	251.67	263.98	277.05	285.68	305.20	306.09	293.53	238.10	194.40	178.70	143.61	150.79	28.79
18 YDAM	MEAN OF YDA	193.1	133.000	145.644	168.45	180.28	193.31	208.98	218.62	206.27	198.76	181.53	166.31	165.75	163.37	131.63	126.73
19 YDA2	MEDIAN OF YDA	173.0	133.000	129.000	157.00	165.00	129.00	188.00	195.00	183.00	175.00	158.00	145.00	144.00	134.50	109.00	90.00
20 YDA1	Q1 OF YDA	127.0	133.000	102.000	121.25	127.00	136.00	144.00	145.00	131.00	128.00	117.00	102.00	95.00	87.00	71.00	56.00
21 YDA3	Q3 OF YDA	233.0	133.000	166.000	201.75	214.00	231.00	251.00	268.00	250.00	238.00	218.25	209.00	217.50	206.00	187.00	182.00
22 CONSM	MEAN OF CONS	1257.8	97.000	556.724	840.82	989.13	1109.89	1255.01	1351.97	1381.89	1444.98	1437.67	1348.09	1345.51	1330.52	1236.24	1085.93
23 CONS2	MEDIAN OF CONS	1193.0	97.000	146.000	695.50	1001.50	1066.00	1215.00	1271.50	1250.00	1307.00	1303.50	1234.00	1233.00	1152.00	1143.00	1112.00
24 CONS1	Q1 OF CONS	664.0	97.000	70.000	112.50	192.00	349.00	642.00	799.25	843.00	880.25	856.00	813.00	822.00	802.25	842.00	486.00
25 CONS3	Q3 OF CONS	1679.0	97.000	787.000	1405.75	1479.00	1572.50	1682.00	1749.00	1774.00	1822.75	1824.25	1703.00	1725.50	1693.50	1649.00	1532.00
26 ARM	MEAN OF AR	1626.6	49.000	576.452	940.47	1167.53	1329.61	1525.11	1671.97	1755.09	1872.93	2136.09	2099.74	1974.12	1823.78	1640.33	1415.47
27 AR2	MEDIAN OF AR	1570.0	49.000	197.000	780.00	1175.50	1291.00	1486.00	1596.00	1634.00	1732.00	2005.00	1996.00	1842.00	1638.00	1544.00	1419.00
28 AR1	Q1 OF AR	1008.0	49.000	90.000	216.00	372.75	561.00	914.00	1115.00	1203.00	1306.25	1534.75	1561.00	1475.00	1286.00	1230.00	783.00
29 AR3	Q3 OF AR	2102.0	49.000	795.000	1503.00	1658.75	1798.00	1957.00	2078.25	2162.00	2266.75	2356.00	2461.00	2357.50	2198.25	2070.00	1838.00
30 AAM	MEAN OF AA	1626.6	49.000	576.452	940.47	1167.53	1329.61	1525.11	1671.97	1755.09	1872.93	2136.09	2099.74	1974.12	1823.78	1640.33	1415.47
31 AA2	MEDIAN OF AA	1570.0	49.000	197.000	780.00	1175.50	1291.00	1486.00	1596.00	1634.00	1732.00	2005.00	1996.00	1842.00	1638.00	1544.00	1419.00
32 AA1	Q1 OF AA	1008.0	49.000	90.000	216.00	372.75	561.00	914.00	1115.00	1203.00	1306.25	1534.75	1561.00	1475.00	1286.00	1230.00	783.00
33 AA3	Q3 OF AA	2102.0	49.000	795.000	1503.00	1658.75	1798.00	1957.00	2078.25	2162.00	2266.75	2356.00	2461.00	2357.50	2198.25	2070.00	1838.00

Means and quartiles of income, consumption, and assets, 1979, two-or-more-person families, other than workers, ¥10,000

Age class			All	<20	21–25	26–30	31–35	36–40	41–45	46–50	51–55	56–60	61–65	66–70	71–75	76–80	81–85	≥86
		Number of observations	5357.0	4.000	63.00	615.00	1417.00	2005.00	2183.00	2050.00	1634.00	1621.00	1623.00	1187.00	615.00	246.00	76.00	18.00
2	YDM	MEAN OF YD	397.0	286.750	301.87	321.12	361.13	398.83	424.72	467.58	509.91	453.60	347.07	271.18	245.32	228.89	205.09	295.39
3	YD2	MEDIAN OF YD	343.0	278.300	276.00	276.00	312.00	348.00	371.00	408.00	449.50	399.00	282.00	186.00	168.00	114.50	72.00	131.50
4	YD1	Q1 OF YD	217.0	211.500	167.00	204.00	230.00	248.00	263.00	280.00	296.75	252.00	152.00	76.00	48.00	25.75	2.25	25.75
5	YD3	Q3 OF YD	500.0	370.250	349.00	388.00	421.50	476.00	501.00	578.00	637.25	587.00	467.00	372.00	332.00	322.75	291.00	549.75
6	YLDM	MEAN OF YLD	333.3	278.750	276.97	294.41	323.35	354.58	369.35	399.59	430.62	371.96	270.56	204.48	179.45	166.58	154.54	173.94
7	YLD2	MEDIAN OF YLD	289.0	272.500	245.00	258.00	281.00	306.00	324.00	351.00	380.50	326.00	213.00	121.00	92.00	71.00	15.50	40.00
8	YLD1	Q1 OF YLD	175.0	206.000	163.00	189.00	206.00	218.00	222.00	238.00	244.75	187.50	97.00	25.00	0.00	0.00	0.00	0.00
9	YLD3	Q3 OF YLD	437.0	357.750	326.00	358.00	382.00	428.00	446.00	491.25	545.00	486.00	377.00	291.00	242.00	208.50	209.75	273.00
10	ZLXM	MEAN OF ZLX	266.3	199.250	270.67	308.05	304.92	335.67	324.12	365.43	361.50	330.97	119.50	0.00	0.00	0.00	0.00	0.00
11	ZLX2	MEDIAN OF ZLX	274.0	221.500	266.00	293.00	272.00	299.00	277.00	320.00	315.00	281.00	0.00	0.00	0.00	0.00	0.00	0.00
12	ZLX1	Q1 OF ZLX	165.0	128.000	256.00	257.00	261.00	279.00	260.00	279.00	265.75	234.00	0.00	0.00	0.00	0.00	0.00	0.00
13	ZLX3	Q3 OF ZLX	372.0	248.250	275.00	341.00	348.00	386.00	373.00	431.25	428.50	433.00	249.00	0.00	0.00	0.00	0.00	0.00
14	ZLM	MEAN OF ZL	377.6	284.105	295.11	318.78	354.88	390.32	411.58	446.87	482.05	425.46	317.67	243.13	217.75	201.32	179.57	246.52
15	ZL2	MEDIAN OF ZL	329.0	277.095	251.03	275.83	305.27	340.48	351.46	391.78	428.31	372.36	259.71	165.19	140.07	94.54	50.83	111.48
16	ZL1	Q1 OF ZL	206.4	209.623	167.31	204.27	225.87	243.41	256.01	269.62	286.09	237.02	136.75	59.25	36.10	16.69	−0.26	15.11
17	ZL3	Q3 OF ZL	480.0	365.596	348.66	386.66	416.28	467.99	485.51	555.99	610.25	553.66	427.20	341.59	295.44	283.01	277.36	448.82
18	YDAM	MEAN OF YDA	309.2	178.250	246.35	251.35	277.29	308.09	331.87	358.62	338.83	318.35	284.63	264.18	247.31	227.82	203.33	295.06
19	YDA2	MEDIAN OF YDA	276.0	178.000	221.00	234.00	258.00	282.00	309.00	320.00	311.00	277.00	246.00	229.00	211.00	179.50	169.50	202.50
20	YDA1	Q1 OF YDA	203.5	130.750	161.00	187.00	204.00	223.00	238.00	235.00	227.00	203.00	183.00	158.00	144.00	130.00	108.00	155.75
21	YDA3	Q3 OF YDA	370.0	226.000	263.00	297.00	326.00	362.00	391.00	430.00	377.00	377.00	342.00	326.00	310.00	304.25	258.25	405.00
22	CONSM	MEAN OF CONS	1726.4	243.000	770.29	973.49	1269.66	1458.61	1624.81	1870.24	2046.83	2014.38	1971.17	1839.05	1864.59	1847.34	1627.32	2355.94
23	CONS2	MEDIAN OF CONS	1579.0	141.000	215.00	822.00	1258.00	1458.00	1525.00	1663.00	1769.50	1781.00	1785.00	1565.00	1636.00	1515.00	1423.00	1804.50
24	CONS1	Q1 OF CONS	948.5	28.500	127.00	147.00	311.00	595.00	890.00	1091.25	1162.00	1165.00	1160.00	1038.00	1080.00	964.75	980.25	1307.50
25	CONS3	Q3 OF CONS	2295.0	559.500	1517.00	1672.00	1923.00	2074.00	2206.00	2371.25	2602.25	2570.00	2512.00	2351.00	2398.00	2290.75	2132.75	3255.25
26	ARM	MEAN OF AR	2558.2	248.500	889.27	1234.83	1666.72	2020.09	2276.32	2578.70	2867.50	2932.85	3398.80	3351.68	3125.64	2860.86	2448.07	3075.50
27	AR2	MEDIAN OF AR	2424.0	218.500	386.00	1083.00	1655.00	2014.00	2175.00	2382.00	2609.50	2708.00	3237.00	3085.00	2920.00	2538.00	2185.50	2630.50
28	AR1	Q1 OF AR	1704.5	−45.750	258.00	422.00	727.00	1170.00	1526.00	1798.75	1978.50	2080.00	2592.00	2543.00	2327.00	1974.00	1639.00	1861.25
29	AR3	Q3 OF AR	3227.0	572.750	1659.00	1941.00	2333.00	2649.50	2887.00	3092.00	3472.75	3507.50	4009.00	3854.00	3646.00	3259.50	3046.00	4204.25
30	AAM	MEAN OF AA																
31	AA2	MEDIAN OF AA																
32	AA1	Q1 OF AA																
33	AA3	Q3 OF AA																

a. Definition of symbols for tables 7.9A and 7.9B:

YD: Current disposable income. Conceptually, it is net of personal income taxes, and also excludes social security contributions by employees; on the other hand, it excludes the social security benefits. This definition was chosen to make it as consistent as possible with AA, defined below, when both components of AA are introduced into the consumption function. YLD: YD less net income from property ownership. ZLX: Estimated "lifetime" labor income between the current period and retirement. ZL: Estimated "lifetime" labor income, the first stage result. YDA: YD adjusted for real capital gains or loss due to the ownership of nominally fixed assets and/or liabilities under inflation. CON: Consumption; it includes gross service flow of consumer durables. AR: Net worth, conventional definition to the extent that data permit. It includes financial assets and liabilities, including, in principle, those indirectly owned through unincorporated businesses, estimated market value of the principal residence, and estimated value of the stock of consumer durables, but does not include the value of real estate properties other than the principal residence, real properties and the value of good will, etc., owned through unincorporated businesses. AA = AR + AS; AS is the net present value of the social security benefits less contributions, plus the present value of the expected lump sums retirement benefits.

Table 7.9B
Means and quartiles of income, consumption, and assets, 1974, two-or-more-person families, workers, ¥10,000

Age class		All	<20	21–25	26–30	31–35	36–40	41–45	46–50	51–55	56–60	61–65	66–70	71–75	76–80	81–85	≥86
	Number of observations	33346.0	50.00	1100.00	3902.00	6173.00	6121.00	5778.00	4558.00	2789.00	1689.00	799.00	292.00	81.00	13.00	1.00	.
2	YDM MEAN OF YD	245.8	166.58	172.05	196.96	218.91	239.81	260.94	288.98	302.13	291.83	228.61	182.99	137.34	120.69	377.00	.
3	YD2 MEDIAN OF YD	225.0	152.50	159.00	183.00	203.00	224.00	246.00	274.00	286.00	269.00	198.00	143.50	121.00	115.00	377.00	.
4	YD1 Q1 OF YD	171.0	100.75	129.00	148.00	166.00	177.00	194.00	208.00	208.00	185.50	128.00	76.25	39.00	75.50	377.00	.
5	YD3 Q3 OF YD	296.0	203.50	199.00	227.25	257.00	288.00	309.00	349.00	378.00	376.00	304.00	256.00	187.50	166.00	377.00	.
6	YLDM MEAN OF YLD	224.0	155.04	161.47	182.98	202.06	220.18	237.86	262.44	273.32	256.34	194.42	147.34	105.42	63.25	357.00	.
7	YLD2 MEDIAN OF YLD	205.0	141.50	150.00	170.00	189.00	206.00	224.00	248.00	259.00	235.00	168.00	117.50	81.00	53.00	357.00	.
8	YLD1 Q1 OF YLD	156.0	98.00	122.00	138.00	152.00	162.00	175.00	190.00	187.00	159.00	103.00	54.50	24.00	9.50	357.00	.
9	YLD3 Q3 OF YLD	273.0	194.50	189.00	210.00	237.00	265.00	283.00	317.00	344.00	329.00	263.00	202.00	154.00	97.50	357.00	.
10	ZLXM MEAN OF ZLX	220.5	151.94	193.52	216.34	213.51	233.61	225.57	246.87	229.03	222.36	102.80	0.00	0.00	0.00	0.00	.
11	ZLX2 MEDIAN OF ZLX	224.0	155.00	193.00	215.00	215.00	235.00	222.00	256.00	238.00	226.00	0.00	0.00	0.00	0.00	0.00	.
12	ZLX1 Q1 OF ZLX	185.0	136.00	168.00	186.00	181.00	198.00	168.00	206.00	190.00	182.00	0.00	0.00	0.00	0.00	0.00	.
13	ZLX3 Q3 OF ZLX	262.0	174.00	226.00	246.00	244.00	272.00	264.00	293.00	276.00	265.00	212.00	0.00	0.00	0.00	0.00	.
14	ZLM MEAN OF ZL	216.4	146.99	159.20	181.53	201.10	218.02	232.02	249.72	255.82	230.17	164.04	110.64	69.25	17.95	309.71	.
15	ZL2 MEDIAN OF ZL	197.1	129.02	145.94	165.29	184.47	200.77	213.79	233.26	241.01	208.18	146.10	92.85	48.39	2.91	309.71	.
16	ZL1 Q1 OF ZL	147.0	85.65	118.65	132.80	146.33	153.97	163.07	172.45	166.78	138.95	79.96	31.49	0.80	−28.86	309.71	.
17	ZL3 Q3 OF ZL	266.2	191.79	186.30	210.50	237.51	264.10	281.53	307.71	322.00	301.04	233.91	172.38	121.99	86.41	309.71	.
18	YDAM MEAN OF YDA	197.2	129.36	147.04	163.80	180.85	192.41	209.47	229.99	226.20	220.02	187.25	174.43	135.90	132.69	279.00	.
19	YDA2 MEDIAN OF YDA	184.0	113.50	147.00	155.00	172.00	184.00	201.00	218.00	226.00	199.00	166.00	160.50	125.00	104.00	279.00	.
20	YDA1 Q1 OF YDA	145.0	94.75	112.00	128.00	141.00	149.00	161.00	170.00	158.00	148.00	124.00	115.25	92.00	76.00	279.00	.
21	YDA3 Q3 OF YDA	233.0	145.25	171.00	188.00	209.00	223.00	245.00	274.00	277.00	267.50	221.00	205.75	163.50	157.50	279.00	.
22	CONSM MEAN OF CONS	955.9	472.14	396.92	579.44	789.75	936.46	1064.17	1156.83	1219.84	1319.47	1266.55	1293.74	1102.02	1220.38	1017.00	.
23	CONS2 MEDIAN OF CONS	958.0	116.00	472.14	184.00	577.00	950.00	1103.00	1164.00	1210.00	1279.00	1223.00	1255.00	1012.00	1051.00	1017.00	.
24	CONS1 Q1 OF CONS	176.0	53.75	116.00	95.00	132.00	187.00	333.50	575.00	720.00	732.50	687.00	757.75	348.00	149.00	1017.00	.
25	CONS3 Q3 OF CONS	1471.0	1019.75	443.00	1082.25	1355.00	1449.00	1515.00	1580.00	1622.50	1787.50	1717.00	1709.75	1498.50	1862.00	1017.00	.
26	ARM MEAN OF AR	1754.5	642.74	758.11	1101.49	1396.04	1969.68	1943.97	2221.96	2322.84	2362.60	2178.18	2060.33	1756.95	1775.77	1812.00	.
27	AR2 MEDIAN OF AR	1710.0	319.50	544.00	857.00	1244.00	1649.00	1933.50	2206.00	2322.00	2309.00	2160.00	2045.00	1655.00	1544.00	1812.00	.
28	AR1 Q1 OF AR	941.0	160.75	330.50	522.00	704.00	965.00	1263.75	1556.75	1682.00	1643.00	1562.00	1506.00	1062.00	706.50	1812.00	.
29	AR3 Q3 OF AR	2422.0	1108.50	1033.25	1551.50	1985.50	2299.00	2531.25	2796.00	2905.00	2993.50	2678.00	2498.75	2094.00	2425.50	1812.00	.
30	AAM MEAN OF AA																
31	AA2 MEDIAN OF AA																
32	AA1 Q1 OF AA																
33	AA3 Q3 OF AA																

Means and quartiles of income, consumption, and assets, 1979, two-or-more-person families, workers, ¥10,000

Age class	All	<20	21–25	26–30	31–35	36–40	41–45	46–50	51–55	56–60	61–65	66–70	71–75	76–80	81–85	≥86
Number of observations	34424.00	32.000	654.00	4050.00	6287.00	6553.00	5748.00	4852.00	3660.00	1616.00	661.00	250.00	51.00	9.00	1.00	.
YDM MEAN OF YD	408.4	220.656	270.43	315.96	352.41	393.43	432.27	476.46	516.51	485.09	361.03	307.77	262.39	190.00	82.00	.
YD2 MEDIAN OF YD	383.0	200.000	248.50	294.00	336.00	378.00	416.00	462.00	497.00	484.00	343.00	270.00	198.00	210.00	82.00	.
YD1 Q1 OF YD	294.0	158.750	201.75	244.75	278.00	308.00	330.25	361.00	387.00	333.00	206.50	146.50	123.00	103.30	82.00	.
YD3 Q3 OF YD	488.0	269.750	319.00	365.00	403.00	459.00	505.00	568.75	641.00	618.00	480.00	407.25	394.00	255.00	82.00	.
YLDM MEAN OF YLD	369.0	208.031	252.40	290.26	321.68	358.67	392.14	431.13	462.46	417.64	295.44	243.46	202.86	138.78	37.00	.
YLD2 MEDIAN OF YLD	345.0	185.000	235.00	271.00	307.00	344.00	379.00	415.00	453.00	405.00	275.00	203.00	155.00	108.00	37.00	.
YLD1 Q1 OF YLD	266.0	155.250	190.00	224.00	252.00	281.00	298.00	326.00	342.00	272.00	156.50	97.50	44.00	64.50	37.00	.
YLD3 Q3 OF YLD	450.0	262.000	296.25	333.00	372.00	420.00	466.00	513.00	570.00	532.00	407.00	349.25	317.00	249.00	37.00	.
ZLXM MEAN OF ZLX	364.6	248.000	316.63	350.30	338.96	378.41	366.35	411.29	407.32	380.48	152.24	0.00	0.00	0.00	0.00	.
ZLX2 MEDIAN OF ZLX	362.0	233.000	304.00	343.00	335.00	375.00	360.00	404.00	398.00	370.00	0.00	0.00	0.00	0.00	0.00	.
ZLX1 Q1 OF ZLX	293.0	206.000	255.00	284.00	280.00	312.50	296.25	331.00	328.00	289.00	0.00	0.00	0.00	0.00	0.00	.
ZLX3 Q3 OF ZLX	425.0	292.250	365.00	402.00	387.00	434.00	415.00	476.16	477.00	445.00	308.00	0.00	0.00	0.00	0.00	.
ZLM MEAN OF ZL	398.4	216.919	266.18	310.84	347.41	387.70	422.96	463.16	498.46	460.23	335.06	279.72	235.52	169.97	65.62	.
ZL2 MEDIAN OF ZL	374.6	196.400	245.52	289.88	332.09	372.63	407.60	447.56	481.83	438.88	318.00	247.49	177.75	157.19	65.62	.
ZL1 Q1 OF ZL	289.0	158.037	197.67	240.21	273.19	303.09	322.98	347.56	377.19	314.97	187.47	135.34	90.94	93.14	65.68	.
ZL3 Q3 OF ZL	478.7	266.774	310.81	358.11	400.89	452.58	495.50	551.90	615.43	585.86	452.91	379.61	361.91	255.00	65.62	.
YDAM MEAN OF YDA	308.4	177.281	226.62	248.68	273.83	296.68	321.82	359.70	372.50	336.70	302.64	280.06	280.78	239.56	201.00	.
YDA2 MEDIAN OF YDA	285.0	166.500	212.00	235.00	260.00	285.00	307.00	338.00	346.50	310.00	267.00	251.50	251.00	209.00	201.00	.
YDA1 Q1 OF YDA	228.0	136.250	175.00	195.00	216.00	237.00	251.00	265.25	258.00	227.25	197.00	180.75	174.00	142.00	201.00	.
YDA3 Q3 OF YDA	362.0	197.750	262.00	284.00	314.00	342.00	372.00	427.00	451.00	414.00	379.50	340.25	366.00	331.50	201.00	.
CONSM MEAN OF CONS																.
CONS2 MEDIAN OF CONS																.
CONS1 Q1 OF CONS																.
CONS3 Q3 OF CONS																.
ARM MEAN OF AR	1340.9	336.938	515.55	770.49	1059.49	1293.74	1464.46	1615.53	1761.00	1900.40	1819.47	1902.18	1795.45	1027.33	1266.00	.
AR2 MEDIAN OF AR	1326.0	118.000	186.00	336.00	936.00	1319.00	1479.00	1561.50	1673.00	1728.50	1682.00	1706.50	1686.00	1113.00	1266.00	.
AR1 Q1 OF AR	391.0	65.750	98.00	151.00	236.00	425.00	786.25	1009.50	1116.25	1161.00	1119.00	1038.50	888.00	208.00	1266.00	.
AR3 Q3 OF AR	1970.0	252.000	733.75	1341.00	1725.00	1906.50	2041.75	2157.00	2294.50	2477.00	2449.50	2611.25	2363.00	1539.00	1266.00	.
AAM MEAN OF AA	2782.6	622.000	1239.60	1791.04	2191.06	2672.15	2948.77	3416.14	3721.94	3669.52	3480.51	3451.88	3106.92	2044.44	2291.00	.
AA2 MEDIAN OF AA	2695.5	459.500	991.50	1573.50	2105.00	2643.00	2921.00	3345.50	3659.50	3515.50	3326.00	3244.50	2974.00	2058.00	2291.00	.
AA1 Q1 OF AA	1757.0	246.250	586.75	1012.00	1289.00	1839.00	2091.00	2491.00	2742.00	2595.25	2624.00	2503.25	2254.00	1274.00	2291.00	.
AA3 Q3 OF AA	3670.0	856.750	1799.50	2413.00	2924.00	3439.50	3750.75	4255.00	4584.50	4593.00	4150.00	4187.25	3893.00	2724.00	2291.00	.

on the value of real estate other than principal residence, and most of the value of unincorporated businesses. The balance sheet items were measured at only one time, so that savings must be estimated as income minus consumption. For these reasons, we have attempted to work mostly with income, consumption, and the value of net worth and have avoided working with savings. We had at our disposal the results of surveys of 1974 and 1979.

We present in table 7.9 the age profile of income, consumption, and net worth for two-or-more-person households, separately for workers and nonworkers. If we take these tables at their face value, it appears that there is some positive savings for all age classes; that is, the standard definition of net worth of households (AR) does not decline significantly after the retirement age of late 50s. Thus, when the growth of productivity per capita is taken into account, we must conclude that net worth of households continues to rise at all ages. This is not the case when we include the net present value of social security benefits less contributions as a part of the household net worth ($AA \equiv AR + AS$) as in the case of the United States. There are a number of serious difficulties in estimating AS, in addition to the question of what the perception of households on the value of AS might be, so that we concentrate our attention on AR in the rest of this section.[16,17]

The sociological environment in which families make a living, including intergenerational relationships, is very different in Japan from that in the United States, and we must note some features that may affect the savings behavior significantly. First, Japanese workers retire early, generally between the ages of 55 and 58, unless they are promoted to be officers of corporations, that is, top ten or fifteen executives. Small entrepreneurs and independent professionals, such as doctors (there are relatively few lawyers), are also exceptions. This feature, coupled with the fact that wives are on average 4 or 5 years younger than husbands, makes the retirement life of most Japanese families considerably longer than that in the United States. Second, primarily because of the extraordinarily high relative price of residential land, older individuals, except those who are unusually wealthy, tend to merge into younger households as they become older. For those who retire, the time of retirement is the natural occasion for the merger, while those who are really poor and must work for whatever small compensation that they may be able to obtain would merge earlier.[18] Of those aged 60, some 40% are living in households headed by a younger person, while of those who are above 65, some 70% are living in younger households. Finally, as a consequence of the processes described above, those who are above the normal retirement age and maintaining independent households tend to be quite wealthy, and this affluent condition at old age has not been anticipated by at least some of them.[19] The recognition of this situation leads us to suspect the presence of serious sampling biases if households in the survey of independent households are treated as a standard normal sample from the entire population. This suspicion was not confirmed in our investigation of the US data, in spite of an extensive formal analysis, but the possibility seems much more serious in Japan with its institutional and family structures.[20]

Taking advantage of the somewhat more detailed information we possess on the demographic characteristics of older persons living in younger households, we shall attempt a different approach to this problem in the Japanese case from the one that we followed in the US case. We will first deal with the savings behavior of those households whose heads are younger than the retirement age or just recently retired, with careful attention to the effects of the presence of older persons in these households. Second, we shall more directly investigate the contribution of the presence of older persons of specific age to the total net worth of the host households, given that we do not know the value of net worth of older persons separately if they are living in a younger household. Finally, we shall analyze separately savings behavior of older persons maintaining independent households.

Equation (16), estimated for households whose heads are younger than the normal retirement age, or immediately after retirement and still remaining independent, is similar to equation (13), used for the US data, although the exact form and definitions of variables are not identical, reflecting differences in availability of data and social conventions in two countries (definitions of variables are given in footnotes to table 7.10):

$$\frac{C(i)}{ZLX(F_j^*, i)} = \sum_a b(a)D(a)\frac{AR(i)}{ZLX(F_j^*, i)} + k_1\frac{AS(i)}{ZLX(F_j^*, i)}$$

$$+ k_2\frac{1}{ZLX(F_j^*, i)} + \sum h(F_j)D(F_j) \tag{16}$$

$$+ h_0 + h_1 DD3 + v(i).$$

The results of estimating this equation using data for 1974 and for 1979 are reported in table 7.10. We have allowed the marginal propensity to consume ZLX, h_0, to take on different values for the top and bottom quartiles of the distribution of ZLX in each age class, taking care to ensure that the consumption function is continuous at points where breaks occur.

Table 7.10
Consumption function for households aged less than 63, summary results[a]

| | All households | | | | Worker households | | | |
| | Without DD3 | | With DD3 | | Without DD3 | | With DD3 | |
	Coefficient	T-ratio	Coefficient	T-ratio	Coefficient	T-ratio	Coefficient	T-ratio
Intercept	0.367	44.3	0.426	48.2	0.453	47.0	0.490	47.8
1/ZLX	28.035	35.2	22.453	26.5	25.212	27.5	21.726	22.3
AR1	0.037	39.2	0.038	40.1	0.033	32.7	0.034	33.2
AR2	0.031	46.0	0.030	44.7	0.027	34.3	0.027	33.4
AR3	0.031	46.4	0.026	44.2	0.026	32.1	0.025	30.7
AR4	0.027	35.8	0.026	33.7	0.023	22.8	0.022	21.2
AR5	0.026	35.4	0.026	35.3	0.024	19.3	0.023	18.6
AS	0.010	12.0	0.007	7.5	0.001	1.0	−0.001	−0.9
F1	0.104	17.4	0.104	17.5	0.117	18.4	0.118	18.7
F2	0.052	12.2	0.049	11.7	0.039	8.1	0.037	7.8
F3	0.075	17.5	0.072	16.9	0.057	11.8	0.055	11.4
F4	0.108	19.5	0.107	19.3	0.090	13.9	0.088	13.6
F5	0.054	11.8	0.052	11.5	0.049	9.4	0.050	9.5
F6	0.057	8.9	0.061	9.5	0.073	9.1	0.079	9.9
F7	0.054	5.1	0.071	6.5	0.053	3.6	0.073	4.9
L1	0.049	11.7	0.051	12.2	0.044	9.4	0.046	9.7
L2	0.063	9.0	0.069	9.8	0.054	7.0	0.059	7.6
M1	0.013	−2.6	−0.011	−2.2	−0.017	−3.2	−0.015	−2.9
M2	0.008	2.2	0.004	1.1	0.007	1.7	0.005	1.1
H1	0.113	21.3	0.106	19.9	0.080	13.0	0.075	12.1
H2	0.085	12.4	0.075	11.1	0.056	7.7	0.049	6.7
H3	0.064	10.7	0.059	9.9	0.029	4.5	0.025	3.9
H4	0.047	3.1	0.042	2.8	0.025	1.6	0.021	1.3
SEX	0.041	6.2	0.061	9.1	0.073	10.0	0.086	11.7
DD3	—		−0.307	−18.6	—		−0.239	−10.4
R²	0.165		0.171		0.140		0.143	
MSE	0.096		0.095		0.086		0.085	
DFE	47534		47533		35328		35327	

a. Dependent variable is C/ZLX.

Definition of symbols:

$F1$: Presence of spouse for the head of household. $F2$: Presence of one child. $F3$: Presence of the second child. $F4$: Presence of the third and more children. $F5$: Presence of one adult other than the head and his (her) spouse. $F6$: Presence of the second adult other than the head and his (her) spouse. $F7$: Presence of the third or more adult other than the head and his (her) spouse. $L1$: Presence of one person above the age of 56 other than the head and his (her) spouse. $L2$: Presence of two or more persons above the age of 56 other than the head and his (her) spouse. $M1$: Household is located in a large city. $M2$: Household is located in rural area. $H1$: Household lives in an independent rental unit owned and operated by the private individual or organization. $H2$: Household lives in a rental unit owned and operated by public agency. $H3$: Household lives in facilities provided by the employer. $H4$: Household lives in a rental room without exclusive kitchen and bathroom facilities, owned and operated by private agencies. SEX: The head of household is female. $DD3$: $d4*(1 - (ZLX3/ZLX))$, where $d4$ is one-zero dummy indicating that the household is in the 4th quartile of ZLX in his age group ($ZLX3$ is the value of ZLX dividing the 3rd and 4th quartiles of ZLX in the age group). ZLX: Estimated "lifetime" labor income between current period and the retirement. AR: Net worth of the household, excluding social security wealth. AS: Social security wealth. ARa: $D(a)*AR$. $D(a)$: Dummy for age class a: $a = 1$, 29 and under; $a = 2$, 30–39; $a = 3$, 40–49; $a = 4$, 50–57; $a = 5$, 58–63. C: Consumption, including services of durables but excluding purchases of durables.

It turned out that the change was not significant for the bottom quartile, while it was for the top quartile, and therefore we have retained the variable $DD3$. We also allowed for the constant term k_2, which is quite large and significant. However, it is larger for 1979 than for 1974, and the change in its value is almost exactly that amount which ensures the ratio of the mean value of consumption to the mean of ZLX to remain the same in both years. The presence of k_2 can therefore be interpreted as indicating the dependence of the consumption income ratio for households on its relative position in the income distribution, not the dependence of the consumption income ratio on the absolute level of income.[21]

Coefficients of demographic characteristics are more or less as we would have expected them. We merely call the attention of the reader to the coefficients of $L1$ and $L2$, dummies indicating the first and second elderly persons in the family. Coefficients of these variables indicate that the marginal propensity to consume ZLX by a household tends to increase by around .05 for each elderly person present. We shall wish to contrast this value with another statistical result to be reported later on.

The coefficient of AR should have increased with age, while in our estimates it appears to decline with age, though only slightly. It is, on the other hand, positive and very significant. We have therefore evidence supporting the proposition that if the household has accumulated larger net worth given its permanent labor income, it will consume relatively more, but we do not have supporting evidence for the finer point of the life cycle theory.

The coefficient of AS, on the other hand, is extremely small, and for all workers it is not significant. This result is consistent with the US case reported earlier, but it is not in accordance with the more common perception of the role of this variable, namely, that such a well-understood social security program should substantially reduce the need of private individuals to make provisions for their old age on their own, and therefore it should reduce private saving. We believe that our result is at least partially due to the difficulty of estimating AS, which is based on statutory provisions and on only minimal information concerning earnings history and prospects for individual households. Thus, it is possible, even probable, that the total variance of AS is denominated by the error of measurement, and this may be the reason why its coefficient is so small.

We now turn to the savings behavior of older persons. As we have indicated earlier, we must separately consider two groups, those that remain independent households and those that have merged into younger households. The basic feature of the former group is that virtually all people in this group continue to save regardless of their age,[22] and therefore their behavior is inconsistent with the standard version of the life cycle theory. This is fairly apparent from simple tabulations such as table 7.9, and it is reconfirmed by an estimated savings function.

As we have indicated earlier, the majority of Japanese become submerged into younger households soon after their retirement at a relatively early age. In some sense, therefore, the behavior of this group can be more important than that of older persons who remain independent. Unfortunately, since they are dependent members of younger households, there is little information on their income, wealth, and consumption separate from those of families in which they have become members. We must, therefore, infer their behavior essentially by comparing behavior of two groups of families that are similar in most respects except that in one group there is one or more older persons present while in the other there is no older person living with them.

By constructing a table similar to table 7.9 covering only those families in which no older persons are present, we can infer that the net worth of households on average and without contribution from older persons merging into them reaches about four to five times their ZLX by the time they are in the age interval of 55–60. Obviously, when these families retire and merge into younger households, they bring along accumulated net worth with them, so that the total net worth of the younger households must increase by this amount (since assets and liabilities of a household are reported in the survey without regard to specific ownership positions by members of the family).

This suggests that a potentially useful analysis can be based on a regression of the following form:

$$\frac{AR}{ZLX} = a_0 + a_1(\text{age}) + a_2(\text{age})^2 + a_3(\text{age})^3 + \sum_{i=1}^{4} b_i^M LMi$$

$$+ \sum_{i=1}^{4} b_i^F LFi + \sum_{i=1}^{4} b_i^{MF} LMFi + \sum_{i=1}^{4} b_i^{FF} LFFi + \varepsilon. \tag{17}$$

AR and ZLX are net worth and lifetime income, respectively, of the younger household to which the older person has merged; age is the age of the head of the younger household; LMi, LFi, $LMFi$, and $LFFi$ are all one-zero dummies indicating the presence of older person (male, female, male and female, and two females, respectively; there are only a few households containing two older males, and they have been dropped from the analysis) in the ith age group. The index i ranges from 1 to 4, and indicates age classes 57–63, 64–70, 71–77, and 78 and over, respectively. When there are a male and a female both present, the age of the male is used, while when two females are present, the age of the older person is used. a and b are coefficients to be estimated.

The polynomial in age traces the pattern of asset accumulation relative to the lifetime income by a household in the absence of older persons.[23] Coefficients b would then measure net contribution of the presence of older person of a particular age class to the net worth of the household, expressed as the ratio of the lifetime income of that household. Note that by construction ZLX is not likely to be affected much by the presence of older persons in the household, except that it is affected slightly by family size. The result of the estimation of the above equation is reported in table 7.11.

Coefficients b are all positive and highly significant, and within each type of older persons, b declines with age, indicating that the net contribution to the net worth of households by the presence of older persons declines with the age of older persons. The value for the youngest group (aged 57–63) ranges between 2.2 and 3.5 for 1974 and 1.8 and 2.2 for 1979. We are not quite sure why the values for 1974 are so much larger than those for 1979, but we believe that those for 1979 make somewhat better sense. Families on average complete their working lives just before their heads become 60, with net worth 4–6 times their lifetime labor income at an annual rate. Since the annual lifetime income of the younger households to which they become merged is larger by the factor of 2 or more because of the increase in productivity per man-hour, it makes sense that the contribution to the net worth of the younger household by the older person when he or she becomes merged is roughly 2 to 3 times the lifetime income at an annual rate of the younger household.

The decline of the coefficients b as the older person ages must then indicate that there is some dissaving by older persons, or reduced saving activities by younger households after older persons join them. The age interval of older persons that we have used is such that there is an interval of a little less than 25 years between the average age in the first group and the average age in the last group, and the decline in the coefficient b is roughly 1.5 for 1979. This means that the presence of an older person increases the consumption of the household on average by a little more than .05 times ZLX. We can now recall that the coefficient of the dummy for the presence of an older person in the consumption function reported in table 7.10 is approximately .05.[24]

This is still not evidence that this group of the Japanese population

Table 7.11
Asset accumulation pattern over age, families aged 58 and under[a]

Variable	1974		1979	
	Coefficient	T-ratio	Coefficient	T-ratio
Intercept	−12.083967	−14.8147	−9.515979	−13.9217
AGE	0.947874	13.7631	0.723214	12.5537
$(AGE)^2$	−0.019633	−10.5872	−0.014396	−9.2797
$(AGE)^3$	0.0001528096	9.5546	0.0001123425	8.3886
LM1	3.883178	13.4614	2.182068	8.8155
LM2	2.221983	9.0133	1.904090	7.8982
LM3	1.475498	6.8077	1.085472	5.8547
LM4	1.185092	5.3174	0.610073	3.3666
LF1	2.441817	19.9549	1.774731	15.8424
LF2	1.686383	16.8818	1.152970	13.5165
LF3	1.391266	14.1512	0.647339	7.8655
LF4	1.282799	10.9219	0.717683	7.5544
LFF1	3.108590	5.3353	1.899177	4.4102
LFF2	3.319778	4.2020	1.479244	2.6333
LFF3	1.839642	0.8068	1.577802	1.6654
LFF4	−1.090871	−0.2762	0	
LMF1	3.474151	11.4247	2.125319	9.8045
LMF2	2.718184	17.4396	1.848275	15.6133
LMF3	1.959807	13.3471	1.320812	11.6382
LMF4	1.685286	8.9342	0.743134	5.2568
R^2	0.1718		0.1769	
MSE	15.593038		11.661401	
DFE	45253		46586	

a. Definition of symbols (dependent variable: AR/ZLX^*; see footnotes to table 7.10 for definition of AR and ZLX^*):

AGE Age of the head of households

LMi One-zero dummy variable for the presence of male older person in the household of ith age class: $i = 1 \to$ age 57–63, $i = 2 \to$ age 64–70, $i = 3 \to$ 71–77, $i = 4 \to$ 78 and over

LFi One-zero dummy variable for the presence of female older persons of ith age class

LMFi One-zero dummy variable for the presence of male and female older persons of ith age class; age refers to the age of the male

LFFi One-zero dummy variable for the presence of two female older persons of age class i; age refers to that of the older person follows the hump-shaped asset accumulation and decumulation pattern popularized by the early literature on the life cycle theory. The pattern presented by coefficients b is that of a cross section of age groups. That is, it is not the pattern followed by a specific age group over time. In order to convert the former to the latter, we must assume, among other things, stability of the pattern among different generations, a very simple pattern over time of the rate of growth of productivity per man-hour, and so on. The resulting pattern depends of course on the choice of assumptions, and its details are not very meaningful, but some basic characteristics appear to prevail under any reasonable choice of assumptions. Net worth does decline moderately after retirement, but even at a very advanced age, older individuals are still carrying a fairly substantial amount of net worth, say roughly one-half of the net worth possessed at the time of their retirement.

Thus, we have, for the first time in our investigation of micro data in the United States and in Japan, reasonably clear evidence indicating that a group of substantial size in the population does follow a hump-shaped asset accumulation pattern. It should be emphasized, however, that evidence is for a very moderate hump shape. First of all, even members of this group by no means reduce the level of net worth to zero at the end of their lives, but only to about a half to a third of its peak. Second, some of these older persons die at various ages before they reach 80 years of age, and the earlier they die, the more bequest they leave behind, perhaps unintentionally.

One should also remember that there is a sizable group, though a minority, of older persons who maintain independent households and continue to earn relatively high income and to save an exceptionally large portion of their income, thus contradicting the classical hump pattern of asset accumulation. Indeed, our preliminary calculations indicate that saving by independent older households outweighs dissaving of older persons living in younger households; that is, even if we had explicit observations on older persons living in younger households, the population mean of net worth by age class including these persons will not exhibit the classical hump shape over age. We must conclude, therefore, that only a part of Japanese households follows the standard life cycle pattern of saving, and even they conform to the pattern very loosely; that is, at most a half of their peak accumulation of net worth is dissaved before their deaths, on average.

Since there are two very distinct groups of Japanese households with respect to their behavior toward asset holdings when they become older, in order to complete the description of their total behavior, it is essential that we be able to indicate what are the processes by which the probability

Table 7.12
Probit analysis of older individual's residential arrangement[a]

Variable	1974		1979		Both years combined	
	Coefficient	T-ratio	Coefficient	T-ratio	Coefficient	T-ratio
Constant	0.193	5.9	−0.150	−4.6	0.015	0.6
AG2	−0.839	−25.5	−0.797	−25.7	−0.807	−35.9
AG3	−1.635	−41.1	−1.632	−42.0	−1.628	−58.7
AG4	−2.252	−38.5	−2.217	−38.4	−2.239	−54.5
SM	−1.073	−21.5	−0.857	−16.8	−0.957	−26.9
SF	−1.279	−41.8	−0.895	−30.5	−1.089	−51.6
Wealth	1.428	48.0	1.670	53.3	—	—
Wealth 74	—	—	—	—	1.573	63.4
Wealth 79	—	—	—	—	1.509	62.3

a. Definition of symbols:

AGi	Age of the older person in question: $i = 1 \rightarrow 57–63$, $i = 2 \rightarrow 64–70$, $i = 3 \rightarrow 71–77$, $i = 4 \rightarrow 78$ and over
SM	One-zero dummy variable for single males
SF	One-zero dummy variable for single females
Wealth	Estimated value of AR belonging to the older persons (see footnotes for table 7.10 for the definition of AR)

of each household eventually belonging to one group or another is determined. As we have indicated several times, we have very little direct information on economic characteristics of older persons living in younger households as dependents. We know the age and sex of older persons and their relationship to the heads of households. Through the use of the result reported in table 7.11, we could estimate net worth belonging to them, and although we know that the procedure is fraught with dangers of biases, we see no alternative to utilizing this information in explaining the probability with which older households are being absorbed into younger households. Thus, we have attempted to estimate an equation for a binary variable showing whether each older household remains independent or becomes absorbed into a younger household by the probit procedure. The result is reported in table 7.12. It is quite clear that the higher the age, the smaller the wealth, the larger the probability that the older household is absorbed into the younger household. When an older person is single rather than married, and such a single person is a female rather than a male, the probability is also increased.

To complete the picture, we also need to explain what are the characteristics of younger households that make them more likely to absorb older individuals than other households. We have also estimated another equation explaining a binary variable by the probit procedure, whose result is given in table 7.13. This result is not as successful as that given in table 7.12, primarily because the coefficient of $ZLX/\overline{ZLX}$ is unreasonably large. We believe that this is a result of the unfortunate fact that, although the survey itself collected fairly detailed information on the breakdown of total family income into categories according to types of income and to individuals receiving them, in the processes of transcribing them into the working tape, they were grossly aggregated, and we have no way of recovering original details. We suspect that relatively younger older persons contribute small but significant labor income to the households to which they have become absorbed, and this is causing the coefficient of $ZLX/\overline{ZLX}$ to become too large. It is our understanding that, for the 1984 survey, all the details of income will be transcribed to the working tape. Assuming that that is so, an equation such as the one reported in table 7.13, among other things, can be better analyzed when data from the 1984 survey is made available for analysis.

There are a number of additional issues concerning savings behavior of households in Japan that could be studied with this set of data. Among them are a somewhat sharper analysis of the dynamic process using two or three rounds of these surveys together and the role of the extraordinarily high price for land in the savings behavior of Japanese households. Some of them have been analyzed and reported in Ando (1985) with some tantalizing results, suggesting that further research in demand for housing may turn out to be helpful in understanding savings behavior of Japanese households.

7   Do We Have a Story? Consistency between Two Studies, and with Aggregate Data

Economists are judged according to how elegant a story they can tell after they have completed either a large-scale empirical study or a very complex theoretical analysis. By these criteria, a set of studies reported here must be classified as a complete failure. We have started with one of the most elegant theories in economics, and we could not find a way to fit abundant bodies of data into its neat framework. Even in failure, however, we learn something, it is hoped, that points a direction for future research, and in this section we summarize a few features of our findings that may be useful in designing future projects in this area.

On the US side, stripped of many complex details, the basic story is that outside of pension programs, most families save a relatively small portion of their income throughout the period of their active participation in the

Table 7.13
Probit analysis of younger households for housing older members[a]

Variable	1974		1979	
	Coefficient	T-ratio	Coefficient	T-ratio
Constant	−1.417	−52.3	−1.575	−53.1
AGE 2	−0.147	6.0	0.245	9.7
AGE 3	0.256	10.6	0.297	11.8
AGE 4	0.219	8.6	0.210	8.0
AGE 5	−0.049	−1.7	0.003	0.1
SEX	0.250	7.3	0.292	8.5
BCITY	−0.159	−5.8	−0.159	−6.2
RURAL	0.295	16.4	0.435	27.2
ZLX/$\overline{ZLX}$	1.543	17.8	1.443	22.7
OD 3&4	0.033	2.0	−0.080	−4.7
OD 5&6	0.170	8.4	0.122	6.2
OD 7	−0.144	−3.1	−0.327	−7.2
OD 8&9	0.012	0.3	−0.043	−1.0

a. Definition of symbols:

AGEI	Age of the-head of household accepting older person: $i = 1 \rightarrow$ age is less than 20, $i = 2 \rightarrow$ age is 20–29, $i = 3 \rightarrow$ 30–39, $i = 4 \rightarrow$ 40–49, $i = 5 \rightarrow$ 50–58
SEX	One-zero dummy indicating that the head of the household is female
BCITY	One-zero dummy indicating that the household lives in a large city
RURAL	One-zero dummy indicating that the household lives in a rural city
OD 1&2	One-zero dummy indicating that the head of household is a manual worker
OD 3&4	One-zero dummy indicating that the head of household ia a clerical worker
OD 5&6	One-zero dummy indicating that the head household is a merchant, tradesman, or small individual enterpreneur
OD 7	One-zero dummy indicating that the head of household is a corporate manager
OD 8&9	One-zero dummy indicating that the head of household is a self-employed or "other"
$\overline{ZLX}$	Sample mean of ZLX (defined in table 7.10)

labor force, and after they retire, they dissave very little, keeping their assets more or less at the same level. In addition, those families participating in private pension programs do not seem to change their behavior toward assets and liabilities other than the value of pension fund reserves, so that contributions to pension funds, by both employers and employees, and interest earnings on pension reserves appear to constitute additional savings for these families; they then dissave benefits from pension funds after retirement. This pattern comes out qualitatively very clearly in all of our data, but quantitative estimates are uncertain because of data defects. Families appear to behave similarly toward the OASI program; their saving and dissaving pattern for assets and liabilities other than social security wealth appears to be little affected by social security wealth. We have not been able to construct a simple and plausible dynamic optimizing model for families with implications that are consistent with the behavior just described.

This rather fragmented behavior of families has a curious consequence. On average, when contributions to private pension programs and interest earnings on their reserves are treated as a part of savings and benefit payments as a part of dissavings, data will show that there is a substantial life cycle component in the household savings behavior, with a twist: the larger the scale of the private pension program relative to other savings, the larger will be the life cycle component of savings. This is visible even in such crude tabulations as table 7.1, although figures here understate the extent of the life cycle pattern created by private pension programs, since in most cases they do not reflect employer contributions and interest earnings. Paradoxically, the savings behavior of American families is conforming more and more to the life cycle pattern over time, at least superficially, because the private pension programs are becoming a more and more dominant part of total household savings, as aggregate data given in table 7.14 clearly indicate. We are not sure, however, that this is a consequence of well-understood, rational decisions by consumers.

We have attempted to carry out comparisons between tables 7.1 and 7.14 in order to assess the reliability of data on pension fund reserves reported in micro data, but our effort was largely unsuccessful because information in micro data is too incomplete in most cases, while, as noted earlier, the editorial process of SCF83 is still incomplete.

It is especially surprising that in 1960, when private pension programs were still a very small factor and social security benefits were not large enough to cover the cost of living, we cannot detect any evidence of dissaving by older households. We are not entirely sure how older families

Table 7.14
Net worth and pension fund reserves for households,[a] end of selected years ($billion)

	Pension fund reserves	Net worth	Ratio
1945	11	672	.017
1950	24	949	.026
1955	51	1341	.038
1960	91	1752	.052
1972	326	3835	.085
1973	322	3996	.081
1979	699	7700	.091
1983	1322	11161	.118

Personal savings, employer contribution to and benefit paid by private pension and profit sharing programs,[b] selected years ($billion)

	Personal savings	Employer contributions	Benefits
1946	13.7	N.A.	N.A.
1950	11.9	1.7	.4
1955	16.4	3.4	.9
1960	19.7	4.9	1.7
1972	52.6	17.9	10.0
1973	79.0	20.9	11.2
1979	86.2	54.9	27.3
1982	136.0	60.4	45.6
1983	118.1	64.8	N.A.

a. Board of Governors of the Federal Reserve System, *Balance Sheets for the U.S. Economy, 1945–83*, 1985, Washington, DC.
b. Bureau of Economic Analysis, *National Income and Product Accounts*, tables 2.1 and 6.15.

covered their expenses then, although indications are that older persons continued to work after 65 if they were poor. More studies of older data are needed to understand this mystery.

The story of the savings behavior of Japanese households was perhaps more understandable to most of us economists. The behavior of those older individuals who maintain independent households may not be rational in some strict sense, but it might be interpreted as at least partly due to large and unexpected earnings opportunities encountered at old age. The behavior of those who merge into younger households must be viewed as coming to an agreement with the younger household, in which the younger households agree to deliver an annuity plus some contingency services to older persons in exchange for the transfer of assets, to take effect gradually over time. This arrangement closely parallels the idea of older persons buying into a private pension program. The question therefore arises why Japanese families enter into these private, intergenerational arrangements when they could presumably buy annuities from insurance companies, especially when most Japanese individuals appear to buy a good deal more ordinary life insurance policies than Americans do. The answer cannot be that Japanese like to live as extended family units; on the contrary, there seems little question that most Japanese would prefer to live in small family units if they had a choice. The answer is probably related to the extraordinarily high price of land, which makes it economically very attractive for an older couple and a younger couple to share a house, perhaps partitioned.[25]

In any event, at the present time, it seems to us to be the case that the life cycle component of savings generated by these older Japanese who merge into younger households and the one in the United States generated by the private pension programs appear to be similar in order of magnitude. On the other hand, savings by independent older households in Japan appear to be far greater than savings by older American households excluding benefits from private pension programs.

In Japan, the social security programs, especially those for old-age pensions and medical care for older persons, have developed and expanded very rapidly in recent years, so that a further question arises why such an expansion of social security programs did not increase the number of older persons living independently. The answer again seems to be the price of the residence. The price of residence is so high that anything like social security benefits, however generous, cannot be adequate to provide private living quarters for older persons.[26]

We now come to the last question that we wish to address in this paper. As we stated at the beginning of this essay, the life cycle theory appeared to be consistent with aggregate data in a number of senses. But we have been able to produce only a very marginal support for the life cycle behavior at the micro level, and for only a part of the population, while for other groups in the population, evidence that their behavior does not conform to the life cycle theory is quite strong. We may therefore be faced with a serious contradiction.

A simple version of the life cycle model can be used to derive, under some additional assumptions, a proposition that the aggregate consumption should be a linear homogeneous function of aggregate expected labor income and the market value of aggregate net worth, and that the coefficients for these two variables should be mildly affected by the population structure, the rate of growth of real labor income, and the rate of return on assets; the model even predicted the approximate range for the numerical value of these parameters. It turned out that the statistical estimates of these parameters did indeed lie in predicted ranges, at least in the United States. Finally, such an aggregate equation implies an equilibrium ratio of net worth to labor income, which indeed turned out to be very close to the observed ratio of net worth to the labor income for the United States. A more elaborate simulation analysis by Tobin and Dolde (1971) also confirmed these correspondences. We are not prepared at present to address this general question of how findings reported in this paper can be reconciled with estimates obtained using aggregate data, since we believe we must resolve a number of very complex technical issues of aggregation, perhaps through micro simulations, before we can directly address this issue. We have, however, made a somewhat startling discovery concerning a closely related but much simpler question, which we wish to report here because this discovery, at the very least, put the earlier, more general question in a different perspective.

In a recent paper, Kotlikoff and Summers (1981) devised a series of very ingenious computations by which they attempted to answer the following question: Of the total existing net worth of households, how much is due to savings by the currently living population, and how much is due to inheritances that they received from earlier generations? They concluded that as much as 80% of existing wealth has been bequeathed by earlier generations; that is, only 20% of the existing wealth is due to savings by the currently living population. Modigliani (1984) has carefully reviewed the work of Kotlikoff and Summers, and after correcting an algebraic slip and modifying the definition of savings so that it conforms more nearly to the standard conventions, he concluded the opposite, namely, that the inherited portion of existing wealth is between 20% and 30%.

Since we find that older families do not dissave much after their retirement, should we not interpret our results as being more consistent with figures reported by Kotlikoff and Summers rather than with those favored by Modigliani? We also realized that we can make computations analogous to those of Kotlikoff and Summers but much more directly by accepting the well-known estimates of historical aggregate savings dating back to the late nineteenth century provided by Goldsmith (1955).

Before we review our computations, however, we should note an important feature of this computation. Suppose all individuals follow the life cycle pattern of savings strictly, so that there is no bequest left in society at all at any time. That is, all individuals consume all their asset holding completely before their deaths. Then the Kotlikoff-Summers-Modigliani computations will indeed show that all assets in society at any time are due to savings by those who are alive at that time. On the other hand, consider the opposite extreme, namely, the case in which no individual dissaves anything at any time, so that everything a person saves, that person bequeathes to a younger person completely. Even in this case, so long as there is growth in the economy, the total amount of assets must increase, and hence, positive savings takes place and some portion of existing assets must be due to the savings of the currently living population. The proportion depends critically on the rate of growth, and hence, the possibility exists of finding that a very substantial portion of the existing assets is due to savings of the currently living population, and this finding is consistent with rather little dissaving after retirement by most members of society.

Our procedure is as follows. We assume that the relative amounts of total savings due to representative members of different age groups at a given time has been approximately fixed over the relevant history, say over 90 years.[27] Next, we take total savings for the economy provided by Goldsmith as given, and allocate it according to this assumed fixed pattern to members of each age group. We thus have

$$s(i, t) = S_t^*(t) \frac{\sigma(i)}{\sum_{j=21}^{89} \sigma(j)N(j, t)}, \tag{18}$$

$$w(i, t) = \sum_{j=21}^{i} s(j, t - i + j), \tag{19}$$

$$W(t) = \sum_{i=21}^{89} w(i, t)N(i, t), \tag{20}$$

where

$S_t^*(t)$ = aggregate household savings as reported by Goldsmith for year t; it includes net investment in consumer durables and undistributed corporate profits after taxes (in $1972),

$\sigma(i)$ = mean value of saving by a household in age class i in the reference year, i.e., 1972 or 1973; SIS is used for table 7.15, and SISP is used for table 7.16 (in $1972),

$N(i, t)$ = the number of households in age class i in the year t,

$s(i, t)$ = implied saving by a representative household of age class i in year t in $1972,

$w(i, t)$ = implied net worth of a representative household of age class i in year t excluding inheritance and gift received, etc. (in $1972),

$W(t)$ = implied aggregate net worth of the household sector in year t, excluding any inheritance left from those who have died (in $1972).

Table 7.15
Implied aggregate household wealth for the period 1960–1980 generated from saving profiles calculated from the CES72–73 and letting assets at the time of death disappear instead of being bequeathed to younger generations

Year	1972 Profile of SISP[a]	1973 Profile of SISP[a]	Actual value[b]
1960	1513	1630	2475
1961	1573	1695	2675
1962	1631	1759	2635
1963	1697	1830	2785
1964	1779	1918	2936
1965	1878	2021	3105
1966	1984	2132	3094
1967	2089	2240	3352
1968	2188	2343	3597
1969	2264	2422	3455
1970	2318	2479	3417
1971	2450	2632	3593
1972	2563	2756	3842
1973	2689	2894	3767
1974	2778	2994	3543
1975	2887	3112	3662
1976	2999	3235	3892
1977	3113	3359	4038
1978	3240	3495	4323
1979	3347	3611	4452
1980	3405	3667	4549

a. The aggregate saving figure used in the calculation is taken to include undistributed corporate profits; that is, most of the real capital gains by individuals are taken account of.
b. Household net worth, fourth quarter of each year, derived from Board of Governors of the Federal Reserve Board (1985).

Since σ, N, and $S*$ are all known, it is easy to calculate $W(t)$ by means of these formulas. We need to go back as far as 69 (89 − 20) years for this purpose, and ignore a few persons who are alive after 90 years of age and those who earn income and save before they are 21. By construction, $W(t)$ is the net worth that has not been inherited from those who have died; that is, $W(t)$ is the current net worth due only to savings of currently living persons. Earlier death is automatically taken care of by the age distribution of population N. Note that our definition of savings includes corporate retained earnings after taxes, so that the most systematic capital gains by households are taken account of in our calculation.

In table 7.15 we present the result of our calculations together with the actual net worth of the household sector as reported by the Board of Governors of the Federal Reserve System, for the period 1960–1980. Since

Table 7.16
Implied cross section age-wealth profiles for 1972 generated from saving profiles calculated from the CES72–73 and letting all assets held at the time of death of a person disappear instead of letting them be bequeathed to younger generation ($1972)

Savings profile used	SIS for 1972[a]	SIS for 1973[a]	Observed cross-section values[b]
Year for which asset profile is projected	1972	1972	1972
Age			
≤ 25	1581	3746	5415
26–35	7395	10994	11929
36–45	14862	16961	17243
46–55	22075	22041	18434
56–64	24649	24677	19950
65–69	22140	16675	18650
70–74	20536	15228	19004
75–79	19108	16773	19991
≥ 80	17908	14848	19126

a. The aggregate saving figure used in the calculation is defined to include undistributed corporate profits; that is, most of capital gains are taken account of.
b. Derived from the Consumer Expenditure Survey, 1972, net end of year wealth including durables.

the concept used by the Federal Reserve Board includes private pension fund reserves, we use SISP for CES72 and CES73 to compute σ. We can see immediately that our computed value of net worth accounts for two-thirds or a little more of the reported value of net worth. This may be surprising because the savings pattern assumed has only a little dissaving at older age, thus implying that most saving is left to younger generations as bequests. This result would not have arisen if the economy was not growing at a reasonable rate.

Table 7.16 reports a similar result, this time disaggregated to age classes. That is, we report the value of $w(i, t)$ for 1972 against those reported in CES72. The impression created by this table is very similar to that given by table 7.15. Here we have used SIS rather than SISP to compute σ, in order to match the concept of wealth against which we are comparing our calculation.

It is easy to show that this is exactly what we should expect. Consider the following stylized saving model. Suppose that people work R years and then live an additional $T - R$ years. At a given time, working people save $s_0 e^{\pi t}$, where s_0 is an arbitrary initial condition, and the retired people have zero net saving flows. If behavior is homogeneous with respect to growth, proceeding at a constant rate π, then the steady state proportion of total wealth accumulated within the lifetime of the currently living population is given by

$$\phi = 1 - R\pi/[e^{\pi T} - e^{\pi(T-R)}]. \tag{21}$$

If $T \approx 50$, $R \approx 40$, and $\pi \approx .03$, then $\phi \approx .62$.

The value of ϕ is not very different from what Modigliani found to be the upper limit of this proportion. In other words, the order of magnitude of the ratio in question that Modigliani found is very close to being consistent with the world in which virtually no one dissaved after retirement. This ratio, therefore, has virtually no power to discriminate between the world in which the traditional life cycle pattern of savings dominates and another in which everything that is saved during a person's lifetime is left as a bequest.

We now see clearly that the macro savings behavior of households is driven by the rate of growth of the population and technological progress with the consequent rate of growth of aggregate income and its interaction with the demographic structure. Whether or not retired persons dissave does not matter all that much in determining the aggregate savings rate when the rate of growth of aggregate income is substantial. Earlier, we presented some evidence to suggest that the distribution of income also matters, provided that the aggregate real income is growing. These are disturbing findings for some of us who have been modeling aggregate savings behavior on the basis of a simple version of the life cycle theory, and believed that aggregate empirical results confirmed the life cycle theory in some indirect sense.

In order that the life cycle theory continue to serve as a basis for describing the savings behavior of households, a number of substantial modifications are necessary, since in its simpler form it fails to capture some essential features of savings behavior as reflected in data. We need to learn much more about multi-dimensional motivations of individuals and households, and their responses to serious uncertainties they must face, especially at old age. Limitations on their knowledge and their ability to carry out complex computations may also be important. It may be that while the life cycle theory in its elegant simplicity is extremely useful in aiding us in our initial conceptual formulation of a model of savings behavior in the abstract, for the practical purposes of characterizing data on actual behavior, we need to abandon some of its elegance and accept a certain degree of tedious complexity. Any theory, to be useful, must balance simplicity and realism, and in this instance, a movement in the direction of realism appears to be called for.

We have also confronted the danger of not analyzing the process of aggregation in complete detail before "macro implications" of a theory formulated at the level of individuals is asserted, and these "macro implications" can be used to test the validity of the behavioral theory using aggregate data. This point is conceded by most economists in principle, but it is seldom observed in practice. It is probably fair to say that the life cycle theory is one of a few instances in economic analysis where some explicit attention was paid to the problems of aggregation, and yet it now appears that the attention was not close enough, and the asserted correspondence between the micro theory and its "aggregate implications" is far from certain.

It is easy to imagine the existence of similar situations in other areas, where we have been claiming to test implications of theories formulated at the micro level with aggregate data, without specifying in complete detail the process of aggregation. A lesson to be derived from this exercise is that theories formulated at the micro level, econometric estimations of such models using micro data, the analysis of aggregation process, and econometric works at the macro level must all be more systematically integrated than current economics practice requires if we are to make progress in understanding how our economy works.

Notes

1. For a number of reasons, we are covering standard, cross-section data in our current study, leaving out at least for the moment data generated by a panel of households. Among other reasons, a panel usually covers a specific demographic group rather than the whole population, and we have found that the effective drop-out rate, including those whose responses in later dates are too incomplete to be usable, is extremely high, requiring difficult and complex adjustments for sampling biases. On the other hand, panel data can be invaluable as a supplementary source of information. We also believe that a series of independent surveys, provided that the design of sampling remains essentially the same and that the sample size in each survey is quite large, can generate cell means that can be thought of as the sampling values of the population cell means, and that they can provide invaluable information on dynamic behavior of economic agents. We have implemented this idea in the case of Japanese data experimentally with reasonable success, and we hope to have an opportunity to utilize it extensively in the future.

2. King and Dicks-Mireaux (1983). Their findings, however, have been challenged by Burbidge and Robb (1982) on the grounds that a removal of a few extreme and

questionable observations weakens the result substantially. Our own investigation into the Canadian data in question tends to support the criticism.

3. Our results so far will be collected into a book, in preparation. Meanwhile, the US and Japanese results are discussed, respectively, in Kennickell (1984) and Ando (1985). This paper is a brief summary of these two large studies.

4. Of three surveys having reasonably complete coverage of net worth, the 1979 survey conducted by the President's Commission on Pension Policy (*HPS79*) was unfortunately so badly organized and edited by those who were responsible for the survey that it is extraordinarily difficult to work with, and its reliability is in serious question. There are some serious problems in the 1962–63 Survey of Consumer Finance (*SFCC*), contrary to its reputation as an excellent source of information on balance sheets of households; for example, there are an extraordinarily large number of households exhibiting totally inconsistent accounts resulting in large negative values of implied consumption; since these households must be very large savers, results of any analysis that we have undertaken relating to savings using this set of data depend critically on how we treat these observations, which are presumably subject to large measurement errors. Indeed, this set of data is more sensitive to our handling of extreme observations than most other data sets with which we have worked. The new Survey of Consumer Finance (*SCF83*) has become available only very recently, and we have not had a chance to work with it extensively. All three surveys suffer from the fact that they are relatively small (4,000 or so observations for *HPS79* and *SCF83*, only a little more than 2,000 for *SFCC*), so that cells for higher age groups in particular contain too few observations to be reliable.

5. For *SCF83*, the values of net worth (in terms of means) follow a somewhat strange pattern for 46–55, 56–64, and 65–69 age groups. The exceptionally high value of net worth for the age group 46–55 results from the presence in this cell of a family whose reported income is quite high ($300,000) but whose net worth is extremely large ($17 million). Because the weighting scheme in computing various means takes into account income but not wealth and income above $50,000 is not distinguished for weighting purposes, this family acquires quite a large weight, thus increasing the computed mean of net worth of this cell. This is probably unwarranted, as the reader can observe that the standard deviation for this cell is three and a half times that for the age group 56–64, although the sample size is larger for the former. Medians of cells follow a much more conventional pattern.

6. For a recent discussion of this type of issue, see the surveys by King (1983) and by Deaton (1985).

7. The result reported here is taken from Kennickell (1984), who has attempted to evaluate a formulation like (1) under several alternative assumptions. For details on the estimation procedure, quality of data used, and the exact procedure for generating future values of variables, see Kennickell (1984). We record here a brief outline of the data preparation. The consumption flows (*C*) were constructed

directly from components including an imputed service flow of houses and consumer durables. Current fungible assets (A) were computed from a combination of recorded values and imputations including consumer durables recorded in an extensive inventory. The expected present value of future labor earnings (YL) was calculated from a system of estimated growth-adjusted income profiles and participation equations. The expected present value of social security benefits (SSW) was calculated by applying actual social security laws to the estimated income profiles for those working and to actual social security income for those either partly or completely retired. Unfortunately, it was not possible to calculate the value of pension wealth from the available data. The path of effective family size was calculated as

$$N_T = \Pr(T, AGE_h) + [.7\Pr(T, AGE_h) + (1 - \Pr(T, AGE_h))]\Pr(T, AGE_s)$$
$$+ .5\sum_{ci}\Pr(T, AGE_{ci})$$

for a married couple with children (the other cases are analogous). $\Pr(T, AGE_h)$ is the probability that agent h (for the head of household, s is for the spouse, ci for the ith child) whose age is AGE_h will survive to time period T. Effective weights of 1, .7, and .5 are given to the head of household, the spouse, and each of the children. Children are assumed to leave home at age 21.

To give the model the best possible chance of explaining the data, we excluded from our sample all those households that may not fit the model because of their characteristics or data problems. Among those excluded were the self-employed, families with rental income, cases with anomalous asset records, families with flows to or from a pension fund, those not participating in either social security or the Railroad Retirement program, households with occupants other than the head and spouse and children aged less than 21, families of single persons aged less than 62, and all households headed by persons aged either less than 26 or greater than 75. For the 1973 data this selection process yields 815 cases out of the original 10,106.

8. These data have been taken from the MPS model data bank, and consumption is defined as expenditure on nondurables and services and the service flow of consumer durables stock.

9. Another attempt to investigate interaction of labor supply, in this case the timing of retirement, with consumption and savings decision is due to Diamond and Hausman (1984). Using a panel data generated by the National Longitudinal Survey, they were able to explain determinants of retirement decisions. Their formulation is, however, not based on the direct use of the Euler equations.

10. For a more extensive survey of the literature on this subject, see Deaton (1985).

11. For more detailed discussion of definitions and the editing of data, see Kennickell (1984).

12. On the other hand, the apparently strong evidence produced by Feldstein and Pellechio (1978) in support of the proposition that the social security replaces private savings on the basis of data from the Survey of Financial Conditions of

Consumers was reviewed recently in detail by Novos (1984). It turned out that the earlier result depended critically on a few extreme and rather implausible observations, and when these observations are eliminated, the results were reversed.

13. A somewhat similar argument of this sort may be found in Hausman and Wise (1977, 1979) and Crawford (1979).

14. It is possible that the assumption of the continuity of behavior between included and excluded agents that is required by these formal analyses is not warranted, making procedures ineffective. Even if this speculation had some merit, however, in the United States, the number of persons not living independently is sufficiently small so that the same selection bias associated with their existence cannot be very large. This is not the case in Japan, however, as we shall discuss in the next section.

15. The sheer size of the sample, which is roughly 5 times the largest sample available in the United States, is an important factor. The reader can judge the importance of this by recalling table 7.1, where the rapidly diminishing size of cells made it difficult to extract significant information. All other aspects of these surveys appear to be extraordinarily conducive to producing as accurate a data base as practicable.

16. Note that because the benefits from private pension programs are all given in the form of a lump sum cash payment at the termination of employment, once a person is retired, it is incorporated into his AR automatically. Before the retirement, however, the issue of recognizing the present value of the benefit is present.

17. A very striking feature of these tables is that the mean and the median of income in most age classes turn out to be virtually equal, suggesting that the income distribution in Japan has very little skewness. This is in sharp contrast to most other countries, especially the United States. Since the population census of Japan does not contain any information on income, and since the tax authority in Japan is unable to consolidate income taxes collected at source and income taxes collected upon filing of returns by individuals, statistics on income distribution in Japan are less complete than in the United States, and a survey such as this one is the primary source of information on income distribution. In the full report of our study of savings in Japan (Ando, 1985), we have made fairly extensive comparisons with data from other sources, and we have concluded that the distribution of income observed in this survey is quite typical in Japan. It is quite plausible to us that there are very few extremely poor persons in Japan, since the Japanese population is very homogeneous and education is universal not only nominally but in reality. It is hard for us to believe, however, that there do not exist very wealthy persons in Japan. We therefore believe that the sample under investigation is biased with respect to the selection of very wealthy households.

18. For a full discussion of this issue, see Ando (1985).

19. There do exist some very poor elderly individuals living alone in Japan, mostly women. They are very few in number, however, and for our purposes they can largely be ignored.

20. Almost any formal analysis must be based on the assumption that those older households that remain independent and those merged into younger households are different realizations from the same stochastic process with continuous random variables. That is, if there are some discontinuous jumps in the behavior of households, such as a big unanticipated change in the resources available to them, as they become merged or as they are induced to remain independent, it is possible that a formal analysis would fail for technical reasons.

21. This interpretation of the result implies the existence of the externalities in the preference ordering of households, thus making the description of their behavior in terms of a simple maximizing model inappropriate.

22. The exception is the small group of single-person families, mostly elderly women, who are very poor and neither save nor dissave.

23. Estimated values of a imply that AR/ZLX increases with age at a declining rate, ending at about 6 at age 56.

24. An additional point should be noted. Since the older person merging with a younger household brings along sizable assets, there will be additional income from assets that must be either saved or consumed. The real return on these assets is likely to be in the range of 3–5%. We observe also that the coefficient of AR in the consumption function reported in table 7.10 is also about .04. Thus, it is a reasonable approximation to say that additional income from assets is mostly consumed.

25. This is clearly not a rational solution from the point of view of society. The price of land is so high because the utilization of land by Japanese residential structures is extremely inefficient. On average, a residential structure in Tokyo is only a little more than two stories high. The price can be brought down dramatically if most residences are converted into high rises, or at least buildings of several stories.

26. Having worked on data for the United States as well as for Japan, we cannot avoid a sense that a part of the differences in the results between these two countries is due to the nature of the data. Not only data for Japan based on vastly larger samples, which are of great value when patterns of cell means and patterns of estimated parameter values rather than a value of a single parameter are at stake, but also individual observations seem to us to be much less erratic, and therefore it was easier to detect some underlying patterns in the Japanese data than in the US data. Surprisingly, at the aggregate level, we believe that the reverse is true, for example, that the national income and product accounts and flow of funds data for Japan are far inferior to those for the United States.

27. For the available cross-section data, this assumption does not seem overly unreasonable. If we can obtain the necessary information for earlier dates, it is quite simple to take a gradual shift of relative contributions to total savings by age groups into account.

References

Ando, Albert (1985). "The Savings of Japanese Households: A Micro Study Based on Data from the National Survey of Family Income and Expenditure, 1974 and 1979," Economic Planning Agency, Government of Japan.

Barlow, Robin (1966). *Economic Behaviors of the Affluent*, Brookings Institution, Washington.

Blinder, Alan, R. H. Gordon, and D. E. Wise (1981). "Social Security, Bequests and the Life Cycle Theory of Saving: Cross-Sectional Tests," NBER Working Paper No. 619, January, Cambridge MA.

Board of Governors of the Federal Reserve System (1985). "Balance Sheets for the U.S. Economy 1945–83," Washington.

Browning, M., A. Deaton, and M. Irish (1985). "A Profitable Approach to Labor Supply and Commodity Demands Over the Life Cycle," *Econometrica*, vol. 53, pp. 503–544.

Burbidge, J. B., and A. L. Robb (1982). "Testing the Life Cycle Theory with Cross-Section Data: The Importance of Outliers," unpublished manuscript, QSEP Research Report No. 54, McMaster University, Hamilton, Ontario.

Bureau of Labor Statistics (1978). *Consumer Expenditure Survey Series: Interview Survey, 1972–73*, Bulletin 1985, Washington.

Bureau of the Census (1973). *Current Population Reports: Consumer Income, Household Money Income in 1972 and Selected Social and Economic Characteristics of Households*, Series P-60, No. 89, July, Washington.

Center for Human Resource Research (1982). *The National Longitudinal Surveys Handbook 1982*, Ohio State University, Columbus OH.

Crawford, David (1979). "Estimating Earnings Models from Truncated Samples," unpublished dissertation, University of Wisconsin, Madison.

Deaton, A. (1985). "Life Cycle Models of Consumption: Is the Evidence Consistent with the Theory?" paper presented at the Fifth World Congress of the Econometric Society, Cambridge, MA., August 16–23.

Diamond, P. A., and J. A. Hausman (1984). "Individual Retirement and Savings Behavior," *Journal of Public Economics*, vol. 23, pp. 81–114.

Feldstein, M. (1974). "Social Security, Induced Retirement and Aggregate Capital Accumulation," *Journal of Political Economy*, vol. 82, pp. 905–926.

Feldstein, M., and A. Pellechio (1978). "Social Security and Household Wealth Accumulation: New Microeconomic Evidence," *Review of Economics and Statistics*, pp. 361–368 (also Harvard Institute of Economic Research Discussion Paper No. 530, January 1977, Harvard University, Cambridge MA).

Fisher, J. (1950). "The Economics of an Aging Population. A Study in Income, Spending and Savings Patterns of Consumer Units in Different Age Groups, 1935–36, 1945 and 1949, "unpublished dissertation, Columbia University, New York.

Fisher, J. (1952). "Income, Spending and Saving Patterns of Consumer Units in Different Age Groups," Part IV in *Studies in Income and Wealth*, vol. 15, Conference on Research in Income and Wealth, NBER, New York.

Goldsmith, R. (1955). *A Study of Saving in the United States*, Princeton University Press, Princeton.

Greene, W. H. (1981). "Sample Selection Bias as a Specification Error: Comment," *Econometrica*, vol. 49, pp. 795–798.

Hausman, J. A., and D. A. Wise (1977). "Social Experimentation, Truncated Distributions and Efficient Estimation," *Econometrica*, vol. 45, pp. 319–339.

Hausman, J. A., and D. A. Wise (1979). "Attrition Bias in Experimental and Panel Data: The Gary Income Maintenance Experiment," *Econometrica*, vol. 47, pp. 455–473.

Heckman, James J. (1976). "The Common Structure of Statistical Models of Truncation, Sample Selection and Limited Dependent Variables and a Simple Estimator for Such Models," *Annals of Economic and Social Measurement*, vol. 5, pp. 475–492.

Kennickell, Arthur (1984). "An Investigation of Life Cycle Savings Behavior in the United States," unpublished dissertation, University of Pennsylvania, Philadelphia.

King, Mervyn (1983). *The Economics of Saving*, Yrjo Johansson Symposium in Finland, June.

King, Mervyn, and Louis Dicks-Mireaux (1983). "Asset Holdings and the Life Cycle," *Economic Journal*, vol. 89, pp. 706–732.

Kitagawa, Evelyn M., and Phillip M. Hauser (1973). *Differential Mortality in the United States: A Study in Socioeconomic Epidemiology*, Harvard University Press, Cambridge MA.

Kotlikoff, Laurence J., and Lawrence H. Summers (1981). "The Role of Intergenerational Transfers in Aggregate Capital Accumulation," *Journal of Political Economy*, vol. 89, pp. 706–732 (also NBER Working Paper No. 445, February 1980).

Lucas, Robert (1975). "An Equilibrium Model of the Business Cycle." *Journal of Political Economy*, vol. 83, pp. 1113–1144.

Mariger, Randall Paul (1983). "Liquidity Constraints, Intergenerational Transfers, and Life-Cycle Consumption," unpublished dissertation, Harvard University, Cambridge MA.

Mathis, Evelyn S. (1969). *Socioeconomic Characteristics of Deceased Persons 1962–63,* Report No. 9, Series 22, National Center for Health Statistics, Department of Health, Education and Welfare, Washington.

Modigliani, Franco (1984). "Measuring the Contribution of Intergenerational Transfers to Total Wealth: Conceptual Issues and Empirical Findings," given at the seminar on Modelling the Accumulation and Distribution of Personal Wealth, Paris, September.

Modigliani, Franco, and Albert Ando (1960). "The 'Permanent Income' and the 'Life Cycle' Hypotheses of Saving Behavior: Comparison and Tests," in I. Friend and D. Jones (eds.), *Consumption and Saving,* University of Pennsylvania, Philadelphia.

Modigliani, Franco, and Richard Brumberg (1954). "Utility Analysis and the Consumption Function: An Interpretation of Cross-Section Data," in Kenneth K. Kurihara (ed.), *Post Keynesian Economics,* Rutgers University Press, New Brunswick, NJ.

Modigliani, Franco, and Richard Brumberg (1979). "Utility Analysis and Aggregate Consumption Functions: An Attempt at Integration," in Andrew Abel (ed.), *Collected Papers of Franco Modigliani,* MIT Press, Cambridge, MA.

Monroe, Day, Maryland Parnell, Mary Ruth Pratt, and Geraldine S. DuPrie, (1942). "Family Spending and Saving as Related to Age of Wife and Age and Number of Children," US Dept. of Agriculture, Miscellaneous Publications No. 489.

Novos, Ian (1984). "Age, Social Security and Wealth Accumulation: Unraveling the Puzzle," unpublished dissertation, University of Pennsylvania, Philadelphia.

Projector, Dorothy (1968), *Survey of Changes in Family Finances,* Board of Governors of the Federal Reserve Systems, Washington.

Shorrocks, A. F. (1975). "The Age-Wealth Relationship: A Cross-Section and Cohort Analysis," *Review of Economics and Statistics,* pp. 155–163.

Theil, Henri (1954). *Linear Aggregation of Economic Relations.* North-Holland, Amsterdam.

Tobin, James, and Walter Dolde (1971). "Wealth, Liquidity and Consumption," in *Consumer Spending and Monetary Policy: The Linkages,* Federal Reserve Bank of Boston, Boston.

Wentworth, Edna C., and Dana K. Motley (1970). *Resources after Retirement,* Office of Research and Statistics Research Report No. 34, Social Security Administration.

Yaari, Menahem (1977). "A Note on Separability and Quasiconcavity," *Econometrica,* vol. 45, pp. 1183–1186.

Comments on "How Much (or Little) Life Cycle Is There in Micro Data? The Cases of the United States and Japan"

Robert M. Solow

This is a very Albert sort of paper. It combines vast industry with a no-nonsense approach to the data. It makes no attempt to wish away damage to received ideas.

The paper raises explicitly a question that has puzzled me for a long time as a passive and partial observer of the literature on saving behavior. Suppose I tell you that I am willing to accept the life cycle approach to saving. Exactly what have I committed myself to believe? Is it merely that the right way to approach the theory of household saving is to imagine a unitary household planning its income stream and expenditure stream over its remaining lifetime, choosing the best feasible combination according to some standard intertemporal preference, and then saving currently the difference between current income and current expenditure along the best feasible path? Is that enough to qualify me as a life cycler in good standing? If so, then I am presumably allowed to remember the long friendship between Modigliani and Simon, which in turn entitles me to smear my original profession of belief with a coating of bounded rationality. Households will satisfice or follow rules of thumb. Like Ando, I would hardly expect to find Euler equations satisfied by individual households and surely not by aggregates of households. I do not know what to make of the impulse to perform solemn tests of that hypothesis on aggregate data. It would be quite enough for the model if some rough expenditure smoothing were widely practiced, with previous plans being amended only when big changes in expectations occurred. The end result would be some sort of stochastic dynamic programming, but with thresholds and other squalid imperfections that might aggregate badly.

But then why all this fuss about bequests? We all know that there are in fact bequests. Specifically planned bequests. I know at least two families whose children will inherit houses on this very island (Martha's Vineyard). There are also unplanned bequests and some bequests whose classification is unclear. The only thing that is necessary to make life cycle theory interesting and important is that "hump saving" should be nontrivial in amount. The sort of abstract life cycle theory whose essence I stated at the beginning does not even exclude in principle the possibility that retired people should save until the very end. It only takes a sufficiently powerful self-interested bequest motive, which could easily be written into preferences to become part of the theory.

But that is too formalistic. At that level of generality life cycle theory would have only consequences as unexciting as those of the pure theory of consumer demand. To be truly interesting, to have palpable macroeconomic significance, as Ando and Kennickell point out, the theory needs to be on to something big and eye-catching. Hump saving really has to matter. That is what gets you nice results like the connection between the aggregate saving rate and the growth rate, whose confirmation in aggregate data has lent support to the theoretical structure. The paper now sows some corrosive doubts about the weight of that inference.

Despite what I have just said, the question about the saving behavior of the old seems to have aroused more passion than it is worth. I suspect there is a little Kuhnian science-as-a-social-process operating there too. When Modigliani and Brumberg and Ando were first developing and exploiting the life cycle model, they wanted a strong simple special case from which powerful conclusions would follow. I would have done the same. So they assumed ("for convenience only; the main results do not depend . . .") that there were no bequests at all. All saving was hump saving. If there were no growth, there would be no aggregate net saving. Most overlapping-generations virtuosi do the same even now, as a reflex. If someone had produced evidence back in 1955 that the old do not dissave as much as the special model would suggest, there would have been no great fuss. ("That is only a pedagogically useful special case, etc.") Now, thirty years later, it seems like something worth defending. If the evidence showed only that the old dissave very little, I would not think the matter so very important.

Ando and Kennickell emphasize the fact that, even in an economy where no one ever dissaves a nickel in old age, quite reasonable rates of growth will have the effect that a substantial fraction of total assets in existence is the accumulated net saving of those still living. So the importance of inheritance cannot be checked out by that route. That particular statistic has low power. I want to mention another arithmetical factor that may blur the picture still further. The quantitative implications need to be worked out, but it would not be hard.

The additional factor is simply that people, even retired people, do not know how long they will live. If they want to be quite sure that they can provide for themselves directly out of the assets they have accumulated before retirement, and even if they would like to leave no bequest, they must plan to dissave rather slowly. If the consequences of outliving your assets are very unpleasant, you will have to conserve those assets. Many people will then die while they still have a substantial part of their initial wealth. They will leave unintended bequests, but they would have no reason to regret their *ex ante* choices.

Using a completely artificial example, but one that is not outlandish by the standards of this particular intellectual game, let me suggest that the quantitative effect of uncertain lifetime could be large. Suppose that the force of mortality $(=m)$ is a constant after retirement, so that the probability that a newly retired person will survive exactly x years is e^{-mx}. The time-additive utility function is age-invariant $(=u(c))$ and, to avoid clutter, there is no time preference. A newly retired person wishes to maximize $\int_0^\infty u(c(x))e^{-mx}\,dx$. To express the notion that it is very bad to run out of assets and become dependent late in life, I require that the planned consumption path be financeable with probability one. Thus if initial wealth is W and the yield on assets is constant $(=r)$, then the constraint on $c(x)$ is $\int_0^\infty c(x)e^{-rx}\,dx = W$. I hope this strong condition takes some of the curse off the artificial expected-utility routine in this context. The first-order condition is $u'(c(x)) = ke^{(m-r)x}$, where k is a Lagrange multiplier whose value is determined to make the present-value constraint just hold. Just for fun, suppose $m = r$, though on the whole you would expect $m > r$, though perhaps not by a lot. (If desired, m can be interpreted as the sum of the instantaneous rates of mortality and time preference. If $m > r$, consumption decreases with advancing age.) If $m = r$, the best $c(x)$ is a constant determined by $u'(c^*) = k$, and it is immediately obvious that $c^* = rW$. The right thing to do in this case is to consume the interest on assets. The retired will neither save nor dissave, and they will die with their postretirement assets intact, to be inherited by the children, or Aunt Aggie, or—God help us—the Commonwealth of Massachusetts, all this without any bequest motive at all. The presence of reasonable heirs makes this a less repulsive scenario.

This is extreme; it happens only because I have taken longevity to be potentially infinite, and used the self-reproducing character of the exponential distribution. Also I have ignored the fact that evasive action is possible, either individually or via purchased annuities, provided you do not resent supporting a lawyer or an insurance company in addition to yourself. That is not the point. The point is that there must be a nonnegligible amount of unintended bequests in real life, and that fact further beclouds the simple inference already beclouded once by Ando and Kennickell. Of course there is no reason why intended and unintended bequests should not coexist. (I was not surprised to discover, after writing all this, that there is even now a literature on this question, including contributions by Andy Abel and Ben Friedman. The starkness of this example may be useful anyway.)

In any case, I do not think the main lesson to be drawn from the paper's empirical analysis has to do with the relative weight of hump saving and bequest saving in total assets. The deeper issue is one that the authors point out very clearly but then sidle away from, probably because it is potentially subversive of life cycle theory and much more besides. The evidence appears to say that retired people conserve their "own" assets almost intact. They do dissave, but they dissave their social security wealth and their private pension wealth. *We* (economists) think of wealth as fungible; *We* think a dollar is a dollar. Why don't *they*? Is it possible that lots of people think it is somehow improper to dissipate their "own" assets but perfectly OK to spend their pension receipts and social security benefits? If so, then how do we know that they do not make similar distinctions among subclasses of their "own" assets? More prosaically, I wonder how much of those conserved assets consists of owner-occupied homes, and whether there is some particular tendency to hang on to the old homestead. That would be easily testable if the data say enough about home ownership and the composition of assets. There might turn out to be less an unwillingness to dissave equity in a home than an inability to do so because the appropriate financial instruments have been until recently unavailable or unknown or available only on unfavorable terms. That would be great for conventional economic ideas, so maybe we should hope it turns out to be the case.

To my way of thinking, the authors adopt the right attitude in contemplating their own regression results. What they see suggests real puzzles about the relation of social security wealth and private pension wealth to saving behavior. Our ingrained habits of thought make it hard to imagine that different forms of wealth could be such imperfect substitutes for one another. Ando and Kennickell are no doubt aware that they could find some defensible specification that would lend more support to their prior beliefs; but they have resisted, and simply recorded that the strong version of life cycle theory does not find confirmation in their data analysis. My own tentative suggestion has already been made. It seems to me that houses, lesser consumer durables, and financial assets of various kinds may not be seen by households merely as alternative forms of wealth. Conventional rules of appropriate behavior may apply to some classes of assets and not to others. That should be a researchable question.

Would that sort of finding really be so terribly destructive of life cycle theory? I do not think so, because I value life cycle theory as a guide to interpreting behavior rather than as a set of equations to live or die by. I like the equations; they are probably the best way to remember what a model is trying to tell you. But life cycle theory will survive as long as there are events you can understand better if you keep in mind the notion that households may wish to achieve a pattern of lifetime expenditures rather different from earnings, and can undertake a complicated menu of transactions to accomplish that goal, along with others. Viewed that way, life cycle theory is secure.

8   1944, 1963, and 1985

Stanley Fischer

Franco Modigliani's 1944 article coming at the end of the period of absorption of the *General Theory* started a remarkable career in macroeconomics that continues to provide insight and inspiration to generations of members of the MIT Money Workshop and a far wider audience outside MIT. "My 1944 article" is certainly the most cited work in the Money Workshop. "My 1963 article" is a distant second, though it has not been clear why the work of the younger Modigliani finds more favor with its author than that of the mature scholar, pointing in 1963 to developments that were soon to be embodied in the MPS model.

The 1944 and 1963 Modigliani articles continue to be worth reading today, both for their insights and as summaries of the state of knowledge at the time.[1] The 1944 article is decisive in its discussion of the role of wage stickiness in generating real effects of monetary policy and unemployment "equilibria" in the Keynesian model. It is interesting too for its grappling with the Hicksian *Value and Capital* argument that the short-term interest rate is determined by the transaction costs of moving between zero interest money and interest-bearing short-term securities. The same issue has been emphasized recently by Neil Wallace (1981); the well-known difficulty of generating a demand for the non-interest-bearing asset, money, when interest-bearing assets are available is typically overcome by modern theorists by postulating that money has to be used to make a purchase (the Clower constraint) or that money holding yields unspecified utility services.

Comments from and discussion with Andrew Abel, Olivier Blanchard, Peter Diamond, Rudiger Dornbusch, Paul Krugman, Merton Miller, Franco Modigliani, Danny Quah, Julio Rotemberg, Paul Samuelson, and Martin Weitzman, none of whom—least of all Franco Modigliani—should be held responsible for the views expressed in this paper, and financial assistance from the Guggenheim Foundation and National Science Foundation, are gratefully acknowledged.

The 1963 article describes its macroeconomics as those of the mid-1950s. The basic macroeconomic model is more sophisticated than the 1944 version in its handling of the banking system and the distinction between inside and outside money, the consumption and investment functions, and the explicit inclusion of a government budget constraint potentially linking monetary and fiscal policy. Most interesting from the viewpoint of current controversies are the brief discussion of markup pricing as an alternative to the Keynesian supply function that makes output a decreasing function of the real wage, the demonstration that credit rationing does not much change the macroeconomic analysis of the operation of monetary policy,[2] and the discussion of the problem facing a monetary authority confronted with real wage rigidity. There is in addition a hint that the author did not at the time regard the Phillips curve trade-off dilemma as a serious one.[3]

In this paper I ask what "my 1985 article" would look like if Franco Modigliani had the time to set out a representative macroeconomic model—or rather two models—of the mid-1980s. The attempt to set our representative models may reasonably be regarded as not only presumptuous but also foolish. I trust that the presumptuousness will be excused as an attempt to smoke out the views of the commentator.[4]

The attempt may be regarded as foolish because no single model can possibly hope to encompass the many substantial analytic contributions to modern macroeconomic theory. To name only a few:

• Overlapping generations models by Samuelson (1958), Diamond (1965), Lucas (1972), Barro (1974), Wallace (1981), Sargent and Wallace (1983), Grandmont (1985), et al. make important points about the role of money and social security in promoting efficiency, capital over-accumulation and the effects of debt on capital accumulation, the Phillips curve and the information-conveying role of prices, discounting of future tax payments, the difficulty of distinguishing between money and bonds in formal modeling, commodity monies, and multiple equilibria arising from non-linearities, each of which is part of the modern canon.

• Disequilibrium models by Patinkin (1965), Mundell (1964a), Clower (1965), Solow and Stiglitz (1968), Barro and Grossman (1976), Benassy (1982), Neary and Stiglitz (1983), et al. show in fixed or sticky price models why quantities enter behavioral equations, identify the wage-price vectors that generate classical or Keynesian behavior, and demonstrate the role of self-justifying pessimism in producing Keynesian unemployment.

• The explosion of work on labor contracting by Baily (1974), Azariadis

(1975), McDonald and Solow (1981), Hart (1983), Hall and Lazear (1984), Stiglitz (1984), et al. has examined the implications of non-spot-market relationships between firms and workers for wage and output determination and shown when contracts will lead to under- or overemployment equilibria.

• The loose notion of efficiency in asset pricing has been made precise by Samuelson (1965), Fama (1970), Merton (1973), Breeden (1979), Tirole (1985), et al., and the efficiency of asset markets has been tested by Shiller (1981), Leroy and Porter (1981), Singleton (1980), Marsh and Merton (1985), et al.

• Rational expectations econometrics has been applied to the testing of standard optimizing models of consumption, fixed investment, inventory investment, labor demand and supply, by Hall (1978), Hansen and Singleton (1983), Flavin (1981), Shapiro (1985), Blanchard (1983b), Eichenbaum (1983), Sargent (1978), Mankiw, Rotemberg and Summers (1985) et al., and to question about the effects of anticipated and unanticipated policy changes by Mishkin (1983) and others.

• The notion of policy making as a game between government and the private sector, implied by the work of Lucas (1973) and Sargent and Wallace (1975), has led far beyond the Tinbergen (1967) approach in the work of Kydland and Prescott (1977), Barro and Gordon (1983), Rogoff (1983), Backus and Driffill (1985), et al.

• The modeling of price and wage stickiness has advanced at the hands of Barro (1972), Fischer (1977), Phelps and Taylor (1977), Sheshinski and Weiss (1977), Taylor (1980), Rotemberg (1982), Blanchard (1983a), Mankiw (1985), Akerlof and Yellen (1985), Blanchard (1985b), Caplin and Spulber (1985), et al.

The list of topics is incomplete—among the missing are indexation, the microeconomics of money, models of banking, information-based macroeconomics, real business cycle theory, and search theoretic models of labor market dynamics and the natural rate of unemployment—and the lists of authors can be multiplied many times. However, in the spirit of the earlier papers, the attempt is not to summarize all of modern macroeconomics but rather to describe the structure most modern macroeconomists should have in mind if and when they think about the way the economy and macroeconomic policy work.

The essential question is what difference do the many contributions described above make to our basic understanding of the way the economy works? Does "my 1963 model" have to be thrown away, or does the basic structure still stand? Modern textbooks, and this paper, say the structure still stands, to be sure with some rooms added, with some altered, and with modern styling replacing the fashions of twenty years ago.

In saying this, I certainly do not mean we have learned nothing in the last twenty years: the sample of topics and papers above is sufficient evidence of the fundamental significance of much of the research of the past twenty years. Nor would I want to encourage any Bourbons who see no reason to go beyond what they knew under the previous regime: the technical level and sophistication of modern macroeconomics demand full-time attention and effort.

While no single model comfortably encompasses the basic views of unreconstructed Keynesians, old-line monetarists, and fresh-water macroeconomists[5] along with those of the eclectic center, the model that comes closest, and that best serves to focus discussion of microeconomic controversies, is the extended Phillips-curve-augmented IS-LM model.[6] The choice of a nonmaximizing model may render the exercise suspect to many in the profession.[7] But it has the benefit of providing a believable account of the operation of the economy.

The major modifications that have to be made to the 1963 model are in the treatment of the Phillips curve and aggregate supply, in the analysis of expectations,[8] and in the openness of the economy. Because dynamics depends sensitively on details of lag specifications in each component of the model, I shall not lay much stress on the specifics of dynamic adjustment.[9]

1   The Simplest Closed Economy Model

The general structure of the models is the same as that of the 1944 and 1963 versions and the standard textbook model in using separate equilibrium conditions for the goods market, the asset markets, and the labor market.

In the closed economy model, the level of output is determined by aggregate demand and supply. Aggregate demand is a function of permanent labor income (Y^p), current income (Y), wealth, the real interest rate (r), government spending on goods and services (G), and taxes net of transfers (T):

$$Y = \phi\left(Y^p, Y, \frac{H+B}{P} + K, r, G, T\right). \tag{1'}$$

Current income enters in addition to permanent labor income because of evidence that consumption demand is more sensitive to current income than is implied by the pure life cycle-permanent income hypothesis.[10] Permanent income may affect not only consumption but also investment demand, as has been emphasized by Eisner (1978). Real non human wealth consists of real high-powered money (H) and government bonds (B) plus the value of physical capital. We discuss below the issue of whether debt is wealth, and the related question of whether future taxes should also affect aggregate demand. The inclusion of just a short-term interest rate is a simplifying assumption; the long rate, or Tobin's q—the ratio of the market value of capital to its replacement cost—is more relevant to the investment decision than the short rate.[11]

Assuming the marginal propensity to consume out of current income is less than unity, (1') can be rewritten:

$$Y = A\left(Y^p, \frac{H+B}{P} + K, r, G, T\right). \tag{1}$$

The demand for real balances is a function of the level of income and output (in some versions spending replaces income), of the nominal interest rate, and of real wealth, designated V. Assuming a constant ratio between the stock of money and the stock of high-powered money,[12] the equilibrium condition in the money market can be written

$$H/P = L(Y, r + \pi, V), \tag{2}$$

where π is the expected rate of inflation and

$$i = r + \pi$$

is the nominal interest rate.

The treatment of capital in the assets markets is the same as that of the 1944 and 1963 papers, implicitly assuming that capital and bonds are perfect substitutes (Tobin, 1961). The more complete treatment in which adjustment costs imply that the price of installed capital—Tobin's q—may vary and in which capital and bonds are gross substitutes does not much affect the analysis of open market operations (Tobin, 1969).

Aggregate supply starts with a wage-setting equation:

$$W_t = P_t^e + f(Y_t^e, Y_t), \tag{3}$$

where W_t is the predetermined wage rate in period t, and P_t^e and Y_t^e are the price level and level of output expected to obtain in period t at the time wages are set;[13] Y_t appears in the wage-setting equation to reflect the possibility that the wage in period t is determined in part on the basis of a predetermined overtime schedule. A price-setting equation completes the supply side:

$$P_t = h(W_t, Y_t). \tag{4}$$

The price-setting equation is consistent with two major alternatives: first that output supplied is a decreasing function of the real wage; or second that price is set as a constant markup on the wage or on costs. The conventional Keynesian supply function with output a decreasing function of the real wage can obtain when the function $h(\ )$ is increasing in both its arguments; the simplest markup pricing equation holds when Y drops out of the function $h(\ )$.

The model is completed by the government budget constraint:

$$G_t - T_t + i_t(B_t/P_t) = (H_{t+1} - H_t + B_{t+1} - B_t)/P_t. \tag{5}$$

In (5), net transfers, T, are defined exclusive of interest payments on the debt. The interest payments are singled out for separate treatment for the later discussion of debt dynamics.

1.1   Comparison with 1963 and Discussion

Equations (1), (2), and (5) are virtually identical to equivalent equations in the 1963 paper.[14] The major differences are in the lack of detail about the banking system in the 1985 version and in the specification of aggregate supply. The details of the 1963 version were heavily influenced by the author's desire to discuss both the Gurley-Shaw inside-outside money distinction and the Patinkin dichotomy-neutrality controversy. The 1985 version shares the judgment of both the 1944 and 1963 papers in placing the main leverage of monetary policy in price stickiness rather than in equilibrium nonneutralities.

On the aggregate supply side, the 1963 version formalized the notion that the wage is constant up to the point of full employment with labor input determined by the demand for labor, and that thereafter the nominal wage adjusts to generate the real wage at which labor supply is equal to demand.[15] As previously noted, there is also a discussion of markup pricing, in which in the short-run output is determined by demand at the price level determined by the prevailing level of wages.

In the 1985 version the wage for each period is mostly predetermined by a Friedman-Phelps-Phillips curve. The length of the period is not specified. Output and labor input is then determined by demand, perhaps even beyond the point of conventional full employment as workers go on over-time. The formulation in terms of output rather than unemployment saves an Okun's law equation relating output to unemployment; it is possible that this formulation beyond its parsimony has served also to reduce the attention paid to unemployment as *the* macroeconomic problem.

The demand determination of output is at the heart of one of the key controversies in macroeconomics. The fact of predetermination of wages is not necessarily disputed, but the Keynesian notion that demand determines output—implying that there might be either under- or overemployment of labor—is (Barro, 1977). I have nothing new to contribute on the issue of whether the labor market should be thought of as clearing in some sophisticated sense in the very short as well as the long period, but record the view that the aggregate supply framework of this paper, which includes the expectation-adjusted Phillips curve, has performed well in recent years in providing an interpretation of the recent disinflation.

The long-run Phillips curve in the 1985 model is vertical: nominal wages adjust to anticipated changes in the price level so that there is no trade-off between output and inflation when the inflation is anticipated.[16] In this framework, the length of the period over which the wage is predetermined is a major determinant of macroeconomic dynamics. The model's dichotomy in which the wage is predetermined for a period is a substantial simplification of the real-world adjustment process in which staggered wage and price setting can generate long-lived adjustments out of comparatively short contracts.[17]

A further controversy centers around the role and determinants of expected price and output levels in the wage-setting process. The spirit of the rational expectations approach is to condition those expectations on expectations of policy and other exogenous variables. Counterposed to this view is the undoubtedly true statement that most people do not know what the money supply—let alone its expectation—is, and thus that they base expectations on the actual behavior of the relevant variable. Adaptive expectations are likely used in routine circumstances when the consequences of error are small and more comprehensively based expectations at times when there are major changes in policy.

Assuming expectations are rational neutralizes expectations as an independent source of economic dynamics; the implications of alternative expectations assumptions can usefully be investigated if there is reason to believe they are not rational. So can questions of the credibility of announced changes in policy. But rational expectations is the right initial hypothesis.

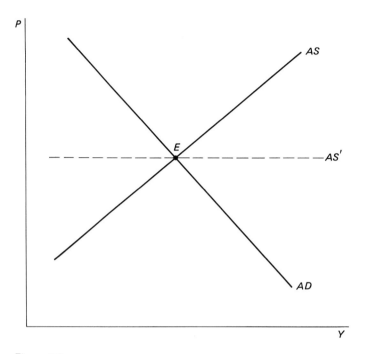

Figure 8.1

1.2   The Aggregate Supply Curve

The aggregate supply curve, *AS*, in figure 8.1 is derived from (3) and (4).
If the markup is constant and the nominal wage is not a function of the
current level of output, the aggregate supply curve is horizontal, as on *AS'*.
If the markup and/or the wage increases with the current level of output,
the aggregate supply curve is positively sloped, as in *AS*. We henceforth
assume the short-run supply curve is positively sloped.

Held constant along an aggregate supply curve are the expected price
level and expected level of output. An increase in either shifts the aggregate supply curve up, raising price at each level of output. Provided output
in equation (4) is a function of the real wage, there is a unique long-run full
employment level of output at which the long-run aggregate supply curve
is vertical.

1.3   Aggregate Demand

The aggregate demand curve *AD* in figure 8.1 represents equilibrium in
both the goods and the assets markets. Substituting for the real interest rate

in (1) from (2) and the relationship between real and nominal rates, we obtain the AD curve as a relationship between the price level and current level of output; its position depends on the expected rate of inflation, the stock of bonds, and fiscal policy parameters. In calculating the slope of the AD curve we assume permanent income increases, but not much, with current income.[18]

The negative slope of the AD curve reflects both the so-called Hicks-Keynes effect that arises from the increase in the nominal interest rate (and with expected inflation held constant, the real rate of interest) as real balances fall, and the wealth effect of an increase in prices on the real value of wealth. The Hicks-Keynes effect is sufficient to produce AD's negative slope.

An increase in the expected rate of inflation, or government spending, or a reduction in taxes, shifts the AD curve up and to the right, increasing output and the price level. An increase in the stock of high-powered money or government bonds likewise shifts the AD curve to the right. We discuss later the question of whether bonds are net wealth. An equiproportionate increase in the stocks of money and bonds shifts the AD curve up proportionately, indicating the potential neutrality of such a policy change.

1.4   Equilibrium

Output and the price level are determined at point E in figure 8.1. We describe E as a position of short-run equilibrium, though the expectations on which wages were determined may be falsified. If either the price level or the level of output is different from the level that was expected, the quantity of labor employed will not be equal to the quantity workers would prefer to supply. Point E can be a position of long-run equilibrium only if workers' expectations are fulfilled, if the budget is balanced, and if the remaining exogenous variables are constant.

We now use the model to analyze a variety of policy changes.

1.5   An Open Market Purchase

An open market purchase increases H while decreasing B by an equal amount. There is no wealth effect at the initial price level. At any given level of income, the larger money stock reduces the interest rate, shifting the aggregate demand curve to the right.

If the change in the money stock was unanticipated, both the level of output and the price level rise in the short run. Then as expectations adjust, the short-run supply curve shifts up, and more of the adjustment takes the form of a price increase. Eventually output returns to the full employment level at a higher price level. The real and nominal interest rates fall because the ratio of money to bonds has risen; the stock of real high-powered money increases, implying that prices rise proportionately less than the money stock.

Because the open market purchase reduces the public's holdings of bonds, disposable income would fall unless there were an offsetting reduction in net texes, which we therefore assume to have been made. In addition, the lower real interest rate increases the rate of investment, implying the full employment level of output rises relative to what it would otherwise have been. We do not take explicit account of this effect of the monetary change.

1.6 Fiscal Expansion in the Short Run

Suppose the government increases spending and reduces taxes; the change has not been anticipated in wage setting. Both the tax reduction and the increase in spending raise aggregate demand; if the expected rate of inflation remains unchanged or rises, the price level and level of output will rise. Again provided the expected rate of inflation does not fall, and if wealth effects on the demand for consumption and real balances are small, both the real and the nominal interest rates will increase. The analysis is entirely that of the conventional IS-LM model, except for the need to consider the effects of the fiscal expansion on the expected rate of inflation.

Except when fiscal policy takes the form of balanced budget changes in expenditure, fiscal expansion implies subsequent changes in the stocks of money and bonds. If the fiscal policy change is transitory, there need be only one-time changes in asset stocks; if the change is permanent there will be ongoing changes in asset stocks. We consider permanent fiscal changes.

1.7 Money-Financed Deficits

Suppose there was initially no government debt and that after the fiscal expansion, high-powered money is printed to cover the deficit. In the new steady state, and absent growth of output, the growth rate of money and the inflation rate will both be θ, where θ satisfies

$$\theta \cdot (H/P) = G - T. \tag{6}$$

Permanent money financing of deficits is possible only if the deficit is small, for the maximum amount of steady state seigniorage is small.

The goods market equilibrium condition can be rewritten

$$Y = A(Y^p, L(Y, r + \theta, V) + K, r, G, T). \tag{7}$$

The fiscal expansion—the increase in G and reduction in T—tend to increase the real interest rate at the full employment level of output. Offsetting that effect is the reduction in real balances that arises from the increase in the expected rate of inflation. But if the wealth effect of reduced high-powered money holdings on consumption demand is small—as it is—the real interest rate will increase to maintain goods market equilibrium in the long run. With the real interest rate higher, the nominal rate too must rise.

Thus permanent fiscal expansion, even if it is money financed, raises the real interest rate in both the short and the long runs. This conclusion would be changed if individuals were infinite horizon maximizers with a constant rate of time preference: in that case saving behavior adjusts so that the real after-tax interest rate is always driven to the rate of time preference. The real interest rate could be changed in the long run in such models only through taxation of the return on capital.

1.8   Bond Financing of Deficits

Pure bond financing of deficits is not possible in the steady state in a nongrowing economy. Holding the stock of nominal balances constant, the government budget constraint is

$$B_{t+1}/P_t = G_t - T_t + (1 + i_t)(B_t/P_t). \tag{8}$$

If interest payments are not included in T (net taxes minus transfers), or if the noninterest deficit does not for any other reason decrease as the stock of bonds increases, then (8) is an unstable equation provided the real interest rate is positive; the simple notion that ever-increasing interest payments overwhelm the budget is true in this case.[19] Even if the budget deficit is defined inclusive of real interest payments, there can be no steady state unless the deficit is zero.[20]

Although pure debt financing of a deficit is not possible in steady state in a nongrowing economy, mixed money and debt financing of small deficits is possible: essentially the seigniorage pays the interest bill on the outstanding stock of debt as well as covering the deficit. This is one sense in which Sargent and Wallace's (1981) argument that deficit financing is inflationary is correct. Similarly, transitory debt financing of a deficit will leave a larger debt and larger interest payments than money financing, so that eventually a higher inflation rate will be needed to finance the larger interest-inclusive deficit.

The contrast between the short run discussed in the previous section and the long run in this section is very sharp. In the short run debt financing probably raises the price level less than money financing; in the long run it does not. Equivalently, short-term debt financing of a transitory deficit, with all future interest-inclusive deficits held constant, raises the price level less than money financing of the same deficit.[21]

1.9   Bonds and Net Wealth

The long-run nonneutrality of money when the ratio of money to bonds is changed results from the assumption that government bonds are net wealth. The assumption that bonds are net wealth was discussed by Patinkin (1965), who recognized that the issue was whether individuals in aggregate regarded themselves as having a future tax liability with present value equal to that of the debt. If the debt was to be paid off by future generations, the logical assumption seemed to be that the debt was net wealth. Barro's (1974) contribution to the debate was the recognition that finitely lived individuals could nonetheless have effectively infinite horizons if they cared in a particular way about their heirs' utility. In this case the debt would not be wealth.[22]

The issue turns out to be suprisingly far-reaching. For instance, does the pay-as-you-go nature of social security affect capital accumulation? Is the national debt a burden in the Modigliani (1961) sense that it leaves future generations with a smaller capital stock? Does deficit rather than tax financing raise the real interest rate? In all cases the answer turns on the same considerations as whether the debt is wealth.[23]

Further, if individuals act as if they are infinitely lived, the life-cycle hypothesis of consumption has to be significantly modified to include the making of bequests. Indeed, recent research by Kotlikoff and Summers (1981) argues that most wealth is the result not of life-cycle saving, but of bequests.

Despite the importance of the issue, there have been no empirical tests sufficiently decisive to move prior beliefs about the issue.[24] The Ricardo—Barro hypothesis implies that private consumption should be invariant to the financing of government spending; private saving should thus rise when the budget deficit increases. Neither this implication of the hypothesis or its opposite, nor the effects of social security on savings, have yet been convincingly established econometrically. Those willing to accept more casual evidence point to reductions in private saving rate and increases in real interest rates as budget deficits have increased since 1981 as *prima facie* evidence against the hypothesis.

Tobin and Buiter (1980) have shown that childlessness, zero bequests, and a variety of other likely events cause the failure of the Ricard-Barro mechanism, all in the direction that causes the debt to be treated as net wealth. Drazen (1978) suggests that a national debt overcomes the difficulty for parents of appropriating some of the return from investing in their children's human capital and thereby raises national wealth. Barsky, Mankiw, and Zeldes (1984) show that in the absence of human capital insurance, future taxes to repay debt reduce the variance of future income, raising current consumption and thus in effect making the debt net wealth. Abel (1984) shows that with uncertain lifetimes, the debt may be net wealth.

The weight of the theoretical arguments[25] and, in my view, the empirical evidence suggests that the debt is to a significant extent net wealth, but those whose priors are sufficiently strong can continue, at least for the present, to believe it is not. In the remainder of the paper we treat the debt as net wealth, recognizing that in practice future tax liabilities fall to some extent on those now living, and that the debt would thus be discounted to some extent.

The short-run effectiveness of *monetary policy* is not dependent on whether the debt is net wealth. So long as wages and prices are sticky in the short run, monetary policy will have real effects. This is very much the message of Modigliani (1963), who downplays the importance of the long-run nonneutralities of money of the type that arise when the debt is wealth. On the fiscal policy side, the issue of whether the debt is net wealth is crucial to the question of whether a tax cut is expansionary and raises the real interest rate.[26]

1.10   The Fisher Relation and the Mundell-Tobin Effect

Because the 1963 paper was written before persistent inflation became a primary concern of US macroeconomics, the Fisher relation and its distinction between the real and the nominal interest rates was not discussed.[27]

The pure Fisher effect, in which the real interest rate is invariant to the inflation rate, does not obtain in the current model, even when the nominal stocks of both money and bonds increase at a constant rate. The Mundell-Tobin effect is responsible for the nonneutrality.

Consider the full employment version of the current model in which inflation has been anticipated in wage setting. Suppose for simplicity that the stock of bonds is zero, and that the growth rate of money has increased from zero to some positive rate. The money enters the economy through transfer payments, but there is an offsetting reduction in disposable income arising from capital losses on existing holdings of money.

Real balances will be constant in the new steady state. Suppose for the moment that real interest rate remained unchanged, with the nominal interest rate increasing one for one with the inflation. Then real balances would be reduced. But this means the goods market cannot be in equilibrium, because aggregate demand is reduced below supply. The real interest rate has to fall to maintain equilibrium, the final result being an increase in the nominal and a reduction in the real interest rates. Because the real high-powered money stock is small, though, this nonneutrality is likely to be empirically unimportant in the long run.[28] Tax distortions of the type emphasized by Feldstein (1983) are potentially a more important source of non-Fisher results.[29]

Perhaps the most interesting Fisher-related result is the claimed rejection of the Fisher effect by Summers (1982). Summers, working with decadal averages, finds almost no relationship between the nominal interest rate and the inflation rate. He interprets this as showing that even in the long run the nominal interest rate barely changes with the expected inflation rate, thus going well beyond Irving Fisher's claim that it takes decades for the Fisher neutrality to obtain.[30]

The question of the Fisher effect is still open though. Barsky (1985) argues that the price level in the nineteenth century essentially followed a random walk, so that the ex ante nominal and real rates were the same; he also shows that the differences in decade average real rates are not significant. Further, controversy still obtains (McCallum, 1984) over whether working with data averaged over long periods, or with the low-frequency end of the spectrum as Summers does in his econometric tests, handles the difficulty of the distinction between actual and anticipated inflation.

2 Opening the Economy

In 1944 it was certainly reasonable for the basic model of US macroeconomics to represent a closed economy.[31] Even in 1963, when balance of payments concerns were serious, recognizing the openness of the economy would not have required much change in the basic model. With the nominal exchange rate fixed and the price level assumed constant, the real exchange rate in an open economy version of the 1963 model would have been constant and the current account a simple function of the level of income. With capital flows relatively insignificant, the current account could be taken as the driving force in international transactions.

In 1985 international transactions play a larger role in determining the behavior of the US economy. Supply shocks that originated abroad were instrumental in the two inflationary episodes of the Seventies; the volume of trade has more than doubled as a percentage of GNP in the last twenty years; the gap between domestic absorption and output amounts at present to several percent of GNP. Under flexible exchange rates and substantial capital mobility, monetary and fiscal policy affect the nominal exchange rate quickly and, because domestic prices are sticky, also affect the real exchange rate and resource allocation.[32] Monetary policy changes, such as in the ill-fated late 1978 contraction, and the October 1979 "regime change," can be triggered by concern over the dollar. No modern forecaster of inflation can ignore the dollar.

The exchange rate directly affects both goods and assets market equilibria, and the aggregate supply or markup equation. In the goods market

$$Y = A(Y^p, V, r, G, T, e/P): \tag{1''}$$

V is real wealth; e is the exchange rate measured as the dollar price of foreign exchange. The variable P now denotes the consumer price index. The variable q will be used to denote the price of domestic output.[33]

The money demand equation remains unchanged, though there is an issue of whether the price of domestic output or the CPI, or some combination, should be the deflator for real balances. The asset market equilibrium condition has to be extended because domestic residents can now hold an extra asset—foreign bonds. The simplest, risk neutral, assumption is that expected returns on domestic and foreign bonds are equalized. If i^* is the foreign interest rate, then

$$i = i^* + \varepsilon, \tag{9}$$

where ε is the expected rate of change of the exchange rate. Attempts to locate a risk premium in the relationship between domestic and foreign rates, perhaps as a function of the outstanding stocks of the assets (Frankel, 1982), have not been successful. We thus shall use (9), together with the assumption that the foreign interest rate is given, as the portfolio equilibrium condition linking domestic and foreign interest rates.[34]

The price of domestic output, q, depends not only on wages and output but also on the exchange rate:

$$q = H(W, Y, e).$$

An increase in e is a depreciation of the exchange rate that increases the price of domestic output. Using the definition of the CPI as a weighted average of the price of the price of domestic output and the exchange rate, the pricing equation can be rewritten as

$$P = h(W, Y, e). \tag{10}$$

Net wealth now consists not only of high-powered money, bonds, and capital, but also net claims on foreigners, measured in foreign currency units, F. Foreign asset accumulation is equal to the current account surplus:

$$V = ((M + B)/P) + K + eF/P, \tag{11}$$

$$e_t(F_{t+1} - F_t)/P_t = NX(Y, e/P) + e_t i^*(F_t/P_t). \tag{12}$$

The analysis of monetary and fiscal policy is essentially that of the Mundell-Fleming model.

2.1   An Open Market Purchase

Suppose the economy starts from a position of equilibrium and that an open market purchase takes place. The domestic interest rate tends to fall, output and the price level to rise. Assuming the open market purchase is a once over event, with budgetary implications neutralized by offsetting changes in taxes, the domestic price level will be expected to rise further next period as wages adjust.

With the domestic nominal interest rate lower, international interest rate equalization implies that the exchange rate has to be expected to fall next period. The real exchange rate therefore depreciates (rises) this period (Dornbusch, 1976). Equivalently, the lower domestic interest rate produces a capital outflow that causes the exchange rate to depreciate. The depreciation increases the inflationary effect of the expansionary monetary policy; to the extent that the trade balance responds in the short run to the exchange rate, the exchange rate effect also increases aggregate demand.

In the longer term as prices adjust fully the exchange rate returns close to its initial level. The increase in the ownership of foreign assets during the adjustment period implies a capital inflow in future years, requiring a slightly appreciated future exchange rate.

2.2   Fiscal Expansion

Expansionary fiscal policy tends to increase the domestic interest rate and appreciate (reduce) the exchange rate. The expansionary impact of the expansion is modified by the exchange rate appreciation. Both domestic investment and net exports are crowded out. The decline in ownership of foreign securities during the adjustment periods requires a slightly depreciated future exchange rate to generate the current account surplus to pay the interest on the foreign borrowing.

Recognition of the openness of the economy thus modifies the analysis of monetary and fiscal policy. For a given increase in nominal aggregate demand, a monetary expansion is more inflationary and a fiscal expansion less inflationary in the short run than they would be in the closed economy. Empirical estimates suggest that the differential effects are not mere theoretical niceties, but are rather empirically significant and to be taken account of in the choice of policy—for instance, during a process of disinflation.[35]

3   Concluding Comments

None of us has not heard the joke about the unchanging questions and the changing answers in economics exams. Contrary to the joke, the basic answers in this paper to how monetary and fiscal policy work are close to those of the earlier papers. But it is only the basic answers to the question of whether changes in monetary and fiscal policy have real effects that are unchanged. The modern answer differ in placing much greater emphasis on expectations, on stock-flow relations, on the openness of the economy, and in the modeling of aggregate supply. They differ also because they are less certain than they were then, and they command less consensus within the profession.

Part of the loss of certainty arises from the complexity of dynamics in model even as simple as the present ones:[36] serious macroeconomics that attempts to describe the behavior of the economy rather than illustrate particular points may no longer be possible with just pen and paper, rather needing more powerful technology. Certainly analysis of the adjustment of the economy to disturbances or policy changes to be used in actual policy making is bound to use a more detailed model than can be solved explicitly. The dynamic properties of the major econometric models, or of maximizing models such as those of Kydland and Prescott (1982), can be understood by means of simulations, but not from analytic exercises. It could be argued that the right way to do macroeconomics is to study the detailed structure of such models and to develop understanding of how they work through a variety of simulation exercises. That is the only way to understand a particular large-scale model; the purpose of simpler models like those in this paper is to develop a sense of the overall structure of the economy and intuition about its working.

The loss of assurance is best explained by asking what view was being contested in the 1944, 1963, and 1985 papers. In 1944 Franco Modigliani was contesting Keynes's claim to have produced an unemployment equilibrium and analyzing Keynesian interest rate theory. In 1963 he was contesting the Gurley-Shaw-Radcliffe view that the basic model would be significantly altered by including financial intermediation, and the Patinkin emphasis on equilibrium nonneutralities. The 1985 paper implicitly contests the views of the rational expectations-market equilibrium school that anticipated changes in money have no real effects and that the only significant fiscal variables are government spending and the microstructure of tax rates.[37]

Two factors are responsible for the loss of mainstream self-assurance. The first is empirical. Lucas and Sargent (1978) emphasize the inconsistency of the 1970s inflation with 1960s vintage Phillips curves. But the expectations-augmented Phillips curve was rapidly assimilated into the mainstream and has stood up well from the early 1970s to the present. The deeper reason for unease is that significant components of the mainstream model have had empirical difficulties, in different ways. The demand function for money has shifted. The investment function refuses to conform to neoclassical theory. The consumption function shows more sensitivity than it should to current income. There is no consolation in these difficulties for competing schools in macroeconomics, for none has produced empirically superior formulations.

The second factor responsible for the loss of mainstream self-assurance and lack of consensus within the profession is the theoretical depth of the rational expectations-equilibrium attack. The models analyzed in this paper are not fully based on maximization—the wage and price setting assumptions in particular are ad hoc.[38] Progress in repairing that weakness is being made by many of those cited in the introduction. But until and unless a new model appears that both satisfies the critical standards of the best theorists and is consistent with the behavior of the macroeconomy, macroeconomics will continue to be faced with a trade-off between theoretical purity and relevance. That will be the macroeconomist's burden for a long time.

As a master macroeconomist, Franco Modigliani has shown the ability to live creatively with that tension.

Notes

1. As the author acknowledges in his *Collected Papers*, (Vol. I, pp. 66–67, and "The Monetary Mechanism . . . ," Vol. I, pp. 69–78), the 1944 article contains errors in its discussion of the controversy over the properties of a monetary economy initiated by Lange (1942) and settled by Patinkin (1965).

2. Recent work on the microeconomics of credit rationing (for example, Jaffee and Russell, 1976; Keeton, 1979; Stiglitz and Weiss, 1981) has not been assimilated into analytic macroeconomic models, though credit rationing is an essential component of the operation of monetary policy in the MPS model. See Blinder (1985) for a recent attempt at a simple macroeconomic model in which credit rather than interest rates is the main transmission mechanism for monetary policy; Friedman (1983) has emphasized the credit-GNP relationship.

3. *Collected Papers*, Vol. I, pp. 80–81. The discussion of the Phillips curve trade-off concludes; "According to some views this is *the* predicament of our times, but I don't propose here to assess this claim or, even less, to propose remedies."

4. Comments on this paper by Franco Modigliani follow.

5. The phrase is Robert Hall's.

6. Policano (1985) expresses some surprise that the IS-LM model is still the basic model used in modern macroeconomics textbooks. The versatility of the model is responsible for its survival: it can be used to analyze both monetary and fiscal policy, in both full employment and unemployment modes; it can generate quantity theory or pure Keynesian results with only minor modifications. The model is capable of accommodating monetarist and Keynesian views, as Friedman's (1970) theoretical framework shows. In my view it can also accommodate a basic rational expectations-market clearing view, though I am not sure adherents of that approach would agree.

7. There is no necessary inconsistency between IS-LM type models and maximizing models; see, for instance, Aiyagari and Gertler (1985).

8. The earlier models assumed unitary elasticity of expectations, which translates into the assumption that all changes that take place are expected to be permanent. The assumption is not fully specified until it becomes clear whether it applies to levels of variables or their rates of change.

9. A view implicit in much recent literature is that each dynamic adjustment mechanism by itself should be capable of explaining business cycle dynamics, which—waiving questions about the existence of a trend—can be summarized by the second-order difference equation for detrended output, $y_n = \alpha_1 y_{t-1} + \alpha_2 y_{t-2} + \varepsilon_t$, where ε is serially uncorrelated, α_1 is about 1.35, and α_2 is about $(-.45)$. The multiplier-accelerator mechanism or Metzlerian inventory dynamics come close to producing this adjustment pattern, but it may rather be the interaction of the many dynamic adjustment mechanisms in the economy—slow price

and wage adjustment, slow adjustment of labor and capital inputs, inventory and fixed investment dynamics, exchange rate dynamics—that is responsible for GNP's hump shape. Rose (1985) in ongoing research asks why so many economic variables appear to have very similar, and very simple, dynamic behavior when lagged adjustment is assumed to be widespread.

10. For example, Flavin (1981) and Hall and Mishkin (1982).

11. In an alternative formulation of the model, q would enter explicitly, both in determining the value of the capital stock and in affecting the investment decision. The model would then be essentially that of Tobin (1969). With q normally inversely related to r, an open market purchase that reduces the interest rate then increases aggregate demand both through a wealth effect on consumption demand and a cost of capital effect on investment (Modigliani, 1971). However, as Tobin shows, the inclusion of q does not significantly change the analysis of the operation of policy so long as bonds and capital are gross substitutes.

12. Movements in the money multiplier have at times, notably in the Great Depression, played a significant role. But they are not normally sufficiently important to carry the money multiplier as a separate variable through the remainder of the paper.

13. Where time subscripts are not used, the subscript should be understood to be t.

14. That model did not explicitly include government spending, however.

15. Equation (6) of the 1963 model comes close to writing down the "min" formulation of disequilibrium economics in which labor input is determined by the minimum of quantity supplied and demanded at the existing wage/price vector.

16. The specification of the wage-setting equation in levels is not innocent. One implication is that past mistakes are forgotten in the wage-setting process. A formulation in which the rate of change of the real wage is made a function of the level of output builds mistakes permanently into the real wage. Another implication is that there is a unique full employment real wage, whereas in the rate-of-change formulation, the steady-state level of employment is independent of the real wage. The latter property would be more plausible if the wage equation (3) were formulated in terms of the unemployment rate rather than output. The two formulations do not differ in their implications for short-run output determination, but have different dynamic and policy implications. The empirical evidence is mixed, though for the period since the mid-1960s the rate of change formulation appears more consistent with the data (Blanchard, 1985b).

17. Taylor (1980), Blanchard (1983a). See also note 10.

18. For the AD curve to slope down, the total effect of a unit increase in current income on aggregate demand, operating on consumption both directly and through permanent income, and on investment through the accelerator, has to be less than unity.

19. Rewriting the left-hand side as (B_{t+1}/P_{t+1}) (P_{t+1}/P_t) and dividing through by (P_{t+1}/P_t), the coefficient on the real stock of bonds on the right-hand side becomes the real interest rate. The effect of (P_{t+1}/P_t) in reducing the real value of $G - T$ on the right-hand side is an artifact of discrete time and should be ignored. Modification of this equation to the case of a growing economy is straightforward.

20. If the budget deficit is defined inclusive of nominal interest payments on the debt, then equation (8) appears to make possible a steady state with positive deficit. But (a) this is purely a result of an inflation illusion in fiscal policy, in which noninterest transfer payments are reduced as the debt increases, and (b) there will be a steady state only if the stock of money is increasing at the same rate as the nominal stock of debt.

21. This implies that future net taxes are increased to offset the effects of higher interest payments resulting from the transitory debt-financed deficit.

22. The question arises whether the government can keep rolling over the debt rather than paying it off. The rolling over strategy is possible only if the growth rate of population exceeds the real interest rate, in which case the equilibrium is inefficient. When the equilibrium is efficient, a transversality condition for the government debt in effect implies that the debt is paid off.

23. That is, provided individuals are not liquidity constrained. Liquidity constraints dominate the issue of Ricardian equivalence in the sense that with liquidity constraints, flows of current income affect aggregate demand whether or not individuals would treat the debt as wealth if they were not constrained.

24. Seater (1985) provides a useful review of research on this issue, with references to much of the literature. See also Modigliani and Sterling (1985).

25. Bernheim and Bagwell (1985) make what they describe as the *reductio ad absurdum* argument that if all individuals are effectively linked—for instance, by the possibility that their descendents might marry each other—then all redistributions have no effects on real resource allocation, being immediately undone by the recipients. Further, tax distortions are nonexistent because individuals internalize the operation of the government.

26. Cf. note 24.

27. The Fisher effect is discussed by Friedman (1968).

28. The mechanism that has been described here is that of Mundell (1964a). The Tobin (1965) nonneutrality of inflation arises from the assumption that individuals consume a constant fraction of disposable income, which includes the value of net (inflation adjusted) transfer payments. In a growing economy, the value of these net transfer payments includes a term $g \cdot m$, where g is the growth rate of the economy and m is the value of real balances. With m falling with the rate of inflation, consumption at a given level of output will fall when the inflation rate rises, producing the same effect on aggregate demand as that in the text.

29. Fisher and Modigliani (1978) list many of these distortions.

30. The early Fama result (1975) of constancy of the real interest rate appeared even then to be a result peculiar to the period of the regression; after the real interest rate changes of the early Eighties, any notion of even approximate real interest rate constancy must be rejected.

31. Keynes's own use of a closed economy model of Britain has frequently been criticized. It is not obvious what features of the Keynesian message would have been changed by recognizing the openness of the British economy: government spending and tax cuts are still expansionary in an open economy, as is an increase in the money supply unless the economy is in a liquidity trap.

32. Dornbusch and Fisher (1984) contains an extended discussion of international linkages of the US economy and presents an open economy model on which I draw.

33. Denoting the price of domestic output by q, and setting the price of foreign goods at unity, the CPI can be written $P = q^s e^{1-s}$; the relative price of foreign goods is then $e/q = (e/P)^{1/s}$; thus e/P in (1″) represents the price of foreign relative to domestic goods.

34. Although there is no compelling evidence for risk premiums, there is also no evidence that suggests the forecast implicit in (9) is a good one. See, for example, Cumby and Obstfeld (1984).

35. Dornbusch and Fischer (1984) and Sachs (1985); Fischer (1987) discusses the effects of exchange rate appreciation on the costs of disinflation.

36. For instance, the analysis of the open economy model in section 2 did not pursue the dynamics of foreign and domestic debt accumulation in detail; the analysis of section 1 did not pursue the dynamics of capital accumulation.

37. Modigliani (1977) directly confronts those views.

38. The use of "ad hoc" as a term of derision makes the point; ad hoc could also be interpreted as fulfilment of the terms of Occam's Razor.

Bibliography

Abel, Andrew B., 1984. "Bequests and Social Security with Uncertain Lifetimes," National Bureau of Economic Research Working Paper 1372.

Aiyagari, S. Rao, and Mark Gertler, 1985. "The Backing of Government Bonds and Monetarism," Journal of Monetary Economics, 16, 1 (July), 19–44.

Akerlof, George, and Janet Yellen, 1985. "A near Rational Model of the Business Cycle with Wage and Price Inertia," Quarterly Journal of Economics, Vol. C (Supplement), 823–828.

Azariadis, Costas, 1975. "Implicit Contracts and Underemployment Equilibria," Journal of Political Economy, 83, 6 (Dec.), 1183–1202.

Backus, David, and E. J. Driffill, 1985. "Inflation and Reputation," *American Economic Review*, 75, 3 (June), 530–538.

Baily, Martin N., 1974. "Wages and Employment under Uncertain Demand," *Review of Economic Studies*, 41, 1 (Jan.), 37–50.

Barro, Robert J., 1972. "A Theory of Monopolistic Price Adjustment," *Review of Economic Studies*, 39, 1 (Jan.), 17–26.

Barro, Robert J., 1974. "Are Government Bonds Net Wealth?" *Journal of Political Economy*, 82, 6 (Nov./Dec.), 1095–1118.

Barro, Robert J., 1977. "On Long Term Contracting, Sticky Prices and Monetary Policy," *Journal of Monetary Economics*, 3, 3 (July), 305–316.

Barro, Robert J., and David Gordon, 1983. "A Positive Theory of Monetary Policy in a Natural Rate Model," *Journal of Political Economy*, 91, 4 (Aug.), 589–610.

Barro, Robert J., and Herschel Grossman, 1976. *Money, Employment and Inflation*, Cambridge University Press.

Barksy, Robert, 1985. "Tests of the Fisher hypothesis and the forecastability of inflation under alternative monetary regimes," Chapter 2, MIT PhD dissertation.

Barsky, Robert, N. Greg Mankiw, and Stephen Zeldes, 1984. "Ricardian Consumers with Keynesian Propensities," National Bureau of Economic Research Working Paper 1400.

Benassy, Jean-Pascal, 1982. *The Economics of Market Disequilibrium*, Academic Press.

Bernheim, Douglas, and Kyle Bagwell, 1985. "Is Everything Neutral? The Implications of Intergenerational Altruism in an Overlapping Generations Model with Altruism," mimeo, Stanford.

Blanchard, Olivier, 1983a. "Price Asynchronization and Price Level Inertia," in R. Dornbusch and M. Simonsen, eds., *Inflation, Debt, and Indexation*, MIT Press.

Blanchard, Olivier, 1983b. "The Production and Inventory Behavior of the American Automobile Industry," *Journal of Political Economy*, 91, 3 (June), 365–400.

Blanchard, Olivier, 1985a. "Monopolistic Competition, Small Menu Costs and Real Effects of Nominal Money," mimeo, MIT.

Blanchard, Olivier, 1985b. "Output, Prices and Wages: An Empirical Structural Investigation," mimeo, Department of Economics, MIT.

Blinder, Alan S., 1985. "Credit Rationing and Effective Supply Failures," NBER Working Paper 1619.

Breeden, Douglas, 1979. "An Intertemporal Asset Pricing Model with Stochastic Consumption and Investment Opportunities," *Journal of Financial Economics*, 7, (Sept.), 265–296.

Caplin, Andrew, and Daniel F. Spulber, 1985. "Inflation, Menu Costs and Endogenous Price Variability," mimeo, Department of Economics, Harvard University.

Clower, Robert, 1965. "The Keynesian Counter-Revolution: A Theoretical Appraisal," in F. H. Hahn and F. Brechling, eds., *The Theory of Interest Rates*, Macmillan.

Cumby, Robert, and Maurice Obstfeld, 1984. "International Interest-Rate and Price-Level Linkages under Flexible Exchange Rates: A Review of Recent Evidence," in John Bilson and Richard Marston, eds., *Exchange Rate Theory and Practice*, University of Chicago Press.

Diamond, Peter A., 1965. "National Debt in a Neoclassical Growth Model," *American Economic Review*, 55, 5 (Dec.), 1126–1150.

Dornbusch, Rudiger, 1976. "Expectations and Exchange Rate Dynamics," *Journal of Political Economy*, 84, 6 (Dec.), 1161–1176.

Dornbusch, Rudiger, and Stanley Fischer, 1984. "The Open Economy: Implications for Monetary and Fiscal Policy," NBER Working Paper 1422.

Drazen, Allan, 1978. "Government Debt, Human Capital, and Bequests in a Life-Cycle Model," *Journal of Political Economy*, 86, 3 (June), 505–516.

Eichenbaum, Martin, 1983. "A Rational Expectations Equilibrium Model of Inventories of Finished Goods and Employment," *Journal of Monetary Economics*, 12, 2 (Aug.), 259–278.

Fama, Eugene F., 1970. "Efficient Capital Markets: A Review of Theory and Empirical Work," *Journal of Finance*, 25, 383–417.

Fama, Eugene F., 1975. "Short-Term Interest Rates as Predictors of Inflation," *American Economic Review*, 65, 3 (June), 269–282.

Feldstein, Martin, 1983. *Inflation, Tax Rules, and Capital Formation*, University of Chicago Press.

Fischer, Stanley, 1977. "Long Term Contracts, Rational Expectations, and the Optimal Money Supply Rule," *Journal of Political Economy*, 85, 1 (Feb.), 191–205.

Fischer, Stanley, 1987. "Real Balances, the Exchange Rate and Indexation: Real Variables in Disinflation," forthcoming, *Quarterly Journal of Economics*.

Fischer, Stanley, and Franco Modigliani, 1978. "Towards an Understanding of the Real Effects and Costs of Inflation," *Weltwirtschaftliches Archiv*, 114, 810–832.

Flavin, Marjorie A., 1981. "The Adjustment of Consumption to Changing Expectations about Future Income," *Journal of Political Economy*, 89, 5 (Oct.), 974–1009.

Friedman, Benjamin M. 1983. "The Roles of Money and Credit in Macroeconomic Analysis," in J. Tobin, ed., *Macroeconomics, Prices and Quantities*, Brookings Institution.

Friedman, Milton, 1968. "The Role of Monetary Policy," *American Economic Review*, 78, 1 (March), 1–17.

Friedman, Milton, 1970. "A Theoretical Framework for Monetary Analysis," *Journal of Political Economy*, 78, 2 (March/April), 193–238.

Grandmont, Jean-Michel, 1985. "On Endogeneous Competitive Business Cycles," *Econometrica*, 53, 5 (Sept.) 995–1046.

Grossman, Herschel I., 1983. "The Natural Rate Hypothesis, the Rational-Expectations Hypothesis, and the Remarkable Survival of Non-Market Clearing Assumptions," in Carnegie-Rochester Conference Series on Public Policy, Vol. 19, *Variability in Employment, Prices, and Money.*

Hall, Robert E., 1978. "Stochastic Implications of the Life Cycle-Permanent Income Hypothesis: Theory and Evidence," *Journal of Political Economy*, 86, 6 (Dec.), 971–987.

Hall, Robert E., and Edward Lazear, 1984. "The Excess Sensitivity of Layoffs and Quits to Demand," *Journal of Labor Economics*, 2, 233–257.

Hall, Robert E., and Frederic S. Mishkin, 1982. "The Sensitivity of Consumption to Transitory Income—Estimates from Panel Data on Households," *Econometrica*, 50, 2 (March), 461–481.

Hansen, Lars P., and Kenneth Singleton, 1983. "Stochastic Consumption, Risk Aversion, and the Temporal Behavior of Asset Returns," *Journal of Political Economy*, 91, 2 (April), 249–265.

Hart, Oliver, 1983. "Optimal Labour Contracts under Asymmetric Information, an Introduction," *Review of Economic Studies*, 50, 1 (Jan.), 3–35.

Jaffee, Dwight M., and Thomas Russell, 1976. "Imperfect Information, Uncertainty, and Credit Rationing," *Quarterly Journal of Economics*, 90, 4 (Nov.), 651–666.

Keeton, William, 1979. *Equilibrium Credit Rationing*, Garland Publishers.

Kotlikoff, Laurence J., and Lawrence H. Summers, 1981. "The Role of Intergenerational Transfers in Aggregate Capital Accumulation," *Journal of Political Economy*, 89, 4 (Aug.), 706–732.

Kydland, Finn E., and Edward C. Prescott, 1977. "Rules Rather Than Discretion—the Inconsistency of Optimal Plans," *Journal of Political Economy*, 85, 3 (June), 473–491.

Kydland, Finn E., and Edward C. Prescott, 1982. "Time to Build and Aggregate Fluctuations," *Econometrica*, 50, 6 (Nov.), 1345–1370.

Lange, Oskar, 1942. "Say's Law: A Restatement and Criticism," in O. Lange, ed., *Studies in Mathematical Economics and Econometrics*, University of Chicago Press.

Leroy, Stephan F., and Richard D. Porter, 1981. "The Present Value Relation: Tests Based on Implied Variance Bounds," *Econometrica*, 49, 3 (May), 555–574.

Lucas, Robert E., 1972. "Expectations and the Neutrality of Money," *Journal of Economic Theory*, 4, 2 (April), 103–124.

Lucas, Robert E., 1973. "Some International Evidence on Output-Inflation Trade-offs," *American Economic Review*, 63, 3 (Sept.), 326–344.

Lucas, Robert E., and Thomas Sargent, 1978. "After Keynesian Macroeconomics," in After the Phillips Curve: Persistence of High Inflation and High Unemployment, Conference Series 19, Federal Reserve Bank of Boston.

McCallum, Bennett T., 1984. "On Low-Frequency Estimates of Long-Run Relationships in Macroeconomics," *Journal of Monetary Economics*, 14, 1 (July), 3–14.

McDonald, Ian M., and Robert M. Solow, 1981. "Wage Bargaining and Employment," *American Economic Review*, 71, 5 (Dec.), 896–908.

Mankiw, N. Gregory, 1985. "Small Menu Costs and Large Business Cycles: A Macroeconomic Model of Monopoly," *Quarterly Journal of Economics*, 100, 2 (Nov.), 529–538.

Mankiw, N. Gregory, Julio Rotemberg, and Lawrence Summers, 1985. "Intertemporal Substitution in Macroeconomics," *Quarterly Journal of Economics*, 100, 1 (Feb.), 225–251.

Marsh, Terry A., and Robert C. Merton, 1986. "Dividend Variability and Variance Bounds Tests for the Rationality of Stock Market Prices," *American Economic Review*, 76, 3 (June), 483–498.

Merton, Robert C., 1973. "An Intertemporal Capital Asset Pricing Model," *Econometrica*, 41, 5 (Sept.), 867–888.

Mishkin, Frederic S., 1983. *A Rational Expectations Approach to Macroeconometrics*, University of Chicago Press.

Modigliani, Franco, 1944. "Liquidity Preference and the Theory of Interest and Money," *Econometrica*, 12, 1 (Jan.), 45–88.

Modigliani, Franco, 1961. "Long-Run Implications of Alternative Fiscal Policies and the Burden of the National Debt," *Economic Journal*, 71, 4 (Dec.), 730–755.

Modigliani, Franco, 1963. "The Monetary Mechanism and Its Interaction with Real Phenomena," *Review of Economics and Statistics*, 45, 1 (Feb.), 79–107.

Modigliani, Franco, 1971. "Monetary Policy and Consumption Linkages via Interest Rate and Wealth Effects in the FMP Model," Consumer Spending and Monetary Policy: The Linkages, Conferences Series 5, Federal Reserve Bank of Boston.

Modigliani, Franco, 1977. "The Monetarist Controversy, or Should We Forsake Stabilization Policies?" *American Economic Review*, 67, 1 (March), 1–19.

Modigliani, Franco, 1980. *The Collected Scientific Papers of Franco Modigliani*, Andrew Abel, ed., Vols. I, II, and III, MIT Press.

Modigliani, Franco, and Arlie Sterling, 1985. "Government Debt, Government Spending and Private Sector Behavior: A Comment," mimeo, Sloan School of Management, MIT.

Mundell, Robert A., 1964a. "Inflation, Saving, and the Real Rate of Interest," *Journal of Political Economy*, 71, 3 (June), 280–283.

Mundell, Robert A., 1964b. "Some Subtleties in the Interpretation of Keynesian Equilibrium," *Weltwirtschaftliches Archiv*.

Neary, J. Peter, and Joseph E. Stiglitz, 1983. "Toward a Reconstruction of Keynesian Economics; Expectations and Constrained Equilibria," *Quarterly Journal of Economics*, 98 (Supplement), 199–228.

Patinkin, Don, 1965. *Money, Interest, and Prices*, 2nd ed., Harper and Row.

Phelps, Edmund S., and John B. Taylor, 1977. "Stabilizing Powers of Monetary Policy under Rational Expectations," *Journal of Political Economy*, 85, 1 (Feb.), 163–190.

Policano, Andrew J., 1985. "The Current State of Macroeconomics; A View from the Textbooks," *Journal of Monetary Economics*, 15, 3 (May), 389–398.

Rogoff, Kenneth, 1985. "The Optimal Degree of Commitment to an Intermediate Monetary Target," *Quarterly Journal of Economics*, 100, 4 (Nov.), 1169–1190.

Rose, Andrew K., 1985. "The Autoregressivity Paradox in Macroeconomics: Implications for Simultaneity, Equilibrium, and the Business Cycle," mimeo, MIT.

Rotemberg, Julio J., 1982. "Sticky Prices in the United States," *Journal of Political Economy*, 90, 6 (Dec.), 1187–1211.

Sachs, Jeffrey D., 1985. "The Dollar and the Policy Mix: 1985," *Brookings Papers on Economic Activity*, 1, 117–186.

Samuelson, Paul A., 1958. "An Exact Consumption Loan Model with or without the Social Contrivance of Money," *Journal of Political Economy*, 66, 6 (Dec.), 467–482.

Samuelson, Paul A., 1965. "Proof That Properly Anticipated Prices Fluctuate Randomly," *Industrial Management Review*, 6, 2 (Spring), 41–49.

Sargent, Thomas J., 1978. "Estimation of Dynamic Labor Demand Schedules under Rational Expectations," *Journal of Political Economy*, 86, 6 (Dec.), 1009–1044.

Sargent, Thomas J., and Neil Wallace, 1975. "Rational Expectations, the Optimal Monetary Instrument, and the Optimal Money Supply Rule," *Journal of Political Economy*, 83, 2 (April), 241–254.

Sargent, Thomas J., 1981. "Some Simple Monetarist Arithmetic," *Federal Reserve Bank of Minneapolis Quarterly Review*, 5 (Fall), 1–17.

Sargent, Thomas J., 1983. "A Model of Commodity Money," *Journal of Monetary Economics*, 12, 1 (July), 163–188.

Seater, John J., 1985. "Does Government Debt Matter? A Review," *Journal of Monetary Economics*, 16, 1 (July), 121–132.

Shapiro, Matthew D., 1985. "Capital Utilization and Capital Accumulation: Theory and Evidence," Cowles Foundation Discussion Paper 736.

Sheshinski, Eytan, and Yoram Weiss, 1977. "Inflation and Costs of Price Adjustment," *Review of Economic Studies*, 44, 2 (June), 287–304.

Shiller, Robert J., 1981. "Do Stock Prices Move Too Much to Be Justified by Subsequent Changes in Dividends?" *American Economic Review*, 71, 3 (June), 421–436.

Singleton, Kenneth J., 1980. "Expectations Models of the Term Structure and Implied Variance Bounds," *Journal of Political Economy*, 88, 6 (Dec.), 1159–1176.

Solow, Robert M., and Joseph E. Stiglitz, 1968. "Output, Employment and Wages in the Short Run," *Quarterly Journal of Economics*, 82, 537–560.

Stiglitz, Joseph E., 1984. "Theories of Wage Rigidity," NBER Working Paper 1442.

Stiglitz, Joseph E., and Andrew Weiss, 1981. "Credit Rationing in Markets with Imperfect Competition," *American Economic Review*, 71, 3 (June), 393–410.

Summers, Lawrence H., 1982. "The Nonadjustment of Nominal Interest Rates: A Study of the Fisher Effect," in J. Tobin, ed., *Macroeconomics, Prices and Quantities*, Brookings Institutions.

Taylor, John B., 1980. "Aggregate Dynamics and Staggered Contracts," *Journal of Political Economy*, 88, 1 (Feb.), 1–23.

Tinbergen, Jan, 1967. *Economic Policy: Principles and Design*, Rand McNally.

Tirole, Jean, 1985. "Asset Bubbles and Overlapping Generations," *Econometrica*, 53, 5 (Sept.), 1071–1100.

Tobin, James, 1961. "Money, Capital, and Other Stores of Value," *American Economic Review*, 51, 2 (May), 26–37.

Tobin, James, 1965. "Money and Economic Growth," *Econometrica*, 33, 4 (Oct.), 671–684.

Tobin, James, 1969. "A General Equilibrium Approach to Monetary Theory," *Journal of Money, Credit, and Banking*, 1, 1 (Feb.), 15–29.

Tobin, James, and Willem Buiter, 1980. "Fiscal and Monetary Policies, Capital Formation, and Economic Activity," in G. von Furstenberg, ed., *The Government and Capital Formation*, Ballinger.

Wallace, Neil, 1981. "A Modigliani-Miller Theorem for Open Market Operations," *American Economic Review*, 71, 3 (June), 267–274.

Comments on "1944, 1963, and 1985"

Franco Modigliani

Fischer's paper provided such good reading for me that it made me think back to the fun and excitement I experienced in writing the 1944 and 1963 papers—excitement that came from the feeling that the structure really helped to understand how the economy worked. I equally remember the thrill when, shortly after the publication of the 1944 paper, Gerhard Tintner told me that the model could be estimated empirically and he was actually doing it (though I must report that I never saw the outcome!).

The fact that I enjoyed the paper does not per se mean that I recognize myself in his model; but, in fact, I largely do.

To begin with, I agree with the basic proposition underlying the whole exercise, that there are a number of basic features that must be added to the 1964 vintage model to bring it up to the state of the arts. They include (i) the "vertical" Phillips Curve and (ii) the implications of an open economy, particularly under a floating exchange regime and reasonably free movements of capital. To this list, Fischer adds (iii) "the analysis of expectations." If he means by that the explicit awareness that actions, nearly always, depend on expectations and not on past events, and that expectations must be carefully modeled, I agree with him. Indeed, much before the craze with rational expectations, the Life Cycle—and the Permanent Income—hypothesis postulated the revolutionary notion that consumption decisions depend on expectations over a very long horizon. Furthermore, the recognition of the role of expectations had important policy implications, as in the case of the choice between permanent and transitory taxes of various types. But, if what Fischer has in mind is "macro rational expectations" and the mechanics that goes with it, I disagree. Even though we cannot avoid drilling our students in this mechanics, I believe it has added little to the analysis and even less to the design of effective policies. On the other hand, I would add to Fischer's list what may be called the "economics of inflation"; after all, the earlier vintage did not even recognize the distinction between nominal and real rates!

It may be noted that all these later enrichments came, to a large extent, not from advances in theory but rather in response to exogenous developments of an economic or institutional type. These included the steadily rising inflation of the late Sixties, the two oil shocks, the growing importance of international capital movements, the breakdown of Bretton Woods, and the ensuing return to (more or less) freely floating exchange rates (though the theory of a floating exchange regime had undoubtedly made important strides before these events at the hands of Fleming and Mundell).

Features (i) to (iii) have little impact on the determinants of aggregate demand, and so the aggregate demand equation (1) looks pretty much as in 1964—provided, however, one is prepared to ignore certain effects of inflation. One is the possibility of inflation illusion—e.g., that consumers may fail to deduct from interest income the loss of purchasing power of the principal. Another possibility is that they may undervalue the equities representing a claim to the stock of capital, K, by capitalizing earning flows at rates closer to the nominal than to the real rate (see Modigliani and Cohn, 1979). Similarly, one must disregard the impact of the price level and inflation on personal and corporate taxation. Finally, in the light of (iii), I would stress that G and T (and r) should be thought of as expectations over some relevant horizon. (The expectation about r should, in principle, be included through the long rate, as Fischer recognizes.) The question of how these expectations are related to current (and past) observables, including the issue of "rationality," might well be left for separate treatment, depending on the application one is making of the model.

Just a minor note of dissent: I do not believe that the earlier vintages, or the new one, assumed that bonds and physical capital (or better yet, "equities") are prefect substitutes, but only that the risk premium by which the required return on (unlevered) equity exceeds the interest rate is not systematically affected by other endogenous variables—this may be a strong assumption, but at least it does not fly in the face of evidence.

The significant difference between the old and the new vintages begins with the supply side and specifically with the Phillips Curve (3), which replaces the wage rigidity assumption of the earlier vintages. However, I find the Fischer formulation a bit obscure and incomplete. I can see the economy of formulating (3) in terms of income instead of the traditional unemployment (though, in my view, it is unemployment that should continue to be at the center of attention). But, I do not see why expected income (unemployment) should play a significant role. Next, I would find it helpful—though admittedly not necessary—to replace Y (by $(Y - \hat{Y})$, where $\hat{Y}$ is the income corresponding to so-called NIRU (Modigliani and Papademos, 1975). Also, I find it easier to work with the traditional rate of change form. But, in any event, the equation should contain a term in productivity—there being, even in short-term anlysis, no reason to assume it constant. In the level form, the productivity variable might be written as $[-(1 - a)n + an^e]$, where n is productivity (output per man per whatever unit of time the wage is measured in), and a measures the extent to which wage settlements reflect productivity increases expected during the duration of the contract. This addition is useful to clarify that the wage bargains aim at roughly maintaining the share and that, at full employment, the expectation of stable prices will be self-fulfilling when technical progress is correctly anticipated. It also helps to account for the fact that, even in the presence of a significant productivity trend, prices, rather than wages, tend to stay constant, and why a productivity slowdown may initially contribute to inflation.

Finally, I find it surprising that his Phillips Curve makes no explicit reference to the role of overlapping staggered contracts, especially in view of the early contributions Fischer has made in this area. I suppose Fischer may try to capture this effect through the assumption that the price expectation term p^e is entirely exogenous. The plausibility of this assumption depends obviously on the length of the time unit. I would prefer to let p_t^e respond partially to p_t, but would at least allow for the role of lagged expectations of inflation.

As for the aggregate output supply function, I agree with Fischer's judgment that there is little new. However, I would stress that time and empirical work (e.g., the MPS) have confirmed the practical usefulness of the stable markup formulation, which is a special case of (4) (once one adds the missing productivity term).

In the central section on the comparison with the 1963 model, and more particularly in the subsection on "Equilibrium," my 1986 story differs from Stan's rendition in one relatively minor and one major respect. The minor respect refers to the way one thinks of unemployment. He thinks of it in Keynesian terms of a supply of labor exceeding the effective demand. I find it much preferable to think of it in terms of a search theoretic formulation plus the Beveridge Curve in the style of, e.g., Holt (1970). When demand declines, the number of jobs is reduced, which decreases vacancies, which lengthens the search time, raising unemployment—on the assumption, roughly consistent with the evidence, that the change in demand does not appreciably change the flow of separation. Finally, the lengthening of the average search period has the effect of dampening the rate of change of wages. Thus, NIRU is not where "demand" is equal to "supply," but rather where the rate of vacancies and associated level of unemployment and length of search (by both employees and employers) is such that there is no significant upward or downward pressure on the wage.

The more substantive difference has to do with the role of rational expectations and the so-called "neutrality" of fully anticipated policy. I begin to take my distance when Fischer asserts that in modeling expectations, "rational expectations is the right initial hypothesis." This, of course, means accepting the usual preposterous implications that the representative agent built into the model must construct and rely on a model of the economy identical to mine, and including the preposterous implication that.... My view on the contrary is that one should model expectations as those of "intelligent laymen," with limited time available to form expectations, especially about arcane variables like the money supply (unless, of course, they make a living in the bond market). This view does not, of course, rule out a priori that in some cases some form of roughly rational expectation may apply. But, in any event, the mechanism of expectation formation should be treated as an empirical issue subject to tests and not as a postulate.

But where I really part company is when Fischer illustrates the working of open market purchases in a way that suggests that monetary policy is neutral, even if with some lag: "As expectations adjust ... output returns to the [initial] full employment equilibrium level." Similarly, it suggests that, to the extent that it works, in the short run it is by fooling people.

It is, of course, true that the model has the property that, as long as the money supply grows at a constant rate not appreciably lower than the growth of real output, then after a shock, output must eventually return to full employment, though it might take a long time. Thus, if we start from full employment, any government policy to change employment will eventually prove futile—except possibly if it affects NIRU, or if it is continuously escalated. But, this conclusion is of little interest. For there is no reason for the government to want to take significant expansionary (or contractive) measures when the economy is already at NIRU—at least once its economists have understood the vertical Phillips Curve (and leaving aside the science fiction subject of the political business cycle).

But there is another story that one could tell and that would ring quite different. Suppose we start again at point E in his graph, but let us now suppose that it corresponds to a sustainable equilibrium, with full employment and steady inflation—say zero. Next, suppose that there is a substantial shock—e.g., a downward shiftof the aggregate demand curve due to a fall in exports because of a world recession. The initial effect is to shift the economy to a short-run equilibrium represented by a point on *AS* but below *E*, with lower output and more unemployment. If the stabilization authorities do not undertake any ad hoc policy, the system will eventually return to *E*. This occurs through a gradual reduction of nominal wages and prices relative to the money supply under the pressure of unemployment above NIRU. This decline continues until it has fully offset the increased demand for money arising from the lower interest. In this way, the system eventually asymptotically returns to full employment, though, presumably, after a substantial lapse of time.

The alternative is for the government to take measures to shift the aggregate demand right back to the initial position. This could be done, in particular, by increasing the money supply to the point where it is appropriate to finance the initial level of income at the initial price level and the new lower level of the interest rate required to increase investment enough to offset the reduction in net exports. Of course, it would be possible to use, instead, fiscal policy—e.g., an increase in expenditure or transfers— though there is a good case for preferring the lower money supply-interest policy. This policy, in fact, may lower the exchange rate (if floating) and thus improve net exports, and reduce the increase in the net inflow of capital that a policy of maintaining income implies.

In reality, of course, the return *E* may require some time—particularly if one is to avoid the danger of "instrument instability." But, this consideration does not change the essential conclusion, that, in this illustration— and, as far as I can tell, in any other relevant case—the effectiveness of the stabilization policy (i) does not rely on fooling anybody but rather in helping everybody by reestablishing the correct real money supply the painless way and (ii) will not depend on whether or not it is fully anticipated—in fact, it may work better if anticipated and understood since it will help form correct price expectations. Furthermore, (iii) once the system returns to *E*, there will be no further adjustment in the private sector to undo what has been achieved by the policy, even though that policy will presumably remain in place until the disturbance has passed, or a new one has come. The implication is clear: there is absolutely nothing in the revised model with "intelligent" expectations, Phillips Curve and all, that would lead one to conclude that stabilization policies must be futile or to reject discretionary stabilization policies in favor of a money rule.

Of course, in a stochastic world, discretionary stabilization policy could get into trouble, and might conceivably even yield a less stable economy than one with rules. As I have suggested in my Presidential Address, the issue is purely an empirical one, and the evidence suggests that stabilization policies have been quite effective. But, the main point, for present purposes, is that vertical Phillips Curves and rational expectations should in no way modify one's prior beliefs as to the comparative merits of rules versus discretion.

I want next to discuss briefly next a fashionable issue on which Fischer seems to be still full of uncertainty and qualms whereas I feel I have "all the answers." I am referring to the issue of whether government debt is regarded by private economic agents—notably for the purpose of consumption decisions—as net wealth (i) to a minor extent, at best as the LCH model suggests, or (ii) instead dollar per dollar as Barro would imply. Stated in terms of flows, the issue is whether consumption, in addition to responding to anticipated disposable income over the balance of life, responds also (negatively) to the prospective deficit (i) only to small extent, if at all (LCH), or (ii) fully as much as to disposable income (Barro). Fischer appears to regard Barro's argument as not implausible. He is particularly impressed by a paper by Kotlikoff and Summers affirming that most wealth is received by bequests. Furthermore, he regards the evidence on the Barro proposition as inconclusive so far.

I differ from him on all counts. First, I regard Barro's argument as highly implausible, because of the very special assumptions it requires on the nature of the utility function and because it has been shown that, even if that utility held for everybody, his conclusions would not still hold for many reasons (e.g., corner solutions, heterogeneity of family composition). Second, in a forthcoming paper, I have shown that the results presented by Kotlikoff and Summers are enormously upward biased because of several errors they have made and because of the unusual definition of bequests received and life cycle income they have adopted. My estimated based on many sources (including K&S) suggests that the share of wealth resulting from bequests is no more than a modest 1/5, and that the contribution of *voluntary* bequests to existing wealth is even smaller. Third, in a recent paper and two forthcoming ones, I have presented what I at least would regard as pretty conclusive evidence, both for the United States and for Italy, that the negative effect of the deficit on consumption given disposable income is modest (Italy) or plain absent (United States). Hence, so far as I am concerned, the Barro fantasy is over.

In the subsection on the "Fisher Relation . . . ," the author's demonstration that inflation is not neutral strikes me as defective. In fact, I would argue that his proposition is true only when the money supply consists of outside money. Furthermore, in this case, the demonstration can be usefully formulated in terms of the Life Cycle Model.

In his demonstration he assumes that, at some point, money begins to grow at a constant rate and correctly infers that this will raise the nominal rate and lower the real demand for money. But equilibrium need *not* be restored by a fall in the nominal and real rate: it can be restored instead by prices rising for a while, faster than money, and thus reducing the real stock of money. If the money is inside money, this is precisely what happens. But suppose money is government debt (and part of private wealth); then the M/P component of wealth shrinks; since the life cycle suggests that the total demand for wealth is unchanged, there must occur a rise in the reproducible tangible wealth component of total wealth, which must result in a fall in the real rate. There might be further consequences as the higher stock of capital will mean larger income, hence a larger demand for money, etc., but these secondary reactions can be neglected since, as pointed out by Fischer, even the main reaction is likely to be pretty negligible.

In the section on international trade—a net addition to the earlier models—I have nothing significant to add to his analysis. Perhaps I would have preferred to his assumption that the adjustment in capital markets is instantaneous a formulation allowing for a gradual response of capital movements to the gap between the domestic and the foreign rate, adjusted for expected changes in the exchange—but I doubt that would make much difference.

And this brings me to the overview provided in the concluding section. Here Fischer is right on target in indicating what views were being contested in each vintage. In particular, he is absolutely right in stating that the views to be contested in 1985 are (i) the relevance of macro rational expectations, (ii) the neutrality of anticipated policy, and (iii) the Barro view that consumption depends on (anticipated) expenditure, not taxes. In fact, my only significant complaint concerning his rendition of the 1985 vintage is that he is much too attentive and timid in rejecting the practical relevance of each of these views. But then I am prepared to accept the fact that it will take some time for the younger generation (and the younger the longer) to cut down to size the contribution of that self-styled "revolution."

I must finally add that in contrast to the younger generation, I feel little qualm about the wage-price unemployment sector. The wage can be satisfactorily accounted for by the Phillips Curve augmented by intelligent price expectations. Unemployment can be understood on the basis of the search model and the Beveridge Curve, and the markup formulation of the price equation rests comfortably on oligopoly theory and other related models.

In conclusion, I wish to thank Fischer for his valiant effort. I trust that between his paper and my comments I can spare myself and others an update of my earlier contributions.

References

Holt, Charles C., "Job Search, Phillips' Wage Relation, and Union Influence: Theory and Evidence," in E. S. Phelps, editor, *Microeconomic Foundations of Employment and Inflation Theory*, Norton, 1970.

Modigliani, Franco, and Richard Cohn, "Inflation, Rational Valuation and the Market," *Financial Analysts Journal*, March/April, 1979, pp. 24–44.

Modigliani, Franco, and Lucas Papademos, "Targets for Monetary Policy in the Coming Year," *Brookings Papers on Economic Activity*, 1:1975, pp. 141–163.

9 Reshaping Monetary Policy

Tommaso Padoa-Schioppa

1 Introduction

The last fifteen years have witnessed important innovations in the financial structure of most industrial countries. This was essentially the consequence of the long inflation, the development of new information and communication technologies, and the floating of exchange rates.

Innovation is often perceived as a "nuisance" to monetary policy, a phenomenon that made the definition, measurement, and control of "money" more and more difficult. This view, however, is unduly restrictive, not only because it reduces financial innovation to a process originating only in the private sector, but also because it assumes that it is predominantly motivated by the desire to avoid regulatory constraints.[1]

As is the case with any other economic agent, the monetary authority maximizes its objective function subject to constraints that are of both an institutional and an economic nature, and it responds to factors that make such constraints more binding. Its tools, however, differ from those available to private agents.

In Italy too, the persistence of double-digit cost and price inflation,

The ideas on which this chapter draws were acquired over fifteen years, largely by accumulating debts that I gladly acknowledge. In Cambridge and Rome, Franco Modigliani taught me to recognize the concepts of economic theory in the complexity of real life and gave me unfailing intellectual inspiration and challenge. Guido Carli, Paolo Baffi, and Carlo A. Ciampi—the three Governors under whom I served in the Banca d'Italia during this period—provided a wealth of experience and offered early involvement in policy problems. By kindly reading and discussing the manuscript, they have further added to their credit. In turn, I am indebted to Antonio Fazio and Giovanni Carosio for the profit I derived from their generous intellectual and professional partnership. None of them can be held responsible for the inevitable biases of an account by someone who was not a dispassionate observer, or for any remaining inaccuracies. I also gratefully acknowledge the valuable help of Francesco Papadia and Valeria Sannucci in preparing this chapter.

a binding external constraint, and the sharp increase in the public sector borrowing requirement called for a transformation of the financial structure.

The importance of the role played by the monetary authority in this process has been a distinctive feature of the Italian experience. The resources that the central bank has devoted to it suggest that rather than a "nuisance," innovation has been an explicit objective.

Two reasons explain this peculiarity. The first has to do with allocative efficiency and the backwardness of the financial market. In this respect the need was felt to affect the supply side of the economy by improving the efficiency of the financial system. The second reason is that the money market and the constraints on central bank behavior had to be reshaped in order to improve monetary control.

This paper leaves the allocative purpose in the background and focuses on the objective of monetary control. This choice, however, does not imply that the long-term goal of improving the efficiency of the Italian financial system is regarded as less important.

In section 2 qualitative and quantitative monetary policy are defined and their mutual relationships illustrated, keeping in mind the specific Italian experience. The general case of substitutability between qualitative and quantitative actions to achieve a given result in terms of monetary control is examined, as well as the main exceptions to this general case. [*]

The following three sections outline the changes induced by central bank qualitative policy on the structure of the financial system over the last fifteen years. Section 3 discusses the increasing difficulties that led to the introduction of direct controls; section 4 illustrates the main features of a two-tier system based on both administrative controls and qualitative actions; section 5 describes the transition to a system of monetary control based on "orthodox" quantitative policies.

Modigliani and Papademos have shown [2] that the "conventional paradigm" of the monetary mechanism, centered on intermediate objectives defined in terms of the supply of a relatively narrow monetary aggregate, is based on specific assumptions that do not hold universally. They have pointed out that Italy is a special case to which, due to its financial structure, the "conventional paradigm" does not apply.

In all possible paradigms, however, the action of the central bank rests on the exclusive license to produce an asset (base money) that is useful to economic activity. And the central bank has not only to make the best "quantitative" decisions concerning the creation of this asset. It has also the "qualitative" task of promoting a financial structure in which the use of its license could be more effective. This paper reviews the efforts made in this

latter field over a period of fifteen years during which Italian central
banking has profoundly changed.

2   Qualitative Policies, Quantitative Policies, and Monetary Control

Economic policy is often described as the choice of the optimal level, or
path, for the control variables given the objective function, the (invariant)
structure of the model, and nonpolicy exogenous variables. In the wider
presentation of Tinbergen, economic policy includes, in addition to these
"quantitative" actions, also "qualitative" actions, which are those in which
"a change in organisation is aimed at, meaning, in mathematical language,
that the type of certain structural relations existing before is changed." [3]
A structural change can, in its turn, be brought about either by means of
what Tinbergen calls "direct policy," [4] i.e., by *imposing* the value of some
parameters, or indirectly, by *inducing a change* in a behavioral parameter
that does not fall under the control of the policy maker.

Recent Italian experience provides ample evidence that Tinbergen's
theoretical concept applies forcefully to monetary policy, which normally
encompasses both the manipulation of policy variables *in* a given structure
and deliberate innovative action *on* the structure itself. In fact, over the
1969–1984 period, qualitative policy has almost played a predominant role
in the strategy followed by the monetary authorities. And qualitative
policy has resorted both to direct actions (introducing ceilings on bank
credit) and to indirect actions (promoting the development of the market
for short-term financial assets that were competing with bank deposits).

It is sometimes argued that quantitative policy and qualitative policy
can be used interchangeably to achieve equivalent results. Suppose, for
example, that the central bank comes to the conclusion that a flatter
(steeper) LM curve than the one "provided by nature," as Tobin puts it, [5] is
desirable so as to reduce the impact on national income of stochastic
disturbances. The central bank may then achieve the desired slope of the
LM either through quantitative policy, i.e., with the *supply of money* being
made to depend on the interest rate, [6] or through qualitative policy, i.e.,
by inducing a change in the interest or in the income elasticity of the
demand for money. [7] In fact, the latter alternative may seem much less
straightforward.

Why, then, should one choose qualitative policy? A few instances will be
examined in which qualitative policy is not equivalent to quantitative
policy and turns out to be more effective. Some of them have been parti-

cularly relevant in Italy, and account for the large recourse to qualitative policy on the part of the Banca d'Italia.

A first set of examples relates to situations in which qualitative policy becomes necessary simply because it is the *only viable* policy to achieve certain objectives.

Monetary policy may be dominated by fiscal policy because of institutional arrangements whereby the central bank is committed—either in the statute book or in practice—to create base money with the sole aim of financing the government, or to be a passive player with respect to the Treasury.[8] In a less extreme situation the market for government paper may be so thin that the central bank, although not formally committed, is neither ready to let the government run out of funds nor willing to accept the large disturbances that may arise if too large an amount of government debt was floated. The higher the importance attached to maintaining orderly market conditions, the stronger is the case for intervening through qualitative policy aimed at thickening the market or through a minimum portfolio requirement on banks.

Similarly, if the money supply is pegged to the exchange rate, then a conflict can arise between this constraint and the desire to use a rule for supplying money in a way that is optimal for the achievement of certain (domestic) objectives. In the Netherlands, where the guilder has traditionally been pegged to the deutsche mark, credit ceilings are used as a means to regain some autonomy in the conduct of monetary policy.

A less frequent, but probably the clearest, example today in which quantitative policy is not viable for stabilization goals is given by seigniorage. If the government were in a position to decide the level or path of the money supply to maximize its seigniorage profits, then no room would be left for rules aimed at monetary control[9] and the central bank would be forced to resort to qualitative action for that purpose.

A second instance in which quantitative policy may be at a disadvantage with respect to qualitative policy occurs when monetary impulses are transmitted to the economy with long and variable lags. If the intervention in the structure ensures a prompter answer of the private sector to stimuli emanating from monetary policy, either because it tends to reduce some "buffers" in the system or because it imposes the value of some relevant parameters, this will have a beneficial effect on monetary control that may not be reached by monetary rule.

A third order of reasons why quantitative and qualitative policies are not perfectly interchangeable is related to the information differential between monetary authorities and private agents.

In the case in which the monetary authority has an informational advantage and knows the source and amount of all shocks affecting the economy, it can perfectly offset them by an appropriate quantitative action, and no need arises for qualitative policy.

If the private sector, however, has an informational advantage, then the monetary authority may resort to qualitative action to shape the financial structure in a way that the response of the agents to the shocks is the optimal one for the purposes of monetary control.[10] In a sense, the idea is to have automatic stabilizers of a monetary kind.[11] Devising a rule that should react to (relatively) unobservable shocks would clearly make no sense. Thus, monetary policy reduces to qualitative policy.

In an intermediate, and more plausible, situation in which the monetary authority knows something more and something less than private agents, it may be reasonable for monetary policy to involve both qualitative and quantitative actions.

Another general instance in which qualitative action can improve monetary control occurs in a stochastic setting in which one of the aims of the policy maker is the reduction of the variance of the goal variable around the target level.[12] It can be shown that, in these cases, a higher number of instruments will increase the effectiveness of monetary control. The principle of not putting all the eggs into one basket applies to economic policy too: relying on the moderate use of many instruments rather than on a single one may reduce the incentive to evasion. The same holds true, even in a deterministic model, whenever there are costs associated with maneuvering policy instruments.[13]

In all these cases, monetary authorities may well decide to act on the financial structure so as to achieve better monetary control. Some of those instances apply to the Italian case: the central bank chose to undertake qualitative reforms that would eventually allow for a more effective use of traditional tools of monetary control and, in the meantime, resorted to direct controls so as to achieve its macroeconomic goals.

3   1969–1974: From Interest and Exchange Rate Pegging to the Generalization of Direct Controls

The main features of the financial structure in which Italian monetary policy was operating in the late Sixties can be summarized as follows:

• A strong preference of households toward liquid assets: with the banking system free to pay interest on deposits and with a relatively low level of per capita financial wealth; in 1969 M2 represented 77% of the public's domestic financial assets, excluding equities.

• The absence of a market for short-term securities: neither the business nor the government sector used to issue short-term marketable debt instruments. Treasury bills represented 0.5% of the public debt (then equal to 8.9% of GDP).

• A thin and not very efficient market for equities: the lack of specialized intermediaries, the preferences of savers, the reluctance of a largely family-owned corporate sector to put at stake the control of firms were the main factors behind a structural weakness of both demand for and supply of new shares. The growth of the business sector, based on profits and debt, was highly dependent on income distribution and interest rate levels.

In practice, monetary policy was conducted with close reference to two key prices that were almost assumed as constraints. First, the exchange rate. Although the Bretton Woods system was already showing signs of weakness, the parity of the lira against the dollar was taken as given, with no significant voices advocating an active exchange rate policy. Second, the interest rate. Since the mid-Sixties, the Banca d'Italia had been pegging the long-term interest rate, thus increasing the liquidity of government securities and favoring the public's demand for bonds.

If neither the exchange rate nor the interest rate put the Banca d'Italia under serious pressure in the second half of the Sixties, it was mainly because in those years cost and price developments were comparatively moderate. Moreover, both nationally and internationally, the short end of financial markets had not yet reached the size and sophistication by which, in the subsequent years, it would magnify "real" imbalances and increase the need for active monetary management.

Beyond these deep factors of stability, the reconciliation between the two pegged rates and the relevant "quantities" (i.e., official reserves and the monetary base) was largely obtained by means of administrative controls and rationing practices. The former were often used to manipulate the net foreign position of Italian banks; the latter took place in the supply of monetary base to the banking system, where the amounts were discretionally managed without moving the official rates.

Thus, in stabilizing the economy the Bank was active "upstream," as it exerted significant, albeit not always visible, influence on "real" trends, while it had less to worry about "downstream" from highly mobile short-term capital. The inadequacy of the apparatus of monetary control placed in between was going to become clear after 1969.

In the same years, drawing mainly on the "Anglo-American" model, the Banca d'Italia was formulating a theory of its own functions and operations in terms of monetary base and multiplier, and developing a scheme for flow of funds analysis. Forecasts for monetary base growth were even published in the Annual Report, subject to certain assumptions concerning income distribution, interest rates, and reserve requirement ratios.[14] The main intellectual influences were Modigliani's and Tobin's.

In a way, that scheme of monetary analysis was ahead of reality; the state of Italian financial markets did not allow for managing the monetary base as actively as the model suggested; short-term (weekly, monthly) operational objectives for bank reserves were not set; the necessary statistics to this purpose were not used; the main component of the deposit multiplier was unstable and volatile, due to a complex regulation concerning banks' compulsory reserves. Furthermore, the degree of independence that the "Anglo-American" scheme assigned to central bank policy was probably higher than the one the Banca d'Italia was then ready to exert. The increasing awareness of the constraints affecting the Bank's ability to adhere to a given path of monetary base creation led, at the end of the 1960s, to the abandonment of the practice by which that path was preannounced. While it did not have much normative effect on the current operations of the central bank (quantitative policy), that model has a decisive influence in setting the path for the financial innovations promoted by the Bank in the years to come.

1969 is a turning point. The rise of inflationary pressures throughout the industrial world led, in that year, to a generalized tightening of monetary policy. In Italy, a wage shock and profound changes in labor legislation put an end to the period of "real" stability. In the years to come, labor costs, fiscal shocks, and eventually oil shocks were going to raise substantially the need for monetary stabilization.[15] The gap between the interest rates in the international financial markets and those prevailing in Italy widened; massive capital outflows more than offset the surplus in the balance of payments on current account.

It had been perceived that the financial and banking structure could hardly be an efficient vehicle for a monetary restriction based on indirect instruments. In fact, the lack of a market for short-term Treasury securities in a period of high and unstable inflation rates meant that the growth of the public sector borrowing requirement would result in an acceleration of money creation. With interventions in the foreign-exchange market geared to maintain exchange-rate stability and with an almost nonexistent open market policy, the short-run control of banks' reserves could rely only on reserve requirements and on refinancing policies.

Both these instruments, however, were difficult to manage.

The dependence of the money multiplier on the distribution of total deposits between commercial banks and thrift institutions, due to different reserve ratios, made the relationship between base money and overall deposits unpredictable; furthermore, reserve ratios were not regarded as an instrument that could be maneuvered for short-run stabilization purposes.

Refinancing policy, on the other hand, exerted its impact basically through rationing mechanisms, with changes in the cost of refinancing following, rather than leading, changes in market conditions; this instrument was therefore rather ineffective in periods of abundant liquidity, in which borrowing at the Banca d'Italia was demand determined.[16]

These drawbacks became more and more evident as the rising borrowing requirement of the Treasury exerted increasing pressure on monetary base creation.

The effectiveness of monetary policy was further weakened by the oligopolistic banking structure and the lack of highly developed financial and capital markets: as the experience of the early 1970s illustrates, interest rates on loans and deposits were fixed by banks in such a way that policy impulses were transmitted to the economy with unduly long lags.[17]

In 1973, when rising inflationary pressures and a worsening in the balance of payments called again for a tightening of monetary policy, the difficulties of acting through the quantitative, indirect policies theorized in the "doctrine" professed by the Bank emerged in full. These difficulties lay essentially in the financial and banking structure and in the inadequacy of the Banca d'Italia's instruments and operational procedures; but they also came from an intellectual reluctance to accept a necessary quantum of monetarism. Moreover, early in that year, with the final collapse of the system of fixed exchange rates, Italy also lost what had been, since 1947, a key reference point for monetary policy.

After a short experiment with a dual foreign exchange market, the lira started to float and Italy also abandoned the European "Snake." New administrative measures limiting capital mobility were applied.

On the domestic front, banks were required to invest in securities a certain proportion of the increase in their deposits so as to sustain the supply of long-term funds (the measure was called the "minimum portfolio requirement"). In addition, a ceiling on the rate of growth of larger-size bank loans was imposed. Meanwhile, notwithstanding its unprecedented rise, the yield offered on Treasury bills often turned out to be lower than the one the market was willing to accept; the Bank of Italy ended up by purchasing substantial amounts of bills in the latter part of the year.

In 1974, when the oil shock boosted the already high inflation and contributed to widening the external imbalance, Italy negotiated a standby agreement with the IMF. The government committed itself to adhere to a target for the expansion of total domestic credit. The recourse to administrative controls was confirmed and extended to the external sector.

In two years a full transition was thus carried out toward a new system of monetary control. The exchange and the interest rates, which for many years had been the key intermediate objectives, were replaced by total domestic credit. Administrative controls, some of which had been occasionally used in the previous years, became a generalized system of monetary and credit management and were extended to all the main components of the flows of funds: long-term external borrowing, the net foreign position of the banking system, bank loans, and banks' investment in securities.

4   1975–1979: Laying the Foundations of a "New System"

At the very time when the architecture of administrative controls was completed, two acts of qualitative policy planted the seeds of a "new system" in which monetary control could mainly rely on "orthodox" quantitative policies. They were the reforms, introduced in early 1975, in the regime of banks' compulsory reserves and in the Treasury bills issuing system.

As required reserves ratios differed widely depending on the type of deposit and bank, the multiplier of the monetary based changed with the composition of deposits. An increase in deposits of 100 lire, given the level of own funds, might thus require additional reserves in monetary base ranging from 0 to 22.5 lire.[18] In January 1975 a uniform required reserves ratio was imposed on the increase in deposits; the marginal ratio was established at 15%; reserves could only be held in monetary base, while previously they could, within limits, be held in securities.

The Treasury bills issuing system was reformed in March 1975, and along with operators other than banks the Banca d'Italia's was admitted to the auction on the same footing as the other participants. The number of operators taking part in the auction and the degree of competition among them increased. It became possible for the Bank to affect the interest rate.

The innovation introduced in the Treasury bills auction system made it possible, for the first time, to organize a system whereby a key interest rate—a rate crucially related to the financing of the Treasury, the interest rate set by commercial banks, and the operations of the central bank—would be determined by a market interplay of these three operators. It paved the way to the development of a marketable short-term instrument that was competing with both bank deposits (in the portfolios of households and firms) and bank loans (in the balance sheet of banks). It created an area where banks' activity, increasingly ossified by direct controls on loans and securities, had to exert an optimizing behavior. Finally, it filled a gap in the mechanism of indirect monetary control: since the disappearance of discount operations of commercial paper, the Italian financial system did not have a short-term asset that the central bank could buy and sell with the aim of controlling the monetary base, and hence money and credit.

The two reforms were also important steps in the establishment of monetary control as a policy function endowed with a degree of autonomy from the budgetary authority and the Treasury. The new reserve requirement could only be satisfied with an asset created by the central bank, and the latter bore the entire burden of its remuneration. Similarly, the participation of the Bank in the auction according to the same rules applied to other participants underlined a distinction between the role of the Treasury and the role of the Bank that was new for Italy.

The auction system, however, had two flaws, which would show all their importance in the years to come. First, a floor-price was fixed by the Treasury for each auction, thus setting a ceiling to the rate. Second, at the inception of the new system the Bank committed itself to act as the residual buyer at the auction. When inflation made nominal rates swell, the combination of these two elements distorted the market mechanism and seriously undermined monetary control.

In early 1976 a slide in the exchange rate opened a monetary crisis that lasted until the autumn, when—after anticipated general elections—a new government based on a new political majority presented a program of severe fiscal stabilization and applied to the IMF and the European Community for conditional balance of payments support.

The methods of monetary control drew two main impulses from the 1976 crisis. On the one side, there was a widening and a strengthening of administrative controls on credit flows. On the other, further steps were taken to allow for conduct of monetary policy to be made through quantitative, indirect methods.

This kind of two-tier system was going to last until the early 1980s. The continuing rise in the Treasury's borrowing requirement—from 9.5% to

15.4% of GDP between 1976 and 1978—played an important role in preserving such a system; the increase in the demand for funds on the part of the Treasury fueled the growth of the market for government debt instruments, thus eventually increasing the scope for open market policy; in the meantime, however, it made the recourse to administrative controls unavoidable for stabilization goals. In terms of final objectives, priority was given to balance of payments equilibrium. Accordingly, total domestic credit remained the primary intermediate target.

On the first tier, administrative controls continued to be applied throughout the period. Even though minimum portfolio requirements gradually became nonbinding and were eased after 1978, ceilings on bank loans—suspended in the spring of 1975—were reintroduced in 1976 and continuously applied thereafter.

Controls related to the external accounts were also tightened. Since the ceiling was referred to lira loans only, it fostered capital inflows through the banking system. The introduction of a compulsory deposit on foreign currency purchases in 1976, the removal, in 1975, of the prohibition on banks to expand their net debtor foreign position, and the active encouragement to borrow abroad helped improving the external position. Meanwhile, the wage indexation scheme introduced in 1975 had tightened the link between exchange rate changes and domestic price behavior.[19] Controls on capital movements were strengthened also by legislative measures: in 1976, illegal capital exports, which were previously dealt with by civil law, came under criminal law.

On the second tier, and under the protective umbrella of such a comprehensive scheme of administrative controls, the central bank's ability to resort to indirect methods was built up. The reforms of 1975 had only touched the multiplier and the Treasury bills primary market. The 1976 crisis had dramatically shown that the Bank of Italy was almost entirely deprived of the operational possibility of acting rapidly on the monetary base through a market mechanism.

To gain this possibility a number of conditions had to be satisfied and steps were taken after 1976. First, full operational flexibility had to be gained in the Treasury bills secondary market: only at the end of 1976 did the Bank start to sell Treasury bills in the open market at a price that was responsive to market conditions, rather than mechanically linked to the allotment price of the previous auctions. In 1979 the Bank began to buy Treasury bills outright in the open market so as to alleviate pressures on bank reserves whenever a generalized need for easing liquidity conditions arose. Specific needs of individual banks continued to be satisfied through refinancing policy. As the attention paid to day-to-day liquidity conditions grew, the role of refinancing was heavily reduced, while that of the open market policy increased. Crucial, in this respect, was the introduction of repurchase aggreements, which endowed the central bank with a more flexible tool for controlling reserves over the very short run.

Second, procedures for short-term policy formulation had to be established: only then objectives for total bank reserves and bank liquidity started to be set within an FOMC-type of monthly decision that involved, besides the Governor, the research and the operational departments of the Bank.

Third, the information basis of the policy process had to be improved: bank reserve objectives started to be set on daily figures and a new statistic was established whereby the information lag on the main items of banks' balance sheets was shortened from 45 to 15 days.

The two-tier system was a rather complex one. When all the constraints on bank behavior were simultaneously binding (which was not always the case) its working could be described as follows: total bank loans and total bank holdings for long-term securities were directly determined by administrative controls; the monetary base policy of the central bank determined the rate on Treasury bills and the distribution of the existing amount of Treasury bills between the banks and the public. Thus the central bank had a direct impact on the total volume of bank intermediation and on its composition.[20]

The year 1979 is important because the central bank was by then endowed with most of the instruments necessary in order to intervene flexibly in the open market. Of no less importance is the fact that, from the beginning of that year, monetary policy was again subject to a formal exchange-rate constraint, due to the decision to join the European Monetary System.

5   1980–1984: The EMS and the Gradual Transition to Quantitative Policy

The third period is characterized by a gradual transition to quantitative monetary control in the context of a restrictive monetary policy. For some years qualitative and quantitative measures have continued to coexist, and they still coexist today with respect to exchange controls and administrative restrictions on capital movements. But the balance has decisively tilted toward quantitative policies.

In 1980–1981 all administrative measures were kept in place and even tightened. Inflation was rising because of the combined effects of the second oil shock and fiscal expansion in 1979–1980. Moreover, monetary policy followed a relatively accommodative line, to help finance a strong rise in investments. It was felt that circumstances did not allow an outright abandonment of direct controls.

In the same two years, however, two events occurred that were to be significant in setting the conditions for a systemic change in policy instruments.

The first was the successful defense of the exchange rate in the summer of 1980. Italian industries had nearly exhausted the margins of competitiveness gained by a slide in the exchange rate managed on the eve of the inception of the EMS. An attempt to impose a devaluation upon the central bank by exerting pressure in the market was resisted in June–July 1980. In September, after a vast reshuffling in its management, Fiat, the largest Italian private corporation, began and, after a 35-day strike, successfully ended a confrontation with the unions on such issues as layoffs, violence in the factory, and flexibility in the use of the labor force. As a result, the rate of absenteeism virtually vanished in a period of a few weeks, productivity rose by 20% in one and a half years, and Fiat regained its leading position among automakers in Europe. The exchange-rate front—which had been the soft front since 1973—had hardened again. The opposite had happened—for the first time since 1969—to the labor front. September 1980 was a turning point in industrial relations for the whole economy. The exchange-rate commitment had been crucial in catalyzing a reversal in a ten-years trend and became again a key element of monetary discipline.[21]

The second event was the discontinuation—agreed upon by the Banca d'Italia and the Treasury in July 1981—of the commitment of the central bank to act as the residual buyer at the Treasury bills auctions. This decision, which went under the name of "divorce," corrected a flaw in the 1975 Treasury bills reform, added another element to a system based on quantitative policy, and significantly strengthened the independence of the central bank.

The divorce was a milestone in the evolution of monetary policy. However, failure to correct the other flaw of the 1975 reform made its application very costly, both in policy and institutional terms. Indeed, the continuing practice of the Treasury to fix a floor price did not allow market forces to determine freely the allotment rate for Treasury bills. This could create a situation in which the interest rate set by the Treasury in the primary market (with the aim of limiting the cost of borrowing) and that set by the Banca d'Italia in the secondary market (with the aim of controlling monetary and credit aggregates) would be inconsistent. Such an inconsistency would, in the short run, lead the Treasury to overdraw from its account with the central bank beyond the limit of 14% of total public expenditures fixed by law, thus causing an expansion of the monetary base in excess of what is consistent with monetary policy objectives.

The years 1982–1984 are those in which the transition to indirect policy was accomplished. In 1983, the ceiling on bank loans was eventually lifted and the portfolio requirement practically abolished. The main burden of monetary control fell on the monetary base, with the help of a reserve requirement that had been hardened at the beginning of the year. Real interest rates were kept in line with those prevailing abroad. In terms of intermediate targets, emphasis on total credit expansion was reduced and somewhat shifted to bank liabilities, to M2, and to credit to the private sector.

The transition was urged by the increasing costs, in terms of allocative efficiency, and the declining effectiveness of direct controls on bank credit. The prolonged enforcement of identical growth ceilings on each bank resulted in widening the gap between the actual and potential growth of single banks and in a negative effect on competition, and hence on efficiency, in the industry. Moreover, such distortions inevitably led to widespread circumvention of the ceilings, both within the banking system and by nonbank intermediaries, which impaired not only the accuracy of control, but also the reliability of statistics. The transformation of the financial structure fostered since the mid-1970s made the suppression of direct controls possible, while administrative measures, which had profoundly changed the size and shape of the money market and affected both bank and households' behavior, were still in place. The growth of a market for securities enabled the Banca d'Italia to exert a more effective control on the money supply, and to reduce gradually the more liquid component of financial assets. Even though the impact of the Treasury's borrowing requirement on the expansion of monetary aggregates was strong and growing, it became possible to prevent it from being systematically amplified through the reserve money multiplier.

The market for short-term government securities had grown at a remarkably fast pace. The stock of Treasury bills in circulation recorded a fivefold increase between end-1975 and end-1981. Between 1981 and 1984 it rose by a further 50%. In this period, the market in Treasury floating rate certificates (CCT) also expanded rapidly, following some changes in the issuing conditions. This made it possible thereafter to lengthen considerably the average maturity of the government debt.[22]

The increase in the overall size of government debt was accompanied by a drastic change in its distribution between banks and nonbanks. At the end of 1978 banks still held 58% of Treasury bills in circulation; the share fell to 50% during 1979 and further declined to 34% at end-1981. During those three years, the share of Treasury bills held by the public rose from 43% to 58%; at the end of 1984, it neared 70%.

Meanwhile, the ratio of M2 to domestic financial assets, excluding equities, fell by 20 percentage points between end-1978 and end-1984, when it reached 64%. These developments resulted from a learning process gradually induced in households' behavior by inflation and by the central bank's intervention in the Treasury bills market; the speed of reaction to changes in the differential between the yield on government securities and deposit rates significantly increased.[23] The rise in the tax rate applied to interests paid on deposits, and the increasing costs associated with compulsory reserves as the reserve coefficient and the level of market interest rates rose, speeded up the process of banks' disintermediation. After 1979, the banking system found it too costly to keep resisting this trend.[24] This change in attitude is highlighted by the behavior of the differential between the deposit rate and the rate on Treasury bills and on Treasury floating rate certificates.[25]

Thus, for a given money supply, the LM schedule has become flatter than it was ten years before. In this respect, in Italy, financial innovation has produced a result opposite to what is observed in those countries where some form of Regulation Q was traditionally applied.[26] This implies that a smaller change in interest rates controlled by the central bank is now required to restore money market equilibrium. If the maintenance of "orderly market conditions" is one of the aims of the monetary authorities, the conclusion should be drawn that such a change in the financial structure has indeed improved the effectiveness of quantitative policy.

The control of the monetary base had also improved and evolved toward a situation in which the financial requirements of the Treasury are satisfied by the banking system and the economy, which in turn get liquidity by selling assets to the central bank.

The active presence of the Banca d'Italia on the secondary market for Treasury securities, combined with the rise in the shadow price of holding idle balances due to the increase in the yield of loans and securities, induced a reduction in the average ratio of excess reserves held by banks against deposits. This was accompanied by a lower variability of the ratio, which helped stabilize the reserve money multiplier.[27]

These developments made the effects of changes in high-powered money more predictable, and shortened the lags with which such changes are transmitted to the banks' supply of deposits.[28]

A shift in the demand function for currency by the public, recorded since the mid-1970s, exerted effects of the same sign on the multiplier: the ratio of currency to deposits, which accelerated its long-run downward trend around 1975, exhibited a lower variability after 1980.[29]

Finally, the rise in the average reserve ratio ensured a higher automatic sterilization of unforeseen shocks originating either in the exogenous sources of monetary base creation or in the market for currency and excess reserves. While reducing the impact of a given change in the monetary base deliberately brought about by the central bank, the higher reserve ratio did not reduce the effectiveness of monetary policy; insofar as it reduced the "noise" affecting the system, the rise in the reserve ratio increased effectiveness.

6 Summary and Conclusions

The last fifteen years of Italian monetary history are reviewed in this paper from the point of view of the evolution of the methods of monetary control and the structure of financial markets. The strategy of actively changing both such methods and structure has been a fundamental component of the action carried out by the monetary authorities during this period.

To follow this evolution it is important to remember that the classical definition of economic policy not only includes quantitative actions, i.e., movements in the policy variables aiming at certain final objectives for a given structure of the model, but also qualitative actions, aimed at changing the very structure of the model. The creation of a new market, the change of certain patterns of economic behavior, or the imposition of parameters falls in the realm of qualitative policy. Qualitative policy may provide useful additional tools for pursuing macroeconomic objectives, or it may be a necessary step toward a situation in which quantitative policy can operate more effectively. This has been the case in recent Italian experience.

The conditions prevailing in Italy at the end of the Sixties made the use of qualitative policy necessary. Key elements of the standard apparatus of quantitative monetary policy were yet to be developed. The end of the Bretton Woods system and the beginning of the long inflation of the Seventies implied the loss of the two policy references that had been essential in the Sixties, i.e., the exchange rate and the interest rate.

Meanwhile, a stronger monetary policy was needed to check growing inflationary impulses.

Qualitative policy was thus used along two lines. First, ceilings on loans and floors on security investments were imposed on banks to achieve intermediate credit and monetary targets set for short-run stabilization and allocative purposes that the monetary authority was unable to pursue with ordinary quantitative instruments. Second, in a more structural sense, the financial system and the methods and instruments of central banking were reshaped with the aim of achieving conditions in which monetary stabilization policy would rely on quantitative actions.

In the late Sixties the Banca d'Italia had practically exhausted its function of financing the economy through the discount window, and was facing a new formidable debtor, the Treasury, which coupled the influence deriving from the size of its financial requirements with that coming from the institutional powers and responsibilities it shares in the very field of monetary policy. In the following years the central bank has endeavored to make the exclusive license to produce base money the basis for managing, in a new situation, the monetary side of the economy through indirect, market-oriented instruments. The distance covered in these fifteen years can be gauged by noticing that open market operations, which are today the chief tool of monetary control, were at the end of the Sixties not only nonexistent but hardly conceivable and that, even if they had been practiced, their effect would have been highly uncertain.

The light thrown on our monetary evolution leaves in the shadow both the allocative and the stabilization objectives of policy. For each of them, an analysis would probably result in a mixed judgment. From an allocative point of view, the creation of a new and rather efficient money market has been a positive result, but loan ceilings and bond floors have inevitably caused allocative inefficiencies. Similarly, direct controls have been a powerful help in limiting the growth of credit aggregates; but if success in stabilization policies has to be measured only by the ultimate objective of price stability, the outcome has been disappointing.

One may ask whether, after the long journey described in the previous pages, Italian monetary policy can effectively aim for monetary stability with a minimum of allocative distortions and relying essentially on indirect methods.

No doubt, essential elements for this to be possible are now in place, and they are elements that could not be set up overnight. These are a wide money market, a fairly stable base-money multiplier, widespread optimizing behavior on the part of the main operators in the financial market, and institutional autonomy of the central bank in conducting its operations.

Yet there are serious reasons for concern. One is that the strong preference for liquid assets by Italian savers has not changed sufficiently. In a system where there has never been a Regulation Q, this preference has been satisfied throughout the period primarily by a high proportion of bank deposits to total financial assets. But it has also been accommodated in other ways that have been evolving over the years: by the transformation of long-term bonds into liquid assets through interest rate pegging policies; by the hypertrophy of the Treasury bills market; and more recently, by the growth of floating rate Treasury certificates. In these conditions the economy always disposes of the fuel to feed inflation. If the creation of a money market was an important objective fifteen years ago, what is imperative today is to develop and strengthen the financial market.

Another reason for concern comes from the fact that the long process of financial innovation described above has still to pass the test of the end of the inflationary climate in which it has been promoted and justified. Disinflation is a threatening experience for financial structures.

The main reason for concern, however, touches the very problem of monetary control and its relationship to fiscal policy. With a public debt and a fiscal deficit approaching, respectively, 90% and 15% of GDP, the conflict between fiscal policy and monetary policy is in the facts. Technically, it takes the form of an inconsistency between the rates set by the Treasury in the primary market and those set by the central bank in the secondary market for Treasury bills. The operational procedures, the instruments of intervention, and the institutional independence are necessary, but not sufficient, conditions for monetary stability. Ultimately, the choice between inflation and price stability is an economic and political one that belongs to society as a whole, and not to the central bank alone.

Notes

1. Hester (1981), Kane (1983), Silber (1983), and Sylla (1982).

2. Modigliani and Pademos (1980).

3. Tinbergen (1952), p. 71. Logically and practically, qualitative and quantitative policies are not autonomous. Lucas (1973) has shown that changes in policy rules may change the structure of the model. Even though he does not seem to imply this, one could imagine a change in the rule governing quantitative action carried out precisely with the aim of achieving a change in the structure. In that sense the

distinction between quantitative policy and qualitative policy would be blurred. However, as it would complicate the analysis in an intolerable way, the two families of tools will be considered as logically autonomous in what follows.

4. Tinbergen (1952), p. 11.

5. Tobin (1983).

6. Poole (1970).

7. As Tobin (1983) point out, "Policy and structure become inextricably combined, their joint product is what matters . . . . One way to alter the operating properties of the system ... is to change the policy rule. Another way is to change the structure."

8. Thomas Sargent and Neil Wallace (1981).

9. In this setup, the term "rule" is not used in a Friedmanian sense, as opposed to discretion, but, rather, as a synonym for quantitative policy.

10. Santomero and Siegel (1981), seem to go as far as saying that in a properly stochastic framework, only qualitative policy (such as changes in reserve requirements) can improve monetary control. The assumption underlying this conclusion must be that the monetary authority cannot use the information on shocks conveyed by interest rates, in the Tobin-Poole meaning, to modulate its policy tools and therefore is precluded, for example, from making (base) money supply responsive to interest rates in a way that would affect the equivalent of the LM curve in their model.

11. Siegel (1979, 1982).

12. In this case the usual Tinbergen principle of equality of the number of instruments and objectives no longer applies (see Brainard, 1967, and Henderson and Turnovsky, 1972).

13. Henderson and Turnovsky (1972).

14. See Baffi (1973), Caron and Cotula (1971), Cotula and Modigliani (1974), and Fazio (1969).

15. In these conditions, it became necessary to raise both the level and the flexibility of Italian interest rates. To achieve this, the Banca d'Italia suspended its pegging policy of the long-term bonds rate; it introduced penalty rates for banks frequently recurring to its refinancing facilities; the maximum issue rate for Treasury bills, which previously had been kept constant at 3.5% since the end of the 1950s, was raised, and it was decided that it would be fixed at each auction; meanwhile, the Bank ceased to stand ready to sell or buy unlimited amounts of Treasury bills at a predetermined price on the secondary market; finally the ceiling on interbank interest rates, imposed in 1962, was abolished. Only then did Treasury bills cease to be classified as a component of the monetary base, a first step on their way to becoming the key instrument in controlling the base.

16. Since in the early 1970s overdraft facilities represented the main source of working balances available to the banking system, the possibility for the central bank of reducing, even temporarily, the limit set for ordinary advances was perceived as a factor that would contribute undesirable sources of uncertainties to the management of running assets on the part of banks' treasures, and was *de facto* ruled out.

17. Between the first quarter of 1969 and the third quarter of 1970, for instance, the rates on bank deposits and on bank loans increased by considerably less than the rate on long-term bonds, with restrictive impulses in the credit market being conveyed by rationing practices rather than merely through price mechanisms, and kept on rising when monetary policy was eased. The spread between loan rates and deposit rates in 1971–1972 remained at a much higher level than in the first half of 1969, in spite of the unfavorable cycle. Investment activity was further depressed by the difficulty that special credit institutions had in raising funds due to the reduction in the demand for long-term bonds.

18. Things became even more complicated if the 100 lire increase in deposits resulted from a fall in deposits at commercial banks being more than offset by a rise in deposits at thrift institutions; in such a case, there might have even been a reduction in required reserves in the monetary base.

19. See Caranza and Fazio (1983).

20. See Padoa-Schioppa (1979).

21. In the following years the parity of the lira in the EMS was periodically changed as a consequence of the still high inflation differential with respect to other European countries. But exchange rate policy kept constant pressure on cost and price developments.

22. The average maturity of the public debt rose from slightly more than one year to nearly two and a half years between 1982 and end-1984.

23. The most recent econometric estimates of the demand for money function—in its M2 definition—elaborated within the Banca d'Italia indicate that the elasticity to the ratio of interest rates paid on Treasury bills and on Treasury variable rate certificates to the own rate of return has been gradually rising over the second half of the 1970s and accelerated considerably at the beginning of the 1980s: in 1983, the long-run elasticity was twice as much as the level reached in 1979. See Cotula et al. (1984).

24. In the previous years banks had repeatedly urged the monetary authorities to transform Treasury bills into an asset reserved to banks only.

25. The ratio between the rate on short-term and indexed government securities and the after-tax average yield on M2 climbed from 6.4% to a peak of 10.5% in 1980–1981; it then declined, but in 1982–1983 it still was twice as large as in 1978–1979. Even though in 1984 deposit rates fell less than those on Treasury securities, the continuing rise in the average compulsory reserve ratio following the increase of the marginal ratio to 20% in 1981 and to 25% at end-1982 suggests

that the ability of banks to complete for funds as aggressively as they did in the past will not be easily restored.

26. Akhtar (1983) and Cotula (1984).

27. This result was also fostered by the introduction, in 1976, of a centralized electronic system for the management of overdraft facilities granted by the Banca d'Italia to the banking system. The contribution of the ratio of excess reserves to deposits to the variability of the money multiplier was halved between 1972–1976 and 1977–1981 (see Zautzik, 1983).

28. Some looseness obviously still remains in the relationship linking base money to bank loans in the short run, due to the role of buffer played by the stock of short-term government securities held by the banking system.

29. The ratio of currency to deposits fell from 15% in 1969–1973 to 11% in 1974–1978 and to 9.5% in 1979–1983; in this last period the variability of the ratio declined by 40% with respect to the previous ten years.

References

Akhtar, M. A., "Financial Innovations and Their Implications for Monetary Policy: An International Perspective," BIS Economic Papers, 9 (December 1983), 5–56.

Baffi, Paolo, "Metodi e programmi di azione monetaria in Italia: uno sguardo a due decenni," in Nuovi Studi sulla Moneta, Milano: Giuffré, 1973.

Brainard, William, "Uncertainty and Effectiveness of Policy," American Economic Association (May 1967), 411–425.

Caranza, Cesare, and Antonio Fazio, "Methods of Monetary Control in Italy: 1974–1983," in The Political Economy of Monetary Policy: National and International Aspects, D. R. Hodgman, ed., Federal Reserve Bank of Boston, 1983, pp. 65–88.

Caron, Massimiliano, and Franco Cotula, "I Conti finanziari dell'Italia," Bollettino Statistico, Banca d'Italia, 6 (1971), 873–919.

Cotula, Franco, "Financial Innovation and Monetary Control," Banca Nazionale del Lavoro Quarterly Review (September 1984), 219–255.

Cotula, Franco, and Franco Modigliani, "An Empirical Analysis of the Composition of Financial Wealth in Italy," Banca Nazionale del Lavoro Quarterly Review, 6 (1974), 140–166.

Cotula, Franco, Giampaolo Galli, Edoardo Lecaldano Sasso La Terza, Valeria Sannucci and Emerico Zautzik, "Una stima delle funzioni di domanda delle attività finanziarie," Temi di Discussione, Servizio Studi della Banca d'Italia, 43 (November 1984), 1–44.

Fazio, Antonio, "Monetary Base and the Control of Credit in Italy," Banca Nazionale del Lavoro Quarterly Review, 6 (1969), 146–169.

Fazio, Antonio, "Monetary Policy in Italy from 1970 to 1978," *Kredit und Kapital,* 2 (1979), 145–180.

Henderson, Dale W., and Stephen J. Turnovsky, "Optimal Macroeconomic Policy Adjustment under Conditions of Risk," *Journal of Economic Theory,* 4 (1972), 58–71.

Hester, Donald. H., "Innovation and Monetary Control," *Brooking Papers on Economic Activity,* 1 (1981), 141–199.

Kane, Edward J., "Policy Implications of Structural Changes in Financial Markets," *American Economic Association Papers and Proceedings,* 2 (1983), 96–100.

Lucas, Richard E., Jr., "Some International Evidence on Output Inflation Tradeoffs," *The American Economic Review,* 3 (1973), 326–334.

Modigliani, Franco, and Lucas Papademos, "The Structure of Financial Markets and the Monetary Mechanism," in *Controlling Monetary Aggregates,* 3rd ed., Boston: Federal Reserve Bank of Boston, 1980, pp. 111–155.

Padoa-Schioppa, Tommaso, "Aspetti istituzionali e strumenti della politica monetaria," *Modello Econometrico dell'economia italiana,* 2nd ed., M2BI, Banca d'Italia, (February 1979), 14–42.

Poole, William, "Optimal Choice of Monetary Policy Instruments in a Simple Stochastic Macro Model," *Quarterly Journal of Economics* (May 1970), 197–216.

Santomero, Anthony M., and Jeremy Siegel, "Bank Regulation and Macro-Economics Stability," *The American Economic Review* (March 1981), 39–53.

Sargent, Thomas J., and Neil Wallace, "Some Unpleasant Monetarist Arithmetic," *Federal Reserve Bank of Minneapolis Quarterly Review* (Fall 1981), 1–17.

Siegel, Jeremy, "The Effectiveness of Monetary Reform under Rational Expectations," *Economics Letters,* 4 (1979), 341–345.

Siegel, Jeremy, "Monetary Stabilization and the Informational Value of Monetary Aggregates," *Journal of Political Economy,* 11 (1982), 176–180.

Silber, William, "The Process of Financial Innovation," *American Economic Association Papers and Proceedings,* 2 (1983), 89–95.

Sylla, Richard, "Monetary Innovation and Crises in American Economic History," in *Crises in the Economic and Financial Structure,* P. Wachtel, ed., Lexington D.C.: Heath & Co., 1982, 23–40.

Tinbergen, Jan, *On the Theory of Economic Policy,* Amsterdam: North-Holland, 1952.

Tobin, James, "Financial Structure and Monetary Rules," *Kredit und Kapital,* 2 (1983), 155–171.

Zautzik, Emerico, "Base monetaria aggiustata e sue interpretazioni: aspetti teorici e applicazioni al caso italiano," *Contributi alla Ricerca Economica,* Servizio Studi della Banca d'Italia, 11, December 1983.

Comments on "Reshaping Monetary Policy"

Giorgio Basevi

My comments on Padoa-Schioppa's paper are addressed to three theses that, more or less explicitly, are contained in it and appear to me to be in need of additional theoretical and empirical support.

The first thesis underpins the dominant theme of the paper, and may be called the theory of the "protective umbrella." The idea is that, in the process of creating the conditions for a monetary policy based on quantitative instruments, the Italian authorities had to keep open—at times even to reopen—the umbrella of administrative controls, the justification being that only under this umbrella could the Italian economy be protected during the stormy periods of the last fifteen years. This theory is based on the assumption that the weather is independent of whether you have an umbrella, and whether keep it open or closed. While I would not deny the realism of this assumption with respect to atmospherical storms, I suggest that it cannot always be extended by analogy to economic events. More specifically, I am convinced that at least one category of the administrative controls that have been maintained in Italy in order to create a wider domestic market for government bills has long been itself a source of potential troubles and an obstacle to further steps toward a more efficient monetary policy. I am referring to the set of controls on the possibility of Italian residents diversifying their financial portfolios abroad. There is now a backlog of potential demand for foreign assets that makes it very difficult to take additional quick steps toward Italian integration into the international financial system—and in particular into the EMS—without losing much of the ground gained domestically in terms of control of the monetary base and management of the government debt in orderly conditions.

Notice that, in saying this, I do not mean to imply that further steps in the direction of opening the economy financially cannot be taken, I suggest, however, that in order to be taken they must be of a different quality and speed. The need for capital controls is itself a function of the type and degree of a country's monetary integration with the rest of the world. Thus, the adoption of a stricter set of constraints for Italy within the EMS (such as the reduction of the width of the lira band and more liberal use of the ECU) must be accompanied by new instruments—such as an adjustable tax on the acquisition of foreign exchange for capital movements—in order for them to constitute a solid and possibly definitive move in the direction of stable and efficient European economic integration.

The danger I see with the "protective umbrella" theory is that it may have landed the Italian economy in the worst of two worlds: it maintained an inadequate degree of competition in the banking sector, and thus crippled the reactiveness of interest rates to changed market conditions, keeping the distribution of private portfolios in a potentially dangerous disequilibrium, and yet constrained monetary policy to the objective of defending the exchange rate in a financially more integrated EMS area.

The second thesis in the paper is less explicitly stated than the "umbrella theory." It maintains that exchange rate policy can be a powerful instrument not just for the objective of price stability but also for inducing the economy to restructure along more efficient lines of production. I must say that this thesis is not openly expressed in the paper, and yet those of you who happen to follow Italian economic affairs know that the idea of keeping the currency overvalued in order to compel industry to resist excessive wage demands and to restructure under the pressure of foreign competition has been popular not only in the United Kingdom but also in Italy, particularly with the monetary authorities.

This thesis is treated sympathetically by Padoa-Schioppa. Thus he stresses the importance of the strong stand taken by the Bank of Italy during the summer of 1980 and the change in industrial relations brought about by the FIAT settlement of a long strike in the fall of the same year. I too am convinced that these were extremely important changes in attitude—and not just for their economic implications but also for their political ones. However, on the basis of this experience the Bank of Italy has built a sort of complacent view of its capacity to keep the lira overvalued: a view that may be very dangerous in the long run, while being theoretically unsound from a wider perspective—dangerous from at least two points of view: it results in a stricter current account constraint, and it builds a crisis potential into the economy—and theoretically dubious for the simple reason that in a multicountry and multicurrency world, this type of policy, if followed by more than one country, leads to competitive overvaluations, with costly consequences to the level of overall demand and employment. If the authorities give a predominant weight to the objective of exchange rate stability, it would be preferable to restrict the band for exchange rate variations within the EMS and defend the parity: there would be less room for prolonged overvaluations followed by periods of prolonged undervaluations.

The third thesis in the paper concerns the Bank's independence from the Treasury, the so-called "divorce." It has been argued by a former Governor of the Bank of Italy that it would have been "subversive" not to finance with base money a public sector deficit that could not be reduced without breaking delicate sociopolitical equilibria. Aside from the question whether a central bank should feel responsible for issues that go well beyond its sphere of institutional duties, this remains an open and hot issue in Italy, notwithstanding the divorce between the Bank and the Treasury. In fact Padoa-Schioppa emphasizes that this divorce has not been completed, with respect to the working of the overdraft facility that the Treasury enjoys with the Bank and to the system of floor prices in the monthly auctions of Treasury bills. The danger here is that a stricter system for the overdraft facility could act as a boomerang on the Bank's independence: in case of need, the ceiling would be changed by Parliament, as happened recently, leaving the Bank with relatively small satisfaction in considering how its independence has been maintained only formally. Clearly these matters lead to the delicate question of determining within constitutional law the role, duties, and rights of the Bank of Italy, as is done in other countries. Trying to find substitutes for this lack of constitutional definition by pushing the game with the government and the social partners to difficult positions is a dangerous strategy, which may easily lead the other players to call its bluff, ending in a loss of credibility on the part of the central bank.

Less than two months after the conference at Martha's Vineyard, I attended the Panel Meeting of Economic Policy, sponsored by a journal based in London. A paper by a group of economists at the Bank of Italy was presented there (Cottarelli et al., 1985), which I discussed, I then asked myself whether, notwithstanding the unfavorable balance that the authors seemed to strike as to the effectiveness of credit controls and their overall desirability, it was likely that those controls would be resumed in the near future. (Notice that in fact they have been resumed since then—in January 1986—in order to meet a foreign exchange crisis, even though they have been announced as a temporary policy change to be soon reversed). I thus said that "[quantitative] credit controls may be in again if in the game between the monetary authorities, on the one hand, and the government and sociopolitical forces, on the other, the bluff is called, and the monetary authorities are compelled to bow to the lack of political will to stabilize the economy on the fiscal front. Moreover, credit controls may also be in again, perhaps accompanied by more efficient tools for controlling capital movements, if the EMS and Italy within it move toward a new phase of turbulence and yet aim at further steps toward monetary unification."

It is sad to say that on both grounds it was easy to be right, as it could already be seen at the time of the discussion that the political unwillingness to face boldly the need to reduce the burden of the public debt, coupled with expectations of exchange rate realignments within the EMS (prompted by the fall of the dollar), would induce the authorities "temporarily" to reopen the umbrella of credit controls. My argument is that the storm, although prompted by the crisis of the dollar, was only partly independent of the policy framework maintained in Italy while moving toward a more liberal, market-oriented economic policy.

Bibliography

Cottarelli, C., G. Galli, P. Marullo, and G. Pittaluga (1985). "Monetary Policy through Ceilings on Bank Lending," mimeo, October.

10

Toward Realistic Policy Design: Policy Reaction Functions That Rely on Economic Forecasts

Robert Anderson and Jared J. Enzler

More than 15 years ago Franco Modigliani played a leading role in the development of the MPS econometric model. Ever since that time the model has been actively used by the Federal Reserve staff as an adjunct to its internal forecasting process and as a vehicle for policy analysis and economic research. Modigliani's influence on quite a number of staff economists goes beyond his contribution to MPS. For many of us his framework for macroeconomic analysis provides a kind of baseline or standard against which other views are inevitably compared. We represent many of our colleagues in recognizing our debt to him on this occasion.

This paper has two goals. The first is to present a simple class of monetary policy reaction functions capable of damping out simulated fluctuations in resource utilization to reveal the model's longer-run properties. Experience has shown that the MPS model is not very stable in long (3–4 years and more) simulations when macroeconomic policy instrument variables are set on rigidly predetermined paths. We do not necessarily regard this as a defect of the model. Indeed, if the model were highly stable in such a circumstance and the real world were not, it would be of little use in studying the complex issues of policy design. Moreover, the major cause of this instability is well understood and has a solid empirical base. However, this same instability makes it difficult to use the model to examine the long-run effects of alternative policies and other phenomena.

We also have a second and far more ambitious goal. We aspire to

Many of the insights useful in preparing this paper were obtained by observing the work of, or engaging in discussions with, our colleagues Peter Tinsley and Peter von zur Muehlen. We have also benefited from extensive discussions with Albert Ando. Tim Grunwald performed the extensions of the simulation code that made the project possible. The opinions expressed here are those of the authors and do not represent those of OMB (in which R. Anderson is Economist), the Federal Reserve Board (on which J. J. Enzler is Associate Director), or their staffs.

simulate and study fairly realistic monetary policymaking procedures. In reality, macroeconomic policymakers make use of intermediate-term economic forecasts. To investigate policymaking procedures of this type we extended the model to create the ability to simulate three groups of actors: (i) the real-world economic agents whose behavior most econometric models are designed to represent, (ii) an imperfect forecaster whose forecasts are used by the monetary policymaker, and (iii) the policymaker himself. Using this extended model, we hope to learn more about how policymakers must behave to achieve their goals.

This paper is divided into four sections. The first presents a general introduction to the topic of reaction functions and how they can be applied in a large-scale econometric model. The second section describes the general form of the monetary policy reaction functions we developed for this project. The third section presents simulations of recent history that demonstrate how the reaction functions we developed can be used to stabilize the model when it is subjected to the economic disturbances experienced historically. In the fourth and final section the specification of our policy rules is extended so that the policymaker can make use of intermediate-term economic forecasts. Using a stochastic simulation technique, we examine how well a number of different reaction functions stabilize key economic variables.

1   Policy Reaction Functions: An Introduction

One approach to policy design is the use of optimal control techniques. Optimal control methods have disadvantages in practice, however. When the planning horizon is long or the number of policy instruments is large, the computations are unwieldy. When uncertainty is introduced the computations are still more burdensome. Even more damaging in our view is the failure of such abstract mathematical techniques to provide much insight into *why* the resulting instrument path is optimal. Policymakers justifiably suspect that policy instrument paths arising from the application of optimal control techniques to any particular economic model may be highly specific to the model being used, and that if the model is misspecified in any significant way, implementation of the calculated optimal instrument path may not produce anything close to the desired result. Finally, instrument paths chosen this way can be quite sensitive to very specific details of the criterion function used in obtaining them. While most people can agree on the general nature of what are desirable goals for policymakers, no such consensus exists for details.

For all these reasons we did not use the optimal control approach in this paper. Instead, we focused on the problem of designing intuitive policy rules using our own notions about how the model really works.

1.1 The Necessity of Choosing a Policy Rule

We cannot emphasize too strongly that *no* model simulation is possible without using either explicit or implicit monetary and fiscal policy reaction functions. Specifying the time path for any policy instrument, a money growth path, for example, merely defines one simple kind of policy reaction function. Nevertheless, there has been little experimentation with more realistic reaction functions. There are at least two reasons. First, it is difficult to estimate empirical reaction functions that can track actual policymakers' behavior. The number of policymakers is small and their identities, objectives, and opinions change over time. While we can rely on the law of large numbers to produce relatively stable aggregate reactions when we model the behavior of large numbers of people, the same logic does not apply to policymakers' behavior.

Second, if a model is to be used to help develop policy, it seems absurd, at first glance, to tie the policymaker's hands by including in it a policymaking rule. The policymaker naturally would like to know the expected outcomes for alternative settings of the policy instruments under his control. A perfectly accurate model would provide enough information to allow him to achieve his objectives. But in view of the substantial errors made by the behavioral equations of the present generation of models, this appears to be a naive view of what actual model simulations can be expected to reveal. In the presence of uncertainty, the nature of the policymaker's reactions to unexpected events is an important determinant of the degree of control over the economy he can achieve. To study the degree of control issue, the ability to simulate the outcomes of various policy rules for reacting to unexpected events is required.

1.2 Expectations Formation

The MPS model structure does not incorporate "rational" expectations formation. Expectations variables are specified as functions of current or past values of the other variables, rather than as functions of simulated future values. Consequently, the behavioral equations in the model do not contain complete descriptions of optimizing behavior that could be expected to withstand all changes in policymaking behavior. How, then, can we rationalize using the model to investigate policy regime changes?

Given recent advances in theoretical macroeconomics, backward-looking specifications may seem naive, but the behavioral equations now in the model generally fit the historical data well. This fact suggests that adaptive expectations formation has proved to be a satisfactory technique to a public subjected to historical policy regimes. We shall subsequently show that if the existing model equations remain reasonably good descriptions of the public's behavior, then some simple, understandable, and realistic-looking policy reaction functions are fairly successful in achieving the objectives policymakers are thought to have. The distribution of economic outcomes resulting from using these rules in simulations is such that it appears adaptive expectations techniques would continue to produce reasonably accurate forecasts of the expectations variables. This suggests that the introduction of such policy rules would not create much incentive for the public to invest in more costly "rational" expectations-forming techniques.

The argument being made here is the "Lucas critique" in reverse. It seems likely that the existing expectations formation mechanisms presently in our model would provide the public with expectations that would prove to be at least as, and perhaps more, accurate if policymakers were to react in the manner described by the more successful versions of our policy reaction functions than they would if policymakers continue to react as they have historically.

2   Developing the Policy Rules

Four types of information are used to create the reaction functions used in this section. The first is a rough idea of policymakers' preferences. It is assumed that in the long run policymakers prefer a constant, low rate of inflation and become increasingly unhappy as deviations from that target occur. It is also assumed that, other things equal, volatile unemployment rates, sharp swings in the growth of output, and large fluctuations in interest rates are undesirable.

Nonvolatility, however, is a somewhat ambiguous goal. The speed with which a disturbed simulated economy can be made to approach a steady-state resource utilization path depends on how violently the policymaker allows certain other variables, particularly interest rates, to fluctuate in the short run. Consequently, there is a trade-off between different kinds of volatility. Policymaker preferences concerning this trade-off could have been described formally using an explicit criterion function, but that has not been done in this paper. Instead, we directly specify reaction functions that reflect those preferences.

This point bears emphasizing in a deliberately positive manner, for nearly every early reader of this paper has at first had a negative reaction to it. Economists are trained to optimize things and tend to regard propositions not based on optimizing principles as being without obvious legitimacy. Practical people, however, sometimes demur. Too often they have been presented with econometric evidence for some proposition that relies on a "best fit" to historical data. Those fits often seriously misrepresent the uncertainty inherent in relating the endogenous to the exogenous elements of the proposition. Thus, contrary to the instincts of most economists, we assert the lack of optimization in this context to be a virtue rather than a vice. By not attempting to find a policy rule optimized against historical data we hope to make our intuitive policy rules more credible to practical observers.

The second type of information we use is our knowledge of some dynamic interconnections between key variables in the MPS model. We know, for example, that the rate of inflation responds, albeit sluggishly, to deviations in the actual from the natural unemployment rate, and that the unemployment rate, in turn, responds to deviations of the actual from the natural rate of growth of output.[1] Thus, it is necessary for policymakers to allow an increase in unemployment and a reduction in the growth rate of output from their natural levels in order to reduce persistent inflation. We believe that our policy rules' reflection of the model's hierarchical causation structure is critical in the success they achieve.

Third, the policy reaction rules take advantage of some simple notions from the literature on the control of imperfectly understood mechanisms. Suppose

$$y_t = f(x_t, \ldots, x_{t-n}; \theta),$$

where y is the variable to be controlled, x is the instrument by which we hope to control it, θ represents other factors influencing y, and t is a time subscript. If θ is only partially predictable, and if knowledge of $f(x)$ and its partial derivatives $\partial y_t / \partial x_t, \ldots, \partial y_t / \partial x_{t-n}$ is subject to error, then it is not possible to control y exactly. If the sign of the derivatives is known with certainty, it is clear in which direction to "turn the steering wheel" when y wanders off course, but just when or how far to turn remains uncertain. The literature suggests that under such circumstances an effective control mechanism should take into account not only the direction and distance the target variable y is from course, but also how fast it is straying from, or approaching, the desired path. Our control rules embody this notion.

Since the function $f(x)$ is not known for certain, the value of x that holds the average value of y on target is also uncertain. The control literature also suggests that control of such mechanisms can sometimes be improved by a reaction rule that responds to the cumulative deviations of y from target, or, in plain language, learns from mistakes. Our control rules also embody mechanisms of this type.

Fourth, and only because it is convenient for simulation, we assume in the early sections of the paper that the monetary policy authorities have one-quarter perfect foresight; they know with certainty the one-quarter-ahead (hereafter called current-quarter) outcome of any particular monetary policy instrument setting. This unrealistic assumption will be dropped when we consider the policy design problem in the final section.

2.1 The Monetary Policy Reaction Function: A Hierarchical Approach[2,3]

The monetary policy reaction functions we create have a very specific form that reflects the MPS model structure. To see why this form was chosen, it is instructive to examine the reasons why one of the most frequently proposed monetary policy reaction functions—a steady growth rate for money—causes large and persistant cycles in MPS model simulations in the presence of disturbances. The model contains a so-called inflation-augmented Phillips curve of the form

$$\frac{\Delta W}{W} = \alpha_0 - \alpha_1 U + \alpha_2 \left(\frac{\Delta P}{P}\right)' + \alpha_3 Z, \tag{1}$$

where W is the wage rate, U is the unemployment rate, P is the price level, and Z represents other factors. The term $(\Delta P/P)'$ may reflect either adaptive price expectations or wage catch-up, but whichever is the case, it is modeled by a distributed lag. The argument is easier to follow if we pretend the lag is the simplest one possible:

$$\left(\frac{\Delta P}{P}\right)' = \left(\frac{\Delta P}{P}\right)_{-1}. \tag{2}$$

The price equation is a markup on unit labor costs. It can be summarized as

$$P = kWe^{-\gamma t}, \tag{3}$$

where k reflects the markup over wage costs and γ is a constant rate of technical change. Assuming k is constant,

$$\frac{\Delta P}{P} = \frac{\Delta W}{W} - \gamma. \tag{4}$$

Substituting (1) into (4)

$$\frac{\Delta P}{P} = \alpha_0 - \alpha_1 U + \alpha_2 \left(\frac{\Delta P}{P}\right)_{-1} + \alpha_3 Z - \gamma. \tag{5}$$

If, as is the case in the MPS model, $\alpha_2 = 1$, we can write

$$\frac{\Delta P}{P} - \left(\frac{\Delta P}{P}\right)_{-1} = \alpha_0 - \alpha_1 U + \alpha_3 Z - \gamma. \tag{6}$$

If Z is constant, the change in the rate of change of prices depends upon the level of unemployment. Furthermore, there is some level of the unemployment rate (the "natural" unemployment rate), consistent with inflation, neither accelerating nor decelerating. The general mechanism described here is quite standard in the empirical literature on aggregate price and wage formation, and it fits historical US data very well.

It is easy to see why holding the money growth rate constant might not result in a stable simulation path for a macromodel containing this mechanism. The fixed money growth path predetermines both the rate of inflation and the price level consistent with the economy's steady-state path at each point of time. Consider what happens if the price level is disturbed upward from the steady-state growth path. The demand for money is increased and interest rates rise. This depresses output and increases unemployment. The increased unemployment, in turn, depresses the rate of change of prices. As long as the price *level* remains too high, a force is created that tends to keep unemployment above its natural rate and the *rate of inflation* continues to fall. The declining rate of inflation eventually returns the price level to its steady-state value, and this in turn allows the unemployment rate to return to the natural rate, but at this point *inflation* is too low to be consistent with the fixed money growth path and the price level falls through the steady-state level. This reduces the demand for money, causing interest rates to fall until unemployment is below the natural rate. Inflation then accelerates until at some point it reaches its steady-state value. But now the *level* of prices is too low. The mirror image of the previous events takes place and overshooting occurs again.

This mechanism virtually guarantees that the model once disturbed will not return smoothly to a balanced growth path, but rather will produce oscillations. The degree to which the cycle is explosive or damped depends on model parameters. With existing MPS parameters the cycle is only slightly damped. The cycle could be eliminated by altering the model structure, of course, but the empirical evidence favoring the inflation-augmented Phillips curve is very compelling.

If the model's price dynamics bear much relationship to those of the real economy, then it makes little sense for the policymaker to attempt to achieve both a target inflation rate and a target price level. It appears more sensible to try to control the inflation rate while accepting whatever price level turns out to be most convenient for achieving this goal.

Inspection of equation (6) suggests immediately how this price cycle might be avoided. If inflation is above its desired level, the policymaker can raise the unemployment rate above the natural rate for a time, then gradually lower it toward the natural rate as the inflation target is approached. This strategy makes sense only if the monetary authorities can control the unemployment rate more directly than inflation. Certainly, that is the case in the MPS model, where virtually the *only* control the policymaker has over prices works through the unemployment rate.[4] The reaction functions developed in this paper take advantage of this hierarchical structure of causation, working backward from inflation, which can be controlled only very indirectly, through unemployment to output, and finally to interest rates (or to financial aggregates), which can be directly controlled.

2.2   Specifying the Monetary Policy Reaction Function

Let *PDOTULT* represent an ultimate target inflation rate chosen by our hypothetical policymaker. However, assume that instead of aiming directly for this target, the policymaker seeks to approach an interim inflation target (*PDOTINT*) computed as the ultimate target rate plus some fraction (β_1) of the difference between current ongoing inflation, *PDOT*, and the ultimate inflation target. This presumes that the policymaker is temporarily willing to accommodate some portion of the deviation of ongoing inflation from his ultimate inflation target (in the text the policy reaction function has been simplified by eliminating a variety of minor details that would have cluttered the exposition; a more complete policy rule specification including parameter values is presented in appendix A):

$$PDOTINT = PDOTULT + \beta_1(PDOT - PDOTULT). \qquad (7)$$

We assume the policymaker next calculates an interim target unemploy-

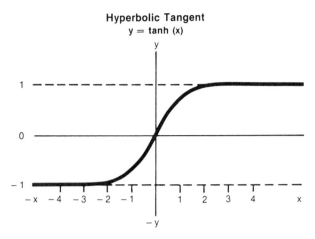

Hyperbolic Tangent
y = tanh (x)

Figure 10.1

ment rate as a deviation from the natural unemployment rate in response to the deviation of the ongoing inflation rate from its interim target. We assume he intends that these unemployment deviations be limited in size. To implement this notion an interim target unemployment rate is calculated that deviates from the natural unemployment rate as a positive, decreasing-slope function of deviations of ongoing inflation from its interim target. A convenient but flexible functional form that has these properties is the hyperbolic tangent (tanh): $y = \gamma_0 + \gamma_1 \tanh(\gamma_2(x - \gamma_3))$.

In this expression y is related to x as in figure 10.1. If $\gamma_0 = \gamma_3 = 0$, and $\gamma_1 = \gamma_2 = 1$, the function crosses the origin ($x = 0, y = 0$) and is bounded by $+1$ and -1. γ_0 shifts the function up or down, γ_1 expands or contracts the distance between the upper and lower bounds, γ_2 controls the steepness of the slope, and γ_3 shifts the function horizontally. The tanh function is used to represent the relationship between the interim target unemployment rate ($UINT$) and the deviation between actual and interim target inflation:

$$UINT = UNAT + \beta_2 \tanh(\beta_3(PDOT - PDOTINT))$$
$$+ \beta_4 \tanh(\beta_5 \Delta(PDOT - PDOTINT)). \tag{8}$$

If, for example, $\beta_2 = 2.0$, the first hyperbolic tangent term causes deviations of $UINT$ from the natural rate ($UNAT$) of up to 2 percentages points depending on the size of the gap between actual inflation and the interim inflation target. If $\beta_4 = 1.0$, the second term can add or subtract up to 1 percentage point from $UINT$ depending on the speed at which actual inflation is approaching or straying from the interim inflation rate target. Equation (8) together with its parameters reflects the policymaker's assumed beliefs about the location of the Phillips curve, represented by the natural unemployment rate, his understanding of the Phillips curve's dynamics, and his preferences about how fast inflation should be returned to its target path. The parameter settings mentioned in the text are the same as those actually used in simulation. While a reader's intuition about appropriate parameter settings may be quite limited at this point, the settings used are certainly of an order of magnitude most would think sensible.

The two tanh terms in equation (8) represent the level and first-difference portions of the control mechanisms suggested by the literature. The integral, or learning from mistakes portion, is incorporated in the calculation of the natural unemployment rate. The exact value of the natural unemployment rate at any moment of time is not known. A preliminary value for the natural rate ($UNAT'$) can be calculated by solving equation (6) for the unemployment rate that sets the left-hand side of equation (6) equal to zero:[5]

$$UNAT' = \frac{\alpha_0}{\alpha_1} + \frac{\alpha_3}{\alpha_1} z - \frac{\gamma}{\alpha_1}. \tag{9}$$

We calculate an improved estimate of the natural rate as we learn from errors by adding an adjustment term ($UNATADJ$),

$$UNAT = UNAT' + UNATADJ, \tag{10}$$

where

$$UNATADJ = UNATADJ_{-1} + \beta_6 \tanh \left\{ \beta_7 \left(\left(\frac{\Delta P}{P} \right)_{-1} - \left(\frac{\Delta P}{P} \right)_{-5} \right) \right. \tag{11}$$
$$\left. + U - UNAT \right\}.$$

The sense of equation (11) is that if inflation rises when $UNAT$ equals U, this constitutes evidence that the policymaker has erred in his estimate of $UNAT$, and that his notion of its location ought to be adjusted upward.[6] Similarly, if inflation does not accelerate when $UNAT$ is less than U, evidence is provided that the policymaker's estimate of $UNAT$ is in error and ought to be corrected. The tanh functional form limits the size of the one-period change in the adjustment.

The next step of the reaction function computes an interim rate of real output growth. It is both a widely accepted fact and a characteristic of the MPS model that unemployment rates react sluggishly to changes in output. Consequently, adhering closely to an unemployment target in the presence of disturbances might require sizable fluctuations in output growth. The reaction functions reflect an assumption that the policymaker recognizes this fact. But it is also assumed that he regards large output fluctuations to be undesirable, so he attempts to control unemployment only indirectly by varying within limits the rate of growth of real output.

Just as there exists a natural rate of unemployment in the MPS model, there also exists a natural rate of output growth defined as the rate of growth that would keep the unemployment rate constant. It is represented here by the symbol $XDOTNAT$. Once again we assume that the policymaker knows approximately what it is and that, other things equal, he would like to keep output growing at the natural rate. Deviations of output growth from its natural rate move the unemployment rate, so it is reasonable to assume that the policymaker might set an interim target rate of growth of output according to a formula like

$$XDOTINT = XDOTNAT + \beta_8(\tanh(\beta_9(U - UINT)) + \beta_{10}\tanh(\beta_{11}\Delta(U - UINT)). \tag{12}$$

This expression makes the interim target rate of output growth a function of deviations of the ongoing unemployment rate from its interim target. By raising the target growth rate when unemployment is above target, the reaction function tends to drive the unemployment rate toward its target value. The tanh functional form is once again used to bound the output growth target. No matter how far unemployment is from its target, there is a limit to how far the real growth target will depart from the natural growth rate. Once again a term in the rate of change of the driving discrepancy is present. In simulations in the next section both β_8 and β_{10} are set at 3.0. Our limited intuition suggests that the values are not unreasonable.

As in the previous step, the integral portion of the control rule is reflected in the calculation of the intercept, which in this case is the natural rate of output growth, $XDOTNAT$.

To obtain an estimate of $XDOTNAT$, a preliminary estimate $(XDOTNAT')$ is made:[7]

$$XDOTNAT' = (1 + .01 * POPDOT)(1 + .01 * TECH) - 1 + \text{other factors}, \tag{13}$$

where $POPDOT$ is the percentage rate of growth of the potential labor force and *TECH* is the estimated underlying annual percentage growth rate of labor-augmenting technical change. The preliminary calculation is then adjusted by a factor *XNATADJ*, to obtain a final estimate of (*XDOTNAT*):

$$XDOTNAT = XDOTNAT' + XNATADJ, \tag{14}$$

$$XNATADJ = XNATADJ_{-1} + \beta_{12}\tanh(\beta_{13}((XDOT - XDOTNAT) \tag{15}$$
$$+ 2.5(U - U_{-4}))).$$

The argument of the hyperbolic tangent function in this case is the observed departure from Okun's law when *XDOTNAT* is accepted as the natural growth rate. Equations (14) and (15) drive the estimate of *XDOTNAT* toward the value that makes Okun's law work.

In the final step our hypothetical monetary policymaker sets the federal funds rate (*RFF*) so that its real, after-tax value $[(1 - t)RFF - PDOT]$ responds to deviations of the level of output (*X*) from its target level (*XTARGET*), determined by applying *XDOTINT* to last quarter's realized GNP level:

$$(1 - t)RFF - PDOT = \varepsilon_1(X - XTARGET) + \varepsilon_0. \tag{16}$$

If we assume *t* (a marginal tax rate) is approximately constant at .3, we have

$$RFF = \frac{1}{.7}PDOT + \frac{\varepsilon_1}{.7}(X - XTARGET) + \frac{\varepsilon_0}{.7}. \tag{17}$$

Differencing once with respect to time yields

$$RFF = RFF_{-1} + \frac{1}{.7}(PDOT - PDOT_{-1}) + \frac{\varepsilon_1}{.7}(XDOT - XDOTINT), \tag{17'}$$

where *XDOT* is the simulated output growth rate and *XDOTINT* is the intermediate target output growth rate that emerged from equation (12).

Adding terms for the first difference and summation of deviations from the output target and using the tanh form to bound the calculated funds rate movements yields

$$RFF = RFF_{-1} + \beta_{14}(PDOT - PDOT_{-1})$$
$$+ \beta_{15}\tanh(\beta_{16}(XDOT - XDOTINT))$$
$$+ \beta_{17}\Delta\tanh(\beta_{18}(XDOT - XDOTINT)) \tag{18}$$
$$+ \beta_{19}\Sigma\tanh(\beta_{20}(XDOT - XDOTINT)).$$

Experiments with trial parameter values in the earlier stages of the monetary policy reaction rule taught us that the differential terms were very important in determining the rule's stabilizing properties, but that the integral terms added very little. In this final stage it was found that both terms were crucial. The differential term turned out to be extremely important for maintaining output stability. This suggests that it is very important for the policymaker to anticipate where the economy is headed in addition to determining where it currently is. It also suggests that economic forecasts beyond the current quarter might be extremely useful to the policymaker.

The integral term of equation (18) also proved useful in long historical simulations for two reasons. First, there appears to be an upward drift over time in the aggregate demand function. This results from a number of factors, including a change in the age distribution of the population, the periodic introduction of new tax incentives for investment, the expansion of income maintenance programs, and an increasing tendency toward deficit financing of federal expenditures. The integral term corrects for these trends. Second, it is important that the reaction function be general enough to accommodate any changes in model structure or fiscal policy that we might wish to investigate. When such changes shift the aggregate demand function, the integral term allows the hypothetical policymaker to learn from his errors and make appropriate adjustments.

The integral term plays an analogous role to that of *UNATADJ* in the calculations of the natural unemployment rate and *XNATADJ* in the calculation of the natural rate of output growth. The constant term in equation (17) can be thought of as a natural rate of interest, and the integral term corrects this estimate of the natural interest rate.

The final stage of the reaction function given by equation (18) represents the policymaker's views of the location of the IS curve, its dynamics, and his preferences about interest rate volatility. Since we have much less certainty about the location and dynamics of the IS curve than we do about the Phillips curve or labor demand functions, we have much less intuition about appropriate parameter values. The ones we used are values that "worked well" and are thus subject to the objection they may have been overfitted. We shall find a way to eliminate our dependence on these nonintuitive parameters in the final section of this paper.

It is our belief that the hierarchical nature of the reaction functions presented here, a nature that is closely related to the model's structure, is absolutely crucial in making the function successful in stabilizing the model. With two exceptions, dropping any of the terms in any of the stages caused the reaction function to perform much less well in historical simulations. The two exceptions were the integral terms in the calculation of the target unemployment rate and output growth rates. These proved unnecessary because recent history has not provided sustained movements of (shocks to) the Phillips curve or labor demand function.

2.3   Fiscal Policy Reaction Functions

Trial simulations demonstrated that the simulated rate of resource utilization could be controlled quite satisfactorily using only the monetary policy reaction rule just described. However, some of our work involved examining the very long-run effects of fiscal policy changes, and this required causing the model to approach a steady-state growth path. We know that if economic policy is to avoid driving the economy away from such a path, then restrictions on fiscal policy behavior are also required. In a steady state, both the government surplus (or deficit) and the outstanding debt must be constant proportions of GNP. This condition is obvious, but it is not as easy to impose as it may seem. To see why one must recall some simple dynamics of debt.

Let D represent the federal debt (consisting only of one-period bills), r the real interest rate, T tax receipts, and E expenditures. Let E' stand for government expenditures other than interest on the debt. Assume temporarily that there is no inflation. Then,

$$D = D_{-1} + E' - T + rD_{-1} \tag{19}$$

describes the evolution of the debt.

Dividing by D_{-1} and rearranging, we have

$$\frac{D - D_{-1}}{D_{-1}} = \frac{E' - T}{D_{-1}} + r. \tag{20}$$

Let g represent the steady-state growth rate of the economy. Then in a steady state,

$$\frac{D - D_{-1}}{D_{-1}} = g,$$

$$g = \frac{E' - T}{D_{-1}} + r, \tag{21}$$

$$g - r = \frac{E' - T}{D_{-1}}.$$

The last expression constrains the possible choices of the deficit (defined to exclude interest payments) relative to existing debt and the growth of real GNP. If the constraint is ignored and the above expression is violated, then debt as a proportion of output grows without limit. Recent experience has shown that $r > g$ is a quite realistic possibility. In that case, if the initial stock of debt is positive, the net-of-interest budget must be in surplus, or else the debt will grow explosively.

These considerations led us to develop an optional fiscal policy rule that could stabilize the debt to GNP ratio at an arbitrary level preselected by an hypothetical fiscal policymaker. The nature of the fiscal policy rule is much like that of the monetary policy rule. The ultimate target is a preselected federal debt to GNP ratio. The federal personal income tax rate is manipulated in such a way that the simulated debt to GNP ratio is gradually driven toward its ultimate target. Movements in the tax rate instrument are, however, restricted to realistic proportions.

Because of space limitations, the details of the fiscal policy rule are not presented here. Only two of the simulations reported in this paper use it. We reiterate that the fiscal policy rule is not needed for the stabilization of resource utilization in ordinary circumstance. It is a very useful tool, however, in long-run simulations (20 years and more) when the usual default rule (fixed government expenditures and tax rates) produces an explosive path for the federal debt (as might well happen starting from the initial conditions of 1985), in long simulations in which steady-state outcomes are the focus of attention, or in simulations where the effects of altering the long-run debt/GNP ratio are under investigation. An example of this last type of exercise is presented in the next section.

2.4   Choosing Policy Rule Parameter Values

Parameter values for the monetary and tax policy functions were obtained through a trial and error process by conducting long historical simulations of the model using various parameter settings and choosing the parameter values that appeared to perform "best" in keeping the economy near its natural rate of resource utilization while at the same time causing inflation to approach and stay near its targeted value. In general, the simulation results were quite robust to the choice of parameter values, at least within a fairly broad range, so parameters were not "fine-tuned." Experience convinced us it was necessary that the general form of the policy rule be something like the one we developed, but, given this form, gains from the fine-tuning of parameters seemed to be quite limited. This, too, we found encouraging because it suggests that a very close correspondence between the parameter values of the reaction function and those of the model is not

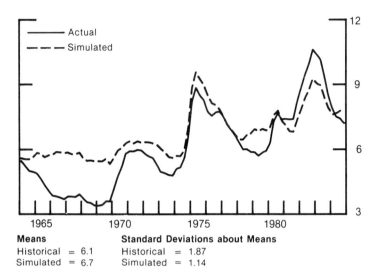

Means	Standard Deviations about Means
Historical = 6.1	Historical = 1.87
Simulated = 6.7	Simulated = 1.14

Figure 10.2
Simulation using monetary policy reaction rule: unemployment rate.

required. It seems likely that the policy rule would work tolerably well even if model parameters could be changed to their "true" real-world values.

3 Toward Realism: Coping with Disturbances

In this section two sets of historical simulations conducted using the reaction functions are presented to demonstrate their stabilizing properties. In these simulations behavioral equation errors were coded into the behavioral equations. Thus, had all policy variables been set at historical values, the simulations would have tracked history exactly. Our goal, however, is to produce "better" outcomes than history.

The first simulation reported here uses only the monetary policy reaction rule in a simulation of 1964:Q1 to 1984:Q4. All tax rates and exogenous federal government real expenditures are held at historical levels.[8] The policymaker's ultimate inflation rate target is set at zero. Figure 10.2 compares the simulated unemployment rates with historical unemployment rates. Several features stand out. First, on average, the simulated unemployment rate is considerably less volatile. The standard deviation of the simulated unemployment rate about the mean of that series is 1.14%. The same statistic for the historical series over this period is 1.87%. The

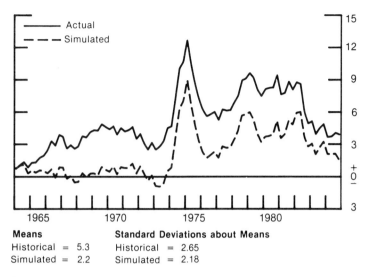

Means   Standard Deviations about Means
Historical = 5.3   Historical = 2.65
Simulated = 2.2   Simulated = 2.18

Figure 10.3
Simulation using monetary policy reaction rule: inflation rate.

simulated average absolute deviation between the unemployment rate and the natural unemployment rate is .95%, compared with 1.50% for the historical numbers. Second, since there was some ongoing inflation at the beginning of the simulation period and since historical inflation gradually accelerated in the late 1960s, the reaction function keeps simulated unemployment considerably above historical levels in that period.

A third feature is that the historical increases in both unemployment and inflation (see figure 10.3) that occurred in 1974 are not reduced. This is what one would expect if the episode was in large part caused by the tremendous increase in the real price of energy. Monetary policy could not do much to improve the available trade-off. A final feature to note is that the runup in unemployment rates in the early 1980s is somewhat reduced. Our reaction function appears to resist the inflation arising from the first energy price shock about as forcefully as did the policymakers of that period, but it resists it a bit less than did the real-world policymakers during the second episode.

The monetary policy reaction rule succeeds in holding inflation far below historical experience, as can be seen clearly from figure 10.3. By 1966, it has succeeded in eliminating inflation entirely. Sustained price increases do not resume until the onset of the oil embargo in 1973. Inflation falls back to about 2% in 1976, rises again in the second energy

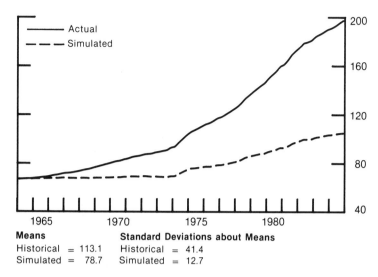

Means

Historical = 113.1
Simulated = 78.7

Standard Deviations about Means

Historical = 41.4
Simulated = 12.7

Figure 10.4
Simulation using monetary policy reaction rule: price level.

price episode, then gradually declines to about 1.5% at the end of 1984. Figure 10.4 further illustrates the reaction function's success in causing price stability by comparing historical and simulated price *levels*. The 1984:Q4 simulated price level is about half the actual price level.

Less encouraging is the fact that the simulated volatility of the federal funds rate considerably exceeds that of the historical series (see figure 10.5). One measure of this volatility, the average absolute one-quarter change in the funds rate, averages about 2.6 percentage points in the simulation, compared with about .9 percentage points over the same historical period. One-quarter movements in the simulated funds rate often exceed 300 basis points—an event that actually occurred only twice in that entire period. It is difficult to imagine the present generation of policymakers allowing such large interest rates fluctuations.

Figures 10.6–10.9 compare two simulations that explore the long-run consequences of using the fiscal policy reaction function to target the ratio of federal debt to GNP at different levels while using the monetary policy rule to stabilize resource utilization. The figures provide a convincing demonstration of the power of our monetary policy rule to damp out the simulated resource utilization and inflation effects of a very large disturbance. In the first simulation the target debt to GNP ratio is set at .2—a setting that leads the model to very roughly replicate the historical ratio of

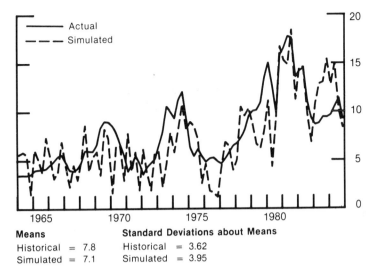

Means   **Standard Deviations about Means**

Historical = 7.8   Historical = 3.62
Simulated = 7.1   Simulated = 3.95

Figure 10.5
Simulation using monetary policy reaction rule: federal funds rate.

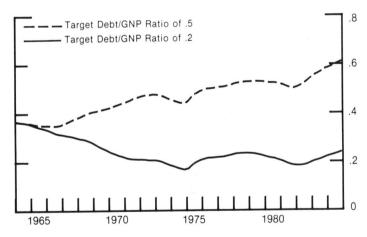

Figure 10.6
Simulations using monetary and fiscal policy reaction rules: federal debt/GNP ratio.

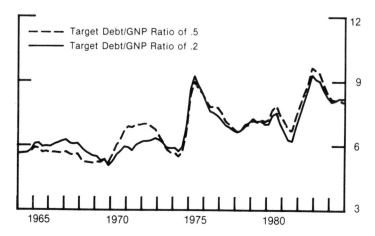

Figure 10.7
Simulations using monetary and fiscal policy reaction rules: unemployment rate.

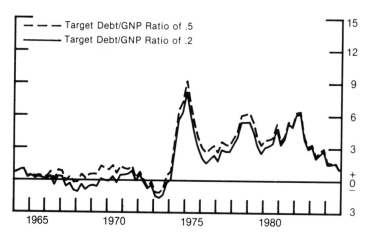

Figure 10.8
Simulations using monetary and fiscal policy reaction rules: inflation rate.

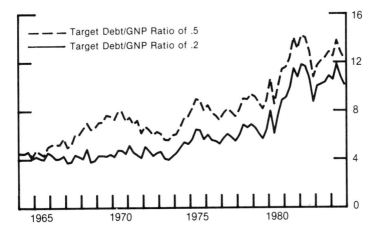

Figure 10.9
Simulations using monetary and fiscal policy reaction rules: corporate bond rate.

debt to GNP prior to 1981. In the second the target ratio is .5, which leads to a substantial increase in simulated debt during the 1960s and 1970s.

Figure 10.6 shows the two simulated debt ratios. In each case, the fiscal policy rule succeeds in achieving a debt ratio near its target value about ten years after the start of the simulation and then keeps it in the appropriate vicinity. Figure 10.7 shows the simulated unemployment rates resulting from the two fiscal policies in the presence of our monetary policy rule. The .5 debt to GNP target ratio results in massive tax cuts early in the period followed by large tax increases later. The monetary policy reaction rule suppresses the resource utilization consequences of these events quite well. Unemployment rates differ by no more than 1 percentage point in a few periods in the first decade. After the debt ratios near their target values and the tax rate changes cease, the unemployment rate paths from the two simulations track each other closely.

Figure 10.8 shows the two simulated inflation rate paths. Unemployment rates are uniformly lower in the first five years of the .5 target ratio simulation, and that results in an inflation rate about 1 point higher by 1969. The monetary policy rule squeezes out this extra inflation during the next three years. Squeezing out inflation is one reason the simulated unemployment rates are higher in that period. After 1972 the simulated inflation rates track each other very closely.

Figure 10.9 shows the two simulated corporate bond rates. The differential between interest rates rises to a maximum of about 400 basis points when the tax rate differential is at its peak, but falls back to around

250 basis points once the debt ratio adjustment is complete. Since the inflation paths are nearly identical in the latter parts of these two simulations, we can interpret the gap between the interest rates as a real interest rate differential. The increase in the simulated federal debt ratio from .2 to .5 raises simulated real interest rates by approximately 2.5 percentage points in this experiment.

Taken at face value, this pair of simulations suggests that fiscal policy has important consequences for the level of real interest rates in the long run. We are not surprised by this result, but must keep in mind that the purpose of the exercise reported here is merely to demonstrate the power of our policy reaction functions to stabilize simulated resource utilization in the face of large fiscal policy changes. It is not a careful investigation of the effects of debt management. To conduct our experiment we had to make a number of assumptions concerning several imponderables about which very little is known. Among them are the response of trade policy, both at home and abroad, to economic changes set in motion by a change in the target debt ratio, capital control policy responses both at home and abroad, and the fiscal policy responses of foreign countries. We have published elsewhere the results of a more serious investigation of the consequences of long-run debt management policies based on simulations using our reaction function mechanisms.

From these simulations on historical data and from a variety of similar tests not reported here, we conclude that our reaction functions are able to stabilize the MPS model in simulations of the recent past even when the model is subjected to severe shocks. On the other hand, they have defects as a description of real-world policymaking behavior. Remedying these defects is the subject of the next section.

4   Fuzzy Foresight: The Use of Imperfect Forecasts in Policymaking

In this section we take away the policymaker's one-quarter-ahead perfect foresight, but give him the ability to forecast imperfectly over longer intervals. Our goal is to simulate the model using an assumption that the policymaker, whose behavior is summarized in various kinds of reaction functions, including some resembling those employed in the previous section, has the same fuzzy medium-term foresight that real-world policymakers employ.

Realistic policy analysis requires the ability to conduct stochastic simulations with the model. Stochastic simulations allow us to estimate the uncertainty associated with any particular policy rule by observing the dispersion of a large number of outcomes found by conducting repeated simulations using the rule. Fortunately, the policy design work of our colleagues Tinsley and von zur Muehlen has already extended the MPS model's capacities in this direction. Their work provides our point of departure.

4.1 The Tinsley–von zur Muehlen Bootstrap Method of Stochastic Simulation and Policy Analysis

The starting point in the Tinsley–von zur Muehlen procedure is a history of errors from the model's structural equations as well as from time-series equations fitted to each of the model's exogenous variables. In the latter case, the assumption is made that the distribution of errors from the time-series equations is roughly similar to the distribution of errors that a forecaster might make in trying to project the exogenous variables. The error series are adjusted to have zero means and then an autocorrelation coefficient (ρ) is calculated for each series (i) according to the formula

$$u_{i,t} = \rho_i u_{i,t-1} + e_{i,t}, \tag{22}$$

where $u_{i,t}$ is the mean-adjusted error of equation i in period t, $e_{i,t}$ is the "innovation" in equation i in period t, and ρ_i is the calculated autocorrelation coefficient. The matrix of innovations and the autocorrelation coefficients is then used to construct a hypothetical series of errors, or pseudohistory, that has the same statistical properties as the historical error sequence using what has been called the bootstrap technique.

A date is chosen at random and the historical vector of innovations for that date is retrieved. By using innovations from the same data for all equations, the historical cross-equation correlations among the innovations are preserved. These innovations are used to shock the model equations and a baseline set of exogenous variables in the first simulation period and the resulting simulation of that quarter is recorded as pseudohistory.

In the next period of the simulation, a new date is drawn at random (with replacement) from the historical period and its associated vector of innovations is recovered. These innovations are passed through the error-persistence equations (22) to obtain shocks for the second simulation quarter. This procedure preserves the historical first-order autocorrelation properties of the equation errors. The same procedure is repeated for each quarter of the simulation—a random drawing from the matrix of innovations followed by the computation of the shocks that are added to the equations as another quarter is simulated. Many such simulations are then conducted. Our main interest will be focused on the range of the simulated outcomes that results from this process, and how the width of the distribution of outcomes is affected by the choice of policy rules.

4.2   Using Reaction Functions in Stochastic Simulations

In Tinsley and von zur Muehlen's work a two-stage policymaking procedure is used. The policymaker makes a one-quarter forecast (represented by a simulation with all innovations set to zero) and chooses a policy instrument setting. He then holds to that setting in a second stage simulation that uses an innovation drawing.

We extended the Tinsley–von zur Muehlen procedure described above in two ways. First, we employed a variety of modified policy rules along the lines of those set forth earlier in the paper to set monetary policy variables in the first step of the Tinsley–von zur Muehlen procedure. Second, the conditional forecast horizon used in the policymaking (first) stage was lengthened from one quarter to several quarters.

These extensions permit us to simulate much more complicated and realistic policymaking procedures than has hitherto been possible. In one interesting case, for example, the hypothetical policymaker first chooses a long-run inflation goal. Based on an hierarchical monetary policy reaction function like the one described earlier, his long-run inflation goal is translated sequentially into interim goals for inflation, unemployment, and real output. The policymaker then selects a target path for an intermediate target variable that results in achieving the output goal in a multiquarter economic forecast. Finally, an instrument variable that the policymaker can control directly is set at a value consistent with causing the intermediate target variable to hit its current-quarter target value in the absence of surprises. Then, using the Tinsley–von zur Muehlen bootstrap technique, we shock the model. We can then repeat the entire process in each quarter of a multiyear simulation, and finally perform repetitions of the simulations using different shocks. The distribution of resulting outcomes provides an estimate of the degree of control over the economy that a policymaker using the hierarchical rule would have.

In order to implement these ideas, it was necessary to modify the model's simulation code to enable it to select a path for the intermediate target variable that would produce a chosen value for some other target variable—GNP growth, for example—more than one quarter into the future in the absence of surprises. There are, of course, an infinite number of paths the intermediate target variable could follow that would produce the given value of the other target variable after four quarters. To determine a unique path for the intermediate target variable some further restriction was needed. We simply assumed that either the intermediate target variable or its growth rate, whichever seemed appropriate, would take on the same value in all four quarters.

One further minor extension of the model's simulation capabilities was made. We modified the simulation code to allow us the option of permitting the forecaster to know the value of the current quarter's disturbances while remaining ignorant of future innovations.

4.3   Simulation Results

With these capabilities in place, we could test the outcomes of a variety of policymaking rules under different assumptions about the policymaker's forecasting abilities. Results of several experiments are reported in the tables in this section. We look at these results from two perspectives. First, we compare the outcomes of the experiments according to how well they correspond with historical experience. The objective of this comparison is to determine whether the policymaking procedure being tested could provide a plausible representation of historical policymaking procedures. Second, we compare various policymaking procedures from the standpoint of the desirability of the distribution of outcomes.

Any number of questions could be asked concerning desirability. We confine ourselves to a broad-brush exploration of three themes:

1. What are the merits of using policy rules of the type we have developed relative to the merits of using rules that track some nominal aggregate?

2. What are the merits of choosing as intermediate targets variables quite responsive to monetary policy instruments relative to the merits of those that are not?

3. What are the merits of using economic forecasts as a part of monetary policymaking procedures?

Table 10.1 reports historical dispersion measures for three variables unaffected by the increases over time in the scale of real output or prices. Dispersion measures are presented for the years 1964–1984, as well as for the 1979:Q4–1984:Q4 period following the change in Federal Reserve operating procedures. The figures in table 10.1 serve as a crude benchmark for comparing the simulations with the results of historical policymaking.

The subsequent tables and the results they report fall into three cate-

Table 10.1
Measures of historical dispersion, selected variables

Variable	Measure	Value
1964:Q1–1984:Q4		
Unemployment rate	Root mean squared deviation about historical mean	1.9 percentage points
Inflation rate (4-quarter percent change in prices)	Root mean squared deviation about historical mean	2.7 percentage points
Federal funds rate	Average absolute one-quarter change	91 basis points
1979:Q4–1984:Q4		
Unemployment rate	Root mean squared deviation about historical mean	1.3 percentage points
Inflation rate (4-quarter percent change in prices)	Root mean squared deviation about historical mean	2.0 percentage points
Federal funds rate	Average absolute one-quarter change	155 basis points

gories. First is a set of three tables that present the results of simulating versions of our hierarchical monetary policy reaction function under three different assumptions about the policymaker's forecasting capability. Second is a set of three tables that parallel the first set in their assumptions about forecasting while replacing our reaction function with a predetermined M1 path. Finally, we include a set of two tables that show variations on our hierarchical monetary policy reaction rule using a four-quarter forecasting horizon.

The results are reported in terms of a statistic measuring the width of the range of simulation outcomes—the 70% confidence interval. This statistic is calculated for a number of macroeconomic variables. The range is based on a sample of 100 simulations from which the highest and lowest 15% of the outcomes are excluded. The resulting confidence intervals are roughly comparable in width to two standard deviations of a normally distributed variable. This relationship provides a crude method for comparing simulated dispersions of outcomes with the historical dispersions reported in table 10.1. Attention is concentrated on the size of the range of outcomes near the ends of the simulations in our discussion.

Experience with our simulation procedures has shown that about 300 simulations are necessary before one can be confident further trials will not

Table 10.2
Hierarchical policy rule using single-period forecasts (current-quarter innovations known)[a]

	Range covering all but the lowest and highest 15% of outcomes (percentage points)			
	Quarter			
	4	8	12	16
(1) Unemployment rate	.9	1.3	1.2 (1.4)[b]	1.8
(2) Fixed weight deflator (4-quarter percent increase)	2.4	3.2	3.7	3.9
(3) Federal funds rate	5.3	7.0	6.6 (7.5)[b]	8.5
(4) Mean absolute 1-quarter funds rate change[c]	2.8	2.6	2.5	2.7
(5) M1 (4-quarter percent increase)	3.3	4.8	5.5	6.5

a. Policy rule:
Ultimate inflation target set at zero, leads to
Interim inflation target one quarter ahead, leads to
Interim unemployment target one quarter ahead, leads to
Interim real growth target one quarter ahead, leads to
Funds rate instrument set according to equation (18).
b. Confidence intervals were not always smooth due to the small size of the simulation sample. Figures in parentheses are the author's subjective notion of a more representative value based on confidence intervals for nearby quarters.
c. Figures represent mean absolute changes, not confidence intervals.

materially affect the measured confidence ranges. Our use of only 100 simulations is a somewhat dangerous concession to high computer costs. Each of the tests reported in one of the tables can be shown to require computations equivalent to an ordinary dynamic simulation covering 8,400 years—hence the dangerous truncation.

4.4 Reaction Function Simulations under Various Forecasting Assumptions

The experiments reported in tables 10.2–10.4 all use some form of the hierarchical reaction function with the ultimate inflation target set at zero. The policy instrument is the federal funds rate. The initial quarter for these and all subsequent experiments is 1985:Q1 and the simulations cover four years. The horizons were limited to four years due to the same cost considerations that restricted the number of trials. In several cases it ap-

Table 10.3
Hierarchical policy rule using single-period forecasts
(current-quarter innovations unknown)[a]

	Range covering all but the lowest and highest 15% of outcomes (percentage points)			
	Quarter			
	4	8	12	16
(1) Unemployment rate	1.2	1.6	1.9	2.1
(2) Fixed weight deflator (4-quarter percent increase)	2.6	3.4	4.7	5.2
(3) Federal funds rate	4.9	6.6	6.5 (7.3)[b]	9.5
(4) Mean absolute 1-quarter funds rate change[c]	1.7	2.1	2.0	2.3
(5) M1 (4-quarter percent increase)	3.4	4.9	5.7	7.0

a. Policy rule:
Ultimate inflation target set at zero, leads to
Interim inflation target one quarter ahead, leads to
Interim unemployment target one quarter ahead, leads to
Interim real growth target one quarter ahead, leads to
Funds rate instrument set according to equation (18).
b. Confidence intervals were not always smooth due to the small size of the simulation sample. Figures in parentheses are the author's subjective notion of a more representative value based on confidence intervals for nearby quarters.
c. Figures represent mean absolute changes, not confidence intervals.

pears the horizon is not long enough to reveal the stabilized width of the confidence intervals. The "best" (and therefore most interesting) policy rules do seem to have stabilized the width of the confidence intervals, however. "Bad" policy rules may not stabilize the confidence intervals over any horizon.

The first experiment creates a link to our historical simulations. In the simulations summarized in table 10.2 it is assumed that the policymaker has perfect one-quarter foresight, so that regardless of shocks, he is able to use accurate current-quarter values of economic variables to calculate the setting of his policy instrument (the funds rate) using the policy rule. His conditional forecast horizon is also, however, limited to only one quarter. These assumptions parallel exactly the ones used in the lengthy historical simulations reported in the previous section. This reaction function keeps the economy under relatively satisfactory control. The 70% confidence interval for the unemployment rate (line 1) remains less than 2 percentage

Table 10.4
Hierarchical policy rule using four-quarter forecasts (current-quarter innovations unknown)[a]

	Range covering all but the lowest and highest 15% of outcomes (percentage points)			
	Quarter			
	4	8	12	16
(1) Unemployment rate	1.1	1.5	1.7	1.7
(2) Fixed weight deflator (4-quarter of change)	2.7	2.9	4.5	4.7
(3) Federal funds rate	3.0 (3.5)[b]	4.8	4.9	7.0
(4) Mean absolute 1-quarter funds rate change[c]	1.5	1.5	1.5	1.5
(5) M1 (4-quarter percent increase)	3.8	4.8	5.3	6.6

a. Policy rule:
Ultimate inflation target set at zero, leads to
Interim inflation target four quarters ahead, leads to
Interim unemployment targer four quarters ahead, leads to
Interim real growth target four quarters ahead, leads to
Constant fund rate chosen to achieve interim real growth target, leads to
Funds rate instrument set at that same level in the current quarter.
b. Confidence intervals were not always smooth due to the small size of the simulation sample. Figures in parentheses are the author's subjective notion of a more representative value based on confidence intervals for nearby quarters.
c. Figures represent mean absolute changes, not confidence intervals.

points after four years. This is a considerably smaller dispersion than recent history provides (see table 10.1 and figure 10.2) and fairly close, as should be expected, to twice the 1.1 percentage point standard deviations about the mean calculated in the long historical simulation using the same policy rule (see figure 10.2). Unfortunately, the confidence interval on the unemployment rate does not appear to have stopped widening at the end of four years. Thus it is somewhat risky to conclude that it would not expand beyond 2 percentage points if the trials were extended further into the future. Meaningful comparisons of alternative policy rules require that these ranges ultimately stabilize.

Finally, as was the case in the corresponding historical simulations, the federal funds rate is highly volatile. The average absolute one-quarter change in the funds rate exceeds 200 basis points, more than twice its historical average. It appears that actual policymakers have placed a higher premium on stable interest rates, relative to stable output and employment, than does this version of the reaction function.

The simulations in table 10.3 repeat the same exercise, but with the forecaster's one-quarter perfect foresight removed. It is to be expected that the reaction function would lose some control over the economy as a result of limiting the forecaster's information about current-quarter disturbances. Ranges of unemployment and inflation are generally wider than in table 10.2. However, it is worth noting that the volatility of the funds rate is somewhat reduced in this experiment. This result is not surprising since the funds rate is not responding to the current quarter's innovations. Of course, this lack of response is precisely what diminishes control over the economy.

In the final experiment in this group we extend the horizon of the imperfect forecast made available to the policymaker from one quarter to four quarters. Once again the conditional forecasts consist of zero-innovation simulations. The lengthening of the forecast horizon permitted other changes toward realism. In previous experiments, the last step of the reaction function was a nonintuitive mechanical rule [equation (18)] that reflected the policymaker's beliefs about the location and dynamics of the IS curve, and his preference concerning the trade-off between interest rate and output stability. We now replace this final step with the assumption that the policymaker chooses a funds rate setting that, when held fixed over the four-quarter forecast horizon, causes forecast output to grow at the interim target rate (calculated by the third stage of the reaction function) in the fourth quarter of the forecast. This specification has the advantage that it does not require the policymaker to rely on parameters reflecting some predetermined knowledge of the location and dynamics of the IS curve. Instead, it delegates any such knowledge to the medium-term forecaster.

Early experience with this alternative caused us to make some further alterations. The first difference terms in the various stages of the original reaction function had served the function of providing a crude proxy for a multiperiod forecast. They were now redundant. In fact, their presence hampered stabilization. Consequently, the first difference terms in the rate of inflation and in the rate of unemployment were dropped from the second and third stages of the policy rule. We also found it helpful to widen the limits [β_8 in equation (12)] on the target rate of output growth. This caused the interim output target to respond more strongly to deviations in unemployment from its target value.

Extending the policymaker's forecast horizon brings about a dramatic improvement in the results. Without a formal criterion function, our evaluation of the relative performance of our different reaction functions must be subjective, but to us the results in table 10.4 look much better. The terminal 70% confidence interval on the unemployment rate is now only 1.7 percentage points and appears to have ceased widening. Inflation and real output growth (not shown) are both more stable than in the experiments reported in tables 10.2 and 10.3. Moreover, all this is accomplished with much less volatility in the federal funds rate. The average absolute one-quarter funds rate change, 1.5 percentage points, is still quite high by historical standards, but about the same as its average variability in recent years (see table 10.1).

How reasonable is this rule as a representation of historical policy? It appears to control resource utilization considerably better than historical experience and it exhibits a funds rate volatility about equal to that of recent years. It is also interesting to note that the 70% confidence interval for M1 growth is 3.8% after four quarters (see line 5). In recent years the Federal Reserve has announced one-year money growth objectives expressed as ranges that are usually 3–4 percentage points wide to allow for contingencies. It is not unreasonable to interpret this range as the Federal Reserve's best guess for the range of money growth outcomes. There is no particular reason, of course, why we should assume that Federal Reserve officials believe that the possibility of falling within the announced ranges is 70% rather than some other number. Nevertheless, it seems to us that the uncertainty of the outcome of money growth in this experiment seems very roughly consistent with the width of announced ranges.

4.5   Money Growth Rules under Alternative Assumptions about Policymakers' Forecasting Ability

Before drawing any final conclusions about the stabilizing properties of our preferred reaction function, its results must be compared with those from some commonly proposed alternative rules for monetary policy. Tables 10.5–10.7 present simulation results where monetary policy is determined by adherence to a variety of rules focused on money growth.

One often-suggested strategy for conducting monetary policy is to have the policymaker hold money on a predetermined growth path. Table 10.5 reports the simulated results of very tightly targeting M1. Note that there is almost no variation in money growth in this set of simulations.

Very tight monetary control bounds unemployment almost as successfully as our preferred reaction function does under the same assumptions (compare tables 10.4 and 10.5) for the first three years of the simulation. Inflation is bounded even more tightly by rigid M1 targeting. However, the control comes at the cost of extreme interest rate volatility. The

Table 10.5

Rigid money targeting rule using single-period forecasts (current-quarter innovations known)[a]

| | Range covering all but the lowest and highest 15% of outcomes (percentage points) | | | |
| | Quarter | | | |
	4	8	12	16
(1) Unemployment rate	1.2	1.6	1.7	2.0
(2) Fixed weight deflator (4-quarter percent increase)	2.3	2.9	3.6	3.8 (4.6)[b]
(3) Federal funds rate	4.9	6.3	7.3	6.9
(4) Mean absolute 1-quarter funds rate change[c]	3.6	3.6	3.7	3.7
(5) M1 (4-quarter percent increase)[d]	.0	.1	.1	.1

a. Policy rule:
Predetermined M1 path, leads to
Funds rate instrument set at the level needed to achieve first-quarter target M1 growth.
b. Confidence intervals were not always smooth due to the small size of the simulation sample. Figures in parentheses are the author's subjective notion of a more representative value based on confidence intervals for nearby quarters.
c. Figures represent mean absolute changes, not confidence intervals.
d. A built-in lower limit on funds rate settings caused M1 target to be missed slightly on occasion.

average absolute one-quarter change in the federal funds rate exceeds 350 basis points in these simulations, a value most observers would regard as entirely unacceptable. It may be true, as some suggest, that introduction of such a policy would in time produce structural changes in the money market reducing this volatility. But since it is these very same movements in interest rates that keep the real economy in check in this experiment, any such reduction in volatility is likely to reduce control of economic activity as well.

The exercise reported in table 10.6 relaxes the control on M1 somewhat relative to the previous experiment. In this case we assume that the forecaster's foresight is both fuzzy and myopic. One-quarter forecasts are made setting all innovations to zero. That allows the calculation of a value for the funds rate instrument that would put M1 on target in the absence of surprises. The funds rate is set at that level by the policymaker as the public's behavior is simulated.

The results are not surprising. The confidence intervals for money are wider, but there is less funds rate volatility. The gain in funds rate stability is not dramatic. The average absolute one-quarter change in the funds rate

Table 10.6
Money targeting rule using single-period forecasts (current quarter innovations unknown)[a]

	Range covering all but the lowest and highest 15% of outcomes (percentage points)			
	Quarter			
	4	8	12	16
(1) Unemployment rate	1.3	2.0	1.9 (2.1)[b]	3.0
(2) Fixed weight deflator (4-quarter of change)	2.7	3.5	4.8	5.2
(3) Federal funds rate	5.0	5.7	7.3	7.2
(4) Mean absolute 1-quarter funds rate change[c]	2.6	2.8	3.2 (3.0)[b]	2.9
(5) M1 (4-quarter percent increase)	1.8	2.7	2.6	2.3

a. Policy rule:
Predetermined M1 path, leads to
Constant funds rate level chosen to put forecast M1 on path one quarter ahead.
b. Confidence intervals were not always smooth due to the small size of the simulation sample. Figures in parentheses are the author's subjective notion of a more representative value based on confidence intervals for nearby quarters.
c. Figures represent mean absolute changes, not confidence intervals.

falls only to about 300 basis points per quarter. Note that the width of the confidence interval on four-quarter M1 growth seems to stabilize at about 2.5 percentage points. This suggests, as does the high funds rate volatility, that the M1 control in this simulation exercise is still tighter than the Federal Reserve expects to achieve (remember official target ranges have averaged 3–4 percentage points).

Relaxing M1 targeting reduces control over the real economy considerably compared to the experiment of table 10.5. The terminal 70% confidence interval on the unemployment rate is increased by 50%. This parallels the experience in the case of the original reaction function when the forecaster's one-quarter perfect foresight was removed. Compared to the reaction function experiment in which the forecasters have fuzzy one-quarter foresight, this money rule does poorly at stabilizing resource utilization (compare tables 10.3 and 10.6).

The final set of simulations in this fixed-M1 targeting group is summarized in table 10.7. This time the forecaster has a four-quarter forecasting horizon and the policymaker chooses the constant level of the funds rate that puts forecast M1 on the predetermined path four quarters into the future. He then holds to that value of the funds rate in the face of the

Table 10.7
Money targeting rule using four-quarter forecasts (current-quarter innovations unknown)[a]

	Range covering all but the lowest and highest 15% of outcomes (percentage points)			
	Quarter			
	4	8	12	16
(1) Unemployment rate	1.2	1.9	1.9 (2.2)[b]	2.6
(2) Fixed weight deflator (4-quarter percent increase)	2.7	3.3	4.6	4.9
(3) Federal funds rate	2.9	3.4	4.2	4.9
(4) Mean absolute 1-quarter funds rate change[c]	.6	.7	.7	.8
(5) M1 (4-quarter percent increase)	2.3	2.9	3.4	3.3 (3.6)[b]

a. Policy rule:
Predetermined M1 path, leads to
Constant funds rate chosen to put forecast M1 on target four quarters ahead, leads to
Funds rate instrument set at same level.
b. Confidence intervals were not always smooth due to the small size of the simulation sample. Figures in parentheses are the author's subjective notion of a more representative value based on confidence intervals for nearby quarters.
c. Figures represent mean absolute changes, not confidence intervals.

surprises generated by the unpredictable part of the public's behavior. This exercise is most directly comparable to the reaction function simulations reported in table 10.4 where the forecaster could look ahead four quarters.

The results of this test look much more realistic than do those in tables 10.5 and 10.6. The degree of control over the economy is roughly similar to that reported in those tables, but the range of variation for the funds rate and its average one-quarter change are both much reduced. The average absolute one-quarter funds rate change is now only about 70 basis points, considerably less than the approximately 150 basis points historical average over the period 1979:Q4–1984:Q4 and even somewhat less than the 90 basis point average for the longer 1964–1984 period. Once again, the extension of the forecasting horizon seems to improve performance greatly. This leads to our first conclusion about policy rules. Apparently there is a great advantage to the monetary policymaker in having available lengthy, even if less than accurate, forecasts. This should provide comfort to the Federal Reserve staff.

Less encouraging for this fixed money-growth policy rule is the fact that the range of outcomes for resource utilization does not seem to have stabilized after four years. This result should not be surprising in view of our earlier discussion of the interaction between inflation-augmented Phillips curves and fixed money-growth policy rules. We believe that had the simulation horizon been further extended, the deterioration would have been more marked.

A comparison of the hierarchical reaction function and the fixed M1 policy rules in the cases where the forecaster has four-quarter fuzzy foresight (tables 10.4 and 10.7) turns up the expected differences. M1 is more responsive to interest rates than is real output, and consequently less in the way of funds rate movements are needed to offset contingencies when M1 is targeted. On the other hand, targeting real output tends to control resource utilization better. The largest gain from using the hierarchical reaction function is that control over economic activity does not continue to deteriorate after the third year. Had we been able to conduct more and longer stochastic simulations, we believe this difference would have been revealed to be more dramatic.

4.6   Variations on the Hierarchical Reaction Function

It could be argued that in testing an absolutely fixed M1 growth rule we are examining a straw man. Some advocates of predetermined money growth paths believe that the paths should be allowed to depend somewhat on economic conditions. In that case, however, we need to find some way to represent money growth path-setting procedures.

Given the focus on money growth in public discussions about monetary policy, it seems interesting to investigate the use of the first three stages of the reaction function to set an M1 growth intermediate target. Table 10.8 reports the results of such an experiment. A search was conducted for the growth rate of M1 that caused forecast and interim target output growth emerging from the first three stages of the reaction function to coincide.

The policy rule used in this exercise is probably more compatible with recent historical experience and with public discussion and understanding of policy procedures than any discussed previously. It does not control resource utilization as well as the rule used in the test reported in table 10.4, but both these rules perform much better than observed historical outcomes. From the perspective of desirability, however, it appears to capture the worst features of the policy rules underlying tables 10.4 and 10.7. Control of the unemployment rate is not as good as in the experiment reported in table 10.4, but the funds rate is nearly as volatile. The only

Table 10.8
Hierarchical policy rule with money as an intermediate target using four-quarter forecasts
(current-quarter innovations unknown)[a]

	Range covering all but the lowest and highest 15% of outcomes (percentage points)			
	Quarter			
	4	8	12	16
(1) Unemployment rate	1.0	1.7	1.6 $(1.8)^{b}$	1.9
(2) Fixed weight deflator (4-quarter percent increase)	2.6	3.1	4.6	4.7
(3) Federal funds rate	2.8	4.7	5.1	6.1
(4) Mean absolute 1-quarter funds rate change[c]	1.0	1.5	1.4 $(1.3)^{b}$	1.4
(5) M1 (4-quarter percent increase)	3.4	4.0	5.2	5.4

a. Policy rule:
Ultimate inflation target set at zero, leads to
Interim inflation target for each of next four quarters, leads to
Interim unemployment target for each of next four quarters, leads to
Interim real growth target for each of next four quarters, leads to
Constant M1 growth needed to achieve average of interim real growth targets, leads to
Funds rate instrument setting needed to hit money growth target in first quarter.
b. Confidence intervals were not always smooth due to the small size of the simulation
sample. Figures in parentheses are the author's subjective notion of a more representative
value based on confidence intervals for nearby quarters.
c. Figures represent mean absolute changes, not confidence ranges.

variables controlled better in this exercise than in the table 10.4 experiment
are M1 and nominal GNP (not shown), neither of which is a particularly
interesting variable to control on its own account.

The policymaking procedure investigated in the exercise reported in
table 10.8 is similar in spirit to merely adding another stage to the hierarchical reaction function to create an interim target money growth rate.
Since the results of the experiment were, if anything, less satisfactory than
the results of the preferred procedure that underlie table 10.4, it might be
interesting to move in the opposite direction by dropping the last stage
(the interim real growth target) and instead targeting directly on the
unemployment rate. The results of this experiment are reported in table
10.9. In this exercise the policymaker sets the funds rate at a value the
forecaster tells him would achieve his interim target unemployment rate
four quarters into the future if held fixed.

We should expect this procedure to achieve better control over un-

Table 10.9
Hierarchical rule targeting unemployment using four-quarter forecasts (current-quarter innovations unknown)[a]

	Range covering all but the lowest and highest 15% of outcomes (percentage points)			
	Quarter			
	4	8	12	16
(1) Unemployment rate	.9	1.1	1.1	1.2
(2) Fixed weight deflator (4-quarter percent increase)	2.6	2.8	3.7	3.5
(3) Federal funds rate	7.5	8.6	12.3	15.2
(4) Mean absolute 1-quarter funds rate change[b]	3.0	3.2	3.3	3.2
(5) M1 (4-quarter percent increase)	5.5	9.0	10.7	11.0

a. Policy rule:
Ultimate inflation target set at zero, leads to
Interim unemployment rate target four quarters ahead, leads to
Constant funds rate chosen to achieve interim unemployment target, leads to
Funds rate instrument set at same rate.
b. Figures represent mean absolute changes, they do not represent confidence intervals.

employment than anything investigated thus far, but at some cost in funds rate volatility. That is exactly what we find. At the end of four years the 70% confidence interval on unemployment is only about two-thirds that of the next best policy rule and far better than historical experience. Inflation is also well controlled, although perhaps no better than in the case of rigid monetary control. Both the terminal confidence interval (15 percentage points) and the mean one-quarter change (over 300 basis points) of the funds rate are very high, however. Few observers would accept that degree of interest rate volatility to achieve the extra control over resource utilization.

Conclusion

We set out to create monetary policy reaction functions that would damp out resource utilization effects of a variety of shocks to the model. We were particularly interested in developing a tool that could be used for investigating the long-run effects of events like changes in fiscal policy and other changes that would affect the steady state. In that effort we clearly succeeded. We were able to accomplish our end, not through the application of some abstract mathematical technique, but rather through a policy rule embodying our intuition about the structure and dynamics of the model.

We also set out to build a simulation system capable of analyzing policy rules that incorporated medium-term economic forecasts. Among that class of rules, we wanted to investigate the properties of some that resembled our stabilizing reaction function. We were able to accomplish this as well.

Finally, we undertook to compare the outcomes of a number of hypothetical policy rules both as potential interpretations of actual policy and for desirability against each other. Many implicit and explicit assumptions are needed to carry out this comparison, so caution should be taken before accepting our conclusions. We found

1. that policy rules incorporating medium-term economic forecasts performed considerably better in our experiments than those that did not;

2. that in rules using medium-term forecasts, attempting to hit targets for variables closely related to long-term goals but unresponsive in the short term to policy (like unemployment or inflation), or for variables highly responsive to policy but tenuously connected to long-term goals (like M1), results in less satisfactory outcomes than does targeting a variable like output growth;

3. that policy rules taking into account some knowledge of the causal structure of the system outperformed those that did not;

4. that those rules appearing to us to be closest to the procedures being used by real-world policymakers generally produced the best results.

Appendix A: Monetary Policy Rection Function

Definitions

P = private, domestic, nonfarm, nonenergy, fixed-weight deflator
$PDOT = (P/P_{-4} - 1) * 100$
$PDOT12 = ((P/P_{-12})^{.333} - 1) * 100$
$PDOTULT$ = policymaker's ultimate inflation target
$Q = (PDOT * PDOT12)^{.5}$ if $PDOT > 0$, $PDOT12 > 0$
$Q = 0$ if $PDOT > 0$, $PDOT12 < 0$
$Q = 0$ if $PDOT < 0$, $PDOT12 > 0$
$Q = -(|PDOT| * |PDOT12|)^{.5}$ if $PDOT < 0$, $PDOT12 < 0$
$PDOTINT$ = policymaker's interim inflation target
$UNAT$ = natural unemployment rate

U = civilian unemployment rate
$UINT$ = policymaker's interim target unemployment rate
$XDOT$ = growth rate of private, nonfarm business output
$XDOTNAT$ = natural growth rate of private, nonfarm business output
$XDOTINT$ = policymaker's interim real growth rate target

Stage 1: Calculation of Interim Inflation Target

$$PDOTINT = .5(Q - PDOTULT) + PDOTULT$$

Stage 2: Calculation of Interim Unemployment Rate Target

$$UINT = UNAT + 2.0\tanh(.5(PDOT - PDOTINT))$$
$$+ \beta_4 \tanh(1.0\Delta(PDOT - PDOTINT))$$

$\beta_4 = 1.0$ in historical simulations and in policy rule simulations involving one-quarter forecasts

$\beta_4 = 0$ in policy rule simulations involving four-quarter forecasts

Stage 3: Calculation of Interim Real Output Growth Target

$$XDOTINT = XDOTNAT + 3.0\tanh(.4(U - UINT))$$
$$+ \beta_{10} \tanh(1.0\,\Delta(U - UINT))$$

$\beta_{10} = 3.0$ in historical simulations and in policy rule simulations involving one-quarter forecasts

$\beta_{10} = 0$ in policy rule simulations involving four-quarter forecasts

Stage 4: Calculation of Funds Rate Setting

$$QQ = .05(XDOT - XDOTINT) + .95QQ_{-1}$$
$$RFF = RFF_{-1} + 1.43\,\Delta PDOT + 1.0[\tanh(.1(XDOT - XDOTINT))$$
$$+ 5.0\,\Delta\tanh(.2(XDOT_{-1} - XDOTINT_{-1})) + 1.0\tanh(1.0(QQ))]$$

Stage 4 calculations are not used in policy rule simulations involving four-quarter forecasts.

Notes

1. The term "natural unemployment rate" in this paper refers to what is often labeled the nonaccelerating inflation rate of unemployment (NAIRU). The term "natural rate of output growth" refers simply to the rate of growth that holds the unemployment rate constant.

2. The idea for specifying the policy rule in hierarchical form was given to us by

Peter Tinsley. This section also reflects discussions with Albert Ando and some earlier work of Lewis Johnson.

3. Tinsley and von zur Muehlen's work in this area predates ours. See P. A. Tinsley and P. von zur Muehlen, "Conditional Intermediate Targeting," unpublished manuscript, October 1983, and "The Reliability of Alternative Intermediate Targets," unpublished manuscript, November 1983.

4. Other, less powerful channels do exist in the model. For example, the international value of the dollar responds to a gap between domestic and foreign interest rates. The exchange rate, in turn, influences export and import prices and the domestic markup of product prices over unit labor costs.

5. The calculations involved in computing $UNAT'$ for the MPS model are quite tedious and the details are not presented in this paper. As equation (6) suggests, the natural rate is largely a function of productivity growth in this model. It is defined in such a way that it is invariant to purely cyclical factors, but moves in response to forces that would alter the steady-state growth path of the economy. Thus a change in energy prices, for example, would temporarily change the computed natural rate through its effect on productivity growth. The time path of the natural rate is not completely independent of economic policy, which might, for example, alter the long-run equilibrium capital stock and hence the *level* of productivity.

6. The actual simulation equation represented here by equation (11) adjusts the simulated change in the inflation rate by subtracting an estimate of the portion of the change caused by changes in real exchange rates and agricultural prices.

7. As in the case of the natural unemployment rate, the details of this calculation are rather tedious and are not presented. Once again, purely cyclical factors are excluded from the calculation, but longer-run factors affecting productivity growth are taken into account. The natural output growth rate defined in this way can be altered for substantial time periods by fiscal and monetary policies.

8. Current dollar exogenous variables were first adjusted by the ratio of the previous quarter's simulated to historical price level, which effectively converts all current dollar exogenous variables to real variables. Exogenous interest rates (primarily deposit rate ceilings) are similarly indexed to simulated values of the corporate bond rate.

Comments on "Toward Realistic Policy Design: Policy Reaction Functions That Rely on Economic Forecasts"

Benjamin Friedman

Yet another of Franco Modigliani's outstanding achievements in economics has been his role in advancing the state of macroeconometric modeling, at both the empirical and theoretical levels, including especially the representation of the financial markets and the monetary mechanism.

Prior to the appearance of the MPS model, the most detailed representation of the financial system in any macroeconometric model of the United States was that contained in the 1964 version of the Wharton model. The financial sector of that model contained six equations. Three represented the nonbank public's demands for currency, demand deposits, and time deposits. The central interest-rate-setting equation determined a representative short-term interest rate as a function of (among other items) the free reserve position of the banking system and the discount rate—both taken to be exogenous. A single term-structure equation then determined a representative long-term interest rate as a simple distributed lag on this short-term rate. Finally, one further equation represented banks' supply behavior in the time-deposit market as the determination of the interest rate paid on time deposits.

The first published version of the MPS model (then called the "FRB-MIT" model), in 1968, contained a financial block consisting of twelve equations. Like the Wharton model, this new model included equations for the nonbank public's demands for currency, demand deposits, and time deposits, as well as an equation (again normalized on the interest rate paid on time deposits) representing banks' supply behavior in the time deposit market. Again like the Wharton model, the initial MPS model also included an equation relating the interest rate on corporate bonds to a distributed lag on a representative short-term interest rate. In addition, this version of the MPS model included four more term-structure equations, determining in a similar fashion the commercial paper rate, the commercial bank loan rate, the home mortgage rate, and the dividend-price yield on equities, as well as an equation determining the nonbank public's supply of one liability (commercial loans).

Beyond this additional detail, however, the fundamental advance embodied in the MPS model was a structural representation of the determination of the model's basic short-term interest rate. In contrast to the Wharton model, there was no equation normalized on the key short-term interest rate. Instead, the two remaining equations in the financial sector of the MPS model represented banks' demand for nonborrowed reserves. One of these equations determined banks' free reserves. The demand for nonborrowed reserves then followed from combining banks' free reserves with an application of the relevant reserve requirement ratios to banks' outstanding demand deposits and time deposits. Hence the model was capable of determining the short-term interest rate, endogenously, not as a simple function of free reserves and the discount rate but instead as an explicit outcome of the clearing of the money and reserves markets.

This fundamental conceptual framework for the representation of the initial stages of the monetary mechanism, which Franco Modigliani had earlier on developed in joint work with Robert Rasche and Phillip Cooper, among others, has remained standard in the literature of the subject through the subsequent two decades.[1]

The interesting paper by Robert Anderson and Jared Enzler applies the modern descendant of this model with two apparent objectives. The objective stated at the outset is to correct the explosive cyclical character that the MPS model exhibits when it is subjected to perturbations, so as more readily to permit either a steady-state analysis or, for that matter, any analysis extending over a simulation horizon longer than just a few quarters. Anderson and Enzler's analysis of the source of this instability is both interesting and credible. In short, they argue that the model's sluggish (and apparently realistic) wage-price dynamics lead to an overshooting of the price level, which is turn creates a continuing cyclical dynamic. This explanation is credible insofar as it describes the initial emergence of cyclical behavior, but it is still far from clear why such cycles should not be highly damped. One objective of the work put forth in this paper is to add additional features of the model, in the form of policy rules, so as to produce an overall model in which such cycles are in fact damped.

The second objective, which dominates the latter half of the paper, is normative: to provide a set of policy rules that, if implemented, would deliver an improved cyclical performance for the US economy. This second objective is more in line with the traditional literature of either model simulations or optimal control exercises aimed at determining an alternative conduct of monetary and/or fiscal policy that, historically, would have improved macroeconomic performance as measured by standard norms.

Although both of these objectives are worth while in the context of the application of the MPS model, they are hardly congruent, and a persistent tension between the two runs throughout the paper.

The basic methodological approach followed by Anderson and Enzler is to eschew any formal optimizing analysis in favor of the derivation of informal, intuitively based rules. Anderson and Enzler state four rationales for choosing this approach: (1) It saves computation. (2) Simpler rules are more likely to be appealing to policymakers. (3) They wanted to exploit their intuition about how the model works. (4) They wanted to avoid the criticism, frequently leveled against optimal control rules, that such rules are model-specific.

All four of these rationales are laudable, but in the end it is not clear to what extent the results presented in the paper bear them out. At the most obvious level, Anderson and Enzler present no argument to the effect that the policy rules they set forth in this paper are any less model-specific than are optimal control rules derived in the standard way. In addition, in the end the value-added provided by their intuition about how the model works is not made clear either.

The construction of the Anderson-Enzler *monetary* rule combines a series of elements: a preference for gradualism in changing the inflation rate; a model embodying a time-varying natural rate of unemployment, with learning about the value of that natural rate at any time; a trade-off of unwanted inflation versus temporary discrepancies between actual unemployment and the natural rate; an Okun's law translation from unemployment to real economic growth, explicitly allowing for population growth, technological progress, and "other factors" (presumably including such important items as changes in labor force participation rates, which have crucially affected such matters in recent years); and a highly compressed IS-type relation between real growth and the real after-tax federal funds rate. All this seems highly sensible, given the initial choice of the underlying intuitive methodology.

By contrast, the Anderson-Enzler *fiscal* rule is highly unusual. For this purpose, Anderson and Enzler choose the stabilization of the ratio of the outstanding federal government debt to gross national product. As they are quick to admit, there is no evidence that the US fiscal authorities have ever implemented such a rule. During the post-World War II period, the ratio of federal government debt to GNP first declined from 1946 until the mid-1970s, then leveled off for the remainder of the 1970s, and, most recently, under the Reagan Administration has risen as rapidly as it declined heretofore. Until 1980, the entire history of the United States in this regard was largely a story of war versus peace. During wartime the federal government ran up its debt in relation to GNP, and then it used the interval until the next war to bring its debt ratio back down again.

Such a departure from what the fiscal authorities have historically done raises an important question about the objective of the analysis in the paper. Since the fiscal rule proposed differs so sharply from the observed conduct of US fiscal policy, it is not clear what interpretation is to be placed on simulations of the model done with the fiscal rule imposed. In this case, the normative objective of devising a rule to recommend to policymakers apparently prevailed over the positive objective of devising a rule that would provide stability to the model to facilitate its wider use. Of course, Anderson and Enzler could have argued that they were simply matching this counterfactual element with some other counterfactual element already in the model, so that the two would offset one another and deliver non-explosive cyclical behavior for the model as a whole, but in the paper they do not make such a case.

As a strictly normative matter, stabilization of the government debt to GNP ratio is a sensible idea.[2] Nevertheless, Anderson and Enzler have nothing to say about the choice of fixed point about which the ratio is to be stabilized. Their simulations demonstrate just how important that choice is, however. In one simulation described in the paper, the government debt to GNP ratio is stabilized around .2, while in the other it is stabilized around .5. As of the mid-to-late 1970s, it appeared as if the government debt to GNP ratio might well be headed toward .2. By contrast, under the Reagan fiscal policy the ratio is now headed toward .5 just by the end of this decade, and presumably beyond .5 thereafter. Anderson and Enzler's simulations clearly show that stabilizing the government debt ratio about .2 is a very different matter from stabilizing it around .5.

In the end, the construction of the policy rules that Anderson and Enzler intuitively derive leads to a combination of integral, proportional, and derivative stabilization devices along the lines suggested by A. W. Phillips more than three decades ago.[3] Given the inherent logic underlying Phillips's original proposal, and given the intuitive nature of Anderson and Enzler's policy rules, this result is hardly surprising. What is surprising is Anderson and Enzler's report that the simulation results are "... quite robust to the choice of parameter values, at least within a fairly broad range."

Given Phillips's well-known proposal for policy rules combining these three standard elements, the reader is therefore left wondering what has been the value-added from Anderson and Enzler's painstaking construction of the policy rules through a step-by-step process reflecting their intuition about how the model works. Since the rules that they eventually use are simply a combination of Phillips's three forms, the initial presumption would be that the use of intuition about the inner workings of the model would at the least have informed the selection of parameter values. Nevertheless, Anderson and Enzler report that the results are not very sensitive to the selection of parameter values anyway. In the end, therefore, it is not clear that the application of this intuition has led to particularly better functioning policy rules than would have been derivable by simply beginning with a Phillips-type rule—for example, relating the federal funds rate (Anderson and Enzler's chosen policy instrument for monetary policy) to integral, proportional, and derivative terms in the inflation rate and real economic growth—and assigning arbitrary parameter values after some limited experimentation.

Finally, the simulation results reported in this paper serve to call attention yet again to a glaring shortcoming in the policy analyses carried out by monetary economists through more than two decades of work with such models. Anderson and Enzler report—as almost every previous analysis of this kind also has reported, whether based on intuitively derived policy rules or on explicitly derived optimal control rules—that the implementation of such rules would improve macroeconomic performance but, in doing so, would lead to substantially greater interest rate volatility than policymakers would presumably accept.

The repeated finding that policy rules designed to improve macroeconomic performance would require higher levels of interest rate volatility makes essential an analysis of whether policymakers' aversion to such interest rate volatility is warranted. To the extent that there are genuine costs associated with interest rate volatility, then, given the apparent importance of such costs in policymakers' decisions, macroeconomic model builders and users ought to incorporate these costs explicitly in their analysis. By contrast, if there are no such costs, or if the evidence suggests that the costs are modest in comparison with the macroeconomic implications of the deviation of actual policy from superior policy rules, then macroeconomists should call upon policymakers to justify their preference for smoother interest rates over superior macroeconomic performance.

Notes

1. See Franco Modigliani, Robert Rasche, and J. Phillip Cooper, "Central Bank Policy, the Money Supply, and the Short-Term Rate of Interest," *Journal of Money, Credit and Banking* 2 (May 1970), 166–218.

2. See Benjamin M. Friedman, "A Credit Market Perspective, 1982 to 1987," and James Tobin, "Budget Deficits, Federal Debt, and Inflation," both in Albert T. Sommers (ed.), *Reconstructing the Federal Budget* (New York: Praeger, 1984).

3. The basic references are A. W. Phillips, "Stabilization Policy in a Closed Economy," *Economic Journal* 64 (June 1954), 290–323, and "Stabilization Policy and the Time Forms of Lagged Responses," *Economic Journal* 67 (June 1957), 265–277.

11

Lessons from the German Inflation Experience of the 1920s

Rudiger Dornbusch

Hyperinflations are the laboratory experiments of monetary economics. In the presence of these rates of inflation and depreciation all other considerations that might normally obscure linkages between money and prices emerge strongly and obviously, beyond discussion or controversy. Stabilization of inflation proceeds if and only when the source of inflation, money creation, is brought under control. This is the traditional view endorsed by Keynes (1923) and particularly developed by Cagan (1956) in his classic essay on the German hyperinflation.

The central emphasis on money creation as the exogenous variable in the inflation process has not gone unchallenged. Already during the hyperinflation experience there was a controversy between the "Quantity Theory School," which took this view, and the "Balance of Payments School," which held the view that balance of payments difficulties, associated with reparations payments, gave rise to exchange depreciation, which in turn led to inflation and monetization. Not suprisingly the government strongly endorsed this view. The special role of money in the hyperinflation process, and particularly in the stabilization phase, has also been reconsidered in a best-selling essay by Sargent (1982). In Sargent's work primary emphasis is placed on budget stabilization rather than on money growth per se. Indeed, he draws attention, as Keynes and other authors had before, to the very large rates of monetary growth following the actual stabilization.

Sargent's message is that *credible* fiscal stabilization is the sine qua non for stopping inflation. This is definitely not viewed as being in conflict with the monetary hypothesis, but it does represent a shift of emphasis. Here is how Sargent (1982, p. 89) puts his findings:

The essential measures that ended hyperinflations in each of Germany, Austria, Hungary, and Poland were, first, the creation of an independent central bank that

---

I am indebted to Olivier Blanchard, Vittorio Corbo, and Stanley Fischer for helpful comments.

was legally committed to refuse the government's demand for additional unsecured credit and, second, a simultaneous alteration in the fiscal policy regime.... We have further seen that it was not simply the increasing quantity of central bank notes that caused the hyperinflation, since in each case the note circulation continued to grow rapidly after the exchange rate and price level had been stabilized. Rather it was the growth of fiat currency which was unbacked, or backed only by government bills, which there never was a prospect to retire through taxation.

The two views are not strictly identical. We can imagine that a deficit persists for some time but does not give rise to money creation because it is entirely financed by external loans. This was, for example, the case in the Austrian stabilization (see Dornbusch and Fischer, 1986). An alternative possibility is the persistence of a deficit, for some time, financed by domestic borrowing. Finally it is possible that the deficit is eliminated altogether but that money creation associated with private credit creation persists vigorously. It is therefore useful to separate the point of emphasis of the two hypotheses even though they may overlap in practice.

In this essay we draw attention to three further aspects of the stabilization of the hyperinflation, namely, the exchange rate and wages, interest rates, and the increase in the real yield of taxation deriving from the mere fact of price stability.

The central weakness of the Sargent position is to present "credibility" as some objective, unquestionable fact—as if passing a budget law or instituting an independent central bank is by itself enough to assure that these institutions will in fact become what they represent on paper. Even though a government may intend or even initiate all the right measures in terms of budget stabilization and brakes on money creation, there remains still the problem of making these measures work once the costs of implementation become apparent (and hence actually being able to sustain them). This is of course the central issue in the transition to accomplishing a successful stabilization. Since policies are not in fact exogeneous, in that the government creates an act on which it cannot, under any and all conditions, go back, the issue of credibility is paramount. In fact the scene is littered with failed stabilization policies, many of which faltered not from inception but on the way.

We argue that exchange rate and interest rate policy in the transition have traditionally formed the vehicle for establishing that credibility by a de facto stabilization. De facto stabilization in turn pays an immediate dividend via the recovery of the real tax yield, thereby creating the potential for a virtuous cycle. The improving budget situation in turn may attract capital flows that reinforce the stabilization. We develop these arguments by discussing the detailed events of the German hyperinflation.

In the German case at least the stabilization was a much more diffuse, accidental matter than a reading of the classics reveals. Exchange rate policy definitely played a key role. Well beyond the early stages of stabilization immensely high interest rates in the face of a sharply appreciating free market exchange rate wiped out adverse speculation, thus helping to establish stabilization until fundamentals—fiscal stabilization and foreign loans—could be brought into place.

The discussion also draws attention to the behavior of the real exchange rate and real wages during stabilization. The real exchange rate sharply appreciated in the final stage and persisted at an appreciated level well into the poststabilization phase. This may well have facilitated the political economy of the stabilization because of the implicit rise in real wages. It reflects the reverse of the coin of real depreciation in the capital flight phase.

1 Some Theoretical Considerations

The conventional or monetary model of hyperinflation centers on the money market. Rational expectations are assumed, and the rate of money creation is determined by the requirement of budget financing.

The budget deficit is a given fraction λ of real output. Deficit finance then implies that the real value of money creation equals the deficit:

$$\dot{M}/P = \mu m = \lambda y, \tag{1}$$

where

μ = the growth rate of money,
λ = the deficit as a share of output,
y = real output,
$m = M/P$ = real balances.

Assume now a linear velocity equation with π denoting the rate of inflation:

$$y/m = \alpha + \beta\pi. \tag{2}$$

Substituting (2) into (1), and assuming that in steady state equilibrium money growth equals inflation, $\mu = \pi$, yield

$$\pi = \lambda\alpha/(1 - \beta\lambda). \tag{3}$$

The equilibrium rate of inflation thus depends positively and in a very nonlinear fashion on the budget deficit as a fraction of output, λ. It also depends on the parameters of the velocity equation. In particular, an exogeneous flight from money (a reduction in α) raises the equilibrium inflation rate.

This model leaves out several important features of a hyperinflation process. Two of these relate to the budget. The first is a point emphasized in particular by Bruno and Fischer (1985), namely, that for many functional forms of money demand there is a Laffer curve of inflation tax revenue. Accordingly there will be more than one inflation rate that can finance a given budget deficit. This raises the question of inflation dynamics. Which equilibrium will the economy move to. How is this path influenced by expectations and policies? What happens, as is possible, if the required inflation tax revenue exceeds the maximum rate that can be raised given the demand for money?

The second point concerns the link between the budget, inflation, and real exchange rates. The inflation rate will affect the budget deficit because it affects the real revenue of tax collection that can be realized from a given tax structure given the inevitable lags in tax collection. These lags can be shortened or their effect can be dampened by indexation. But there remains, in hyperinflations, an inevitable erosion of real tax revenue that is more substantial the higher the rate of inflation. It is worth separating here short-run and long-run effects: In the short run an acceleration of inflation, given lags, will inevitably reduce the real value of tax collection, and thus it widens the deficit, raises money creation, and thereby increases inflation. Over time the government may offset at least in part the erosion by shortening delays for tax collection. The dynamic influences then involve a race between the acceleration of inflation with its tax erosion effects and the acceleration of tax collection, or increased indexation, which exerts stabilizing effects.

But the deficit will also be affected by the real exchange rate. This is particularly the case if service of an external debt or reparation payments denominated in foreign exchange appear as a significant government outlay. With these two points in mind the budget deficit in (1) now becomes

$$\mu m = \lambda(\pi, \sigma)y, \tag{1a}$$

where σ denotes the real exchange rate.

The introduction of the real exchange rate in (1a) raises the question of exchange rate determination in a hyperinflation economy. The tradition has been to emphasize PPP because a hyperinflation was viewed as the ultimate, pure case of a monetary experiment. But it is quite apparent from the facts that real exchange rates varied widely, certainly in the short run.

But if PPP is not a satisfactory model of exchange rate-price relationships, then a more complete model of portfolio choice and real exchange rates needs to supplement the monetary model above.

A related point concerns financial markets. The monetary model cuts this topic short by viewing the inflation process from a money-goods margin of substitution. But clearly financial markets did exist, and part of the reason for inflation, along with deficit finance, was the creation of credit for the private sector. Money creation therefore depends not only on the budget but also on the policy defining discounting of private paper. The behavior of real interest rates therefore appears to be an important feature of hyperinflation processes.

The final point concerns dynamics of wages, prices, and the exchange rate. Escalation of inflation, from moderate rates to a hyperinflation—defined by Cagan (1956) as an inflation rate in excess of 50% per month—involves systematic shifts in the timing relationships. We can imagine an economy where initially wages are adjusted in a backward-looking fashion at infrequent intervals, say every 6 months. Prices are adjusted more frequently and exchange rates perhaps weekly. As the inflation rate increases these lags shorten until ultimately all pricing takes place on the basis of the exchange rate. The shift to hyperinflation may be associated with the move from backward-looking wage adjustment to exchange-rate-based wages. The analysis is further complicated by the role of expectations, specifically expectations regarding such fundamentals as the budget, which is at best only partially exogeneous.

To formulate a realistic model of hyperinflation, taking account of the issues raised here, is clearly beyond the scope of this paper. The purpose here is too look at the details of the German hyperinflation to point out that each of these complications was in fact an important part of the story, so that a simple budget-money-credibility story is not enough, even if in the final analysis stabilization cannot take place without them. They are necessary, but it is not apparent that they are also sufficient conditions.

2   Initial Conditions

In the immediate aftermath of World War I, Central Europe resembled Latin America of the past twenty years: political turmoil mixed with economic inequality, precarious democracy, and financial instability. Although the German hyperinflation stands out, problems of high inflation or even hyperinflation prevailed in many countries, including Russia, Austria, Poland, and Czechoslovakia. In fact, it is doubtful that there was any country at all

Table 11.1
Comparative price levels and exchange rates (indices 1914 = 1, annual average)[a]

	United States	United Kingdom		France		Germany	
	P	P	e	P	e	P	e
1914	1	1	1	1	1	1	1
1919	2.6	2.5	1.1	3.4	1.4	3.9	7.8
1920	2.6	3.1	1.4	4.9	2.8	14.1	13.5
1921	1.4	2.0	1.4	3.4	2.6	18.1	10.2
1922	1.3	1.6	1.3	3.1	2.4	323.3	101.8

a. P denotes the Wholesale Price Index, e the index of the local currency price of the US dollar.

that escaped altogether a significant increase in prices during World War I. Even in Switzerland the price level doubled during the war. The main difference is how various countries coped with the subsequent stabilization effort.

It is interesting to start our analysis well before the hyperinflation got underway and compare Germany with other major countries. Table 11.1 offers a comparison focusing on the price level and the dollar exchange rate. The benchmark is the United States and the comparison countries are France and the United Kingdom.

The central point emerging from table 11.1 is the large wartime price increases everywhere, including the United States. In the war years prices more than doubled in the United States and in the United Kingdom. In Germany and France the increases were much larger, more than 200%, and nearly 300%. But in this respect Germany was not much different from France.

The large change occurs between 1920 and 1922: The United States and the United Kingdom experience a sharp deflation as price *decline* nearly 50%, in France prices fall less than 40%, and in Germany they increase by a factor of 23, or 2200%. The United Kingdom returned to gold at the prewar par in 1925. France stabilized in 1926–1928 with a large depreciation and a much higher level of prices, 7 times the 1914 level. Germany by contrast suffered a hyperinflation before prices were stabilized in a new currency. Clearly one decisive point is 1921, when other countries moved to *de*flation while Germany went into inflation.

Germany emerged from World War I with significant losses of territory and with a burden of reparations to be determined by an Allied Commission. The immediate postwar years were overshadowed by expectations of the reparation payments and by domestic political turmoil. There were

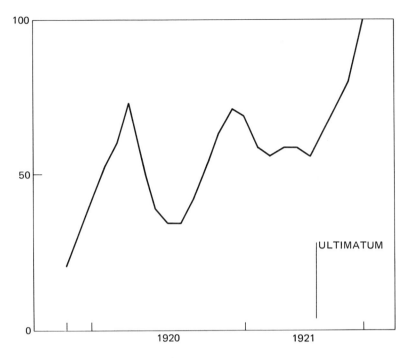

Figure 11.1
The nominal exchange rate (Reichsmarks/dollars).

revolutions and revolts ranging from Soviet Republics in various states, including Bavaria, to right-wing activity of the demilitarized professional army. It was said that $100 could buy you a minor revolution. Uncertainty about the political and economic future is reflected in the erratic behavior of the exchange rate (marks/US dollars) shown in figure 11.1.

In the brief period from October 1919 (the Treaty of Versailles had been concluded in June 1919) to March 1920 the price of the dollar tripled. The depreciations was a reflection of the uncertainty in Germany, but it fed back to prices and fueled the turmoil. The sharp collapse in the spring of 1920 was one of the few points of potential return. Several factors helped create a moment of stability. The Erzberger fiscal measures strengthened the budget, the right-wing Kapp Putsch had been suppressed, and many other countries perhaps did not look that much better. But these improvements did not last, in part because of a sharp deterioration in the external balance.

A definite deterioration in the inflation outlook occurred in late spring of 1921 and relates to reparations. The terms fixed by the Reparations Commission required Germany to pay 2 milliard (2 billion in US terminology) gold marks a year, plus 26% of German exports in addition to occupation expenses. The London Ultimatum of May 1921 required a front end payment of 1 milliard gold marks by August 1921 in foreign exchange, and a second slice of 500 million gold marks by November 15 of that year. The 1.5 milliard payment amounted to about half of total tax revenue. Using 1925 data, a payment of 2 milliard gold marks plus 26% of exports would amount to about 6% of GNP. The payment of reparations was associated with the massive exchange depreciation in the second half of 1921.

Further complications of the political climate arose when the League of Nations imposed the separation of Upper Silesia from Germany. Germany's foreign policy in respect to reparations and other peace terms was a "policy of fulfillment." At least as a matter of policy, if not in the full delivery, Germany sought to implement the terms of the London Ultimatum. While the 1921 payments were in fact met in early 1922, Germany protested its inability to fulfill these stiff terms and in June 1922 suspended all payments.

A commission of experts, including Keynes and Cassel, was invited to consider stabilization. The experts reported at the end of November 1922 to the German government, arguing three points (an excerpt from the report of the experts is reproduced at the end of the paper): They were satisfied that the budget was balanced under conditions of reasonable price stability and excepting reparations and that stabilization could not proceed if reparations were to be continued. But they also made this observation (*Gutachten*, 1922, p. 14): "We conclude that, in the conditions we postulate [suspension of reparations] an immediate stabilisation is possible by Germany's own efforts. . . . At the rate of 3500 marks to the dollar the gold in the Reichsbank now amounts to about twice the value of the note issue. This is an unprecedented situation. No other currency has fallen into decay with so great a potential support still unused."

But for the moment the possibility of stabilization disappeared as French and Belgian troops, in response to the suspension of reparations payments, occupied the Ruhr area. The occupation was met by German "passive resistance," the financial costs of which completely outstripped any chance of price stability.

3   The Hyperinflation

The prelude to the hyperinflation was the first part of 1923, when, in the face of the Ruhr occupation, the government attempted to stabilize the exchange rate. Figure 11.2 shows the official dollar exchange rate. Follow-

Reichsmarks/US Dollars (X 1,000)

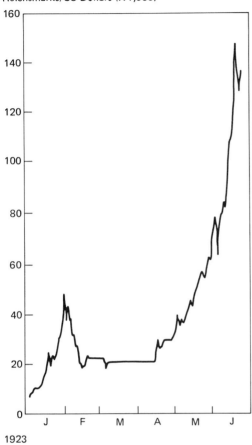

1923

Figure 11.2
The exchange rate.

Table 11.2
The German hyperinflation in 1923 (percentage change from previous month)[a]

	Wholesale prices	Exchange rate
February	55	101
March	−13	−24
April	15	7
May	57	95
June	137	131
July	286	221
August	1,162	1,307
September	2,432	2,035
October	29,586	25,957
November	10,133	8,462

Source: *Wirtschaft und Statistik.*
a. Stabilization occurred on November 15, 1923.

ing the collapse in January, at the time of the occupation, the rate recovered and was stabilized between mid-February and mid-April. Inflation that had run at 28% and 89% per month in December and January rose to 111% in February and in March. After the stabilization of the exchange rate, there is actual deflation of 17% and only 7% inflation in April. As soon as the exchange rate support was abandoned, because of huge reserve losses, the hyperinflation got underway.

Table 11.2 shows the dollar exchange rate (paper marks per dollar or gold mark) as well as the monthly rates of depreciation and of inflation for the critical period in 1923. During the Ruhr occupation in January and February 1923, prices had doubled each month, as did the dollar rate. But from the middle of February to the middle of April there was a brief reprieve, with falling prices and currency appreciation. The episode is explained by significant Reichsbank intervention in the exchange market.

By May inflation and depreciation accelerate, and for the rest of the year the German economy disintegrates as inflation rates reach at their peak 30,000% per month, or just above 20% *per day.* At 20% inflation per day the price level doubles in less than four days!

The stories of life in the most dramatic stages of hyperinflation are well known. Keynes reports how people would order two beers at a time because the beer would grow warm and stale more slowly than the price was rising. Taxis were preferred to streetcars because one paid at the end of the trip. Other accounts include stories on how firms made payments of workers by furniture van. Schacht (1927) reports that the demand for notes was so immense that 133 printing firms produced notes for the government on more than 1783 machines with 30 factories working full time to supply the paper.

In July the inflation rate was still 3.5% per day. In August it rose to 6.5% per day, in September to 11.2%, and finally to an average of 20.9% in November. In the final stages of the inflation, prices and exchange rates became closely tied because even weekly reports on the cost of living or wholesale prices were far out of line with current developments. Quotations of the exchange rate and thus of the gold mark became the central pillar for calculating prices. The government had throughout resisted a dollarization of the economy, but in the middle of the year could no longer prevent much of pricing from shifting to gold or the dollar, even though German money continued to be used as required by law. The shift to the gold mark or foreign-exchange-based pricing led in July–August to a big upsurge in inflation via the once-and-for-all elimination of lags. Perhaps it is this shift to foreign-exchange-based pricing that is the ultimate element in the shift toward hyperinflation. Clearly, in September–November prices were changed more than once a day, and ultimately all inertia disappeared in a process that Pazos (1978, p. 93) has described as follows: "The reduction of intervals [for setting wages and prices] to their shortest possible duration and the pegging of wage adjustments—both upward and downward—to the freely fluctuating quotation of foreign currency give hyperinflation a mechanism different from that of intermediate inflation. The day to day adjustments of all contracts puts an end to all connections between the value of transactions in successive periods. . . ."

4 The Stabilization

Elements of the stabilization occurred even before the extreme explosion got underway. As early as August 1923 the government had issued a loan of 500 million gold marks, in part in small denominations. These bonds had started circulating and had come to be accepted as hard currency even though they carried no backing other than the government's promise to redeem in gold. Where the political improvement offered the prospect of budget improvement the acceptance of the gold mark bonds (for which convertibility in gold was certainly not assured) had paved the way for a new monetary instruments. In fact the gold mark loan bonds served as backing for gold mark liabilities issued by municipalities and other government bodies.

But the deciding event was clearly political stabilization. On the political front the Streseman government, formed in August 1923, put an end to passive resistance in October. On the threat of resolution of parliament, an "empowering law" was enacted that allowed the government to pass regulations and laws, even suspending the constitution wherever the national economic interest so required.

Plans for stabilization focused on two alternatives: a Gold Bank or a Roggenbank (Rye Bank). In the end the idea of a Roggenbank won out, although in a somewhat different form, as the Rentenbank (Mortgage Bank). The key institutional elements of the stabilization were three:

• Legislation in mid-October introduced the Rentenbank as a semi-public body with capital represented by fictious claims on industry and land. The assets of the bank were to be claims on the government and credit to the private sector. The total loans were not to exceed 2,400 million Rentenmarks or gold marks, half to the government, half to private borrowers. Of the government part 300 million were to be set aside to retire the government floating debt held by the Reichsbank.

• The liabilities of the Rentenbank were the Rentenmark. They had a convertibility feature that linked them to the successful gold mark loan: upon request 500 Rentenmarks could be converted into a bond having a nominal value of 500 gold marks, thus establishing the 1 : 1 link between the Rentenmark and the circulating gold mark loan certificates. Because these certificates were accepted as hard currency, the convertibility linkage of the Rentenmark could readily take advantage. But the Paper Mark remained legal tender, and the Rentenmark had the only claim that it had to be accepted by government agencies in payment.

• The same legislation instituted the rule that the Reichsbank would no longer be entitled to discount government bills. Reichsbank note issue had to be backed at least one-third by gold and the remainder by commercial paper. But the Reichsbank remained entitled, subject to the gold backing requirement, to discount commercial paper.

On November 15 the Rentenbank came into operation and issue of the Rentenmark started. Prior to the actual issue the government had already placed at the end of October a small denomination gold mark loan. The loan was issued to cope with the *cash crisis*, namely, the fact that the real money supply had declined to levels so low that the payments mechanism had substantially collapsed. Queues at the commercial banks and the Reichsbank trying to obtain paper money grew longer, and more and more of the demand for paper money went unsatisfied. Depreciation and inflation wiped out the real value of money much faster than the government, municipal

Table 11.3
The aftermath of the stabilization (index December 1923 = 100)

	Money stock	Wholesale prices
1923		
November 15	20	22[a]
November 20	41[b]	118
November 30	70	119
December (end)	100	100
1924		
June	138	92
December	188	104

Source: *Wirtschaft und Statistik*, various issues.
a. November 13.
b. November 23.

authorities, and practically anyone could create paper money (see Yeager, 1966, p. 271).

Within a month price and exchange rate stability had been restored. Extra taxation and even more so the sharply increased real value of tax collection in January 1924 and beyond eliminated fiscal difficulties as a source of inflationary deficit finance. But there remained a different threat, namely, Reichsbank commercial lending. During December 1923 and in early 1924 credit expanded so rapidly that a risk of renewed inflation and depreciation in March 1924 had to be checked by a credit crunch.

One of the striking features of the stabilization that is often emphasized is the comparative stability of prices and exchange rates. Monetarists are fond of quoting a well-known remark of Havenstein, the President of Reichsbank, to the effect that the arrival of new, high-speed printing presses would cope with the cash crisis. The remark is construed as reflecting complete ignorance of the source of inflation and the inflation-induced adjustment in velocity. But it may well reflect a more sophisticated model of inflation in which in fact, real balances were inadequate rather than burning holes in pockets. This is brought out in table 11.3. Between the date of stabilization, November 15, and the end of the year, Reichsbank credit increased fourfold. Over the same period the quantity of Reichsbank notes outstanding nearly doubled.

Another important feature of the stabilization that needs comment is the behavior of unemployment and of real wages. Figure 11.3 shows that the German real wage increased strongly in the stabilization. The real wage gain (relative to 1922–1923, not 1913) persisted. The increase in unem-

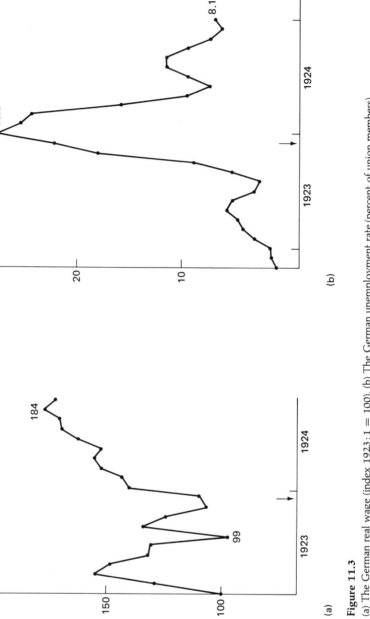

Figure 11.3

(a) The German real wage (index 1923:1 = 100). (b) The German unemployment rate (percent of union members).

ployment was dramatic, but did come down from the record levels of December 1923. Of course, tight money and the overvalued exchange rate set the stage for the "Stabilisierungskrise"—the decline in activity that follows successful stabilization.

5 Why Did Stabilization Succeed?

There is no single obvious explanation for the successful stabilization of the German currency. The standard explanations are five, involving in each case a combination of a gain in confidence based on one or more of the following fundamental factors:

• monetary stabilization via the discounting restraints imposed on the Reichbank and the Rentenbank,

• fiscal stabilization,

• exchange rate stabilization,

• political stabilization through the end of passive resistance and the appointment of an expert group of the Reparations Commission, and

• the reduction in the real money supply prior to stabilization.

The question of how stabilization was achieved is not exactly the same as that of why hyperinflation occurred in the first place. But the latter question provides a good starting point. There are broadly two schools of thought: One emphasizes the budget and money creation as *active* sources of the hyperinflation. Adherents of this theory would make exchange rate adjustments passively respond to the domestic inflation developments along Purchasing Power Parity (PPP) lines. The alternative theory is the balance-of-payments approach. This theory claims that adverse balance-of-payments developments force exchange depreciation, which then deteriorates inflation and, with that, budgetary performance. In a setting of passive money, exchange rate disturbances then *cause* inflation. Political disturbances fit in either setting as the proximate sources of disruption. For the monetary-fiscal approach they initiate deficit finance. For the balance-of-payments approach reparation payments are the source of extraordinary foreign exchange demands, which force depreciation of the currency, which then spreads to domestic inflation and a widening of the budget deficit.

For either of these schools the consolidation of the political events via an end of passive resistance and the improved prospect of stabilization loans was thus an important ingredient. But beyond that there are differences on what is *the* essential element in gaining stability.

Table 11.4
The budget (millions of gold marks fiscal year April–March)

	1922	1923	1924	1925
Expenditure	3,951	8,979	7,220	7,444
Receipts	1,508	2,620	7.757	7,334
Budget deficit	2,442	6,359	−537	110

Source: *Wirtschaft und Statistik*, various issues.

Sargent (1982, p. 83) attributes the stabilization to the institutional limit on monetization deficits and the resulting need for fiscal correction. The limit on government credit from the Rentenbank and the prohibition of discounting of government debt by the Reichsbank combined to separate completely deficit finance and the monetary system. He notes that the government was forced into budget balance, and thus the objective conditions for inflation were removed "by a series of deliberate, permanent actions to raise taxes and eliminate expenditures." He refers in particular to the cuts in employment in the public sector. The proposed cuts were in fact very substantial: a reduction of 25% in government employment to be implemented in several stages. Of course, the data show that the gain tax revenue was much more important for budget stabilization than the cut in spending.

The success of fiscal stabilization is seen in the budget shown in table 11.4. There is no question that Germany in fact moved to a balanced budget and beyond. GNP data for the early 1920s appear to be unavailable and hence it is difficult to express the budget relative to GNP. But an estimate for 1925 is possible. For that year budget receipts represent 10.4% of GNP.

Figure 11.4 shows the value of tax receipts in gold marks. The figure makes apparent the erosion of tax revenue in the hyperinflation and the very rapid recovery of real revenue once price stability returns.

The monetary-fiscal view would certainly be reinforced by the change in personnel, when in December, Schacht, a self-confessed gold standard man, replaced Havenstein as President of the Reichsbank. Graham (1930) is quoted by Yeager (1981, p. 59) as writing of Havenstein's death as "a demise which cannot be thought of as other than opportune."

The Reichsbank effectively withstood the pressure to resume monetization of budget deficits. As already noted, the Reichsbank was prohibited from discounting government paper. When the Finance Minister turned in December to the Reichsbank for a bridge loan, he could not secure credit

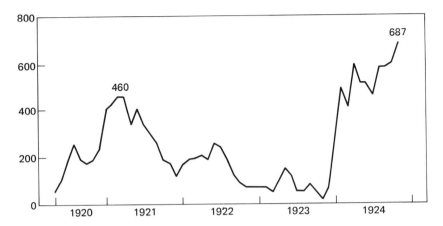

Figure 11.4
Tax collection (millions of gold marks).

and had instead to raise emergency taxes, anticipate taxes, and issue gold
mark bonds.

Table 11.5 shows that most of the monetary expansion that does occur
in the early phase of the stabilization is in fact in the form of small
denominations of the gold loan and Rentenmark, not Reichsbank money.
An institutional feature worth recording is the extreme difficulty of putting
Rentenbank notes into circulation: a printer's strike was taking place at the
very time the Rentenmark was to be issued. As a result the printing was
delayed and the note issue proceeded very slowly. Accordingly, at no time
in the early stabilization did the Rentenmark lose in scarcity.

The monetary-fiscal control is, of course, a central part of the stabilization and indeed the fundamental factor. But this does not really answer the
more basic question: *How does a government that plans to do all the right
things and, indeed, puts them on paper secure the credibility that then makes it
possible to live with the policies?* It surely is not the case that there is an
objective way of doing things right that, when hit upon, always and
invariably yields instant public recognition and success. Observers of the
time (as opposed to, say, Sargent's analysis) recognized this deeper problem. They were sensitive to it because they had seen earlier attempts in
Germany and in other countries that started off right, but then fell apart
because they were not supported by stabilizing speculation. A case in point
might be the first Poincaré stabilization of 1924, which evaporated while
the second, in 1926, stuck. Where is the difference?

Students of the German stabilization were keenly aware of the issue.

Table 11.5
Composition and level of the nominal money stock (million of gold marks)

	Reichsbank	Rentenbank and gold loan	Emergency money	Coin	Total
1923					
November 15	155	286	18	—	459
December 31	497	1,666	111	—	2,274
1924					
March	690	2,081	28	26	2,833
June	1,097	1,837	—	139	3,073
December	1,941	1,835	—	383	4,159

Bresciani-Turroni (1937) refers to the stabilization as a "miraculous event" and notes (p. 355), "The stabilisation of the German exchange showed, as did that of the Austrian crown, this characteristic: The exchange was stabilised *before* there existed the conditions (above all the equilibrium of the Reich Budget) which alone could assure a lasting recovery of the situation."

Of course, one might argue today that the fact of stabilization is immaterial; what counts are the fundamentals, the firm expectation. With the expectation of reduced money creation and inflation, there is growth in real money demand, which will be split between the transitory blip due to the Rentenmark issue and a fall in prices. But that, once again, begs the question of the certainty about the budget. Various observers note that it was the very fact of the cessation of inflation that provided the stabilization of the budget via increased real values of tax collection. This argument makes the termination of inflation a precondition for fiscal stabilization rather than the other way round. That argument, however, is not completely right. The fiscal stabilization had, in fact, four elements:

• the increase in the real tax collection that came from the end of inflationary erosion of the tax yield caused by collection lags,

• the elimination of the real value of the long-term government debt in the hands of the public via the hyperinflation,

• the elimination of part of the floating debt in the hands of the Reichsbank by the substitution of the (interest-free) Rentenmark credit, and

• the creation of new taxes and cuts in outlays.

The important part, in respect to timing, concerns the long-term public debt. The service of the debt amounted at the end of the war to more than half the budget outlays. By 1924 it was less than 3%. To achieve that result there was a need for a sufficiently large cumulative increase in prices before the other three factors could complement the real debt reduction to stabilize the budget. In this sense the timing of the stabilization is not altogether indeterminate. This point is certainly reinforced by the fact that the reduction in outlays associated with the end of passive resistance was a precondition for financial stability.

A very interesting suggestion comes from the analysis of Keynes (1923, pp. 46–48) and Bresciani-Turroni (1937). The argument is that the rise in velocity, because of hyperinflation, ultimately reduces the real value of cash balances to so negligible a level that two factors are at work. First, *any* sort of external loan will be sufficient to place the entire currency outstanding on a gold cover, making it possible to implement convertibility. Second, the extreme rise in velocity is not sustainable (furniture vans delivering daily payments). As Keynes (1923, p. 47), writing before the actual stabilization, puts it,

... a minimum is reached eventually from which the least favorable circumstance will cause a sharp recovery.... When the overvalue of the currency has fallen to a very low figure, it is easy for the government, if it has any external resources at all, to give sufficient support to prevent the exchange from falling further for the time being. And since by that time the public will have carried their attempts to economise the use of money to a pitch of inconvenience which it is impracticable to continue, even a moderate weakening in the degree of their distrust of the future value of money will lead to some increase in their use of it; with the result that the aggregate value of note issue will tend to recover.

Comparison of a number of stabilization programs highlights this critical aspect of exchange rate stabilization. It appears invariably as *the* key step in a program. It is not sufficient by itself—this is shown by the February–March 1923 attempt to stabilize—but it is the critical step that coordinates expectations, at least temporarily, around a new trend of prices and thus gives a chance to fiscal stabilization via the revenue effects. It might be argued that stabilizing private speculation, in the face of the right kind of objective evidence, would perform the same function. It might well, but it would be difficult to disagree that enticing private speculators to perform the stabilization might require even more monetary-fiscal overkill than if the government itself takes the steps.

It is quite clear that the government was aware of the need to establish a sound base of departure for the stabilization. Schacht (1927) makes a point that between November 14, when the Rentenmark was about to be

Table 11.6
Official and Cologne exchange rates (billion of marks/US dollars)

	Official	Cologne
November 12	.630	3.90
November 13	.840	6.85
November 14	1.26	5.80
November 15	2.52	6.50
November 20	4.20	11.70
November 20	4.20	11.00
November 30	4.20	7.80
December 6	4.20	4.90
December 10	4.20	4.20

Source: Schacht (1927).

issued, and November 20 the government devalued by 333% so as to raise the value of reserves relative to the quantity of Reichsmarks outstanding. With money issue practically ceasing, at least for a while, this meant a huge contraction of the money stock in terms of foreign exchange and also in terms of domestic prices. The devaluation was also designed to move the official rate more in line with the free market rate observed in the occupied territories. The quotations for the official rate in Berlin and the free Cologne rate are shown in table 11.6. Figure 11.5 shows the same fact using the Berlin and Amsterdam rates.

The exchange rate data make the point that the stabilization was not an immediate, obvious set of measures reflected instantly in the exchange rate in the free market. Even by November 30, when prices had stopped rising, the free market rate still exceeded very significantly the official now fixed rate of 4.2 gold marks per US dollar. Only toward the middle of December, a full month after stabilization, did the market accept the policy. And as early as February–March 1924, because of excessive commercial credit expansion of the Reichsbank, a new depreciation of the free rate ensued.

The exchange market was perhaps slow in recognizing the viability of the policies merely because they could prove themselves only over time. The request of the Finance Ministry for accommodation, in late December 1923, really shows that there was at best a potential stabilization, with institutions that were there on paper and on probation.

Quotations from the weekly report of the *Economist*'s reporter in Berlin read as follows:

The currency question continues to be in a mixed condition and it is very dangerous to predict how things will develop. (November 27, 1923)

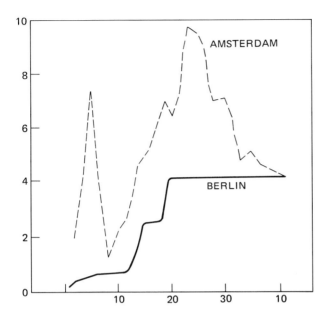

Figure 11.5
The Reichsmark/dollar exchange rate (billions of Reichsmarks/dollars).

The finances continue to be in a hopeless condition and as the provisional Renten mark currency reform, which is at best doubtful, cannot possibly succeed without budget balancing the general situation is gloomy. (December 4, 1923)

The currency condition has distinctly improved, owing to the price-fall now followed by a relative stability which creates the impression in the public mind that the Renten mark, gold loan currency and even the paper mark are, for some reason not known to the science of currency, really stable. This view cannot be held. The dominating influence is that for the moment the same views seem to be held abroad (as far as there is any dealing in German currency) and that so long as foreign Bourses do not depress the mark, causing a paper mark price-rise ... the stability will be maintained. (December 16, 1923)

In that perspective a major credit for de facto stabilization must go to the actual fixing of the official exchange rate combined with supertight credit. The view that emerges from this perspective does recognize the importance of institutions (no government discounting, fiscal correction, printers' strike), but goes further to argue that these measures must, in fact, be made sustainable by actual success. Huge real interest rates and a stop to capital gains on the exchange market are a way, though a very expensive one, to bring hyperinflation to a screeching halt.

Table 11.7
Interest rates in the aftermath of the stabilization (percent per day)

November 19	8–4%	December 3	1–3–1/2%
November 22	5–8–15–20%	December 4	2–1/4%
November 26	5–10–5%	December 5	1/2–2%
November 27	5–6–10–14%	December 7	2%
November 28	10–15–10%	December 8	1–1/2%
November 29	5–8–4%	December 10	1/4–1.5%
November 30	5–2%	December 11	1/2%
		December 12	1/2%
		December 13	1/6%
		December 17	1/2%
		December 18	1/4–1/2%
		December 19	1/4–3/4%
		December 20	1–1.5%
		December 21	6.5%
		December 22	2.5–3/4%

Source: *Berliner Borsen Courier.*

We now turn to the interest rate question, which seems a strikingly neglected factor in the literature.

6   The Real Interest Rate Problem

A fact that has received no attention at all in the literature (with the exception of Prion, 1924, and Pfleiderer, 1976) is the striking behavior in interest rates. Table 11.7 shows the interest rate *per day* quoted on the Berlin stock exchange for overnight loans (*Tagesgeld*).

To place these interest rates in perspective we need to remember that prices were actually falling over the period and that the free market rate for foreign exchange was collapsing. Thus a *daily* interest rate of 0.5%, or nearly 500% per year, combined with falling prices implies a fantastic real interest rate. An interest rate of 3% per day, as prevailed in November–December, after the stabilization, amounts to a monthly cost of credit of nearly 150%. In the face of an official exchange rate that remained fixed, the mere postponement of a resumption of hyperinflation and hyperdepreciation by a few days meant dramatic capital losses for foreign exchange speculators. The fact of a depreciation of the dollar by nearly 100%, combined with the huge cost of credit, operated as a forceful stabilizing device. This was in fact the strategy of consolidating the stabilization success. Schact in particular makes much of the fact that in November–

Table 11.8
Interest rates, the dollar, and prices in 1924

	Interest rate (% per year)			
	Day money	Month money	Dollar[a]	Prices[a]
January	87.6	28.3	99.6	92.9
February	34.9	22.6	104.1	92.5
March	33.1	30.0	103.2	95.5
April	45.9	44.5	103.2	97.3
May	27.8	44.3	99.5	95.0

Sources: *Wirtschaft und Statistik*, 1925, p. 276, and Board of Governors.
a. Index December = 100.

December the main game was to ruin speculators ("to serve them with their tail in their mouth").

This regime of extremely high real interest rates carried through for more than half a year. This is apparent from the dollar exchange rate, the price level, and money market interest rates reported in table 11.8.

Note that the day-to-day money, for lack of a daily price index, is not indexed, while monthly loans are indexed. The large difference between the rates in January 1924, a full month after the stabilization, reflects the ongoing possibility of a resumption of depreciation and inflation.

One might ask how, conceivably, interest rates can be so high. Who would borrow and who would not lend? The active margin in all likelihood is foreign exchange. Given earlier experience with stabilization, and especially in the period February–April 1923, the public had every right to expect that from one day to the next, because of political events, the exchange rate could collapse and hyperinflation might resume. But even the indexed rate is extremely high; in fact it is Latin American. The difference here reflects, in part, the fact that indexation is stated in terms of prices and not the exchange rate. To the extent that a collapse would start with the exchange rate, the indexed rate should in fact also reflect somewhat the risk of renewed depreciation.

Table 11.8 also brings out the renewed credit squeeze in April 1924. Following a substantial credit expansion, the exchange rate in the free market (i.e., abroad) weakened and confidence in the sustainability of the reforms softened. The Central Bank reacted by a complete freeze on money creation, which proved effective in reversing the adverse expectations. With prices falling and the stabilization established, the nominal rate now falls below the indexed rate. Table 11.8 thus suggests that only a few months after the stabilization, and after repeated demonstrations of the new rules, was the reform in fact established. In the meantime, of course, realized real interest rates had been very large, thereby creating a burden on real activity that was reinforced by the strong real exchange rate.

The real interest rate problem can easily be understood in terms of the standard model of interest rate determination. It is an issue that Mundell (1971) has particularly emphasized. Now we present the condition of monetary equilibrium in terms of the nominal interest rate, i,

$$M/P = L(i, \ldots), \tag{4}$$

which yields the equilibrium nominal interest rate

$$i = h(M/P); \qquad h' < 0. \tag{4a}$$

The stabilization program involves policies that stabilize the price level via exchange rate fixing and a stop to (or drastic slowdown in) money printing. Through the combined channels M/P is more or less frozen at a level close to the hyperinflation low. Therefore the equilibrium nominal interest rate, which now is also the real rate, stays extraordinarily high. This fact persists because M can only rise to the extent that the Rentenmark is issued or the Reichsbank discounts commercial paper and monetizes reserve inflows. Discounting of private bills, although clearly taking place, was still limited in the first six months, and the reflow of capital that did occur was not monetized but rather used to satisfy foreign exchange demand at the rationed rate. Reserves actually did not rise until late 1924. Prices did fall some, but the fixed exchange rate certainly precluded a massive deflation.

It is clear therefore that even with a 600% increase in nominal money, real interest rates still remain exceptionally high. The surprising fact is that capital inflows should not have occurred on a much more dramatic scale. It is worth noting that exactly the same problem of high real interest rates (or insufficient capital inflows) is now occurring in the Argentine stabilization. The problem is reinforced in Argentina because the central bank is not even expanding commercial credit so that capital inflows are the only way to money creation.

7   Exchange Rates and Inflation

The discussion of the German hyperinflation, and of other inflation explosions, invariably brings up the question whether the exchange rate depreciation is the "source" of inflation. The argument is immediately rejected on the ground that without validating monetary policy the depreciation

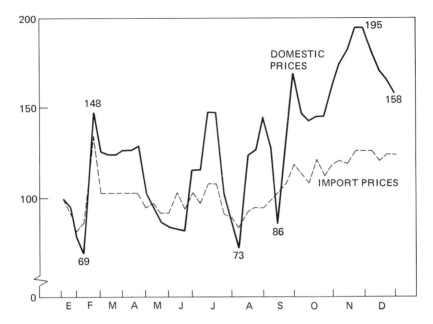

Figure 11.6
Import and domestic prices in gold (index 1923 : 1 = 100).

could not be sustained. But that argument may be too simple once it is recognized that money creation is endogenous via the budget, and that the budget may be affected by the rate of inflation and by the real exchange rate.

Consider figure 11.6, where we show at ten-day intervals the prices of domestic goods and of imports in gold marks, that is, paper mark prices translated into foreign exchange at the going official exchange rate. A rise in the gold mark price of domestic goods thus represents a rise in inflation relative to depreciation, and conversely for a decline in the gold mark price. It is quite obvious from the figure that there are huge shifts in the relative prices. During periods of exchange rate stability, in early 1923 and in late 1923, prices are stable or declining. By contrast, following an exchange rate collapse, as in April 1923, July 1923, and August 1923, there is an outburst of inflation. It is this sequence, running from exchange rate collapse to domestic inflation, that motivates the balance-of-payments approach.

The exchange rate issue enters the analysis in still another way. One of the striking features of many stabilizations is the sustained real appreciation. Figure 11.7 shows the real exchange rate in Germany. One explanation is that the exchange rate is driven by the portfolio holders' decision to

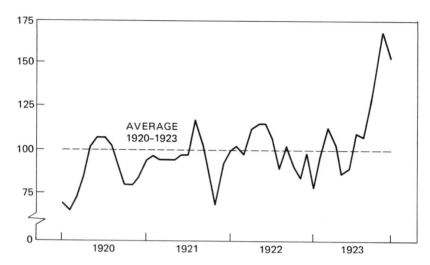

Figure 11.7
The German real exchange rate.

move out or into a currency. In the face of economic and political instability there is capital flight, which leads to real depreciation (and hence sharply accelerating inflation). In the stabilization phase, there are net capital inflows and stabilization loans that allow current account balances or deficits and hence a real appreciation. This fact is important because it helps explain, in part, the success of stabilization since it raises real wages.

8   Concluding Remarks

The detailed description of events in the German stabilization draws attention to the fact that stabilization appears a much more diffuse, multi-faceted issue than a simple monetary model would predict. Two points in particular stand out: The government defended a fixed exchange rate, following an initial sharp depreciation, and extremely high real interest rates were maintained for more than half a year, even after actual budget balancing was in sight or even achieved. Were these steps essential? Could the hyperinflation have been stopped as effectively, or even at lower costs in terms of unemployment, if the government had on November 15 simply withdrawn from the foreign exchange market, allowing a flexible exchange rate without any controls on transactions? And, second, were extremely high interest rates required to establish the credibility of the reform? Could the government have got by with a larger issue of Rentenmark and with lower interest rates? Finally, what role did expectations about relief from reparations and/or foreign loans play in supporting the government's monetary and fiscal policy? Had the Dawes loan not arrived in 1923, would the government have had to maintain huge real rates, and could it have afforded to do so?

None of these issues arises in the simple monetary model, but each is crucial in real life stabilization contexts. Only a broader model of the hyperinflation economy that models real exchange rates, portfolio balance, and credibility can hope to answer these questions. In the meantime, exchange rate fixing (and wage-price controls) seem an effective means of giving the economy both guidance as to the equilibrium price level and an initial dose of inertia.

Extract from the Report of the Group of Experts

II. Outlines of a Plan for Stabilising the Mark.

1. In return for a suspension of payments under the Treaty of Versailles for a period of two years, the German Government should offer to the Reparation Commission the following definite guarantees:

a) that an independent Board of Exchange Control would be constituted as a special department within the organisation of the Reichsbank and that the Reichsbank would hold adequate gold from their reserves at the service of the Board.

b) That so long as any part of such gold is unpledged, paper marks shall be purchased by the Board of Exchange, on demand, at a fixed rate to the dollar; this fixed rate to be determined on the principles of outlined in the first part of our Report.

c) that the aggregate value of the net floating debt shall not be increased beyond a defined figure; all other government requirements for credit to be covered by funded loans.

No modification to be made in the above without the permission of the Reparation Commission.

It would be necessary, further, for the Reparation Commission on the one hand and the German Government on the other to exempt the resources of the Board of exchange from interference.

2. On the consent of the Reparation Commission being obtained to the above, the following measures to be taken:

a) The financial cooperation and support of an International Financial Consortium to be invited.

b) A foreign currency reserve, on such scale as may be required, to be created on the basis of the gold at the disposal of the Board of Exchange, in conjunction with the credits which may be negotiated with the International Consortium from time to time on such security as may be acceptable.

c) The abolition of all exchange regulations and the restoration of free and un-restricted dealings in exchange and foreign securities.

3. The Board of Exchange to buy and sell foreign exchange on demand (on gold-exchange standard principles) against paper marks at fixed rates, the selling rate being not above 5 percent dearer than the buying rate in the first instance.

4. The Bank Rate to be raised to a high rate and dear money to be maintained until stabilisation is quite secure; but discounts and advances to be made freely at this rate for regular trade transactions against all normally approved security.

5. In order to concentrate into its foreign-currency reserves as large an amount as possible of the free foreign assets of German nationals, under conditions which would inspire confidence:

a) The Board of Exchange would issue gold bonds, guaranteed by the Reichsbank, at an adequate rate of interest, repayable in gold in one or two years, in exchange for foreign bank notes, bank balances etc.

b) The Board of Exchange would buy foreign exchange spot and sell it forward at appropriate corresponding rates for various periods.

6. The additional notes required to carry on the business of the country, as it returns to more normal conditions, would be issued,

a) by trade discounts and trade advances by the Reichsbank and

b) the sale of marks by the Board of Exchange against the receipt of foreign currency; and, to the least possible extent and for a period not exceeding six months, against further Treasury Bills issued to cover the budgetary deficit during the transitional period before the budget can be balanced.

Berlin, November 7th 1922.

Signed: R. H. Brand,
„ Gustav Cassel,
„ Jeremiah W. Jenks,
„ J. M. Keynes.

References

Angell, J. W. (1929). *The Recovery of Germany*, Yale University Press.

Bresciani-Turroni, C. (1937). *The Economics of Inflation*, Allen and Unwin.

Bruno, M., and S. Fischer (1985). "Expectations and the High Inflation Trap," unpublished manuscript, Massachusetts Institute of Technology.

Busch, O., and G. Feldman, eds. (1978). *Historische Prozesse der Deutschen Inflation*, Colloquium Verlag.

Cagan, P. (1956). "The Monetary Dynamics of Hyperinflation," in M. Friedman, ed., *Studies in the Quantity Theory of Money*, University of Chicago Press.

d'Abernon, V. (1926). "German Currency: Its Collapse and Recovery: 1920–26," *Journal of the Royal Statistical Society*, vol. xc, part I.

Deutschlands Wirtschaft, Wahrung und Finanzen (1924). Im Auiftrag der Reichsregierung, Zentral Verlag, Berlin.

Dornbusch, R., and Fischer, S. (1986). "Stopping Hyperinflation: Past and Present." *Weltwirtschaftliches Archiv*, April.

Graham, F. (1930). *Exchange, Prices and Production in Hyperinflation Germany*, Princeton University Press.

Gutachten der Internationalen Finanzsachverstandigen uber die Stabilisierung. (1922). Published by the German Foreign Office.

Guttman, W., and P. Meehan (1975). *The Great Inflation*, Saxon House.

Haller, H. (1976). "Die Kriegsfinanzierung und die Inflation," in Deutsche Bundesbank, *Wahrung und Wirtschaft in Deutschland, 1876–1975.*

Holtfrerich, C. L. (1980). *Die Deutsche Inflation*, de Gruyter.

Keynes, J. M. (1923). *A Tract on Monetary Reform*, Macmillan.

Laursen, K., and J. Pedersen (1964). *The German Inflation: 1918–1923*, North-Holland.

League of Nations (1944). *International Currency Experience. Lessons of the Inter-War Period.*

League of Nations (1946). *The Course and Control of Inflation.*

Mundell, R. (1971). *Monetary Theory*, Goodyear.

Pazos, F. (1978). *Chronic Inflation in Latin America.*, Praeger.

Pfleiderer, O. (1976). "Die Reichsbank in der Zeit der Grossen Inflation, die Stabilisierung der Mark und die Aufwertung von Kapitalforderungen," in Deutsche Bundesbank, *Wahrung und Wirtschaft in Deutschland: 1876–1975.*

Polak, J. (1943). "European Exchange Depreciation in the Early Twenties," *Econometrica*, vol. 11, 151–162.

Prion, W. (1924). "Zinspolitik und Markstabilisierung," in *Schmollers Jahrbuch*, 48, 843–868.

Sargent, T. (1982). "The Ends of Four Big Inflations," in R. E. Hall, ed., *Inflation*, University of Chicago Press and National Bureau of Economic Research.

Sargent, T. (1984). "Stopping Moderate Inflation: The Methods of Poincaré and Ms. Thatcher," in R. Dornbusch and M. H. Simonsen, eds., *Inflation, Debt and Indexation*, MIT Press.

Schacht, H. G. (1927). *The Stabilization of the Mark*, Allen and Unwin (reprinted by Arno Press, 1978).

Statistisches Jahrbuch for das Deutsche Reich (1923, 1924/25, 1926).

Williamson, J., ed. (1985). *Inflation and Indexation*, MIT Press.

Wirtschaft und Statistik, various issues.

Yeager, L. (1966). *International Monetaty Relations*, Harper and Row.

Yeager, L. (1981). *Experiences with Stopping Inflation*, American Enterprise Institute.

Young, P. (1925). *European Currency and Finance*, US Government Printing Office.

Comments on "Lessons from the German Inflation Experience of the 1920s"

Luigi Spaventa

Contemporary events—Latin American hyperinflations, cases of extreme exchange rate instability, mounting domestic and external debt in many countries—have contributed to a revival of interest in the monetary and financial history of the Twenties, often used as a peg for, or taken as a proof of, modern theories and models (not always so modern in view of what we read in the relevant literature of the period). In this vein, Dornbusch's paper (1987) provides a compact and vivid account of some main features of German hyperinflation and especially of the successful stabilization of the fall of 1923: a success story that puzzled many observers at the time and that defies the ambition of modern economists to fit facts into a neat and precise model.

In his brief sketch of the hyperinflation phase and in his account of stabilization process, Dornbusch is well aware of the complexity of factors at work and of the impossibility of singling out any of them as the one responsible for the failure or success of policies. It is on these grounds that he criticizes less eclectic interpretations of the events, such as Sargent's (1982) "budget-money-credibility" story. I fully agree with his concluding remarks in section 8 that stabilization (and hyperinflation, I would add) "appears a much more diffuse, multifaceted issue than a simple monetary model would predict" [and, contrary to what Dornbusch seems to think in introductory remarks preceding section 1, this is precisely the impression one gets from a "reading of the classics," from Bresciani-Turroni, to Angell, Haberler, and Nurkse]. If anything, Dornbusch himself is at times not eclectic enough : if not in his narration, which brings many threads together and shows how the extreme pathology of hyperinflation itself created some of the conditions necessary for stabilization, then in his general remarks, where he still seems to be looking for a character able to perform the major role of the villain in the first part of the piece and of the hero in the second, and where, though with some hesitancy,[1] he assigns such a role to the exchange rate.

It is of course out of the question that the commitment of the authorities to the 4.20 exchange rate was a major, though by no means the only, component of the stabilization policy: the somewhat rhetorical question posed by Dornbusch in section 8 whether inflation could have been stopped as effectively, had the government withdrawn from the exchange market, leaving the rate to float without controls, can probably receive an unambiguously negative answer. Neither this conclusion, however, nor the obvious fact that domestic hyperinflation and the external depreciation of the mark chased each other with alternate leads and lags allows us to infer, as Dornbusch is tempted to do at places, that external depreciation was the *leading* factor of domestic hyperinflation. This inference appears to be based on two arguments, one of which is, as it were, Dornbusch-specific, while the other reopens an old debate that subsequent literature seemed to have settled.

The Dornbusch-specific argument is that, while money creation depends on the budget deficit, the latter is itself affected both by domestic inflation *and* by external depreciation. An acceleration of inflation causes a decline in the real value of tax revenues, owing to the lags in tax collection. This could be an indirect effect of external depreciation if the latter leads on domestic inflation. But Dornbusch also sees a direct effect of the exchange rate on the deficit, "particularly ... if service of an external debt or reparation payments denominated in foreign exchange appear as a significant government outlay" (section 1; see also section 7). German data of the period, however, provide no evidence of this direct effect of external depreciation on the size of the budget deficit: between the second half of 1919 and the beginning of 1920, while the external value of the mark fell at an accelerated pace, the budget deficit actually diminished; it increased instead in the course of 1920—a period of remarkable stability of the exchange rate. Also the evidence of the effects of domestic inflation on the deficit is, at best, mixed, except in the very final phase of the hyperinflation, between the second half of 1922 and 1923; in earlier phases, the decline in the real value of revenues was offset, and at times more than offset, by a decline in the real value of government expenditures.[2] This is not surprising, for in earlier phases the effects of inflation on real interest payments on domestic debt prevailed upon those on revenues and on those, of opposite sign, on other expenditures.

I now come to the more general problem of the causal links between exchange rate depreciation and domestic inflation. Dornbusch briefly supports the view, held by a number of writers of the period and criticized by later contributions, that causality ran from the balance of payments to exchange rate depreciation to domestic inflation.[3] The criticism that without validating monetary policy depreciation could not be sustained "may be too simple once it is recognized that money creation is endogenous via the budget," which is itself affected by the rate of inflation and by the real exchange rate (section 7). Further, inspection of import and domestic prices in gold in 1923 shows a "sequence, running from exchange rate collapse to domestic inflation, that motivates the balance-of-payments approach" (section 7).

The view mildly supported by Dornbusch was inherently that of a vicious-circles model *ante litteram*. Its critics used subtler and more modern arguments than the one cited by Dornbusch: neglect of the role of expectations; of the difference in the price formation mechanism between auction and contract markets, except under extreme hyperinflation, when such difference vanishes; of the dynamics of inflation. The critics agreed that movements of domestic prices and of the exchange rate interact, but pointed out that it was impossible to establish in general a genuine causal relationship between them; nor could such a relationship be inferred from the mere fact that one of the two variables moved before the other. In the first period after the war, external depreciation lagged behind domestic inflation in many countries, as there was a belief that European currencies would return to their prewar parities.[4] Once these expectations were reversed, the exchange rate was more prone to lead on prices and to oscillate more freely.[5] The greater rigidity of internal prices disappeared in the more acute stage of hyperinflation, when costs and prices "became more and more sensitive to variations of the exchange" and when "a 'system' of internal prices which represented a kind of centre of gravity of the oscillation of the exchange ... no longer existed."[6] The critics of the causality from the exchange rate to inflation, though pointing out that monetary accommodation was necessary, all agreed that as inflation and depreciation accelerated money supply and velocity would become endogenous variables, and they all agreed that foreign exchange speculation was in general destabilizing.[7] The difference of views was on policy remedies: on whether control of money supply was necessary and sufficient or priority should be given to stabilization of the exchange market, complemented by "an appropriate credit policy."[8] Support of the second view, correctly shared by Dornbusch, does not, however, require that a precise causal link be established as to what determined what in the first place—also, because Dornbusch is careful to list all the other factors that contributed to the success of stabilization: a credit crunch; the wiping out of the real value of the debt stock and the reduction to a negligible level of the real value of the currency stock; the readiness of the public to accept and trust any new standard; and, it may be added, exchange controls.

To conclude, there is one question that lies outside the scope of Dornbusch's paper, but on which it would be interesting to know Dornbusch's opinion. Granted that stabilization of the exchange rate was and can be an essential ingredient to ending phases of extreme hyperinflation, can the exchange rate be used in more normal cases as a costless tool for achieving price stability and staving off external inflationary pressures? The question is particularly relevant for small open economies pegging their exchange rates and for an evaluation of the EMS experience. The latter and other European experiences of the Seventies seem to show that the magic of virtuous circles probably works only after the hell of very high inflation rates has been experienced.

Notes

1. An earlier version of the paper (Dornbusch, 1985) was more sanguine, especially on the relationship between the exchange rate and the budget deficit.

2. See Bresciani-Turroni (1937), chapter II, part I.

3. A comprehensive survey of the debate is in Angell (1926). For a brief flashback, see Spaventa (1983).

4. See Nurkse, in League of Nations (1944), p. 113.

5. The difference in price formation in the exchange rate market and in the products markets is repeatedly made by Bresciani-Turroni (who points out that the distinction was lucidly made by Thiers in his *History of French Revolution*, when dealing with the collapse of the assignates: "Les marchands ne peuvent se donner le mot aussi rapidement que des agioteurs réunis dans une salle.").

6. Bresciani-Turroni (1937), p. 144.

7. For references, see Spaventa (1983).

8. Nurkse, in League of Nations (1944), p. 118.

References

Angell, J. W., 1926. *The Theory of International Prices*, Cambridge, Mass.

Bresciani-Turroni, C., 1937, *The Economics of Inflation*, London (English edition of *Le vicende del Marco tedesco*, Milano, 1931).

Dornbusch, R., 1985, "Stopping Hyperinflation: Lessons from the German Inflation experience of the 1920s," NBER Working Paper Series, no. 1675, August 1985.

Dornbusch, R., 1987, "Lessons from the German Inflation Experience of the 1920s", in this volume.

League of Nations, 1944, *International Currency Experience: Lessons of the Interwar Period*, Geneva.

Sargent, T., 1982, "The Ends of Four Big Inflations," in R. E. Hall, ed., *Inflation*, Chicago.

Spaventa, L., 1983, "Feedbacks between exchange-rate movements and domestic inflation: vicious and not so virtuous cycles, old and new", *International Social Science Journal*, Vol. XXV, no. 3.

12 Modigliani-La Malfa Revisited: The Italian Economy from the Sixties to the Eighties

Giorgio La Malfa and
Edoardo Lecaldano Sasso
la Terza

1 The 1966 Article by Modigliani and La Malfa

Twenty years ago, Franco Modigliani and Giorgio La Malfa (MLM), reviewing economic policy in Italy during the early '60s, argued that in the medium term incomes policy was the only effective means of controlling inflation without affecting levels of employment and economic growth.[1] The main assumptions of the model they used were

1. Money wages are exogenous in the short run. In the long run, they tend to move with the level of prices, the time scale depending on the degree of indexation in the wage system.

2. Prices are set by a markup over unit cost, the markup varying with the level of economic activity.

3. Given the money supply and nominal wages, the level of economic activity influences nominal demand for money directly, through the volume of transactions, and indirectly, through the markup and hence the price level. Equilibrium in the money market determines the rate of interest, which in turn interacts with the level of activity through its effect on investment decisions.

4. In an open economy, with fixed exchange rates and no capital movements, the balance of payments is a function of aggregate demand and the ratio of domestic to international prices.

The reference framework employed by MLM was thus mixed, combining classical elements (the investment function) with Keynesian (liquidity preference and rigid money wages) and post-Keynesian ones (the markup and an exogenus income distribution).

The authors wish to thank the Bank of Italy for the assistance provided. The views expressed in this paper are, like any errors, of course the authors'.

Applying this model to an increase in nominal wages in excess of productivity, it was argued that a new equilibrium with higher domestic prices and lower real income and employment would follow. As for the effects on the balance of payments, these would depend on the Marshall-Lerner condition being satisfied.

Expansionary monetary and/or fiscal policies would reestablish full employment, at the price of worsening the external balance. In the medium-to-long term, however, the wage-price spiral would make both inflation and the balance-of-payments deficit unbearable. Accordingly, MLM suggested the adoption of an incomes policy to circumvent the inflation-unemployment dilemma; as for monetary and fiscal policies, it was suggested that they should be directed to controlling the level of activity, income distribution, and the allocation of resources between consumption and investment.

The purpose of this paper is to establish whether the conclusions and policy prescriptions of the MLM article still hold, in the light of both theoretical developments (section 2) and of the evolution of the Italian economy in the '70s and '80s. To summarize the findings of the paper:

1. Developments in the international economic environment following devaluation of the dollar in 1971, two oil crises, and the rise of the newly industrialized countries have worsened the trade-off between growth and external balance as compared to 20 years ago (section 3).

2. Domestically, structural changes in the labor market account for a shift inward of the trade-off between real wage growth and employment (section 4).

3. In failing to perceive these two basic developments, the effectiveness of demand management policies was grossly overestimated, while problems on the supply side were neglected. This in turn generated rapidly expanding public sector deficits, leading to inflation and external imbalances first, and to a dramatic debt management problem thereafter (section 5).

4. Throughout this period monetary policy has been largely accommodating, the alleged purpose being to avoid crowding out private investment (section 6).

5. Once these new elements are introduced into the analysis, the policy prescriptions may be formulated as follows (section 7):

• Incomes policies, though still necessary to control inflation, are no longer sufficient to relax structural constraints on growth.

• MLM considered fiscal and monetary policies basically interchangeable, with a preference for the latter, given its flexibility and speed of response.

Nowadays, the complexity of financial markets, the size of the public debt, and the supply side nature of Italy's unemployment and balance-of-payments problems require a well-defined mix of fiscal and monetary policies.

• A less expansionary fiscal policy in the aggregate, together with a substantially greater share of public investment in investment expenditure, could be coupled with a monetary policy of lower interest rates, thus easing the debt problem without jeopardizing the internal and external stability of the lira.

• Price stability would be assured by both incomes policies and a less expansionary fiscal policy in the aggregate.

Italy's experience over the last twenty years strongly confirms the final conclusion of the MLM paper: inflationary pressures should be faced with decision, from the beginning, without "postponing tough measures." MLM felt that the longer the delay, the greater the cost of adjustment. This paper suggests a somewhat stronger conclusion, namely, that a long period of inadequate policies may cause serious economic problems to become intractable.

2   Advances in the Theory of Economic Policy

Three major developments in the theory of income and price determination have occurred over the past twenty years:

1. Attention already paid to flow variables has now been extended to stocks of real and financial assets. Hence, the effectiveness of economic policies is tested taking into account resulting changes in the economy's endowment of real and financial resources.

This issue has been forcefully aired in the debate on the effects of alternative forms of deficit financing. The traditional IS-LM framework would imply that money-financed deficits lead to less crowding out of private investment. This result does not necessarily hold, once income and wealth effects are considered. The extent of crowding out will come to depend on both the way the deficit is financed and the volume of the outstanding debt. If government bonds are net wealth, and if the interest elasticity of savings is less than the income elasticity of consumption, an expansion of public debt, by generating a simultaneous increase in both wealth and incomes, may push interest rates onto a dynamically unstable path.

2. From the end of the '60s, increasing attention has been paid to the role of expectations. The early Keynesian models' assumption of static expectations was at first replaced by the more flexible notion of adaptive expec-

tations. Under this hypothesis, in long-run equilibrium, actual and expected values will coincide, or else, in the case of constant growth, they will differ by a fixed percentage. The hypothesis of rational expectations came next, postulating that expectations can only be wrong because of random, inherently unpredictable, factors.

It follows from this that the effectiveness of any given economic policy tends to peter out over time. With adaptive expectations, policies would have to be progressively strengthened; with rational expectations, they can only be effective if unexpected, or if the adjustment process is hindered by institutional rigidities.

3. The third major innovation is careful modeling of the transmission mechanisms of monetary policy. In the early Keynesian models bonds and cash were the only financial assets, the latter exogenously supplied by the central bank.

The portfolio approach makes it possible to investigate more fully the channels of transmission of monetary impulses through to real economic variables. The wider the range of financial assets, the more the final impact of monetary policies will depend on initial conditions in the economy. Furthermore, the greater the proportion of financial flows going through intermediaries, the more effective policies based on control of money supply will be, and the less effective will be those based on short-term interest rate management.

By focusing attention on the structure of financial markets, a greater emphasis is laid on the institutional factors that must be taken into account by the monetary authorities. This weakens the case for fixed monetary regulations.

Evidence of a changing economic environment prompted the analysis behind these developments. In Italy, the debate on the sustainability of debt heated up as first private and then public debt grew rapidly, the debt ratio to GNP rising to well above levels seen in the '50s and '60s. Increasing attention was paid to the role of expectations given the accelerating inflation of the '70s. Research on the portfolio approach paralleled developments in financial markets, in part as a consequence of changes in the techniques of intermediation and in part as a response to structural changes in the real economy.

3 Developments in the International Economic Environment

The collapse of the Bretton Woods system at the end of the '60s had been preceded by mounting concern over the increase of dollars held outside the

Table 12.1
Exchange rate variability[a]

	Nominal effective rate		Real effective rate[b]	
	Italy	Major industrial countries[c]	Italy	Major industrial countries[c]
1961–1964	0.09	0.14	0.30	0.36
1965–1969	0.16	0.25	0.30	0.40
1970–1974	0.88	0.85	0.96	0.97
1975–1979	1.10	1.07	1.04	1.10
1980–1983	0.89	1.01	0.74	1.30
1980	0.83	1.20	0.69	1.37
1981	1.30	1.55	0.83	1.57
1982	0.64	1.28	0.79	1.23
1983	0.80	1.04	0.64	1.04

Source: IMF (1984).
a. Monthly average of absolute percentage variation in average exchange rate (weighted according to IMF exchange rate model).
b. The real effective exchange rate utilizes changes in the consumer price index.
c. Average, weighted according to their shares in world trade, for France, West Germany, the United Kingdom, Italy, Canada, the United States, and Japan.

United States, the result of persistent US balance-of-payments deficits (see section 2, item 1). It was followed by a period of high exchange rate volatility, only incompletely controlled by cooperation among monetary authorities. As indicated in table 12.1 exchange rate fluctuations increased in frequency and amplitude during the '70s, a trend only partially moderated in Italy in the early '80s.

Soon after the end of the "dollar standard" came the first oil crisis, to be followed some six years later by a second. Energy import prices per unit of GDP soared from an index of 100 in 1970 to stand at an average of 500 during the first five years of the present decade. The percentage of energy products in total imports rose to reach 33% in 1981, then dropped to 27% in 1984 (table 12.2). The problem was not one merely of cost: security of supplies was no longer guaranteed.

At the same time, international competition accentuated the emergence of economies able to compete in many of Italy's traditional manufacturing and agricultural export markets. Italy's dependence on foreign trade appeared more precarious, with export prices falling relative to import prices, causing a progressive deterioration in the trade-off between the achievement of domestic growth and equilibrium in the balance of payments, for any given rate of international growth (table 12.3).

Table 12.2
Energy prices and imports[a]

	GDP deflator (A)[b]	Deflator of domestic price of energy imports (B)[b]	B/A (in %)	Energy imports as percentage of total imports at current prices
1970–1974	119.8	193.9	150.7	17.6
1975–1979	249.2	763.9	307.3	24.8
1980–1984	550.8	2,752.2	499.6	29.6
1980	395.9	1,731.8	437.4	27.3
1981	468.6	2,650.7	565.7	32.8
1982	551.8	2,950.6	534.7	31.0
1983	634.8	3,000.0	472.6	29.8
1984	702.9	3,427.8	487.7	27.0

a. Based on Bank of Italy data.
b. 1970 = 100.

Table 12.3
GDP growth rate and the balance of payments[a]

	GDP real growth rate (A)	Net balance of trade as % of GDP (B)	Net balance of payments on current account as·% GDP (C)
1961–1964	5.7	−3.2	0.7
1965–1969	5.8	1.1	4.7
1970–1974	4.3	−1.6	−0.5
1975–1979	2.3	−0.4	0.7
1980–1984	1.1	−2.4	−1.4
1980	3.9	−4.1	−2.4
1981	0.2	−3.0	−2.3
1982	−0.5	−2.3	−1.6
1983	−0.4	−0.9	0.2
1984	2.6	−1.8	−0.8

a. Based on Bank of Italy and ISCO data.

Table 12.4
Exchange rate and export competitiveness (1970 = 100)[a]

	Relative prices (A)[b]	Exchange rate (B)[c]	Competitiveness (B/A in %)
1971	102.6	101.9	99.4
1972	104.7	103.0	98.3
1973	114.0	114.6	100.5
1974	127.4	126.2	99.0
1975	138.4	131.8	95.2
1976	158.2	160.1	101.2
1977	178.0	175.2	98.4
1978	186.4	189.2	101.5
1979	196.6	195.3	99.4
1980	215.3	203.2	94.4
1981	238.4	231.7	97.2
1982	255.4	249.6	97.8
1983	263.8	263.0	99.7
1984	284.7	278.8	97.9

a. Based on Bank of Italy data.
b. Weighted average price of manufacturing exports relative to international prices; calculated according to the share of Italy's manufactures exports.
c. Weighted average exchange rate (weighted as in previous note).

It has to be emphasized that price competitiveness played a minor role in this process. Indeed, the exchange rate depreciation over the period was roughly equivalent to the difference between domestic inflation and world price inflation (table 12.4). Hence, to offset the worsening of the trade-off, a higher rate of productivity growth and a radical recasting of both product mix and production methods would have been called for. This, in turn, would have required a substantial increase in investment.

Such conditions have not been met. Energy requirements per unit of output decreased by 17% between 1973 and 1984, substantially less than in West Germany, the United States, Britain, and Japan (table 12.5). As for exports, the qualitative performance has been disappointing. The share of low-technology products in Italy's total manufacturing exports in 1973 was already appreciably higher than the OECD average: 40% as compared to 32%. In 1983, the figures were 42.3% as against 25.4% (table 12.6). As a consequence, Italian exports have been more and more directed toward markets where international competition from newly industrialized countries has been growing vigorously. These markets are characterized by lower value added per unit of output and by relatively higher price elasticity of demand. This narrows the margin for Italian firms to shift onto foreign customers any loss of domestic profitability.

Table 12.5
Energy requirement per unit product[a]

	Italy	France	West Germany	United States	United Kingdom	Japan
1970	96.5	98.7	99.7	105.8	103.0	100.2
1973	100.0	100.0	100.0	100.0	100.0	100.0
1976	95.9	90.4	95.5	90.6	98.1	94.4
1978	92.8	89.5	91.5	87.7	95.4	87.3
1980	86.8	88.5	86.3	84.9	90.0	80.6
1981	84.7	85.7	82.9	82.7	85.2	75.7
1982	83.0	81.8	80.5	80.5	83.7	71.1
1983	82.7	82.4	80.0	78.3	80.9	69.6
1984[b]	83.0	82.5	79.5	76.5	79.5	71.1

Source: OECD and Italian Treasury.
a. Tons of oil equivalent per unit of GDP at 1975 prices and exchange rates.
b. Provisional, partially estimated.

Table 12.6
Exports of manufactures by level of technology (percentage composition)[a]

	OECD			Italy		
	1973	1978	1983	1973	1978	1983
High-technology	16.8	17.9	20.5	11.6	10.4	11.7
Medium-technology	51.2	52.9	54.1	48.0	46.0	46.0
Low-technology	32.0	29.2	25.4	40.4	43.6	42.3

Source: Pagliano Rebecchini, and Vona (1985), based on OECD data.
a. "High-technology" exports include the output of industries 1–9 according to the SITC classification; "medium-technology," those of industries 10–16; and "low-technology," those of industries 17–24.

4 Domestic Developments

As for developments in the domestic economy, a substantial increase in real wages took place at the beginning of the '70s. The average annual rise in labor costs in mining and manufacturing in the period 1970–1974 exceeded growth in prices and labor productivity by 2.6%. For the decade as a whole, the gap is 1.3% (table 12.7).

Conflict over income distribution was not new to the Italian economy. It had indeed been the spur to the MLM analysis. That which occurred at the end of the '60s and the beginning of the '70s was, however, a structural rather than a cyclical conflict. It resulted in an irreversible shift in the trade-off between real wages and employment. Institutional changes in the labor

Table 12.7
Prices, productivity, and labor costs (% changes)[a]

	GDP			
	Labor costs (A)	Prices (B)	Productivity (C)	Real wage gap (A − B − C)
1960–1964	13.2	5.9	6.5	0.8
1965–1969	7.9	3.0	6.2	−1.3
1970–1974	16.1	10.1	4.0	2.0
1975–1979	19.5	16.9	1.7	0.9
1980–1984	18.1	16.5	0.7	0.9
1980	22.6	20.6	3.1	−1.1
1981	21.9	18.3	−0.3	3.9
1982	17.3	17.8	−0.3	−0.2
1983	16.4	15.0	−1.3	2.7
1984	12.1	10.7	2.2	−0.8

	Mining and manufacturing			
	Labor costs (D)	Prices (E)	Productivity (F)	Real wage gap (D − E − F)
1961–1964	12.9	3.5	6.1	3.3
1965–1969	7.6	0.8	7.7	−0.9
1970–1974	17.1	9.9	4.6	2.6
1975–1979	19.3	16.7	2.6	0.0
1980–1984	17.0	15.2	2.4	−0.6
1980	19.0	19.0	4.1	−4.1
1981	20.2	13.3	0.6	6.3
1982	17.8	17.8	−0.3	0.3
1983	15.3	15.6	0.3	−0.6
1984	12.5	10.1	7.0	−4.6

a. Based on ISCO and Bank of Italy data.

Table 12.8
Gross fixed investment (as a percentage of GDP)

	Total investment			Investment in mining and manufacturing		
	Private	Public	Total	Private	Public	Total
1960–1964	—	—	23.3	5.2	2.1	7.3
1965–1969	—	—	19.8	3.2	1.9	5.1
1970–1974	—	—	20.9	4.0	2.4	6.4
1975–1979	13.5	6.0	19.5	3.9	1.7	5.6
1980–1984	13.3	5.7	19.0	3.4	1.6	5.0
1980	14.4	5.4	19.8	4.2	1.6	5.7
1981	14.7	5.5	20.2	3.9	1.6	5.6
1982	13.1	5.9	19.0	3.4	1.6	5.0
1983	12.4	5.6	18.0	2.6	1.6	4.2
1984	11.9	6.0	17.9	3.1	1.6	4.7

Source: Bank of Italy.

market, legislation more favorable to employees, and the upward revision of indexation mechanisms altered firms' ability to maintain profit margins.

The squeeze in profits drastically affected capital expenditure. The percentage GDP going to gross fixed investment declined from 23.3% in 1960–1964 to 19% in 1980–1984. The decline witnessed in mining and manufacturing was even more pronounced (table 12.8).

Conditions in the labor market and rising energy costs in turn caused investment to be directed toward factor substitution rather than expansion of capacity. As a consequence, the growth rate of GDP fell by 2.5 points in '70s as compared to the decade before, and by a further 2.2 points in the early '80s. The average growth rate in mining and manufacturing declined 7.4 percentage points, to 0.5% in the '80s (table 12.9).

As for employment, the proportion of the labor force engaged in mining and manufacturing—which rose between the mid-'60s and mid-'70s by 1.4 points as a result of the employment policies followed by state-controlled enterprises and the reduction in the wroking week—fell on average by 3.4 points in the period 1980–1984. Employment in the private sector declined even more sharply (table 12.10).

The simultaneous changes in Italy's trading position and in income distribution—which redirected purchasing power away from social groups primarily oriented toward capital formation to groups primarily motivated by consumption—explain the gradual deterioration in the state of the Italian economy. When a substantial rise in investment was required to

Table 12.9
GDP and mining and manufacturing output (% changes)[a]

	GDP	GDP at 1970 prices	GDP deflator	Mining and manufacturing output	Mining and manufacturing output at 1970 prices	Mining and manufacturing output deflator
1961–1964	11.9	5.7	5.9	11.1	7.4	3.5
1965–1969	9.0	5.8	3.0	9.3	8.4	0.8
1970–1974	14.8	4.3	10.1	16.3	5.8	9.9
1975–1979	19.6	2.3	16.9	19.6	2.6	16.7
1980–1984	17.8	1.1	16.5	15.7	0.5	15.2
1980	25.4	3.9	20.6	24.6	4.7	19.0
1981	18.5	0.2	18.3	12.2	−0.9	13.3
1982	17.2	−0.5	17.8	15.3	−2.1	17.8
1983	14.6	−0.4	15.0	12.7	−2.5	15.6
1984	13.6	2.6	10.7	13.8	3.3	10.1

a. Based on ISCO and Bank of Italy data.

reshape the productive system, the Italian propensity to save declined. Personal saving, adjusted for inflation, fell from 13.9% of disposable income in the second half of the '60s to 8.7% in the '70s, and to 1% in the first five years of the present decade.[2]

The evidence presented above explains why the economic difficulties encountered during the '70s differ so substantially from previous experience. During the '60s inflation was curbed by bringing aggregate demand in line with productive capacity. Incomes policy may have been a more efficient way to achieve the same result, but monetary policies were also effective, given the nature of the imbalances to be corrected.

The shift in domestic and foreign supply and demand schedules in the '70s called for measures aimed at adjusting the system to the new equilibrium conditions. Economic policy, however, in the absence of a full appreciation of these differences persisted with a '60s approach, in the belief that the troubles came from aggregate demand rather than supply. As a consequence, economic policies were not only largely ineffective; they actually hindered adjustment of the sytem.

5   Government Policy

The social tensions developing throughout the '70s led to a steady expansion of government intervention.

First, government sought to maintain the level of employment, both by

Table 12.10
Private and public employment and the unemployment rate (annual average data)[a]

	Total labor force (%)			
	Private sector[b]	Public sector	Total	Unemployed
1960–1964	85.1 (—)	10.2	95.3	4.7
1965–1969	82.2 (24.5)	12.0	94.2	5.8
1970–1974	79.7 (26.2)	14.2	94.0	6.0
1975–1979	76.4 (25.5)	16.0	92.4	7.6
1980–1984	73.1 (22.5)	16.4	89.5	10.5
1980	75.5 (24.9)	16.2	91.7	8.3
1981	73.9 (23.4)	16.4	90.2	9.8
1982	72.9 (22.7)	16.5	89.4	10.6
1983	71.8 (21.4)	16.4	88.3	11.7
1984	71.3 (20.2)	16.5	87.7	12.3

	Rates of change				
	Private sector	Public sector	Total	Unemployed	Labor force
1960–1964	−0.9	3.6	−0.4	−6.5	−0.8
1965–1969	−1.2	2.1	−0.8	6.4	−0.5
1970–1974	−0.4	4.3	0.3	0.4	0.3
1975–1979	0.3	2.4	0.6	9.3	1.2
1980–1984	−0.1	1.3	0.1	9.5	1.0
1980	1.3	1.0	1.3	1.1	1.2
1981	−1.0	2.1	0.5	19.8	1.2
1982	−0.8	1.2	0.5	9.0	0.5
1983	−0.3	1.0	0.0	11.8	1.2
1984	0.2	1.0	0.3	5.7	1.0

Source: Bank of Italy.
a. Workers on the Wage Supplementation Fund are included in the unemployment figures.
b. Employment figures for mining and manufacturing are given in parentheses.

expanding the number of public sector employees and sustaining aggregate demand through increased transfer payments to individuals. Second, it tried to offset the impact on profits of increases in real wages in excess of productivity growth, so as to curb inflationary pressures and support private investment. To this end, it proceeded to absorb social security contributions, to take control of companies in financial difficulties, to raise controlled prices and charges by less than the amount needed to cover inflation, and to grant a variety of subsidies.

Both kinds of government intervention contributed to the growth of the public sector deficit as a percentage of GDP. Comparing the first years of the present decade with the '60s, public sector spending has risen by about 20 percentage points with respect to GDP. This increase has occurred mainly in wages and salaries, social security benefits, and interest payments (table 12.11).

Between 1960 and 1984, total employment in the public sector rose by about 1,800,000 units. This compares with an increase of less than 1,500,000 units in the total labor force and a fall of 1,900,000 in the private sector. Had the number of public employees grown after 1970 at the same rate as in the private sector, public expenditure on wages and salaries for 1984 would have been 23 trillion lire less than the actual figure.[3] Even taking into account resulting loss in tax revenues, the deficit would have been about 20% smaller. The rate of unemployment would, however, have been about 5 percentage points higher, climbing above 17% in 1984.

Of comparable importance, though not easily quantifiable, have been government measures to support business profitability through various kinds of transfers.[4] As a percentage of the gross product of the private sector, transfers to firms rose from 4.1% in 1976 to 7.9% in 1984. Over the same period, that position of lending to firms included in the definition of total domestic credit dropped from 14.2% to 9.5% of GDP, whereas total lending to firms declined from 15.6% to 11.2% (table 12.12). In recent years traditional channels of fund raising have been of parallel importance to public sector transfers to firms, at least in terms of quantity. True, public sector funds have partly been used to offset current operating losses, rather than to finance capital expenditure. In the absence of government support, however, industrial output would have been seriously affected in the aggregate.

Both types of government actions aimed at increasing the average propensity to consume and to invest, by expanding financial wealth in the form of public debt. As structural difficulties prevented the productive system adjusting to changes in nominal demand, interventions of this kind were

Table 12.11
Public sector revenues and expenditures (as a percentage of GDP)

	Current revenues (A)					Capital account revenues (B)	Total revenues (A + B)	Current expenditures (C)					Capital account expenditures (D)			Total expenditure (C + D)	Net indebtedness	PSBR
	Direct taxes	Indirect taxes	Social security contribution	Other[a]	Total			Wages salaries	Social security	Interest payments	Other[b]	Total	Fixed investment	Other[c]	Total			
1960–1964	5.7	11.9	10.6	4.9	33.1	0.1	33.2	11.5	10.3	1.5	6.7	30.0	3.8	0.7	4.5	34.5	1.3	2.5
1965–1969	6.4	11.6	11.4	4.4	33.8	0.0	33.8	12.8	12.4	1.7	6.5	33.4	3.6	0.9	4.5	37.9	4.1	4.6
1970–1974	6.1	10.4	12.5	4.4	33.3	0.2	33.5	13.2	13.4	2.6	7.0	36.2	3.4	0.9	4.3	40.5	7.0	9.3
1975–1979	8.6	9.6	14.1	4.1	36.4	0.2	36.6	13.3	15.7	5.2	7.6	41.8	3.8	1.3	5.1	46.9	10.3	12.6
1980–1984	13.8	10.5	15.5	4.3	44.0	0.2	44.2	15.8	18.3	8.3	8.4	50.8	4.5	1.7	6.2	57.0	12.8	14.9
1980	11.2	10.1	14.5	3.9	39.7	0.2	39.9	14.1	15.8	6.4	7.3	43.6	3.9	1.3	5.2	48.8	9.0	11.1
1981	12.8	9.7	14.7	4.3	41.5	0.2	41.7	15.9	17.7	7.3	7.8	48.7	4.3	1.4	5.7	54.4	12.6	13.3
1982	14.2	10.1	15.7	4.2	44.2	0.2	44.4	16.0	18.7	8.6	8.8	52.1	4.6	1.5	6.1	58.2	13.7	16.3
1983	15.5	11.2	16.3	4.3	47.3	0.2	47.5	16.4	20.0	9.2	9.1	54.7	4.8	1.9	6.7	61.4	13.9	17.0
1984	15.3	11.3	16.2	4.4	47.2	0.2	47.4	16.4	19.5	9.9	9.0	54.8	4.8	2.5	7.3	62.1	14.7	16.7

Source: Bank of Italy.
a. Income from capital, from sales of goods and services and other current revenues.
b. Intermediate consumption, subsidies to firms and other current expenditures.
c. Capital grants and other capital account transfers.

Table 12.12
Public sector transfers to firms (in % of private sector total output)[a]

	Net financial transfers (A)					Social security contribution (B)[c]	Total (A + B)	Financing to firms[d]	Total financing to firms[e]
	Current account	Capital account	Partial grants	Loans	Total[b]				
1960–1964	—	—	—	—	2.8	—	—	—	—
1965–1969	—	—	—	—	3.7	—	—	—	—
1970–1979	—	—	—	—	3.9	—	—	—	—
1976–1979	1.2	1.5	1.3	0.5	4.3	1.1	5.6	11.7	13.7
1980–1984	1.6	1.6	2.1	0.8	6.1	1.8	7.9	9.1	11.9
1980	1.5	1.2	1.7	0.9	5.3	1.6	6.9	11.0	15.0
1981	1.5	1.3	1.6	1.1	5.6	2.2	7.8	8.1	12.7
1982	1.7	1.7	2.4	0.7	6.5	1.6	8.1	8.8	11.0
1983	1.3	2.1	2.8	0.7	6.7	1.9	8.6	8.1	9.7
1984	2.1	1.8	1.8	0.6	6.1	1.8	7.9	9.5	11.2

a. Based on Treasury and Bank of Italy data.
b. Data for 1960–1974 are from Cotula, Masera, and Morcaldo (1983).
c. Reduction in social security contributions.
d. Financing by banks and special credit institution and funding through bond issues.
e. In addition to items in table note c, includes all other sources of funding except those already included in the aggregate "total transfers from the public sector."

bound to affect the balance of payments and the price level. Success of similar economic measures depends on purchasers of government securities not entirely discounting any additional future tax that may be needed to service the debt. Even assuming ultrarational expectations, however, uncertainty as to who will have to bear the burden of higher taxes and the exclusion of consumer durables from the tax base would cause debt-financed policies of income redistribution to modify the average propensity to spend.

Direct government contribution to capital formation during the '60s and the '80s has instead been very limited. Public sector capital expenditure rose by less than 1 point as a percentage of GDP between the '60s and the first half of the present decade (table 12.11), though its intensity fluctuated from year to year. Investment support should have been targeted at raising productivity and at easing adjustment to domestic and international changes. No such policy was implemented, however, and state intervention, when not contrary to the above aims, was not selective in its targets.

On the whole, government action in the '70s and the '80s, though very extensive, was unable to solve the problems of the Italian economy. Being mainly directed toward relaxing social tensions caused by the crisis in the productive system, it did not attempt to deal with its causes. Such a policy, however, by expanding public debt, entailed future obligations that could be only met by ever-increasing borrowing, thereby shifting the burden of problems originating in the real sector to the financial sector.

6   Financial Markets and Monetary Policy

From the early '60s to the mid-'80s, Italy's financial wealth, as measured by total liabilities, rose faster than GDP (table 12.13). Although it is difficult to determine a long-term equilibrium level of the ratio of financial wealth to income its continuous increase is incompatible with the stability of the economy. Persistence of such an imbalance tends to trigger adjustment mechanisms that bring the aggregate in question back toward its equilibrium value. These mechanisms can act either on the numerator or on the denominator of the ratio, depending on whether assets are created to finance the private or the public sector.[5]

If capital markets are efficient, excess formation of financial assets within the private sector, while able to generate financial instability, does not, however, lead to a corresponding increase in total wealth of the economy, which in turn would generate excess demand in the market for goods. Other things being equal, an increase in corporate debt unmatched by an

Table 12.13
Financial assets and interest rate

| Year | Against domestic financing of[a] | | | | Against total financing of[b] | | | | Average rate interest on public debt[g] | Rate of growth of nominal GDP |
| | State sector (A)[c] | Public[d] | | Total (A + B)[c] | State sector (D)[c] | Public[d] | | Total D + E[c] | | |
		B[e]	C[e]			E[e]	F[e]			
1960–1964	30.8	54.4	69.0	85.2	32.8	107.6	130.4	140.4	4.0[h]	11.9[h]
1965–1969	29.2	67.1	86.9	96.3	30.7	103.7	134.5	134.4	4.4	9.0
1970–1974	35.4	77.0	101.8	112.4	36.4	109.6	144.9	146.0	5.4	14.8
1975–1979	48.8	69.3	91.7	118.1	49.7	90.1	119.1	139.8	10.2	19.6
1980–1984	61.6	54.6	75.3	116.2	60.3[f]	95.5[f]	131.1[f]	155.8[f]	13.6	17.8
1980	53.1	57.0	76.9	110.1	54.1	92.3	124.5	146.4	12.0	25.4
1981	55.2	55.2	76.6	110.4	56.8	98.5	134.9	155.3	13.6	18.5
1982	59.7	53.5	72.6	113.2	61.7	94.5	128.3	156.2	15.0	17.2
1983	66.5	53.1	74.9	129.6	68.7	96.8	136.6	165.5	14.1	14.6
1984	73.4	54.3	76.7	127.7	—	—	—	—	13.4	13.6

a. Financing by banks and special credit institutions and funding through bond issues.
b. In addition to items in table note a, includes foreign financing and issuing of shares.
c. Yearly average stocks as a percentage of GDP.
d. The public includes households, firms, insurance companies, and social security institutions.
e. Yearly, average stocks as a percentage of gross product of the private sector.
f. 1980–1983 average.
g. Interest payments of the public sector as a percentage of the yearly average stock of public debt, excluding debt with the Bank of Italy.
h. 1961–1964 average.

equal increase in firms' assets would be offset by a fall in their capital value, reducing the numerator of the financial wealth/GDP ratio.

Alternatively, expenditure financed by issuing new financial assets may not be able to generate output whose value at current prices matches demand as determined by financial wealth. In this case the general price level will increase, reducing the real value of financial wealth and eliminating the excess demand for goods. The ratio of financial wealth to GDP thus comes down as a result of the increase in nominal terms of the denominator.

This alternative adjustment mechanism is specific to those assets created as a counterpart of public sector deficits, to which in general there is no corresponding increase in productive capacity. The government, however, is always able to guarantee its solvency, at least domestically. Consequently, the wealth/GDP ratio tends to return to its equilibrium level by a revaluation of the denominator, since the numerator cannot be devalued in nominal terms.[6]

The growth in financial assets at a faster rate than GDP in the '60s and early '70s was due to increasing private sector debt. This situation gradually changed during the '70s, when the proportion of GDP required to finance the public sector deficit, which had been small and stable throughout the '60s, increased steadily from 3.6% in the '60s to 14.9% in period 1980–1984 (table 12.11). At the same time, the private sector's recourse to external funds fell, following the slow down in investment and increased government transfers.

Changes in the composition of financial assets helps to explain the difficulty of reducing inflation in Italy. Public deficits raise the ratio of financial wealth to income. To the extent that the real interest rate does not rise to accommodate this change, and to the extent that in the short run wealth is not promptly reallocated from financial to real assets, inflation will bring the ratio back to its original level. The cause of Italian inflation thus lies in the nature of government intervention undertaken to face the crisis of the '70s. Had this been directed toward increasing supply so as to match demand, inflation would not have been required to balance the markets. Failure to follow this path caused the Italian economy to move from a situation where the high level of corporate debt endangered the solidity of financial structures to one where the large volume of financial assets rendered a slowing down of inflation difficult.

Monetary policy has been strongly conditioned by mistakes in government intervention. Until the first oil crisis, monetary policy aimed at controlling aggregate demand: the central bank intervened to cool the economy down when strains in the goods and labor markets threatened to push up prices and to worsen the balance of trade. During recessions, monetary authorities sought to stabilize interest rates in order to support investment.

In 1974, negotiation of a standby loan from the IMF led to the adoption of an intermediate quantity target, i.e., total domestic credit. Several factors underlay this change. Growing instability of the real economy made quantity targets more suitable for stabilization policies. Moreover, increased variability of the inflation rate made it difficult to determine inflation expectations and hence the underlying expected real interest rate.

The choice of total domestic credit as the specific intermediate target was aimed at ensuring external balance without having to resort to continuous exchange rate adjustment. The same intermediate target could, however, have been used to regulate GDP growth.

Under certain simplifying assumptions,[7] it can be shown that demand for financial assets by households, SF, can be expressed as

$$SF = TDC + CM + CA,$$

where TDC = total domestic credit expansion, CM = capital movements, and CA = current accounts of the balance of payments.

Once the targets have been fixed for inflation and the exchange rate, and given exogenously determined international demand, the current account balance is a decreasing function of domestic demand. This, in turn, is determined by the decisions of the public sector regarding revenues and expenditures. Fiscal variables are only indirectly influenced by the choices of the monetary authorities; in Italy, moreover, they have escaped all control in recent years. Consequently, consumption and investment choices—which, by our earlier assumptions, determine not only households' financial balance but also that part of firms' demand for credit met domestically and the current account balance—can only be reconciled by movements in the interest rate or in the level of income.

On the assumption that firms' foreign borrowing is small compared with their domestic borrowing, this implies a decreasing relationship between income and the real interest rate in the short run. The combination adopted for these two aggregates can be obtained by adding a target for external balance:

$$CM + CA = 0.$$

Alternatively, as mentioned earlier, income can be fixed at a predetermined level and the exchange rate left to absorb external disequilibria.

The TDC approach thus rests on the assumption that it makes sense to aggregate lending to the public and to the private sectors. For this to be

Table 12.14
Total domestic credit, public sector borrowing requirement and finance to the nonstate sector (yearly changes)[a]

	Total domestic credit		Domestic finance to the public sector		Finance to the nonstate sector	
	A	B	A	B	A	B
1974	20,015	89.4	8,796	95.6	12,513	94.8
1975	35,633	144.3	14,237	178.0	16,936	101.4
1976	33,961	115.1	14,208	103.0	19,753	125.8
1977	35,262	115.2	17,973	137.2	17,289	98.8
1978	49,261	129.6	31,763	—	17,498	—
1979	53,748	101.4	28,531	92.0	25,217	114.6
1980	63,271	106.7	34,015	89.7	29,256	136.7
1981	73,334	113.7	45,242	125.3	28,092	98.9
1982	100,391	137.5	68,987	160.4	31,404	104.7
1983	120,545	114.8	85,542	131.6	35,003	87.5
1984	138,476	113.0	91,364	108.1	47,112	124.0

a. A = billions of lire; B = in percentage of the target established by the Interministerial Committee for Credit and Savings.

valid, however, in the short term the import content of investment must be equal to that of public sector expenditure. In the long term, moreover, the public expenditure multiplier must be equal to that for investment.

Actually, neither of these conditions is satisfied. A fall in credit to the private sector, serving primarily to finance investment in plant and equipment, buildings, and inventories has a greater impact on imports than does a fall in the public sector borrowing requirement. In the long term, however, if the economy lacks sufficient supply elasticity, public deficits on current account, which only influence demand, tend to increase prices and to generate external account deficits, without affecting the level of real economic activity. By contrast, a credit policy that expands investment helps loosen the structural constraints on growth.

In light of these differences, it is difficult to decide whether changes in the composition of *TDC*, due to unforeseen changes in the public sector borrowing requirement, should be offset by altering the level of finance to the private sector. From the adoption of *TDC* in 1974, private credit was kept below the target level in the face of public deficit overshooting only in 1983 (table 12.14). From the mid-'70s onward, no declining trend for the ratio of total funds to the economy (including public sector transfers to firms) to the gross product of the private sector is apparent (table 12.12). This suggests that the monetary authorities, faced with a policy of government intervention based on an incorrect understanding of the problem, accepted the consequent high rates of inflation and progressive depreciation of the lira in order not to undermine investment.

At the same time, to minimize negative feedback on the financial system, the central bank made great efforts to modify the structure of the financial markets. The aim was to improve the trade-off between inflation and depreciation of the currency on the one hand and recession on the other. At the beginning of the '70s, Italy's financial markets, in the face of high and variable inflation, were poorly equipped to tackle the strains originating in the goods and labor markets, which were transmitted to the financial system through large public deficits. Until the later '70s, medium- and long-term fixed rate securities represented the only alternative to bank deposits for the majority of households. Initially, therefore, the authorities made use of administrative measures to guarantee the financing of the public sector deficit, assisted in this by the money illusion of savers.

As attention focused increasingly on the real rate of interest, it became necessary to raise nominal rates in line with inflation. At the same time, to reduce the equilibrium value of the real interest rate, the monetary authorities promoted the creation of new financial instruments, such as Treasury bills, variable rate securities, and convertible bonds, which met savers' preferences better with regard to yield and risk.

The latter was virtually eliminated, thus reducing the short-term sensitiveness of investment in securities to changes in the nominal rate of interest and making it easier for financial instability to arise. In the first few years of the '80s, the average effective rate of return on public debt gradually approached the GDP growth rate, until in 1984 they coincided (table 12.13). Further movement in this direction would put the ratio of public debt to GDP on a dynamically explosive path.

7 Economic Policy in the 1980s[8]

In the mid-'80s, damage produced in the previous fifteen years by inflation, low growth, and loss of international competitiveness have made trade unions, management, and government more conscious of the need to tackle Italy's structural problems. The present situation, however, leaves very little margin for a policy designed at one and the same time to reduce unemployment, bring down the inflation rate, and keep within the constraint imposed by the balance of payments.

If Italy's external accounts are to balance in the medium term, current items will have to be in balance, since Italy is not in a position to collect international seigniorage on its currency. In turn, this implies that domestic demand has to grow at a rate consistent with that of the world economy.

If movements of the exchange rate are to offset differences in domestic and foreign inflation and if world demand is to expand over the next five years at an average annual rate of 4–5%, GDP will have to grow at an average annual rate of no more than 2.5–3.5% if balance on current account is to be maintained. These values will have to be reduced by 1 percentage point if the exchange rate is not to offset the difference between foreign and domestic inflation, assumed to be 4 percentage points. Moreover, as there was a substantial current account deficit in 1984, the GDP growth rate will have to be cut still further to keep the deficit constant and thus gradually reduce its ratio to GDP.[9]

Consequently, external constraints conflict with the target of reabsorbing unemployment. Assuming an average 2.5% rise in productivity over the next five years, the increase in GDP compatible with balance on the external account will likely entail a reduction, or at best no change, in employment, while the labor force will expand by about half a point per year.

A further increase in unemployment will make it even more difficult to reshape public finances. There will nonetheless have to be a gradual reduction in the ratio of the public sector borrowing requirement to GDP, in order to curb the inflationary potential of financial wealth and allow the real interest rate to be safely brought down. In view of both the present and likely future levels of unemployment and the proportion of the public sector's financial liabilities—bearing floating rates, cutting back public expenditure alone will not be enough to achieve this objective. The solution to the problem is to be sought over the medium term, by making faster growth of GDP possible.

This negative feedback hinders the simultaneous pursuit of the various targets of economic policy and make it necessary to establish priorities. Top priority, as pointed out, has to be given to loosening the external constraint on growth, primarily through government action. Even though the size of today's imbalances make it difficult to reduce public expenditure in the immediate future, it is nonetheless possible to improve its quality and composition. The aim should be to reduce Italy's dependence on energy and food imports, to increase the technological level of both output and production processes, and to raise both the average level of skills and the sectoral and geographical mobility of the labor force. As pointed out above, public sector measures in these areas have been inadequate, as regards both quantity and quality. Improving their quality, however, appears to be even more difficult than preventing an expansion of government intervention along the lines discussed above from causing total public expenditure to increase even further.

Given the constraint imposed by the balance of trade, the greater the social consensus on the distribution of income, the lower inflationary pressures will be. If investment is to be of the kind and amount needed to reduce unemployment, any increase in productivity achieved in the next few years will have to accrue to profits. With moderation in wage demands, new investment will be directed toward broadening the productive base rather than toward saving labor.

In the case of substantial changes in the productive structure, however, real wages are not necessarily the major factor in the choice of output and production processes. The earlier and ongoing shifts in the structure of international trade force Italy to change the composition of its exports, expanding their high-technology content. Discontinuities in the production function mean, however, that there is no guarantee that labor-intensive processes can be used to manufacture these products.

The more government intervention and incomes policy are successful in reducing the external constraint and ensuring noninflationary growth, the smaller the imbalances falling on the financial markets will be. While monetary policy is effective in controlling aggregate demand in nominal terms, it is much less so when the difficulties originate on the supply side. When this is the case, monetary policy is faced with two alternatives: it can accommodate fiscal policy, ensuring the stability of financial markets, or it can rigidly pursue a fixed policy rule so that fiscal policy decisions are fully reflected in the cost and/or availability of credit to the private sector.

In Italy, despite the adoption of a quantity target suitable for nonaccommodating monetary policies, the central bank has until recently chosen the first option. This policy has been justified on the grounds that private credit is used mainly to finance production and investment. If government intervention does not change, however, the central bank will be faced with a crucial dilemma. To impose on fiscal policy the discipline of a quantitative target would undoubtedly penalize production and investment. On the other hand, accommodating the creation of financial assets by the public sector without generating inflationary pressures might prove impossible. Owing to the high proportion of floating rate debt, the income effect of an increase in the rate of interest might exceed the consumption substitution effect, reducing savings and making extraordinary financial measures unavoidable.

Twenty years after the MLM article, the Italian economy shifted from a near full-employment equilibrium to an unemployment equilibrium. Under present conditions, incomes policy can still ensure control of inflationary pressures, but it is no longer able on its own to loosen the constraint that the requirement of external equilibrium imposes on economic growth and employment.

Compared with the '60s, economic policy must now aim not at the control of demand but at the reshaping of industry. Public spending will have to be rethought, with priority being given to measures that improve the productive structure, with less attention paid to redistribution of national income.

Notes

1. Modigliani and La Malfa (1966).

2. See Lecaldano Sasso la Terza, Marotta and Masera (1985).

3. See Giucca and Salvemini (1985).

4. Public transfers to firms are different in kind: net financial transfers, net trade credits to the public sector, reduced social and Wage Supplementation Fund contributions, tax breaks. There are doubts whether such differing items can be aggregated. Furthermore, coherent statistical data are available only from 1976 onward and are limited to net financial transfers and to reductions in social contributions.

5. See Caranza and Lecaldano Sasso la Terza (1985).

6. Unexpected changes in interest rates would affect the market value of bonds and, possibly, the willingness to hold financial assets. Strong empirical doubts exists on this last point, however, and the virtual disappearance of fixed interest rate financial assets during the mid-'70s eliminates the first effects.

7. Let us assume that taxes are paid entirely by households, which also account for all expenditure on consumer goods; that corporate profits are fully distributed and that only firms invest in real assets (and do not invest in financial assets); that the financial balance of financial intermediaries is zero; and that the government does not own domestic financial assets.

8. See Grilli, La Malfa, and Savona (1985).

9. See Castaldo, Palmisani, and Rossi (1985).

Bibliography

Caranza, C., and E. Lecaldano Sasso la Terza, "Sostenibilità del debito e politica monetaria," Bank of Italy, manuscript, 1985.

Castaldo, P., F. Palmisani, and S. Rossi, "Il vincolo esterno: primi elementi per un'analisi empirica comparativa," Bank of Italy, manuscript, 1985.

Cotula, F., R. S. Masera, and G. Morcaldo, "Il bilancio del settore pubblico e gli effetti di spiazzamento: un esame dell'esperienza italiana," in Banca Commerciale Italiana, *Spesa pubblica e sviluppo dell'economia*, Edizioni di Comunità, 1983.

Giucca, P., and G. Salvemini, "Occupazione e retribuzioni nel settore pubblico," Bank of Italy, manuscript, 1985.

Grilli, E., G. La Malfa, and P. Savona, *L'Italia al bivio: ristagno o sviluppo*, La Terza, 1985.

International Monetary Fund (IMF), "Exchange Rate Volatility and World Trade," Occasional Papers No. 28, 1984.

Lecaldano Sasso la Terza, E., G. Marotta, and R. S. Masera, "Households Saving and the Real Rate of Interest: the Italian Experience, 1970–83," *Temi di discussione*, Bank of Italy, 1985.

Modigliani, F., and G. La Malfa, "Su alcuni aspetti della congiuntura e della politica monetaria italiana nell'ultimo quinquennio," *Moneta e Credito*, 1966.

Pagliano, P., S. Rebecchini, and S. Vona, "Il declino della CEE nel commercio internazionale: la dimensione del fenomeno e il ruolo di alcuni fattori strutturali," Bank of Italy, manuscript, 1985.

Index